Of Centaurs
and Doves

Of Centaurs and Doves

Guatemala's Peace Process

SUSANNE JONAS

University of California at Santa Cruz

Foreword by Sir Marrack Goulding

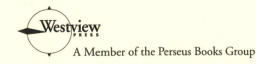

A Member of the Perseus Books Group

Copyright © 2000 by Susanne Jonas.

Published in 2000 in the United States of America by Westview Press, 5500 Central Avenue, Boulder, Colorado 80301-2877, and in the United Kingdom by Westview Press, 12 Hid's Copse Road, Cumnor Hill, Oxford OX2 9JJ

Find us on the World Wide Web at www.westviewpress.com

Jonas, Susanne, 1941–
    Of centaurs and doves : Guatemala's peace process / Susanne Jonas.
      p.   cm.
    Includes bibliographical references and index.
    ISBN 0-8133-3467-5 (hc)—ISBN 0-8133-3468-3 (pb)
      1. Guatemala—Politics and government—1985–   2. Negotiation—Guatemala—History.
3. Guatemala—Relations—United States.   4. United States—Relations—Guatemala.
5. Human rights—Guatemala—History.   I. Title.
F1466.7 .J66   2000
972.8105′3—dc21

                                                                                          99-053442

The paper used in this publication meets the requirements of the American National Standard for Permanence of Paper for Printed Library Materials Z39.48-1984.

10   9   8   7   6   5   4   3

I dedicate this book to my parents, Gerald and Hilda Jonas, and to my late grandmother, Anne Klestadt—all of them refugees of a different holocaust, in Europe sixty years ago. From their example I learned about strength, grace, and humor in the face of adversity.

Come, let's go, my country, I will go with you.
I will descend the depths you show me.
I will drink from your bitter chalices.
I will remain blind, so that you may see
I will remain voiceless so that you may sing
I must die so that you may live. . . .

I have grown tired of bearing your tears.
Now I want to walk with you in lightning step.
To accompany you on your journey, because I am a man
of the people, born in October to face the world . . .

Ay, Guatemala,
When I say your name, I return to life.
I arise from a flood of tears in search of your smile . . .

—From "Vámonos Patria A Caminar" by
Guatemalan poet Otto René Castillo, 1965

Contents

Illustrations

Foreword

The peace process in Guatemala has the potential to become one of the standard-setting achievements of the second half of the twentieth century, in the same class as the Camp David Agreement between Egypt and Israel, the peace settlement in Namibia, the Paris Accords on Cambodia, and the peaceful transitions that took place in Czechoslovakia, Germany, Hungary, and Poland after the collapse of communism in the Soviet Union. It is an ambitious attempt, by visionary Guatemalans and the international community as a whole, to end an ostensibly internal conflict that has torn a country apart for almost two generations. This makes Susanne Jonas's book essential reading for anyone interested in the prevention, management, and resolution of conflict.

It remains to be seen, however, whether the Guatemalan peace process will realize that potential. One of the fascinating things about Dr. Jonas's book is that it is published at a moment when the result still hangs in the balance. She has, as it were, written the first four acts of a five-act drama. Neither she nor her audience knows at the end whether Act V will be a tale of triumph or of tragedy.

As she herself observes, the first half of the book is imbued with the optimism generated by the signature in late 1996 of a package of agreements designed not only to end a thirty-six-year war but also to remove the causes of that war by transforming the Guatemalan polity. The second half, on the other hand, reflects the doubts, even pessimism, created by the difficulty of implementing those agreements and especially by the electorate's rejection in mid-1999 of the constitutional reforms they prescribe. The voter turnout in that referendum was only 18.5 percent, recalling the worst days of the pseudo-democracy that characterized the years of military rule.

But those who continue to strive to implement the peace agreements can take comfort from an observation by Machiavelli (in chapter VI of *The Prince*):

> It must be considered that there is nothing more difficult to carry out, nor more doubtful of success, nor more dangerous to handle, than to initiate a

new order of things. For the reformer has enemies in all those who profit by
the old order, and only lukewarm defenders in all those who would profit
by the new order, this lukewarmness arising partly from fear of their adver-
saries, who have the laws in their favour, and partly from the incredulity of
mankind, who do not truly believe in anything until they have had actual
experience of it.

Amongst the outside players in the peace process, the United Nations
has been the most important. Although every conflict is a law unto itself,
the UN was able in Guatemala to draw on lessons learned in its previous
endeavours in Central America. In Nicaragua, it had supervised the 1990
election, facilitated the subsequent political transition, and helped demobilize the Contras. In El Salvador, it had mediated the negotiation of a peace
settlement, signed in 1992, which contained many features that were to re-
cur in Guatemala, and had deployed a multifunctional peacekeeping operation to help the government and the FMLN implement that settlement.

But the United Nations has never pretended to a monopoly in peacemaking and peacekeeping. A feature of the Salvadoran process had been
the support provided to the Secretary-General by a group of interested
states from the region and beyond—Colombia, Mexico, Spain, and
Venezuela, who were later joined by the United States. The same occurred
in Guatemala, with Norway added to the group. An innovation in
Guatemala was a sustained effort to supply information about the negotiations to the intergovernmental agencies, including the Bretton Woods institutions, whose help would be needed when the time came to implement the eventual agreements. In some cases, agencies were directly
involved in the negotiations. The International Labor Organization (ILO),
for instance, made an important contribution to the agreement on the
identity and rights of indigenous peoples, which was one of the boldest
and most innovative ingredients in the peace package.

The outside players thus had an important role. But, as emerges so
clearly from this book, it was the Guatemalans themselves who really mat-
tered. The international community could help, but it could not impose.
Susanne Jonas describes well the distinct way in which Guatemalans express themselves, aptly dubbed by her as "affirmation by denial." In none
of the other peace processes with which I have been involved have I had
so strong a sense of a society turned in on itself, a society with its own private way of doing things, a society that would be slow to accept that outsiders had anything to contribute to the solution of its problems, and a society, therefore, which had to be approached with infinite patience and
with the knowledge that its reaction to one's efforts would sometimes
seem irrational and perverse.

This being so, it is remarkable that the peacemakers in Guatemala
were more ambitious than ever before in addressing the sensitive inter-

nal factors that had caused the conflict. One of the lessons the UN had learned from its previous peace efforts was that it is not enough to mediate a peace agreement, put in a peacekeeping operation for a year or two to help implement its military aspects, and then move on elsewhere. Peace would not stick unless action was taken to deal with the root causes of the conflict. In Guatemala, as in most other internal conflicts, those factors are largely economic and social in nature and were summarized by President Arzú in his inaugural address as "impunity, discrimination, and poverty." The bulk of the Guatemala peace package consists of agreements whose purpose is to correct those ills. This redounds to the credit of the outside players, and especially of my colleague and friend, Jean Arnault, who has led the UN team in the negotiation and implementation of the agreements. But even more does it redound to the credit of the Guatemalan players, in successive governments, in the armed opposition and in civil society, who defied Guatemalans' traditional mistrust of outsiders and insisted that the imperative of peace required them to allow the international community to give them help.

Another strength of this book is the length, depth, and breadth of the author's knowledge of Guatemala and its people, based on hundreds of interviews at all levels of society over more than a decade. Reading the book, I have been repeatedly struck by her understanding of Guatemalans and their country and have found myself wishing that we the mediators had been as well informed. This is another lesson that the UN has learned, but perhaps not well enough yet: Those in intergovernmental agencies who aspire to help resolve conflict must draw on all the resources available to them, including the underutilized resource of scholars and other nongovernmental actors.

There is another lesson that shouts from Susanne Jonas's pages. Great powers must be careful about the allies they choose. "My enemy's enemy must be my friend" is not a sound principle. It can create alliances that will fail to achieve the desired objective; and when all is later revealed, those alliances will bring shame to the democracy that has been unwise enough to enter into them. It is sad that that lesson has not been remembered in recent years in the Balkans.

Susanne Jonas is to be congratulated on a work full of drama and wisdom and scholarship and illuminated by her love of Guatemala and its people. Her book will, for many years to come, be of value to academics and practitioners alike, whatever the dénouement in Act V. I commend it to all.

Sir Marrack Goulding,
former Under-Secretary General, United Nations
Oxford, England
July 1999

Acknowledgments

Thinking back on the ten-year lifespan of this book, I am increasingly aware of how much I owe to the extraordinary cooperation and generosity of many individuals and institutions. As is explained in more detail in the Prologue, the analyses in this book have been distilled primarily from the hundreds of interviews I conducted during the decade of the 1990s with virtually all of the key Guatemalan and international players. Year after year in many cases, they took time from busy schedules to speak with me. A number of Guatemalan interviewees graciously shared their views with me despite their doubts about the peace process (or about my interpretations). Overall, this level of cooperation made it an exhilarating experience to do the research for this book.

None of the interviewees would have been so open if I had not assured them that their observations were off the record; hence, I cannot recognize them individually here or in the text. I will mention here only two of them, who did not live to read this book to which they contributed so much. To Msgr. Juan Gerardi, Auxiliary Bishop of Guatemala, whose brutal (April 1998) assassination remains unsolved, I owe much of my intellectual grounding in Guatemala. From 1987 until shortly before his murder, I was never in the country without spending several sessions with him and benefiting from his wisdom, his wit, and his razor-sharp comments on my writings. And from the first time I met him in 1990, Rolando Morán, who spent thirty-six years as a URNG guerrilla commander and died suddenly in 1998 as secretary-general of the URNG political party-in-formation, always made time to see me and often reminded me to take the long view, to "think in Maya time." Doubtless, both of them would have taken issue with some of my analyses here, but they both believed deeply in the peace project and supported my endeavors to write about it.

Several research organizations in Guatemala and in the United States were most generous in facilitating my access to information and analysis. Chief among these was the Facultad Latinoamericana de Ciencias Sociales (FLACSO)/Guatemala, which has been my in-country "home base" over the years. FLACSO/Guatemala's director, René Poitevín, was a constant source of assistance and encouragement as well as intellectual exchange. FLACSO/Guatemala's researchers and staff provided a level of collegiality and friendship that greatly enriched and enlivened my summers in Guatemala. Among the other institutions whose researchers and staff cooperated with me on an ongoing basis in Guatemala were Informess Centroamericana, Asociación de Investigación y Estudios Sociales (ASIES), Instituto de Relaciones Internacionales e Investigaciones para la Paz (IRIPAZ), the UN verification mission (MINUGUA), and the Guatemala office of the UN Development Program.

In the United States, I benefited greatly from cooperation offered by the Bay Area's Guatemala News and Information Bureau (GNIB) and Data Center. In Washington, a host of organizations were very helpful—chief among them on an ongoing basis, the Washington Office on Latin America (WOLA), as well as the Guatemala Scholars Network, Network in Solidarity with the People of Guatemala (NISGUA), National Security Archive, Latin American Working Group, Americas Watch, Amnesty International, Center for International Policy, and the Robert F. Kennedy Memorial Center for Human Rights. In New York, I received great assistance from the UN Department of Political Affairs and its Guatemala Unit, as well as the Lutheran Office for World Community.

I am very grateful to several institutions that provided financial support for the research in this book: the Dante B. Fascell North-South Center at the University of Miami, the Stevenson Program on Global Security at the University of California at Santa Cruz, the University of California's system-wide Institute on Global Conflict and Cooperation, and FLACSO/Guatemala. Funding to support the Spanish translation of this book, to be published by FLACSO/Guatemala in 2000, has come primarily from the Fundación Soros/Guatemala. Several individual donors who wish to remain anonymous have also contributed.

Intellectually, this book was greatly enriched by written comments and verbal feedback/discussions on chapter drafts from a wide range of colleagues—in Guatemala, elsewhere in Latin America, and in the United States: Arne Aasheim, Gabriel Aguilera, Nelson Amaro, Bernardo Arévalo, Jean Arnault, Aura Marina Arriola, Dinorah Azpuru, Ian Bannon, Stephen Baranyi, Raúl Benítez, John Booth, Jim Boyce, Amilcar Burgos, Terry Burke, Hugh Byrne, Violeta Carpio, Ingemar Cederberg, Chris Chase-Dunn, Denise Cook, Juan Pablo Corlazzoli, Hector Dada, Guillermo Delgado, Alvaro de Soto, Larry Diamond, Ricardo Falla, Lars Franklin, Juan Alberto Fuentes, Victor Gálvez, Gisela Gellert, Pablo González Casanova, Marrack Goulding, Alain Joxe, Norma Klahn, Cristina Laurell, William LeoGrande, Leila Lima, Ronnie Lipschutz, Margarita López Maya, Hugo Lorenzo, Mario Lungo, Betita Martínez, Charles William Maynes, Rafael Menjivar, Tommie Sue Montgomery,

Manuel Montobbio, June Nash, Arnoldo Ortíz Moscoso, Luis Padilla, Silvia Irene Palma, Manuel Pastor, Jenny Pearce, René Poitevín, Alvaro Pop, Alicia Rodríguez, Roberto Rodríguez, Fred Rosen, Gert Rosenthal, Rachel Sieder, Paul Sigmund, Jorge Solares, Raquel Sosa, Jeff Stark, Nancy Stein, Ricardo Stein, David Stephen, Suzie Dod Thomas, Edelberto Torres Rivas, Carlos Vilas, Tom Walker, Kay Warren, Teresa Whitfield, Staffan Wrigstad, and Raquel Zelaya. Needless to say, given the highly contested issues addressed here, none of these good colleagues are responsible for my particular constructions and interpretations of events.

I have been fortunate to have assistance from several extremely competent researchers who served as my "eyes and ears" in Guatemala during the times when I could not be there: Karen Ponciano, María Victoria García, and Aura Patricia Aparicio. In the United States, I was assisted by a number of highly motivated student researchers at the University of California, Santa Cruz—chief among them, Kerry Dudman, Karen Biegel, and Laura Alvarez. Jonathan Moller deserves particular thanks for his spectacular photographs.

At Westview Press, I am most appreciative and grateful to my editor, Karl Yambert, for his collaboration and his patience as this book evolved and took on a life of its own. Thanks also go to Michelle Trader at Westview, and the rest of the Westview staff for steering this book through a blitzkrieg production process.

As during earlier years, I am grateful to Marvin Stender for contributing to my peace of mind and safety during my research summers in Guatemala.

A very special thanks to my daughter, Rebecca Bodenheimer, and my *compañero*, Tom Holleran: Both of them were a source of ongoing moral support for—and relief from—my work on this book. In addition, my travels with each of them in Guatemala at different moments during the 1990s enabled me to see that incredible country for the first time all over again, through their eyes.

Susanne Jonas

Prologue

The Emotional Roller Coaster

Objectively, a peace negotiation is a matter of cold calculations of power and advantage by two warring parties—by all standards, the most Machiavellian of events. How, then, is it possible for an observer/chronicler of such a process (a foreigner, at that) to become so emotionally involved with the course of such a negotiation as to experience ups and downs more typical of affairs of the heart? And how can such an observer/chronicler claim to write a reasonably accurate account and interpretation?

I have been living with this contradiction for many years now, so I owe readers some explanation. The personal and anecdotal stories in this prologue will hopefully help readers to understand the emotional tides and undertows of Guatemala's peace process. Keep in mind that I am dealing here not just with any country, but with Guatemala, the anything-can-happen country that throws spectacular physical and human beauty up against equal parts of brutality and tragedy. By all measures, Guatemala is a country of high drama, at times melodrama or *telenovela,* but always of epic proportions. Guatemala reveals the highs and lows of human interactions.

Guatemala is also impossibly convoluted. Nothing is simple, straightforward, or easy to understand. Nothing is what it seems. But within this devilish reality lies, as well, the fascination, the intrigue, the intellectual challenge from Guatemala: "Dare to understand us in our full complexity!" Or, more accurately, "Dare to try! Just as you think you understand, we'll show you that you understand nothing at all."

Of course, this draws me even deeper into the labyrinthian puzzle. But if I obey Guatemala's siren song and try to understand with any degree of honesty, I must be prepared for the consequences: Without even intending to, I have paid to get on this emotional roller coaster. Every time I catch a glimpse of a better future, my hopes will be dashed. And every time I begin the inevitable descent into despair, Guatemala will save itself, somehow, in the most unimaginable way. And so, I continue on for the next round.

This round opened in 1990, with the beginning of dialogue about a possible peace process. Such a process was the only way to end Guatemala's decades-long civil war between leftist insurgents and rightist counterinsurgents, yet Guatemala's elites had vowed "never" to accept such a solution. After initial meetings in Oslo, word came from Madrid that Mario Sandoval Alarcón, leader of the ultra-rightist "Liberation Movement" in the 1950s and founder of death squads in the 1960s, had embraced leaders of the leftist insurgent URNG (Unidad Revolucionaria Nacional Guatemalteca) at the end of a meeting to discuss elections and future constitutional reforms. Impossible, but true. Somehow, something had moved off the dead center of traditional Guatemalan politics.

The dismal 1990–1991 election (less than one-third of the electorate voted) was alleviated by newly elected President Serrano's promise to begin serious negotiations with the guerrillas. Not that very many Guatemalans took the initiative seriously; most of my friends and colleagues were skeptical about *la danza de la paz,* the dance or charade of peace. I believed that a peace process had to happen in the long run, because the war had come to an impasse and none of the players had anywhere to move but forward. But the "long run" was taking a long time to materialize. By mid-1992, after a few initial advances, the talks ground to a halt and in August came within an inch of being torpedoed altogether. To those of us who observed that breakdown in the negotiations, it felt like being on the edge of a great abyss, because an outright rupture in peace talks would have meant a return to no-holds-barred total warfare.

Within Guatemala, while I was there during the summer of 1992, the army kidnapped university student and secret URNG member Maritza Urrutia. They held her for days, drugged and interrogated her, and put a videotape on the evening news, having her read a "confession" as a guerrilla, petition for "amnesty," and deny that she had been kidnapped. In the process, she mentioned that she had met her compañero "at a FLACSO party in Mexico." In Guatemala's "message system," the mere mention of FLACSO (one of Guatemala's leading research institutes) under these circumstances was taken as an expression of the army's dislike of FLACSO's intellectual work, a warning or threat. Instead of just watching the film on TV, FLACSO was now part of it, without knowing exactly why. Guatemalan researchers have always been dangerous in the army's eyes; and in 1992, the memory of the brutal 1990 assassination of anthropologist Myrna Mack (still an "unsolved" political murder) was an open wound.

The Maritza affair was also a warning to anyone doing political work that might pave the way for the URNG to become a legal political party—

an obsession within the army, now that the peace process was giving the URNG more legitimacy, as reflected even in private presidential polls. Others had been assassinated for the crime of preparing for the URNG's return and legalization. Thanks to international pressure, Maritza was finally released and saved from becoming another "disappearance" statistic; but she had to be smuggled out of the country clandestinely in order to avoid appearing before a tribunal, which would have meant coming under the government's control again.

The only tension relief in 1992 came from gallows humor:

At a jail where some political prisoners were being held, the warden arrived to tell them: We have good news and bad news for you. The good news is that half of you will go to Mexico, the other half to El Salvador. The bad news is that the top half of you [each] goes to Mexico, the bottom half to El Salvador.

And then, there were the real-life happenings that were worse than bad jokes: The army, attempting to induce the return of indigenous populations living in highlands "resistance communities," was offering food rations; since there were one hundred people in one case and only fifty rations, the army's plan was to kill the other fifty. A group of peasants from rural Cajolá demonstrating in the capital was brutally attacked by riot police; the Minister of Interior said, "Don't blame us; [the peasants] put their heads in the way of police batons." Meanwhile, the government furiously lobbied the world to prevent Rigoberta Menchú from getting the 1992 Nobel Peace Prize—even submitting the name of a ruling-class philanthropist (unknown outside of Guatemala City) as an alternative. But the government's desperate maneuvers were no match for world opinion.

It was during the summer of 1992 that I first discovered how to keep sane by making up mind games, turning Guatemala's perversity, complexity, and opaqueness into the subject of a new book. The collage/book I invented would mix a large dose of gallows humor with indigenous stories and folktales; it would deconstruct the aberrations in Guatemalan political culture, such as denial in order to affirm, the Guatemalan way of dealing with repression; it would celebrate the absurd as well as the magical; and above all, it would recount the hundreds of personal stories that Guatemalans had told me during the past thirty years.

The allegorical street names in Guatemala City's historic center seem made for such a book: Street of Liberty, Street of Purgatory, Street of Bitterness, Street of the Tortoise, Street of the Storm (Tormenta also meaning Adversity), Street of Oblivion, Street of Sorrows. . . . That book will be called No Hay Parada—taking its name from the ubiquitous signs ("no bus stop here") at all of the places where Guatemala City buses actually do stop. Denial in order to affirm. (Naturally, I've often seen those buses pass me by when I'm waiting at the designated *paradas*.) I am only slowly writing that book, but ever since 1992, it has been my companion, my alternative to despair when things get bad in Guatemala. Meanwhile, I can always measure the political climate by how fast my back goes out from the tension.

In postwar El Salvador, I saw TV ads urging people to come forward and give testimony to the Truth Commission. Would this ever happen in Guatemala? 1992 and 1993 stretched out forever, with virtually no visible progress in the peace talks. 1993 was interrupted by the most Guatemalan of events: the attempted *auto-golpe* (self-coup) by President Serrano. That crisis or implosion of the old system had a totally unexpected, almost miraculous, outcome with the rise of Human Rights Ombudsman Ramiro de León Carpio to the presidency (June 1993). But it was not to be a simple story with a happy ending. Our briefly raised hopes and optimism were quickly, diabolically thrown to the ground. It took only two months for the human rights president to grab a rifle at a PAC (civilian self-defense patrol) meeting in Huehuetenango and bow before Guatemala's triumphalist counterinsurgency army, adopting the army's agenda of undoing the few gains in the peace process made by the previous government. Yet one more false political opening bit the dust, reinforcing ingrown Guatemala-think: Nothing will ever change here. But there was something new in 1993: A "cultural revolution" arrived with the opening of La Bodeguita del Centro, Guatemala's first Peña. At last, a place where you could have a drink while listening to Latin American protest songs or arguing politics with friends.

The 1994 conjuncture was a tangle of contradictions. In January the peace negotiations finally came under the aegis of the United Nations (UN), the only conceivably credible mediator, and in March the human rights accord was signed. But none of that stopped government negotiators from proclaiming that the postwar role of the army would never be negotiated with the URNG; rather, the army itself would define its role and impose it on the enemy. The army envisioned itself continuing to control internal security (inventing "new" enemies, mainly indigenous Mayan "terrorists"—possibly allied with the Zapatistas in Chiapas); but at the same time, the army proposed to become the protector of the Mayan "cultural heritage." (That one struck me as so surreal that I had to ask the army general who said it to repeat himself, just to make sure I'd heard him correctly.) Worse yet, almost no one in Guatemala seemed to doubt that the army would indeed impose its own terms on the negotiating table. "This is not normal maneuvering within a serious peace process but psychological warfare, ideological bombardment," I wrote at the time in an article subtitled "Tales of the Absurd":

The distorted logic that rules the small world of Guatemala can drive even veteran observers to desperation. Many times in recent months, the Guatemalan peace process felt like climbing a very high mountain: the closer you get to the top, the farther away it seems.

After an interminable wait, a tiny light appeared at the end of the tunnel, with the arrival of the UN human rights monitoring mission, MINUGUA, at the end of 1994; perhaps now, finally, the world would take notice and force the government, kicking and screaming, into the twentieth century. Perhaps there would be a chance to realize the dream quoted by Nobel Peace Prize laureate (former Costa Rican president) Oscar Arias at a conference on Guatemala: "We'll be secure when we hear that knock at the door at 6:00 A.M. and we know it's only the milkman."

And then, on March 23, 1995, the front page of the *New York Times* jumped off my breakfast table, with the revelations that a Guatemalan army officer on the payroll of the CIA was directly involved in the assassinations of U.S. citizen Michael DeVine and an indigenous URNG leader married to American lawyer Jennifer Harbury. Harbury's hunger strikes had finally forced out the truth. On that March 23, history changed, as Guatemala's dirty secrets (and Washington's dirty secrets in Guatemala) became the breakfast-table reading of millions of Americans for weeks to come. I was in New York doing interviews with UN officials that day. I remember thinking that this scandal could do for Guatemala what the case of the six assassinated Jesuits had done in El Salvador: The U.S. role, always murky, was now out in the open. And the Guatemalan army, now on the defensive, would have to get serious about the peace negotiations, despite all its posturing to the contrary.

From here on in, until the signing of the final accords at the end of 1996, the peace negotiations acquired an irreversible rhythm. The new government of Alvaro Arzú that took office in January 1996 left no doubt that it seriously intended to conclude the negotiations quickly and on reasonable terms. Meanwhile, a magnificent Springtime began to unfold in Guatemala—even despite one last terrible army massacre of returning refugees at Xamán, Alta Verapaz, in October 1995. (In Guatemala, "Springtime" has a double meaning: In tourist brochures, the country is advertised as the land of "eternal spring"; but Guatemalans themselves use the term to refer to the democratic decade of 1944–1954.) It was Springtime again in 1996, because average Guatemalan citizens, and even human rights activists, began to conduct their business normally and to unlearn the brutally learned reflex of fear. Springtime, because new spaces were opening up within an exclusionary system for broader participation in politics, and indigenous and women's organizations were blossoming.

Springtime, because Quetzaltenango, Guatemala's second-largest city (half indigenous, half ladino), elected an indigenous mayor, the candidate of an autonomous indigenous "civic committee." (Not that his election dispelled ladino racism. Several prominent city walls bore the graffiti, "*Indio! que me compone las calles*": "Fix up the streets for me, you Indian.") Quetzaltenango also became a center for multisector "consultas populares" that brought together grassroots representatives from around the highlands to discuss the peace agenda. The *consulta* for Mayan priests and priestesses that I was invited to attend was a sophisticated discussion that crossed the boundaries between the spiritual and the political—another example of how people were appropriating the new spaces for participation. (See photos on page 159.)

In Sololá, a community (85 percent indigenous) that had been in the heart of the conflict zone, residents decided to choose their 1996 Reina (Queen) not on the basis of bathing-suit beauty but on the ability of the young women to explain the (1995) accord on indigenous peoples' rights. This was a special touch of Springtime because of the contrast to an earlier beauty queen: 1968's Miss Guatemala, Rogelia Cruz, known to have leftist sympathies, had been assassinated, her body stabbed, beaten, raped, poisoned, brutally tortured, and left naked for the vultures. The message had been deliberate and unmistakable, an early harbinger of the insidious message system that was to characterize Guatemala's thirty-six-year war. And in the late 1990s, the Sololá community, led by its elected indigenous mayor, unanimously rejected the army's decision to "donate" a new military institute at the site of its former base—that base so unforgettable because of the awful "monument" at the entrance—a gigantic army helmet over gigantic army boots. After extensive internal discussions, the community mobilized to have the facility converted into a branch of the national university. They were emphatic about demilitarizing the community and gaining new opportunities for higher education.

Sololá and Quetzaltenango in the late 1990s signify the beginning of the end of the counterinsurgency logic—and the opening of space for Guatemala's magic to emerge. This is the *Guatemala profunda* and the *Guatemala posible* of the future.

December 1996: Vámonos, Patria, a Caminar

December 28, 1996, was the night I never could have imagined. On the eve of the signing of Guatemala's peace accords, the Central Plaza was the scene of unprecedented—previously inconceivable—popular ceremonies and celebrations. A variety of indigenous groups danced and marched with banners in Mayan languages. At the Plaza's Acoustic Bandstand, URNG supporters were holding a public rally. As if they them-

Sololá before and after the end of the war: As late as the mid-1990s, the predominantly indigenous town of Sololá, in the middle of a major conflict zone, was kept "under control" by the army base, with the gigantic monument of the army helmet over boots at its entrance. By 1998, Sololá residents were demanding that the former army base be converted not into a military academy ("Adolfo Hall"), as the government initially proposed, but into a public university facility.

On the eve of the signing (the night of December 28, 1996), indigenous, popular, and civil society organizations celebrated in Guatemala City's Central Plaza; organizational banners depicted here include Saqb'ichil-COPMAGUA (Coordinating Office of Organizations of the Maya People of Guatemala), CONIC (National Coordinating Committee of the Indigenous and Peasants), Movement of Women Weavers of History, and Association of Guatemalan Lawyers and Notaries.

selves couldn't quite believe it, some of them still covered their faces with kerchiefs, the mark of the old clandestine mentality. A young man thrust a URNG women's-rights flyer into my hand. Slightly jaded, I remembered the battles of women to be treated as equals in the URNG. But this was not a night for judgmental thinking.

The lights of the majestic Catedral Metropolitana gave off a surrealistic glow, while the buildings surrounding the plaza were draped with banners: *La paz es tu oportunidad de dar felicidad* ("Peace is your chance to spread happiness") and (from the Colegio de Abogados or Lawyers' Association) *Construyamos la paz: Guatemala lo merece* ("Let's build peace: Guatemala deserves it"). There was an enchantment to that evening that I had never felt in Guatemala. This was the magnificent Guatemala, the subject of poet-*guerrillero* Otto René Castillo's ode, *"Vámonos patria a caminar, yo te acompaño"* ("Come, let's go, my country; I will go with you").

I thought back to my first "celebration" in that same plaza—on the eve of September 15, Independence Day of 1967—when the civil war was already raging. (The night before, I'd been awakened by gunfire between the army and the guerrillas.) It had been a strange celebration, without jubilation, surrounded by armed police and bayonetted soldiers in Vietnam-style fatigues. How many of the people in that plaza softly singing the national anthem had already been affected by violence and repression? That was thirty years ago, when Guatemala first drew us in, a whole generation of us from abroad, with her beauty and her violence and her never-ending drama.

The formal signing on December 29 of the final peace accord in the National Palace was a lavish affair, featuring visiting presidents from several Latin American countries and Boutros Boutros-Ghali, outgoing UN secretary general. The entire cast of characters involved in the peace process since 1990 was on hand. Watching the ceremonial signings by government functionaries and URNG leaders, I could hear the shouts from outside the palace, where thousands had gathered to celebrate. I would have liked to be out there and inside at the same time. Later, during the post-signing reception, came the most magnificent moment, as I looked out from the palace balcony and saw the plaza filled with thousands of people determined never to return to the past. Surely there hadn't been an occasion like this since the Revolution of 1944. This was the moment of an unequivocal *"adios"* to forty-two years of bloodshed and pain—one of those rare moments in deeply polarized Guatemala when national reconciliation seemed a real possibility.

During the entire week I was in Guatemala for the signing of the peace accords, I couldn't process anything analytically. Mainly, I felt happy. Was I alone in my jubilation? Apparently not. One friend of mine, part of the government team, described himself as being in an "emotional coma"—a combination of exhaustion with delirium, I think. On a more objective note, a telephone poll taken on the night of the signing by the conservative newspaper *Prensa Libre* showed that 77 percent of those polled responded that they felt "happy." Of course it was not so simple. Big business leaders, someone told me, had taken the day to go to the beach—but I saw some of them at the signing ceremony, anyway. Certainly, there were many skeptics among those attending the signing and outside in the plaza, but even some of the skeptics ended up celebrating after all. There were a thousand different subtexts, and I wanted nothing more than to stretch out this historic moment, to stay for a month and ask everyone where they were on the day of the signing and what they were thinking. . . .

Mid-1999: Guatephrenia

As I was in the last few months of finalizing this book, which had been my daily companion for nearly ten years, Guatemala once again dashed my hopes. In May 1999, after two years of political maneuvers among politicians in Congress, the long-awaited referendum on the constitutional reforms designed to lock in the peace accords finally took place. A bare 18.5 percent of registered voters went to the polls and blocked the reforms by a margin of 55/45. Because I had once been flying so high, I now came to feel the depths. Even my friend "gallows humor," who had gotten me through difficult times before, was hiding from me now.

Looking back on it, I can see that the defeat of the reforms was not an isolated event but the culmination of a process of deterioration. It took only a few weeks for the magic of that moment in December 1996 to begin being dispelled by the realities of actually existing Guatemala, with its stubborn resistances to change. Like others concerned about Guatemala's peace process, I have been suffering from a kind of "Guatephrenia"—a condition where I am caught between hope for a better future (*la Guatemala posible*) and exasperation, even horror, at how slowly things change here.

Like everyone else, I suffered the first real postwar shock from the deliberately grotesque assassination of Msgr. Juan Gerardi in April 1998: The bloody image of his skull crushed by a cement block and spread across the floor of his garage was an unmistakable reminder of the brutality of Guatemala's war. All the worse because the war was over, and this was a "peacetime" political crime; it came two nights after Gerardi presented his Human Rights Office's monumental report (ironically titled *Nunca Más [Never Again]*), documenting the army's atrocities during the war. A giant of a man, he had also been my friend and intellectual guide (see Acknowledgments). Today, more than a year after his assassination, after pursuing outrageous "personal motive" leads for months, the government's "investigation" has not made one inch of progress. Watching from his grave, the bishop is probably not surprised; after all, this is Guatemala.

I return to where I began in 1990–1991. Like others who have accompanied or participated in Guatemala's peace process, I got into this because I could see nowhere to move but forward. I can still see nowhere to move but forward. At its height, this process showed me the vision of a *Guatemala posible*. And even at its most painful moments, it remains compelling. Wherever it ends up, I have been privileged to accompany this roller-coaster process as one of its observers/chroniclers. I desperately wanted to end this book with some certainty (presumably through ratification of the constitutional reforms), some guarantee of a better future. But I was forgetting that there are no certainties here. Guatemala mocks me: "Just as you think you understand, we'll show you that you understand nothing at all."

The Project of This Book

Centaurs and Doves

Some years ago, Carlos Figueroa Ibarra (1986) gave us the unforgettable image of the "centaurization" of the Guatemalan state, that is, its domination by a counterinsurgency apparatus that was half-beast, half-human, a mix of civilian and military power, with the prevalence of the military component. As I have used this construction in a previous book (Jonas 1991, 148), it refers to a creation by the entire ruling coalition, composed of the bourgeoisie or large propertied interests, the army, and its civilian allies in the state apparatus. What was negotiated in the peace process was the *de-centaurization* of the state and society, as the precondition for strengthening civilian power and constructing a multiethnic democracy—and ultimately, for assuring the governability of Guatemala.

At the heart of the first half of this book is the obvious question (and one that is most frequently asked): How did it become possible to have a successful peace negotiation in Guatemala? Why did this seemingly invincible army agree to negotiate and sign substantive peace accords with the rebels that went far beyond ending the war? How did that army and its civilian allies—the "centaurs"—come to negotiate with Guatemala's "doves"? By "doves" I mean a broad spectrum of those who believed in (or came to believe in) the project of a meaningful peace settlement—among them, most organized sectors of civil society, most of the URNG (most of the time),[1] and a few visionary individuals in the ruling coalition, even in the army. The Guatemalan settlement did not reflect a purely military calculus. Herein lies the fascination of the political dynamics that led to the Guatemalan peace accords.

But the saga does not end there. Concluding this book with the peace accord signing would have been easier and less painful, perhaps, but only half of the story. The two and a half years of attempting to implement what was signed on paper, and to identify the dangerous obstacles, both visible and invisible, have raised many new questions: Did the centaurs and "peace resisters" ever have any intention of implementing the accords? Or did they lay a trap to achieve their goal (demobilization by the guerrillas) without really conceding a thing? What is likely to be the lasting significance of the peace process, and what are the limits of change in Guatemala?

Readers will note a shift in tone between the first half of this book and the last half. I knew ahead of time that the implementation process—turning paper agreements into realities—would be more difficult than the negotiation; but I didn't realize just how much more difficult. Detractors of the peace process will argue that it was my mistake to have been hopeful in the first place; but if that was a mistake, it was one shared by many Guatemalans. Thus, the optimism in the first half of the book is muted in the second half, which tells the tales of the implementation wars. Rather than try to make everything fit together (too) neatly, I have preferred to allow these differences in tone and mood to emerge as part of the still unfinished story.

Methodology: Binational and Multiperspective Constructions

Having written about Guatemala throughout its decades of war, I began to follow the peace process since its inception in the late 1980s and early 1990s. After the formal peace talks began in 1991, I spent around two months of each year in Guatemala, interviewing virtually every relevant player (both formal and informal). These individuals came from all sectors of Guatemalan society and spanned the entire social and ideological spectrum—from presidents and defense ministers to the URNG rebels and their leaders, Catholic Church bishops and priests from many denominations, a broad range of grassroots and indigenous activists, businessmen, and politicians. During the times when I was not in Guatemala, I maintained ongoing direct phone and e-mail contact with major participants and observers. In addition, during those times, several wonderful in-country research assistants served as my "eyes and ears" (see Acknowledgments).

Also on a yearly basis, I interviewed virtually all informed and participating actors in the international community. These interviews with diplomats from the United Nations, the United States, and various countries of Europe and Latin America were conducted not only in Guatemala but also in Mexico, where most of the formal negotiations took place. I regularly interviewed the highly informed and interested officials of Mexico's Ministry of Foreign Relations and knowledgeable diplomats in the embassies of the Friend countries. Mexico was also the site for interviews with the URNG leaders who negotiated the peace. In the United States, I made numerous research trips to New York for interviews with UN officials and other knowledgeable diplomats in the country missions to the United Nations and to Washington for interviews with U.S. policymakers, members of Congress, and officials in the International Monetary Fund (IMF) and World Bank, the Organization of American States (OAS), and the Inter-American Development Bank (IDB).

This book, therefore, is informed by a multiplicity of perspectives. Many of them will doubtless be presented in books by the primary actors, who will tell the story as they lived it. One particularity of my perspective is that it is *binational*. I have been privileged (as well as financially obligated) to have one foot in Guatemala and one foot in the United States, and hence to be informed by the dual logic of an inside/outside view. From inside the country, events seem less linear, more multidimensional, complex, and nuanced; all that is part of the Guatemalan logic, whereby things happen in the most indirect manner possible. But on the other hand, everything is also more emotionally charged—and distorted if informed *only* by being in the world of Guatemala, distanced from any larger picture. Indeed, there were times when I felt that I could see Guatemala more objectively by entering, sinking roots, and then leaving, to return again later.

Another element of binationality is the vibrant and growing community of Guatemalans surrounding me in the United States. Many of them are in the United States precisely because of Guatemala's protracted civil war, and their lives here (or between here and Guatemala) will be greatly affected by the quality of Guatemala's peace. (I take up this theme more analytically and systematically in the Conclusion.) A final element of binationality is related to my intended audience: Because of the deep U.S. involvement in all of Guatemala's affairs during the twentieth century, I have always written, and I am writing this book, for Guatemalans and interested readers worldwide, but especially for the U.S. public.

At the core of this book are the hundreds of interviews (conducted on a not-for-attribution basis) during the six years of the negotiation process and the first two and a half years of the peace accord implementation. (Perhaps today, some of the interviews could be on the record, but particularly during the negotiations, confidentiality was a precondition for most interviews.) The interviews were usually more than an hour in length and sometimes lasted three to four hours. Some of those I interviewed year after year have become friends. Many of them did not follow the script I would have expected, and I found "doves" in some of the most unlikely places. The interviews were so multilayered and multidimensional that I have been tempted to write the full "inside story," in order to allow the richness of all the different voices and viewpoints to emerge. (This is especially the case for Chapter 2.) If I had done that, however, I would not have finished until well into the twenty-first century, too late for the book to make any difference. So I have constructed this story by synthesizing, weaving together, and distilling an interpretation from all the hundreds of interviews, cross-checking different versions against each other.

The experience of doing the interviews has been personally gratifying and often exciting. There was intellectual excitement—"light bulbs" going off in my head—for example, when the interviews forced me to examine my own preconceptions. But excitement also came in other forms. One top European diplomat who had been involved with Guatemala's peace process since the beginning arranged, through his embassy in Guatemala, to speak with me when our paths crossed for twenty-four hours in Mexico City. We did finally have an extended breakfast interview—but only after he contacted me (from his car phone) during the one hour I was reachable. That same week (in 1996), at the Mexico presentation of the first book to be published about the peace process, by Teresa Bolaños de Zarco, I was finally able to arrange a long-awaited interview with a key behind-the-scenes player—a Guatemalan whom I had never been able to catch in his office in Guatemala during the previous six years.

In addition to my interviews, this book is based on consultation of all of the relevant written sources—the primary documents and analyses listed in the References. I have monitored Guatemala's daily press, as well as weekly and monthly publications. In addition, I have drawn on excellent on-the-ground analyses presented at forums and conferences organized by a host of Guatemalan universities and research institutes, international and national foundations, and private sector institutions, as well as indigenous, women's, human rights, religious, and other popular organizations. In short, virtually every sector of Guatemalan society has engaged the issues addressed here, and my interpretations owe a great deal to their efforts.

I was fortunate to be a consultant and participant in a multisector roundtable conference held in San Francisco's Presidio in October 1994 ("Imagining a Post-War Guatemala"), sponsored by the (Oscar) Arias Foundation for Peace and Human Progress and the Vesper Society. For three full days—at a time when the formal peace negotiations were not going well—forty of us sat in a closed room in a frank but difficult dialogue; some of the relationships established through this dialogue later proved significant. (It was at this conference that Alvaro Arzú, at the time a "pre-candidate" for the 1995 presidential election, engaged in dialogues that led to his informal contacts and then his formal on-the-record negotiations with the URNG after he took office in 1996.)

Finally, in order to gain a comparative perspective on the Guatemalan experience, I have studied and interviewed participants and observers in other peace processes—in El Salvador and elsewhere in Latin America, South Africa, the Middle East, Northern Ireland, and Bosnia. I have been involved in organizing as well as participating in conferences on comparative peace processes and coedited a volume based on one conference that I co-organized (Lipschutz and Jonas 1998).

Lecturas *or Readings of History*

It is said that history (especially after wars) is written by the victors. But what happens in an ambiguous case such as this, where there were no clear winners/losers but a negotiated solution? This aspect of the Guatemalan situation convinced me that the only way to write about this peace process, even as it unfolded, was to conduct the hundreds of interviews with participants from all sides.

Since my method involves a distillation from these interviews, I hope to achieve some measure of credibility and faithfulness to reality, if not total "objectivity." In the end, of course, I am presenting an analysis, a particular *lectura* or reading or recounting of events. I shall address the many embedded issues of interpretation as they arise—among these, responsibilities for the war and during the war, agents of (versus obstacles to) peace and democratization, and responsibilities for successes and failures in implementing the peace accords. This is "committed history," insofar as I have felt committed to a successful outcome of the peace process. But it is informed by all possible viewpoints—including many that were difficult for me to hear—and my own analyses have been modified by many interpretations that differed from my own.

Of all the "other" interpretations, perhaps the most difficult for me is the argument that the peace process is meaningless except as a cease-fire, that it has made very little difference to Guatemala and nothing very significant has changed. Even in my most pessimistic moods—and even after the unkindest cut of all, the defeat of the constitutional reforms—I believe that a great change has *begun* in Guatemala. I feel privileged to have been allowed to accompany and share in this process of change, with all its ups and downs. I hope, therefore, that this book can serve as a mirror to Guatemalans, to remind them of their remarkable achievements during the last decade.

Susanne Jonas
San Francisco

Note

1. This is not to portray the URNG leaders uncritically but simply to recognize that they were instrumental in initiating the project of a meaningful peace settlement and in pressing it forward. In characterizing their role overall, I am reminded of the answer given by Nicaragua's Sergio Ramírez when asked recently what the lasting legacy of the Sandinistas was: He answered, "in spite of themselves, democracy."

1

Background: Guatemala's Thirty-Six-Year Civil War

Modern Guatemalan history has been characterized by a unique dynamic, in which the country's structural problems have given rise to popular and revolutionary movements time and again; but they have also provoked responses by repressive forces that prevented those movements from achieving their goals. The counterinsurgent forces, strong enough to prevent a popular or revolutionary victory, were unable to address the sources of revolt, to triumph definitively over the carriers of revolt, or to control the social forces unleashed by chronic crisis. This dynamic has been expressed in Guatemala's thirty-six-year civil war, the longest and bloodiest in the hemisphere, leaving some 200,000 civilians dead or "disappeared."[1] It was a "Cold War civil war" insofar as it was ideologically, politically, and militarily part of the U.S. Cold War confrontation with the Soviet Union and communist forces (real or labeled as such) in the Third World.

This chapter focuses on the two most recent phases of Guatemala's civil war, during the 1970s and 1980s, as the backdrop for the peace process of the 1990s.[2] But in order to understand these phases, we must go back to previous events, beginning with the democratic nationalist Revolution of 1944 and its violent CIA-sponsored termination in 1954. The Revolution of 1944–1954 and its overthrow created the conditions for the civil war's first phase: the armed insurgency during the early 1960s (inspired also by the Cuban Revolution) and the ferocious response of 1966–1968, when, under U.S. tutelage, Guatemala's army was shaped into the first modern counterinsurgency army of Latin America. The second phase of the war, to be analyzed here in more detail, reached genocidal proportions in the early 1980s and consolidated the counterinsurgency state.

As a consequence of the war, "normal" electoral politics came to have very little meaning. Virtually all political arrangements from 1954 until the mid-1990s were dominated by the coalition between the army and economic elites; they were based on an explicit rejection of reformist options and political exclusion of the majority of the population. As will be seen, even the return of elected civilian government in the late 1980s did not signify a return to democracy in any meaningful sense, nor did it address any of the glaring socioeconomic disparities. Hence, the popular and indigenous majorities of the population were not able to seek redress of grievances through electoral means; instead, they pressured through extraparliamentary (mainly unarmed) organizations, which the army and government deemed "subversive" and subjected to levels of repression unmatched anywhere in Latin America.

The vicious cycle of war and exclusionary politics continued for several decades. Although the army twice dealt the revolutionary movement nearly fatal blows (in 1966–1968 and in 1981–1983), it was unable to prevent the rebels' resurgence again in the late 1980s. Like its historic enemy, the counterinsurgency army, the insurgent movement had to learn through bitter mistakes; but it seemed to have nine lives and several times was reborn from its own ashes. At the same time, the revolutionary movement itself underwent profound crises and redefinitions of strategy, leading to its subsequent initiatives for a negotiated end to the war.

After decades of civil war, upheaval, and political violence, neither side was able to win outright; finally, some of the main players began to see that the war could be ended only through a genuine political settlement. Meanwhile, the country remained in a chronic social crisis, and profound issues of social injustice remained foremost on the agenda.

Antecedents:
U.S. Intervention and Its Aftermath

Under the weight of the economic and social crises caused by the world depression of the 1930s, Guatemala's neocolonial order cracked in 1944, when a broad middle- and working-class coalition overthrew military dictator Jorge Ubico. Thus was initiated the Revolution of 1944–1954, the only genuinely democratic experience in Guatemala's entire history. The two governments of Juan Jose Arévalo (1945–1950) and Jacobo Arbenz (1951–54) guaranteed basic democratic liberties (including free elections), abolished forced labor (which had been nearly universal for the indigenous population), granted minimum wages and basic rights for workers and peasants, and increased social welfare and equality. In addition, the Revolution modernized Guatemalan capitalism, undertaking agricultural diversification and industrialization programs, fomenting national enterprises, and regulating foreign investment to serve national priorities. Most significant was Arbenz's far-reaching (but capitalist) agrarian reform of 1952, which distributed land to over 100,000 peasant families.

Coming on top of other nationalistic moves by Arbenz, the expropriation of unused land belonging to the U.S.-based United Fruit Company (the largest landowner in Guatemala) prompted an angry response from the U.S. government. Charging that Guatemala was serving as a "beachhead for Soviet expansion" in the Western Hemisphere, the CIA worked with Guatemalan opposition forces to organize the overthrow of the Arbenz government in June 1954 and to install in its place a pro-U.S. counterrevolutionary regime. This regime immediately reversed the democratic and progressive legislation of the Revolution, including the land reform, and unleashed widespread repression. The legacy of the Revolution of 1944–1954 and its violent termination was to compound the social polarization already characteristic of Guatemala, throwing the country into permanent crisis.

Nevertheless, even under the post-1954 counterrevolutionary order, history could not be "reversed," since the same underlying structural dynamics and contradictions that had caused the Revolution continued to develop. The Guatemalan economy, like that of all Central America, enjoyed a thirty-year period (1950–1980) of growth based on the expansion and diversification of agricultural exports to the world market and a minimal industrialization during the 1960s and 1970s, carried out mainly by foreign capital. But even export-led growth generated turmoil, because of the extreme inequities in resource and income distribution. The most telling indicator for Guatemala was that 2 percent of the population continued to control 67 percent of the arable land. In the 1970s, the diversification of exports brought significant new expropriations (from peasants) and concentrations of land; the main beneficiaries were army generals using their control over the state apparatus to accumulate personal wealth. Thus, impoverishment stemming from land concentration intensified geometrically, as Guatemala became virtually the only country in Latin America not to have sustained even a minimal land reform.

At the social level, the diversification of the productive structure significantly modified Guatemala's traditional class structure and reshaped the ruling coalition (between the army and economic elites). Among other things, diversification of the ruling class meant incorporation of the upper ranks of military officers and a redefinition of the alliance between the army and the bourgeoisie. But rather than "opening up" the class structure, these modifications only accentuated its overall polarization. At the bottom pole of Guatemalan society, meanwhile, industrialization and agricultural diversification did not significantly expand the proletariat as a fully employed labor force. Rather, the countryside saw the growth of a semiproletariat: Land-starved peasants from the highlands were forced to work on the southern coast as seasonal migrant laborers during part of the year. In the cities, migrants from rural areas swelled the ranks of an underemployed informal proletariat. As a consequence, the "development" of the 1960s and 1970s actually left a decreasing proportion of the economically active population fully employed on a permanent basis. As will be seen below, these tendencies were compounded during the 1980s.

Because 60 percent of the population is indigenous, class divisions in Guatemala become much more explosive through their intersection with ethnic divisions. For centuries, the indigenous population has been subjected to one or another form of forced labor; the state, in particular the army, has defined for itself the vocation of disciplining, controlling, and repressing the indigenous majority of the population. In a situation approaching de-facto apartheid, issues of ethnic identity and democratic rights for the indigenous majority have become central. As will be seen, the combination of class and ethnic tensions accounted for the revolutionary upsurge of the early 1980s and remains a source of social unrest. The crises of recent decades have also laid the objective foundations for a new protagonism of women, but this only began to find specific forms of organized expression in the 1990s.

The profound changes in society produced new generations of social movements (labor, peasant, indigenous, community)—first in the 1960s, then in the late 1970s, and (after they were destroyed in the early 1980s) again in the second half of the 1980s. In the absence of any serious attempt to meet the needs of the poor or the indigenous or to use the benefits of growth during the 1960s and 1970s to redistribute wealth, these movements continually exerted new pressures upon the state and the established social order. These pressures were contained by a level of repression at times unmatched anywhere else in Latin America; one generation after another of movement leaders and activists, as well as centrist political opposition leaders, was eliminated by the army and illegal paramilitary forces. Even the systematic repression failed to stop the reemergence of popular movements in one form or another, although it severely restricted their functioning.

These massive social conflicts have defined Guatemalan politics during the past four decades. Within an overall framework of direct military rule, there was a civilian interlude (1966–1970) and beginning in 1986, a more definitive return to civilian rule, during which the army dominated politics from behind the scenes. But largely as a legacy of the experience of the 1944–1954 Revolution and its violent overthrow, these hard-line regimes faced constant challenges. In fact, the illegitimacy of the ruling coalition and the refusal to permit even moderate reformist political options created the conditions for the growth of a revolutionary guerrilla movement. Quite literally, there was no alternative "within the system." (Issues of interpretation on this and other points are taken up in the last section of this chapter.)

The first wave of guerrilla insurgency, during the 1960s, was centered in the eastern region, where the peasants were ladino rather than Mayan; although small and without a base among the indigenous population, the insurgency was contained only after a major counterinsurgency effort, organized, financed, and run directly by the United States along the lines of its operations in Vietnam. (See Jonas 1996a and Chapter 5.) This was a turning point in Guatemala, with U.S. military advisers playing a decisive role in "professionalizing" the Guatemalan military—transforming that army (previously "weakened" by nationalist tendencies and inefficiency) into a modern, disciplined, brutal counterinsurgency army that subsequently came to dominate the state directly. The counterinsurgency state was institutionalized after 1970, when the head of the 1966–1968 campaign, Colonel Carlos Arana Osorio (the "butcher of Zacapa"), used that victory to win the 1970 presidential election. Since the goal of this first "dirty war" had been to eradicate the civilian support base of the guerrillas, it cost the lives of over 8,000 civilians. It was also within this context, in Guatemala, that such artifacts of counterinsurgency war as semiofficial death squads (based in the security forces) and "disappearances" of civilian opposition figures were introduced to Latin America. Since that time, Guatemala has had more than 40,000 civilian disappearances, accounting for over 40 percent of the total for all Latin America.

The insurgents, in no way prepared for the army counteroffensive and having made serious mistakes in their own organizing strategies, suffered a temporary defeat in 1968. However, they were able to reorganize and reinitiate their struggle in the early 1970s, this time in the western indigenous highlands, with some Mayan communities becoming central participants. The active involvement of up to half a million Mayas in the uprising of the late 1970s and early 1980s was without precedent in Guatemala, indeed in the hemisphere. Coming in the wake of the 1979 Sandinista victory in Nicaragua and the outbreak of civil war in El Salvador, this remarkable "awakening" in the indigenous highlands provoked a revolutionary crisis, threatening the army's century-old domination over rural Guatemala.

Insurgency and Counterinsurgency
in the 1970s–1980s

As suggested above, the structural transformations of the 1960s–1980s caused Guatemala's indigenous populations to redefine their class identity. These same factors also profoundly affected their self-conceptions and identities as indigenous people and became the basis for the vast

Mayan uprising in the late 1970s and early 1980s. Economic growth followed by economic crisis broke down the objective barriers that had kept the Mayas relatively isolated in the highlands. This was greatly intensified by the economic and political crises of the 1970s and 1980s, when growing numbers of Mayas were forced to migrate to the southern coast as seasonal laborers and to Guatemala City. These changes and displacements brought them into increased contact with the ladino, Spanish-speaking world. Rather than "ladinizing" or acculturating them, however, this experience reinforced their struggle to preserve their indigenous identity, although in new forms—as Guatemalan Jesuit priest/scholar/activist Ricardo Falla (1978, 546) put it, to discover "new ways of being indigenous." These factors form the background for understanding why Guatemala's Mayan peoples became one of the powerful social forces driving the insurgency of the 1970s and 1980s.

In the countryside, structural contradictions—the crisis in subsistence agriculture, compounded by a massive earthquake in 1976—uprooted and displaced thousands of indigenous peasants, causing them to redefine themselves in both class and cultural terms. As producers, they were being semiproletarianized as a seasonal migrant labor force on the plantations of the southern coast, meanwhile often losing even the tiny subsistence plots of land they had traditionally held in the highlands. The combination of their experiences of being evicted from their own lands and their experiences as a migrant semiproletariat radicalized large numbers of highlands Mayas. Even the more developmentalist influences were contradictory, in that they raised hopes and expectations in the 1960s, only to dash them in the 1970s. The clearest examples of this dynamic were those peasants who received land from the government's colonization programs in the 1960s, only to have it taken away again in the 1970s, as powerful army officers grabbed profitable lands in colonization areas.

Culturally, highlands indigenous communities were being transformed and redefined throughout the 1960s and 1970s, as they "opened up" to contact with the ladino world. Increased contact had the paradoxical effect of reinforcing their defense of their ethnic/cultural identity, and this became a factor in mobilizing their resistance to the ladino state. Politically, "reformist" parties, such as the Christian Democrats, made incursions into indigenous communities, raising expectations of change—only to leave those hopes unfulfilled for most people. Meanwhile, indigenous organizations were defined by the government as "subversive" and excluded from "normal" political expression.

Finally, increased army repression against indigenous communities had contradictory effects: Rather than terrorizing the Mayas into passivity, by the late 1970s it stimulated some of them to take up arms as the only available means of self-defense against state violence. All of these contradictory experiences of the 1970s must be seen in interaction with the transformation of grassroots organizations of the Catholic Church, the rise of Christian Base Communities, and the gradual emergence of a "Church of the Poor." These new religious currents became central to the radicalization of the indigenous highlands.

All of these strands were woven together by 1976–1978 in the emergence of the Comité de Unidad Campesina (CUC) as a national peasant organization, including both peasants and agricultural workers, both Mayas and poor ladinos, but led primarily by Mayas—by definition a "subversive" organization from the viewpoint of the ruling coalition. CUC came into the limelight after a major massacre at Panzós, Alta Verzpaz, in 1978, and the 1980 massacre at the Spanish embassy, in which Guatemalan security forces burned alive several dozen indigenous protesters, as well as functionaries of both governments. In February 1980, CUC staged a massive strike of workers on the southern coast sugar and cotton plantations; from the viewpoint of landowners and the army, this strike was their worst nightmare come true.

Equally important in the growth of a politicized indigenous movement was a change in the stance of the revolutionary insurgents vis-à-vis the Maya population, within the context of a much broader reevaluation of strategy and organizational recomposition after the defeat of 1968. This involved a recognition of the failures of the *foco* strategy of the 1960s as fundamentally militaristic and not rooted in a solid mass base. Even more serious, the insurgents had to rectify having virtually ignored the indigenous population during the 1960s. By the time of their resurgence in the early 1970s, the three major organizations had generally come to understand some of these errors; two of them, Ejército Guerrillero de los Pobres (EGP) and Organización del Pueblo en Armas (ORPA), spent several years being educated by the indigenous population and organizing a political support base in the western highlands (and other areas) before renewing armed actions later in the 1970s.

The guerrilla military offensive reached its height in 1980–1981, gaining 6,000 to 8,000 armed fighters and 250,000 to 500,000 active collaborators and supporters and operating in most parts of the country. In the context of the Sandinista triumph in Nicaragua and the outbreak of civil war in El Salvador (both in 1979), the new wave of armed struggle in Guatemala was taken very seriously by the ruling coalition as heralding a possible seizure of power by the insurgents. In early 1982, the various guerrilla organizations united in the Unidad Revolucionaria Nacional Guatemalteca (URNG), overcoming years of sectarian divisions.

Even as unity was proclaimed, however, and even as the revolutionary movement achieved its maximal expression during 1980 and 1981, a change in the balance of forces between the insurgents and the army began during the second half of 1981, as the army initiated an unprecedented counteroffensive. By the spring of 1982, the revolutionary movement had taken very serious losses to its infrastructure in the city, where security forces had already, in 1978–1980, decapitated the unions and other popular movements and political opposition forces. In the highlands, the army unleashed a virtual holocaust upon the indigenous communities. Blinded by its own triumphalism, the URNG had in fact lost the initiative, and some of its fundamental weaknesses came to the surface. As a result of the URNG's weaknesses and of major changes within the ruling coalition, the army gained the upper hand and dealt decisive blows against the insurgents. For the next several years, the URNG was on the defensive and did not recover a capacity to take new initiatives until the late 1980s.

A major reason for this second defeat of the guerrillas and the suffering inflicted on its supporters among the population was the failure to have anticipated the scorched-earth, genocidal war unleashed by the Guatemalan security forces; hence, tens of thousands of highlands Mayas were left unprepared to defend themselves. The statistics are staggering: From mid-1981 to 1983 alone, 440 villages were entirely wiped off the face of the map; up to 150,000 civilians were killed or "disappeared." There were over one million displaced persons (one million internal refugees, up to 200,000 refugees in Mexico). Accompanying these massive population displacements was the deliberate destruction of huge areas of the highlands (burning of forests, etc.), causing irreversible environmental devastation. The aim of these genocidal policies was not only to eliminate the guerrillas' popular support base but also to destroy the culture, identity, and communal structures of the indigenous populations.[3]

These goals were carried out, in the first stage (1981–1983), through scorched-earth warfare and, in the second stage (after 1983), through the imposition of coercive institutions throughout the countryside, designed to consolidate military control over the population. Among these institutions were mandatory paramilitary "civilian self-defense patrols" or PACs (at one point involving one million peasants, one-fourth of the adult population); "development poles," rural forced resettlement camps where every aspect of people's lives was subject to direct army control; and militarization of the entire administrative apparatus of the country. These counterinsurgency institutions were legalized in the new Constitution of 1985, which provided the juridical framework for civilian government in the late 1980s.

At the entrance to Chichicastenango (world-famous for its culture and for its Sunday marketplace, but located in a conflict zone), the army was still using obligatory PACs or "Civilian Self-Defense Patrols" (renamed "Voluntary Civil Defense Committees," but equally involuntary) to maintain military control in the mid-1990s. The sign reads: "The defense of the country is the obligation of everyone," and "The army fulfills its mission; the people trust their army."

Recomposition of the Counterinsurgency State and Return to Civilian Rule

As seen above, the beginning of revolutionary insurgency in Guatemala during the 1960s generated a counterinsurgent response on the part of the United States and the Guatemalan ruling coalition, which was institution-alized in state power after 1970.[4] During the late 1970s, the ability of the military regimes to govern Guatemala deteriorated seriously as a conse-quence of relatively weakened internal cohesion within the ruling coali-tion and the lack of any consensual basis or societal legitimacy. The clear-est examples were the openly fraudulent elections of 1974, 1978, and 1982. By 1982, these divisions were serious enough to spark recognition of the need for a change in the nature of military rule in order to recover some modicum of legitimacy, at least among the ruling sectors, and to end Guatemala's international isolation as a pariah state, and hence its re-stricted access to international financial assistance.

The change or "recomposition" is generally seen as beginning with the coup of March 1982 (following the third successive electoral fraud), which brought to power the regime of General Efraín Ríos Montt. Nevertheless, the Ríos Montt government (March 1982–August 1983) presided over the bloodiest era and the majority of the massacres. It was only after this most brutal phase of the counterinsurgency war had accomplished its goals under Ríos Montt that army leaders and their civilian allies, now under the military government of General Oscar Mejía Víctores, took concrete steps toward a return to civilian rule. They recognized that a facade of constitutional democracy was needed to overcome the contradictions of direct military dictatorship. This understanding was the background for the political process of 1983–1985, during which a Constituent Assembly was elected to write a new constitution containing basic guarantees of citizens' rights, at least on paper, and presidential elections were held in late 1985.[5]

The 1985 presidential election, although free of fraud, was severely restricted and unrepresentative of large sectors of the population, as only rightist and centrist parties that had reached agreement with the military were allowed to participate (see Trudeau 1993; Jonas 1989). Aside from the exclusion of the left, there were no real choices on substantive issues. Nevertheless, the election did permit nonmilitary candidates for the first time in fifteen years; it was overwhelmingly won by Christian Democrat Vinicio Cerezo, the most progressive of the candidates. Cerezo's victory was greeted with high hopes for a real change from the many years of military dictatorship.

Despite these hopes and despite having come into power with a significant popular mandate, however, Cerezo chose not to fully use the space that he had—that is, not to wage the struggle that would have been needed to achieve a real transfer of power from the military to civilians. His government did very little to control the army or address the country's underlying socioeconomic problems; he accepted the army's priority of defeating popular and revolutionary forces, and this significantly limited the possibility for genuinely pluralistic politics or for ending the civil war. In this regard, the Cerezo period (1986–1990) turned out to be not so much a genuine "transition to democracy" as a necessary adjustment for trying to deal with Guatemala's multiple crises and to reestablish minimal international credibility. It evolved into a civilian version of the counterinsurgency state, in some respects a continuation of what had been imposed in the late 1960s.

A second nonfraudulent election was held in 1990; it was viewed as significant insofar as it established the continuity of civilian rule. Nevertheless, abstention was extremely high, with only 30 percent of eligible voters participating; and once again, no leftist opposition parties were permitted. By 1990, however, there were new currents in the "informal" arena of Guatemalan civil society (outside the electoral process), and these began to undermine the foundations of the counterinsurgency state. One major expression of these currents was an emerging national consensus, articulated primarily in dialogues led by the Catholic Church, for an end to the civil war. Virtually all political sectors began to recognize that Guatemala could not be truly democratized until the civil war was ended through political negotiations (rather than a military victory by either side), until the country was demilitarized, and until the underlying structural inequalities and ethnic discrimination were acknowledged and addressed.

Social Crisis and Reemergence of Social Movements

Structural social crisis—ironically, a product of macroeconomic growth during the 1970s—was compounded during the 1980s, when the international capitalist crisis hit Central America (and all Latin America) as severely as the depression of the 1930s. Among its principal manifestations were rising prices for all industrial imports (largely a consequence of the "oil shocks"), coupled with falling prices for Central American exports. These crises left the Guatemalan economy suffering negative growth rates during the 1980s; both unemployment and inflation soared to unprecedented levels. As a result, purchasing power in 1989 was 22 percent of what it had been in 1972, and the overall poverty levels of 1980 jumped markedly during the second half of the decade.

The central social characteristic of Guatemala during the 1980s (and into the 1990s) remained increasing concentration of wealth amid pervasive poverty. All of the Central American countries shared this characteristic, but Guatemalan poverty has been particularly extreme, on several counts. First, the inequality of resource and income distribution has been greater, and no measures have been taken since the overthrow of Arbenz to alleviate it (i.e., no land or tax reform). The second particularity of Guatemalan poverty has been the number of social indicators on which it ranks worst (illiteracy, physical quality of life, infant mortality). The third particularity is the ethnic component of poverty, with all statistics for the indigenous population being far worse than the national average. As elsewhere, there has also been a marked feminization of poverty.

The above characteristics of extreme underdevelopment and inequality were not new to Guatemala, but a number of things did change dramatically during the 1980s. First, under the impact of the international crisis of the 1980s, all of Guatemala's economic and social problems were seriously aggravated. Even at the macroeconomic level, Guatemala lost more than fifteen years' growth during the 1980s, reversing the growth pattern of the previous thirty years. Second, after the mid-1980s, the government began to implement austerity policies more aggressively, culminating in the structural adjustment measures of the late 1980s and early 1990s; these policies only further aggravated the grave social crisis. Third, informalization of the urban proletariat left only slightly over one-third of the workforce fully and permanently employed.

This last indicator was among the important modifications in Guatemala's class structure during the 1980s, which left close to 90 percent of the population living below the official poverty line by the end of the decade (up from 79 percent in 1980); nearly three-fourths of the population lived in extreme poverty, that is, unable to afford a basic minimum diet.[6] During the late 1980s, the impact of the economic and social crisis in regenerating social ferment among the poor proved greater than the ability of the counterinsurgency state to repress such ferment. In spite of the reescalation of repression against labor and other popular movements, the constitution of this huge majority of the population that was united by being poor led to a slow rebuilding and reemergence of popular movements after the disasters of the early 1980s; a stream of austerity protests began in 1985 and continued with surprising vigor.

Guatemala's new popular movements were the product not only of austerity measures but also of the country's multiple crises, including the many crises of uprooted populations. The war alone left over 10 percent of the population displaced. Natural disaster, war, and economic crisis during the late 1970s and 1980s brought significant migration to the capital, causing its population to double. Increasingly, the urban poor were indigenous; and more than half of the households came to be headed by women. A significant number of the new urban poor (250,000 to 500,000 people) lived in the city's massive shantytowns in precarious squatter settlements. The absence of basic social services (running water, sewage, electricity, transportation) sparked new community struggles, which became as important as the more traditional labor union struggles among organized sectors of the labor force.

In the rural areas, meanwhile, hundreds of thousands of those displaced within the highlands or to the southern coast joined together with the landless already living there to form a national movement for land. The reconstituted popular movements of primarily rural indigenous peoples also included human rights groups organized around demands that were openly political and directly related to the ongoing counterinsurgency war: for example, the Grupo de Apoyo Mutuo (GAM), an organization of wives and mothers of the "disappeared" and other human rights victims; the mainly indigenous widows' organization CONAVIGUA; CERJ Runujel Junam, founded to empower highlands Mayas to resist service in the PACs; and CONDEG, the Council of Displaced Guatemalans, representing internal refugees. Many thousands of Mayas also resisted army relocation and control programs by fleeing to remote mountain areas and forming permanent "communities in resistance" (CPRs), which finally began to gain national and international recognition in the early 1990s.

Among the main new characteristics of Guatemala's popular movements in the late 1980s and early 1990s were the following: The first and most important was the centrality of the indigenous population with its double condition of exploitation and ethnic discrimination in both rural and urban settings. This was reflected in the rise of diverse movements and organizations fighting for a broad range of indigenous rights (see Warren 1998a; Esquit and Gálvez 1997). The second novelty was the slowly emerging protagonism of women, although their participation was often invisible. Third was the growing role of the Catholic Church within popular movements. Liberation Theology was a major influence throughout the 1970s and 1980s; even after the appearance and rapid growth of evangelical Protestant groups during the 1980s, the Catholic Church remained a leading force in articulating the demands of the popular movements.

In short, Guatemala experienced the gradual emergence of a bloc of popular and indigenous organizations.[7] These organizations continued to suffer from many serious weaknesses—above all, continued vulnerability to the endless stream of kidnappings, disappearances, death threats, and assassinations. Their articulation as a social force was also hindered by continuing problems of disunity and inability to organize among the huge informal proletariat. Because repression forced them to operate semiclandestinely, their advances were often imperceptible. Nevertheless, their continued existence and growth was in itself a form of defiance of the counterinsurgency state.

By the late 1980s the context for political action was also shaped by the resurgence of the URNG. Even though the army had destroyed much of the URNG's social base in the highlands in the early 1980s, it had been unable to inflict a "final" defeat upon the insurgent forces or to "win" the war definitively. Hence, the organizations of the URNG survived the holocaust; they remained the nuclei of future resistance, even at their low point, and gradually began to recover their ability to take initiatives, both militarily and politically. Nevertheless, their inability to resist the army's counteroffensive of the early 1980s, combined with the recomposition of the counterinsurgency state in the mid-1980s, required once again a profound reorganization and redefinition of strategy.

Such redefinitions became necessary, first, in response to the clear lesson of the early 1980s that military victory over the counterinsurgency

forces was a totally unthinkable objective—and that the cost of the second round of the war for the civilian population had been so high as to
preclude a strategy based simply on continuing the war. Second, in view
of the 1985 election and transition to civilian rule, that is, to a potentially
legitimate government, the Left had to find new ways of becoming a significant force in civil society. Hence, as will be seen, shortly after the 1985
election, the URNG began to propose dialogue/negotiations for a political settlement to the war. For the URNG, the emphasis on negotiations
was part of several larger modifications of strategy: giving more weight
to political aspects of the struggle, while at the same time maintaining a
military capacity; broadening its social and political alliances; slowly beginning to recognize the role of popular and indigenous sectors acting
autonomously; and the importance of an ideological pluralism that
would allow the popular movements to follow their own organizational
dynamic. As will be seen in subsequent chapters, this was also a response to the growing complexity and the growing plurality of interests
in Guatemalan society.

Context for Beginning a Peace Process

Because of its profound contradictions, the Guatemalan counterinsurgency project was unlikely to be stabilized. In the first place, it did not
and could not win the battle for legitimacy, given its intrinsic brutality.
Second, its basic premise, that the army had definitively won the war
against the guerrilla insurgency, was disproven in practice, causing discontent and destabilization within the ruling coalition. Finally, this was
combined with economic policies designed to expand the economy solely
through world-market-oriented "nontraditional exports." Aside from intensifying social conflicts, these policies limited economic growth precisely because they did nothing to develop the internal market.

By the late 1980s, Guatemala was by no means in an insurrectionary situation or "ungovernable," but it was in a chronic social crisis. The counterinsurgency state made reformism by itself unviable, by precluding partial solutions to the staggering problems of poverty and ethnic
discrimination. Gradualist approaches to change were simply not permitted. But faced with the deepening of these problems, important sectors of
the population made continual efforts to organize in self-defense—increasingly around issues of ethnic discrimination and indigenous rights,
as well as poverty. Hence, basic issues of social transformation remained
on Guatemala's agenda, although not in the traditional forms.

The URNG, for its part, experienced another resurgence during the late
1980s, but its "revolutionary" or transformatory project required redefini-

tion. Guatemala is one of the few countries in Latin America where the armed insurgent movement had operated continuously since the 1960s. But armed struggle is not what people choose; after thirty years of counterinsurgency war, and particularly after the holocaust of the early 1980s, the URNG could not simply propose another decade of war. (In fact, the mid-1980s saw several splits within the organizations of the URNG, with dissidents arguing that the insurgents should have laid down their arms altogether after the defeat of 1981–1983—see below.) For these reasons, the URNG leadership recognized the need for significant modifications of strategy.

Most important, the URNG recognized that the goal of "taking state power" militarily was unthinkable and that, in any case, the cost of pursuing that strategy would be far too high, particularly for the civilian population. In addition, the URNG, like the Salvadoran FMLN (Frente Farabundo Martí de Liberación Nacional), learned some painful lessons from the Sandinista experience in Nicaragua: "Taking state power" could be quite relative and did not reduce the vulnerability to all-out attack by the United States; moreover, Washington simply would not permit "another Nicaragua." The URNG gradually moved toward a strategy of gaining a share of power for the popular classes through political means. Hence, after Guatemala's return to civilian rule in 1986, even while continuing the war, the URNG began pressing for political negotiations with the government and army to end the war.

For four years the Guatemalan government stubbornly insisted that the insurgents must "lay down their arms." But by the first half of 1990, the war was intensifying, and even army and government spokesmen were finally forced to acknowledge the significant upsurge in guerrilla actions. (Indeed, the various rightist coup attempts during the Cerezo years stemmed in good measure from discontent on the Right over the army's inability to win the war.) The implicit admission that the war could not be "won" militarily by either side created the conditions, for the first time beginning in the spring of 1990, for the negation of the war: serious discussions about ending it.

However, it was also clear that the process would be protracted and convoluted. For one thing, ultra-right sectors staunchly opposed any such process; hence, the process was certain to be accompanied by continuing violence and periodic escalations of the war. Further, many of those who verbally supported and participated in the process (certainly the Guatemalan and U.S. governments) thought of negotiations as a way to pressure the guerrillas politically into laying down their arms rather than addressing the root causes of the war; and the Guatemalan army was still dominated by a mentality of political/military victory over the guerrillas rather than negotiations involving mutual concessions. Even among the various sectors of civil society committed to negotiating an end to the war, each of the major players had its own agenda and responded to its own pressures. Nevertheless, it seemed clear, particularly after the signing of a final peace accord in neighboring El Salvador in early 1992, that this process was the terrain on which the battle for Guatemala's future would be fought in coming years. Certainly it was the only possible avenue for demilitarizing and democratizing Guatemala and for eroding the structures of the counterinsurgency state.

A Note on Contested Issues
Concerning the War

This background chapter would not be complete without at least acknowledging, if not presuming to answer, some of the most controversial and hotly debated issues regarding the war. It is impossible to ignore these profound questions about the war because of their relevance to interpretations of the peace process.

Indeed, there are many different questions that should not be conflated. Some go back to the very beginning: What gave anyone the right to take up arms as a means of struggle "on behalf of the Guatemalan people"? Lest this sound like a rhetorical question or one that could come only from rightist landowners or army generals, let me clarify that this question has been put to me by Guatemalans of the center-left and ex-members of the revolutionary organizations and by some Guatemalanists in the United States. They argue that armed struggle guaranteed massive repression before all other means had been exhausted and hence brought unnecessary suffering upon the civilian population.

But looking honestly at the political system of Guatemala in the 1960s, in the aftermath of the 1954 CIA intervention, it is not difficult to see that electoral politics offered no way to bring about social change. It can be argued that those who took up arms in 1960 were partly inspired by the Cuban Revolution and had not totally exhausted political mechanisms in Guatemala. But in any case, the 1963 election, which seemed certain to be won by moderate progressive ex-President Arévalo, was preempted by a military coup that had the blessing of the U.S. government. A few years later, Julio César Méndez Montenegro based his 1966 campaign on a platform of social change (promising "the third government of the Revolution of 1944–1954"); the insurgents of the FAR (Fuerzas Armadas Rebeldes) agreed to give his government a chance and even began a partial demobilization. But the deals he was required to make with the army before taking office and the U.S. decision to become directly involved in the counterinsurgency war closed off the possibilities that had seemed to exist. Ironically, the civilian Méndez government ended up presiding over the transformation of the Guatemalan army into a counterinsurgent killing machine. So it seems reasonable to argue that there were no real options "within the system" during the 1960s. Subsequent elections until 1985 were totally dominated by the army, with three of them (1974, 1978, and 1982) being fraudulent as well.

A far more troubling set of issues concerns the responsibility of the URNG and its relationship to the indigenous civilian population in the highlands conflict zones during the second wave of the insurgency (late 1970s and early 1980s). A wide range of critiques has been made. The harshest is exemplified by David Stoll (1993), who argues that the highlands indigenous civilian populations in the Ixil area were, by and large, caught "between two armies"; whatever support they gave the guerrillas was based on coercion or deception.[8] Rather than playing an active role in the war, they were victims of the revolutionaries' decision to challenge the Guatemalan army in their villages. Moreover, the revolutionaries deliberately or knowingly brought down repression on the highlands population in order to recruit; the population voluntarily joined the PACs in "self-defense" against both the guerrillas and the army. Some versions of the "two armies" thesis have been used to imply that the URNG bears a responsibility equal to that of the army and that it used tactics equally brutal (whether or not in equal proportion).

A significant part of the answer to such sweeping accusations lies in facts that have just recently begun to be systematized for the historical record. The April 1998 report *(Nunca Más)* by the (Catholic Church) Archbishop's Human Rights Office (ODHA 1998)—a report based on over 6,000 testimonies taken throughout the country over a period of several years—was very clear in attributing responsibility for more than 85 percent of the war atrocities to the army and/or (army-controlled) paramilitary units, and slightly under 10 percent to the URNG. The February 1999 report of the official Truth Commission (CEH 1999), based on over 9,000 testimonies, went even further, attributing 93 percent of the atrocities to the army and paramilitary forces, versus 3 percent to the URNG (and 4 percent not determined). Both reports (discussed in more detail in Chapter 6) documented and criticized the abuses committed by the URNG. But they both revealed that the army, unlike the URNG, deliberately engaged in levels of brutality far beyond what was militarily necessary. Furthermore, the CEH report demonstrated that the army committed acts of genocide, as defined by international law, as part of state policy during the 1981–1983 period.[9]

But leaving aside the question of "two armies," equally responsible for the carnage, there are more nuanced critiques of the URNG's role. Yvon Le Bot's incisive book (1995) poses central questions that have troubled

In a CPR (Community of Population in Resistance) of the Sierra, Quiché, a young
girl, with her younger brother, holds an exploded mortar shell that had been fired at
the community during an army offensive.
SOURCE: Jonathan Moller, 1993. By permission.

many Guatemalans: To what extent was the war of the early 1980s really a
war of the Maya—as contrasted with a war waged on Mayan territory by
revolutionary organizations? In fact, was armed struggle a method that
would have been taken up by the Maya had they not been forced to do so
in self-defense against the army? Unlike less careful analysts, Le Bot does
not accuse the URNG (his study focuses mainly on the EGP) of waging a
war against the Maya, but he does hold the guerrillas to account for un-
leashing the army's war against them and of not knowing how to contain
it or defend the civilian population once it was unleashed. This is unquestionably the historical responsibility of the insurgents.

Finally, an important current of opinion in Guatemala, from ex-members
of the URNG among others, maintains that after the genocidal counterinsurgency offensive of 1981–1983, the URNG should have laid down its

arms in order to avoid any further suffering by unarmed civilians. (Some even refer to an "offer" made by Ríos Montt in the middle of the scorched-earth campaign for the URNG to disarm—surrender—in exchange for their legalization.) Indeed, as mentioned above, several of the organizations within the URNG (most notably, the EGP) suffered splits over the issue of whether to continue armed struggle or lay down their arms in the mid-1980s to prevent further bloodshed. (See Payeras 1996, and summaries in Jonas 1991, 139 ff. and 189 ff.) Coming at the end of a genocidal counterinsurgency offensive, and coming in large measure from ex-militants of the URNG, these criticisms of the URNG had a great deal of legitimacy. However, they assumed that the URNG in 1984 was a defeated force and could do nothing further.[10] Within this logic, any new initiative such as prolonged, substantive peace negotiations would have been inconceivable. Yet from the perspective of 1999, that argument is belied by subsequent developments. As it turned out, the URNG was able to use its remaining military strength and its political capital to get the government/army to the negotiating table; the peace negotiations resulted in substantive agreements that could truly benefit the civilian population—above all, the indigenous population. That, at least, is the argument of the rest of this book. Whether the end results will justify the massive effort of the peace process is another question, discussed here in subsequent chapters.

Notes

1. The statistic of 200,000 unarmed civilians killed or "disappeared" has its own mini-history. I used that statistic in my last book (Jonas 1991, 2, 9) on the basis of extensive research in both Guatemala and the United States—including information from former U.S. officials and the Inter-American Commission on Human Rights of the Organization of American States, as well as human rights organizations and the Guatemalan Catholic Church. *Foreign Policy* did its own independent fact check regarding that figure for my article (Jonas 1996a, 146). Nevertheless, when that article appeared, a State Department official—who had served in Guatemala but refused to be identified for the record—contested the figure, insisting that "more than 100,000" was more accurate (*San Diego Union-Tribune*, July 21, 1996). Subsequently, the 200,000 figure was used in a *New York Times* editorial (Sept. 23, 1996) and other sources of record both in the United States and in Guatemala. More recently, the exhaustive reports by the Guatemalan Catholic Church (ODHA 1998) and the official Truth Commission (CEH 1999) used the 200,000 figure—the latter suggesting that it might even be low. By now, this once-contested figure is used routinely, even by defenders of U.S. policy (e.g., Mark Falcoff in *Wall Street Journal*, March 3, 1999). On all of the above, see also Ball et al. 1999.

2. Much of this chapter, except the last section, summarizes portions of my previous book, *The Battle for Guatemala* (Jonas 1991). Readers interested in detailed documentation and references regarding the immense literature on Guatemala's

war will find them there. Some of the debates over issues of interpretation are also discussed there; others are raised at the end of this chapter.

3. Regarding the U.S. relation to the Guatemalan army during this phase of the war, see Chapter 5.

4. For a more theoretical discussion regarding the counterinsurgency state and its civilian versions, see Jonas 1991, 171 ff.

5. Different interpretations of the 1982–1985 transition from direct military rule to elected government and of the 1986–1990 Cerezo presidency are presented in Chapter 4.

6. For a fuller discussion of these and other statistics, see Jonas 1991, 177–180, and the sources given there.

7. The notion of a "bloc" indicates that the social subject is not one class in the traditional sense but a combination of exploited and dominated sectors, whose political expression is a coalition or "front" of popular and indigenous movements; it incorporates conditions related to (ethnic) identity and (gender-based) reproduction as well as (class-based) exploitation.

8. Full critiques of Stoll's "two armies" thesis have been developed by anthropologists such as Kay Warren, Charles Hale, and Linda Green and historians such as Piero Gleijeses and Greg Grandin.

9. For systematic studies of the army's strategies and actions, see Schirmer 1998; Arévalo 1998a; and Aguilera 1990, among others.

10. Torres Rivas goes even further, arguing that there was never a real civil war in Guatemala (but only a counterinsurgency war), primarily because the insurgents never posed a real threat to state power (Torres Rivas and Aguilera 1998, 58–68). Aside from definitional issues regarding what constitutes a "civil war," this interpretation diverges significantly from the perceptions of both the Guatemalan army/government and their U.S. backers at key moments during the armed conflict (particularly 1966–1968 and 1981–1983). Even in the late 1980s and early 1990s, perceptions about the war varied greatly between the major conflict zones and Guatemala City—with repercussions lasting into the postwar era (see Chapter 8).

2

The Mined Road
to Peace

The December 29, 1996, signing of the final peace accord ending Guatemala's thirty-six-year civil war opened up a new chapter in the country's history. Guatemala's was the longest and bloodiest of Latin America's Cold War civil wars. Taken as a whole, the accords, brokered by the United Nations (UN), went far beyond ending the civil war; they declared an "adios" to forty-two years of painful Cold War history and projected major changes for the country. Like the accords in neighboring El Salvador five years earlier, they constituted a truly negotiated settlement; rather than victors imposing the terms upon vanquished, they represented a splitting of differences between radically opposed forces, with major concessions from both sides.

The process by which the accords were reached was long and difficult. As late as 1993, Guatemala's military and civilian elites were still insisting that they would "never" negotiate a UN-moderated and -verified peace settlement with the leftist insurgency. Resistance by Guatemala's elites to international peacemaking, indeed to any kind of political settlement, was nothing new. The URNG made initial overtures proposing peace talks in a public letter to President Cerezo in the fall of 1986 (*New York Times*, Nov. 3, 1996) but received no government response. And in August 1987, even as the historic Central American Peace Accords were being signed in Guatemala City, Defense Minister Héctor Gramajo declared pointedly that the accords did not apply to Guatemala's civil war; having "defeated" the insurgent leftist guerrilla movement, the army insisted that it had no reason to negotiate. A low-level pro-forma meeting between government-identified politicians and URNG representatives was held in Madrid in October 1987, but it produced no result.

Shortly thereafter, in the fall of 1987, as the Central American region began to move toward peace, the Guatemalan army launched a major "final offensive" designed to consolidate its announced "triumph" over the URNG. The army was also determined to prevent the *aterrizaje* (landing) of the URNG as a legal political force—as became evident in the pattern of extrajudicial killings during this period. But more than three years (and several military offensives) later, in April 1991, the army had not achieved its goal of military victory and finally agreed to begin formal peace talks with the URNG. At that time, army officials and their civilian backers were still convinced that they could win a political victory, forcing the URNG to lay down its arms in exchange for minimal, pro-forma concessions. And in the wake of the Salvadoran peace accords of January 1992, bringing with them an extensive UN presence, the resistance to such a prospect in Guatemala stiffened.

But despite the odds, the Guatemalan peace negotiations continued, in a process that involved not only the main belligerent parties (the government/army and the URNG) but virtually all organized sectors of Guatemalan society, plus the UN as moderator, several Friend governments, and other international players. As it unfolded, the Guatemalan peace process was anything but pro-forma; its results were to be binding and internationally verified, and promised to shape important aspects of the country's future.

This chapter presents a political history and interpretation of this extraordinary process, its key turning points and crises. Beyond its significance for Guatemala itself, the story of the Guatemalan peace negotiations holds fascinating and surprising lessons, both positive and negative, for a conflict-ridden world (discussed in the Conclusion). This chapter also describes how the UN became a central player in that process, traces its interactions with the key Guatemalan players, and suggests some hypotheses about the effects of its involvement. These issues are best understood by beginning from the previous period, when the UN was less central and various Guatemalan players were resisting its participation.

As will be seen below, central UN involvement, which took several years to achieve, dramatically raised the stakes of the peace process for all parties concerned, both within Guatemala and internationally, and made the process much less reversible. This did not reduce the importance of domestic players; what was striking about this process in its totality was the endlessly shifting interaction between domestic and international peace efforts—and the many forms of resistance to those efforts. I shall also suggest how (and why) Guatemala became important to the UN and the international community and came to be viewed as one of the best possibilities for a "success story"—although, as we shall see, success was by no means guaranteed, even after the signing of the accords in December 1996. In the end, a viable peace rests on the political will of the Guatemalan actors on all sides and at all levels.

The dramatic shifts and turns in this often convoluted process serve as a constant reminder that Guatemala is a country where anything can happen, where nothing is linear, straightforward, or predictable; every advance toward peace has been met by new resistances and destabilizations. I emphasize this because El Salvador is the implicit point of comparison. Ultimately, some important aspects of the written accords are similar (e.g., demilitarization and a very limited role for the army in exchange for guerrilla demobilization). But in addition to some obvious particularities of the Guatemalan case, such as the indigenous issues, the process itself has been very different. The hidden dangers and endless resistances of the Guatemalan experience call to mind the Middle East more than El Salvador—a point to which I shall return in the Conclusion. Furthermore, at the level of political culture, El Salvador is fairly transparent. By contrast, Guatemala is the country where people deny in order to affirm; even today, when almost everyone speaks the discourse of peace, there are many different constructions of the word.

A final introductory note: As suggested in the Prologue, this chapter is the one where my method of distilling an interpretation out of hundreds of interviews has required the most self-discipline (in order to finish the book). I was continually tempted to present the full "inside story," with all the different versions of each crisis and turning point. But if I had done so, this chapter would have been an entire book in itself.[1]

1986–1990: Initial Dialogues

As seen in Chapter 1, even as the civil war went into its third, low-intensity phase during the late 1980s and into the early 1990s, outside factors helped lay the bases for peace talks. Regionally, the Central American Peace Accords of August 1987 (Esquipulas II) effectively ended the Contra war in Nicaragua and established a framework for negotiated settlements in El Salvador and Guatemala. The successful negotiations in Nicaragua (late 1980s) and in El Salvador (early 1990s) were examples that could not be ignored, despite the army's emphatic rejection of this route for Guatemala. In addition, a larger international shift was occurring during the late 1980s: the beginning of the end of the Cold War.

Finally, by the late 1980s, considerable pressure for peace was building up within Guatemalan society. During 1989, the National Reconciliation Commission (CNR) created by the 1987 Central American Peace Accords sponsored a National Dialogue; although boycotted by the army, the government, and the business elites, this Dialogue expressed a clear consensus among all other organized sectors in favor of a political settlement to the war—indeed a clamor for peace with political pluralism and social justice. The CNR was chaired by Msgr. Rodolfo Quezada Toruño of the Catholic Church Bishops' Conference. The dialogue process was formalized at a March 1990 meeting in Oslo between the URNG and the CNR. This agreement projected a series of URNG meetings with the political parties and subsequent meetings with the "social sectors" (labor/popular groups, religious groups, private sector, and so forth), and finally with the government/army.

These initial steps, which also involved a personal representative of the UN secretary general as observer, yielded results far beyond what had been expected. In the June 1990 meeting between the URNG and the political parties in Madrid, agreement was reached, at least in principle, on the need for modifications to the 1985 Constitution, and the guerrillas agreed not to disrupt the 1990 elections. Later in 1990, even the powerful umbrella organization for big business, CACIF (Coordinating Committee of Agricultural, Commercial, Industrial, and Financial Associations), held initial discussions with the URNG in Canada—an event unthinkable during the previous thirty years.

Beyond the formal meetings, the dialogue process opened up spaces within a repressive context for public debate about issues that had been undiscussable for decades; in this sense, it became an important avenue for beginning to democratize Guatemala. But at this stage, aside from the Catholic Church,[2] the pro-peace forces were still relatively unarticulated in comparison with the organized power of those resisting a substantive peace process. The Cerezo government left office without having undertaken any formal peace talks; but in its last year, it did authorize the CNR's participation in the 1990 Oslo meeting and the political parties' meeting with the URNG in Madrid, and these meetings left the door open for possible negotiations in the future.

1991–1993: Bilateral Negotiations, Guatemalan "Conciliator"

In April 1991, newly elected president Jorge Serrano, responding to domestic and international pressures and building on his own experience in the CNR, opened direct negotiations with the URNG. In fact, he had used a pro-negotiation stance to differentiate himself from the other, also conservative candidates in the campaign. For the first time, top army officials agreed to participate in meetings to set the agenda and procedures for peace talks. The occurrence of these preliminary meetings, dropping the precondition that the URNG first disarm and accepting a full substantive agenda, represented a small but very significant step forward. During the next year, there was an agreement in principle on democratization (1991) and partial "pre-agreements" on human rights (1992). Additionally, during the spring of 1992, the URNG issued a document describing its overall vision of the future (URNG 1992), and the government responded with its own document (Government of Guatemala [GG] 1992); according to Manuel Conde, who headed the governmental Peace Commission (Comisión de la Paz, COPAZ) under Serrano, although these were called "proposals to Guatemalan society," they were equally directed toward the international community (even the UN), in order to demonstrate "political will" on both sides and have the Guatemalan process taken seriously.

Nevertheless, amid a generalized skepticism in Guatemala toward the peace process, the economic and military elites remained totally opposed to a fully negotiated peace. CACIF was pressuring the government to discuss nothing but the terms of a cease-fire, and sectors of the army considered COPAZ "traitors." The resistance from these forces emerged most clearly in their "never in Guatemala" backlash response to the UN-supervised accords signed for El Salvador in January 1992, and subsequently to El Salvador's Truth Commission Report in March 1993.

The precariousness of the process became evident when it stagnated in August 1992 over human rights issues and moved toward total breakdown during the last months of Serrano's crisis-ridden government,[3] leading up to the May 1993 *Serranazo* or *auto-golpe* (self-coup). The Serrano government turned out to be much more interested in imposing a cease-fire deadline than in resolving the substantive issues—a stance unacceptable to the URNG. During early 1993, for example, even while presenting himself at the UN as the great architect of the peace process, Serrano was offering, in exchange for an early cease-fire, agreements only on human rights (including their verification) and demilitarization. The URNG, in turn, was insisting on negotiation of the entire agenda and was pressing for representation of the civilian sectors at the negotiating table. Knowledgeable participants on the government negotiating team considered this URNG stance to be "maximalist" and concluded that the URNG's commitment to negotiations was tactical rather than absolute. This conclusion by government negotiators was confirmed by my own interviews during the early 1990s; I also found that it was more true of some URNG leaders than others.[4]

The May–June 1993 political crisis unleashed by the *Serranazo* (the president's attempt to seize absolute power, dissolve Congress, and suspend the Constitution) interrupted the peace talks altogether. Paradoxically, even the resolution of that crisis, through the ascendance of former Human Rights Ombudsman Ramiro de León Carpio to the presidency in June 1993, further postponed the resumption of serious peace talks. (For detailed accounts, see McCleary 1997; Jonas 1994b.) The new government, in close alliance with the "institutionalist" wing of the army high command (i.e., those favoring formal civilian rule but maintaining the army's power intact), presented unrealistic proposals for negotiations that would have discarded previously signed agreements and, in essence, would have required the URNG to disarm without any substantive settlements. These proposals by the new coordinator of COPAZ, Hector Rosada, were rejected almost unanimously throughout Guatemalan society (except by the army and CACIF) and were viewed as completely nonviable by key international players in Guatemala and at UN headquarters in New York.

During the Serrano years (1991–1993), the negotiations had been chaired and coordinated by Msgr. Quezada Toruño as "conciliator," with the UN as observer.[5] In the world of Guatemala, even this represented a significant advance, insofar as the idea of a negotiated end to the war was finally accepted by the government, and a serious peace process began. However, both parties still had the idea that the UN would verify but not mediate the peace, and neither side seriously expected anything like the Salvadoran model to work for Guatemala.

This bilateral phase was a necessary first stage in Guatemala, given the strong resistances by the army and big business (CACIF) to any negotiations with the URNG. It also provided space and time for the coalescence of political forces in civil society with a strong interest in resolving the substantive issues and with enough accumulated strength to be taken seriously. Eventually, however, this process ran up against the limits of operating in a purely Guatemalan context, without the added weight of the UN and the international community to overcome strong internal resistances. The importance of the international community became evident during the *Serranazo* (May–June 1993), when leading governments such as the United States and Germany threatened to withhold trade as well as aid unless the constitutional order was immediately restored; faced with the specter of economic sanctions, CACIF (previously divided over the *Serranazo*) was persuaded to abandon the pro-*golpe* forces and leaned on the army as an institution to do likewise.

By late 1993, after the efforts of the de León Carpio government to scuttle the previous gains of the peace process were rejected both domestically and internationally, both sides were more inclined toward a central role for the UN. The URNG came to appreciate more clearly the necessity of UN involvement in getting its full agenda discussed and reaching binding agreements. For its part, the government was anxious to remove Quezada Toruño from his central role, believing him to be partial to the URNG. (As he later put it, he was being viewed as the "Fifth URNG Comandante.") Furthermore, despite the fact that the elites were generally distrustful of a UN role in Guatemala, both the Serrano and de León Carpio governments had tried to use the UN as an international forum for strengthening their hand against the URNG (respectively, in January and

October of 1993). These efforts did not succeed, but structurally they may have served to gain wider acceptance for the idea of UN involvement. By this time, in addition, the Serrano government had successfully insisted that the UN replace its initial observer, Francesc Vendrell, viewed by the Guatemalan government as "pro-URNG";[6] the new UN representative was a more junior official, Jean Arnault.

Toward the end of this first period before the negotiations came formally under UN moderation, there was at least one other channel, an informal negotiating "track" sponsored by Norway, which had been playing a similar role in the Middle East; even some of the same individuals were involved.[7] In 1993, when the formal negotiations were stalled, Norway prepared for a totally secret "Second Track"—also to involve Israel, because of its ties to the Guatemalan army. It also helped that two members/advisers of the Guatemalan COPAZ had the necessary ties—one to Norway, one to Israel. According to key players from all sides of this "Track II" initiative, it was never designed to replace formal negotiations, but rather to pave the way for their resumption, this time under UN moderation. Subsequently, Norway continued to play a significant public role, earning its image as the "honest broker," as is discussed below.

1994–1995:
Initial UN-Moderated Negotiations

In January 1994 the negotiations were resumed, but this time on a significantly different basis: At the request of both parties, the UN became the moderator, paving the way for significantly increased involvement by the international community. The agenda-setting Acuerdo Marco (Framework Accord) of January 1994 formalized the role of the "Group of Friends" governments—primarily Mexico, Norway, Spain, and the United States, and more nominally, Venezuela and Colombia.[8] Some of the Friend governments had been very actively engaged with the process in its earlier stages. At the same time, the Acuerdo Marco established a mechanism for participation by the organized sectors of Guatemalan civil society. By this time, grassroots popular and indigenous organizations had come to view the peace process as an arena for discussing issues that were not being addressed in the formal political arena and had become increasingly vocal in their demand for participation in the peace talks.

During the *Serranazo*, these popular forces had come together for the first time to play a role in mainstream national politics, and they even participated in a national dialogue with CACIF within the context of a broad multisectoral forum, the Instancia Nacional de Consenso. Building on these experiences, popular and indigenous forces—and eventually even women's organizations, although they initially had to struggle to be included—joined with established political parties and other sectors (including even small and medium business, but by its own decision, not CACIF) in the Asamblea de la Sociedad Civil (ASC) established by the Acuerdo Marco. The ASC's functions were to make consensus proposals to the negotiating parties and to endorse (or not endorse) accords once they were signed. Chaired by Msgr. Quezada Toruño, the ASC was by no means a unified bloc. It even included representatives from the ultra-rightist Frente Republicano Guatemalteco (FRG), the party led by General Efraín Ríos Montt, who had headed the military dictatorship of 1982–1983 and presided over the worst phase of the scorched-earth counterinsurgency war. In fact, the ASC's diversity and the autonomy of many of its organizations made it a vital forum for hammering out consensus. Unlike El Salvador, there was no one "party line" guiding all popular organizations—much less indigenous organizations, which had been mobilizing autonomously for years.

The plurality of collective actors (organized sectors), each with its own agenda and vision for Guatemala's postwar future, gave the Guatemalan process a unique character and dynamic. This plurality, both between and within sectors, can be captured in the image of a symphony orchestra with a multiplicity of sections—as contrasted with the Salvadoran process, more of a trio between the government, the FMLN, and the UN.[9] It also explains why the Guatemalan peace process was not limited to the negotiating table in Mexico, but rather reflected the interactions between the negotiations per se and the opening of democratic spaces in Guatemalan society as a whole. Ultimately, the peace process became the political terrain on which competing agendas about the country's future were being played out.

Beginning in 1994, then, the ASC became a central actor in making proposals to the negotiating table on each of the substantive themes on the agenda; its proposals were not binding, but they could not be dismissed or ignored. None of this, however, stopped government and army officials from continually attempting to downgrade its role or from accusing it of being a facade or "ideological relative" of the URNG and of trying to open new "fronts" for the URNG. Indeed, the government engaged in various forms of psychological warfare to intimidate not only the popular movement but virtually all sectors of society.

Under the new negotiating arrangements, a breakthrough Comprehensive Agreement on Human Rights was signed in March 1994, calling for immediate steps to be taken by both parties and for the immediate establishment of UN verification mechanisms to monitor human rights. (Days after the accord was signed, the head of the Constitutional Court was assassinated in broad daylight—a typical message from Guatemala's peace resisters.) Two further accords were signed in Oslo, in June 1994: one on the resettlement of populations displaced by the war, and a second establishing a Truth Commission—formally called the Historical Clarification Commission (CEH). But the latter accord produced a major crisis in the process, which was seriously compounded by delays in the implementation of the human rights accord.[10] For one thing, the government took no steps to comply with its obligations under the accord; in fact, human rights violations worsened dramatically and the war intensified during this period (April–October 1994). In August, the URNG refused to return to the negotiating table until the provisions of the accord were implemented.

Second, months passed before arrival of the UN Verification Mission that had been mandated to begin functioning immediately—even though virtually all participants and observers agreed that the presence of such a UN mission could significantly change the situation on the ground.[11] During the tense interim before arrival of the MINUGUA mission in November 1994, government and army officials repeatedly objected that the planned mission was too large and, in any case, should not be empowered to initiate investigations into human rights abuses. These delays, coinciding with the Truth Commission crisis, undermined the credibility of the entire peace process.

As this crisis moved toward resolution during the fall of 1994, negotiations were resumed on the next theme, indigenous rights. Both because of the complexity of the issues and because of serious tensions over the timetable for the negotiation process—tensions so serious as to require top-level UN intervention—the Accord on Identity and Rights of Indigenous Peoples was not reached until March 1995.[12] The accord itself contained far-reaching changes—including a constitutional reform declaring the country to be "multiethnic, multicultural, and multilingual"—and was considered a landmark achievement for a country whose population is 60 percent indigenous. By no means did it fulfill all the demands of Guatemala's organized indigenous movements, but it did lay the basis for future gains.

Internationally, however, the signing of the indigenous accord was considerably overshadowed by the simultaneous eruption of a major scandal in Washington concerning the involvement of a Guatemalan military officer on the CIA payroll in the early 1990s murders of U.S. citizen Michael DeVine and URNG commander Efraín Bámaca, married to U.S. lawyer Jennifer Harbury. These revelations blew the lid off an explosive Pandora's box, increasing pressures on Washington to break long-standing secret ties to the Guatemalan army (see Chapter 5). Within Guatemala, the immediate effect was to seriously rattle the peace negotiations, as the army officer corps closed ranks to defend itself. Structurally and in the longer term, however, the scandal had a more positive effect, as it put the Guatemalan army, already beleaguered by endless human rights criticisms, even more on the defensive, both at home and abroad—despite the army's posturing to the contrary—and weakened the hand of peace resisters in the military high command.[13]

A separate international factor was the message from the June 1995 Paris meeting of the Consultative Group of Donor Countries (mainly the United States and Europe and international lending institutions): Major funding for Guatemala would be withheld until a final peace accord was signed and until tax reforms in Guatemala guaranteed internal financing. This message seemed to particularly affect the attitude of some big-business sectors, and thereafter, the more modernizing groups within CACIF became much more interested in the peace talks. They were also becoming involved because "their issues," socioeconomic issues, were now on the negotiating table.

Within Guatemala, meanwhile, the peace process began to be directly impacted by the dynamics of the November 1995 general election campaign. During the first half of the year, the URNG issued an unprecedented call urging Guatemalans to vote; this was interpreted as signaling an implicit shift toward political means of struggle. A few months later, for the first time in forty years, a leftist coalition of popular and indigenous organizations came together as a political party (Frente Democrático Nueva Guatemala, FDNG) to participate in the elections. The FDNG was nominally independent from but considerably influenced by the URNG, and its formation was taken as a further sign of the latter's shift to political forms of struggle. Equally significant, in an August agreement brokered by the Central American Parliament on the Panamanian island of Contadora, the URNG promised to suspend military actions during the last two weeks of the electoral campaign, in exchange for a commitment from the major political parties that the peace negotiations would continue under a new government and that the accords already signed would be honored. For the first time, Guatemala's political class accepted that the negotiated agreements constituted "accords of state" and hence could not be jettisoned by any future government or Congress.

UN-moderated negotiations continued throughout the rest of 1995 on the next theme, socioeconomic issues, including the ever-prickly question of land reform. But the negotiations took second place to the November elections, and no agreement had been reached by that time. Still, by mid-1995, one could sense a significantly greater commitment to the peace process on all sides. As always in Guatemala, progress generated strong resistance, including calls from the more recalcitrant hard-line sectors to halt the entire peace process;[14] but increasingly, these were seen as coming from minority factions. Hence, even the period when no new agreement was signed (April 1995–April 1996) was a critical time for confidence-building among the Guatemalan players. By this time, as later stated publicly by COPAZ coordinator Hector Rosada, the government team had learned "to listen to the URNG's arguments without considering them our enemies, even though the war continued."[15]

Both sides were strengthened by the outcome of the 1995–1996 electoral process. Despite his extremely narrow victory in the runoff election (by a margin of less than 2 percent), new president Alvaro Arzú of the Partido de Avanzada Nacional (PAN) entered office on a strong note, bolstered by his party's majority in Congress and well articulated with the economically powerful CACIF. The URNG, for its part, was implicitly strengthened by the surprisingly strong showing of the newly created FDNG. Despite its lack of political experience and resources, the FDNG won 7.7 percent of the presidential vote and 6 of the 80 congressional seats, becoming the third-strongest political party in Congress. In addition, several indigenous *comités cívicos* allied with the FDNG won important mayoralties, including Quetzaltenango, Guatemala's second-largest city. Until they actually occurred, such results had not been believed possible in Guatemala.

During the course of 1995—even before, and certainly after, these election results—the URNG leadership had decided not to sign any further agreements with the de León Carpio government. Aside from their doubts about what this government would be willing to sign, they recognized that it had always been a transition government and was by this time a lame-duck government with little political legitimacy.[16]

The other decisive novelty of 1995–1996 that strengthened the impetus toward peace was the presence and active functioning of MINUGUA throughout Guatemala. Although the actual human rights situation remained fairly dismal, MINUGUA represented the first direct, on-the-ground, ongoing international presence in Guatemala, and this shifted the balance of forces within the country.

MINUGUA I (1994–1996):
The Human Rights Mission

Although my purpose here is not to provide an in-depth institutional analysis of MINUGUA's functioning,[17] I shall briefly discuss the mandate and functions of MINUGUA beginning in late 1994, as part of the larger UN investment in Guatemala. Despite the delays in its deployment, MINUGUA represented a crucial commitment from the international community—in the UN lingo, a "confidence-building" institution—particularly coming prior to the signing of final peace accords and at a moment

of stagnation and high tension in the negotiations. Since it embodied resource expenditures, MINUGUA became the most concrete expression of
the international community's interest in Guatemala. It also represented a
promise of what the international community could do for Guatemala after the signing of final peace accords, a down payment of sorts.

In their content, MINUGUA's periodic human rights monitoring reports served as a signal to the international community regarding the human rights climate in Guatemala. One message emerged clearly from
MINUGUA's first four reports (issued in March, June, and October of
1995 and March 1996): The main obstacle to human rights improvements
was impunity—not, as the government had long maintained, the continuation of the war (meaning that there could be no improvement in human
rights until after a cease-fire). According to MINUGUA's fourth report, issued in March 1996 and summarizing the first year of its operations, "the
Mission saw no decisive progress in the commitment to fight impunity."
The persistence of impunity was "attributable basically to the absence of
a State policy for combatting it"; the government failed to investigate,
identify, and punish those responsible for human rights violations. Although it identified some areas in which progress had been made, the report expressed "deep concern" that "during the period covered by its reports, no effective measures were taken to follow up the majority of [its]
recommendations." More concretely, the MINUGUA reports focused attention on specific cases and violations by both sides (government and
URNG) and indicated to each side what steps to begin taking immediately. Two subsequent reports, issued respectively in August 1996 and
March 1997, covering the Arzú government's first year in office, were significantly affected and overshadowed by the endgame dynamics of the
negotiations, as is described below.

Although MINUGUA by itself could not correct Guatemala's abysmal
human rights situation, the very presence of a 400-plus-person mission
throughout the country changed the human rights context, most notably
during 1995. For one thing, its presence had a "dissuasive impact,"
serving as a tangible, on-the-ground reminder that the world was watching the human rights situation in Guatemala very carefully. (One top
MINUGUA official saw the angry responses to the mission's first report
as a sign of its effectiveness; at least it was being taken seriously.)
MINUGUA's presence also contributed to overcoming the pervasive fear
experienced by many Guatemalans, by providing a neutral place or
haven to take their testimonies; particularly in remote rural areas where
many people had never had contact with pro–human rights officials, this
opened spaces for freer expression. And in the high-profile case of the
massacre at Xamán, Alta Verapaz (October 1995) killing eleven refugees
returned from Mexico, MINUGUA's rapid arrival and pronouncements

preempted the army's attempts to blame the victims. This prompt response contributed to the resignation of the defense minister and the eventual (unprecedented) consignment of the case to a civilian court.

The other significant innovation in MINUGUA's mandate (doubtless a "lesson" from the experience in El Salvador) was to couple verification with the strengthening of national institutions charged with human rights protection (the UN term is "institution-building"). The MINUGUA reports evaluated reasons for the "defective functioning" of the judicial system, the Public Prosecutor's Office, the National Police, and other public security forces in investigating and prosecuting criminal activities as well as human rights abuses; among these reasons were the autonomy of the army and its adjunct units and forces. Beyond pinpointing these structural problems, MINUGUA (together with the United Nations Development Program, UNDP) began to work on strengthening institutions in a number of areas. It was beyond MINUGUA's purview, however, to correct the root problems of militarization, which remained to be resolved at the negotiating table. This would require the dismantling (not the strengthening) of existing structures under the army's control and the creation of new institutions, above all, a truly autonomous civilian police force.[18]

Aside from the limitations of its mandate and separate issues related to its funding,[19] MINUGUA faced several external constraints. The most immediate of these came from Guatemala's "peace resisters," taking several forms. The first was a series of overt attacks against MINUGUA, including shooting up the office, as well as ongoing threats, harassment, and even kidnappings directed against MINUGUA personnel; in none of these cases did the government arrest those responsible. In short, MINUGUA was experiencing the effects of the impunity documented in its reports. Another set of attacks came from hard-liners in the army and private sector, accusing MINUGUA of defending *"izquierdas humanas"* rather than *"derechos humanos"* (i.e., of favoring the URNG)—despite MINUGUA's sharp criticisms of the URNG for charging "war taxes" (accompanied by threats and reprisals) in rural areas and engaging in other armed activities that endangered civilian lives. CACIF never accepted the idea that property damage was considered a less serious human rights violation than assassination.

Finally and most important, the government engaged in a pattern of passive resistance and undermining MINUGUA's work behind the scenes, particularly on the part of government institutions that were supposed to be strengthened. There were ongoing attempts to limit MINUGUA's functions on the grounds of "national sovereignty," as well as generalized resistance to implementing MINUGUA's recommendations by institutions of the judicial system.[20] While chafing under MINUGUA's presence, the government tried at the same time to use it as an argument for getting rid of Mónica Pinto, the independent expert mandated by the UN Human Rights Commission; but in the real world of Guatemala, there certainly was room for an expert who was not permanently based in the country and hence would not operate under the pressures affecting MINUGUA as an in-country mission.[21]

In short, MINUGUA was operating amid the minefields of Guatemala's subterranean message system. Many of the messages directed against MINUGUA were, in reality, expressions of resistance to the peace process as a whole. In particular, the Guatemalan army's goal was to outlast MINUGUA (wait for it to leave) and, more generally, to "survive the peace." The most serious hidden danger for MINUGUA was that this war of attrition could eventually end up undermining its effectiveness or credibility. On balance, nevertheless, MINUGUA's presence affected the human rights context in Guatemala in important constructive ways and, whatever its problems, was being evaluated as "successful" overall. Beyond its human rights and incipient peacekeeping functions, then, MINUGUA was structurally part of the calculus of the peacemaking process.

Changed Chemistry in 1996: Arzú and the Endgame Dynamics

Even before his hair-raisingly narrow victory in the cliff-hanger January 1996 runoff election (less than 2 percent margin over the party of ex-dictator Ríos Montt, openly opposed to the peace process),[22] incoming president Alvaro Arzú and his representatives had begun to hold direct, secret meetings with the URNG in different venues, sponsored by various governments and the Vatican (through the Community of San Egidio).[23] After taking office, the new government—recognizing, among other things, that international funding was contingent upon signing a final peace accord—took a very positive stance toward the negotiations, raising expectations that a final peace accord would be signed in 1996. Arzú's government included a center-left "peace cabinet" component, with the new COPAZ headed by ex-URNG militant Gustavo Porras, as well as strongly pro-peace ministers of foreign affairs (Eduardo Stein) and defense (Julio Balconi) and special presidential adviser Ricardo Stein. The new government also ceased to engage in the direct and indirect, heavily ideologized attacks on the URNG as a "defeated force," "subversive terrorists," and so on, that had been the prevailing discourse of previous governments. Unlike its predecessors, this government viewed the URNG as its negotiating partner—a key element in any successful negotiation—and even respected its "patriotic motives." Perhaps this changed chemistry owed something to Arzú's patrician/ruling-class background, which enabled him and his appointees to feel less beholden to or intimidated by the army than the governments of Cerezo, Serrano, and de León Carpio.[24]

In any case, the actions taken by the new government in its first months, including shake-ups in the army and police to purge the most corrupt elements shortly after taking office, paved the way for the URNG's unprecedented "good-faith" gesture in March 1996 of calling an open-ended halt to offensive armed actions. The government responded by halting offensive counterinsurgency operations. This marked, if not the end of the war overall, at least the end of armed confrontations.

Alongside the vastly improved bilateral dynamics between the government and the URNG, one could detect an effort by the government to sideline the UN and decrease international community pressures under the guise of the "new understandings" between the two belligerent parties. (The implicit message: "We love each other so much that we need no intermediary.")[25] In fact, as is described in Chapter 6, this dynamic—indirectly a new expression of old antagonisms of the Guatemalan elites toward the UN—was to emerge more clearly in early 1997, immediately after the signing of the final peace accords, in connection with implementation and verification of the accords. According to top UN officials, the PAN, Arzú's party, and CACIF had been warned by their colleagues in El Salvador's rightist party, ARENA, to limit the UN role. It took a combination of the URNG's insistence on a central UN role and sensitivity by UN officials in dealing with the government to defuse open hostility. Hence, some believe, both MINUGUA and the UN negotiating team assumed a "lower profile" during the first part of 1996—which coincided with the budget crisis of the UN General Secretariat and the attendant uncertainties about MINUGUA's future (see Note 19).

In May 1996, the Accord on Social and Economic Issues and the Agrarian Situation was finally signed. The accord reflected the new correlation of forces that was to characterize the Arzú government: greater direct involvement by CACIF and a somewhat lower profile for the corruption-ridden and increasingly discredited army. The accord was initially embraced by CACIF and received with strong criticism from popular organizations;[26] although it recognized poverty as a problem and committed the government to increase taxes as a percentage of GDP, it did not contain an outright land reform or even a direct job creation program (with unemployment and underemployment at two-thirds of the economically active population). No one could have any illusions that people's daily lives would be improved directly by the accord, and this raised the specter of a socioeconomic deterioration such as the one experienced in El Salvador after the 1992 peace accords. Despite these shortcomings (which were predictable, given the need to bring CACIF on board), the

ASC was eventually (in July) persuaded to *avalar* (endorse) the accord. UN and other international officials viewed the accord as reflecting a number of lessons from the Salvadoran experience, particularly concerning coordination between the UN and the international financial institutions (International Monetary Fund, World Bank, Inter-American Development Bank) during both the negotiation and the implementation phases (see Chapter 7).

Meanwhile, the negotiators moved on to the next difficult issue, demilitarization. Several months of intense negotiations culminated in the signing of this most central accord of all, the core of the entire peace process: the Accord on Strengthening of Civilian Power and the Role of the Armed Forces in a Democratic Society. The accord mandated constitutional reforms to limit the functions of the previously omnipotent army to defense of the national borders and of Guatemala's territorial integrity. The accord also eliminated the PACs and other counterinsurgency security units, reduced the size and budget of the army by one-third, and created a new civilian police force to guarantee civilian security. Finally, it mandated necessary reforms of the judicial system to eliminate the pervasive impunity. In short, this represented on paper a plan for the "de-centaurization" of Guatemala, the dismantling of the Cold War counterinsurgency apparatus. It held the potential, if fully implemented, to initiate important democratic transformations of the state. (Its loopholes and omissions surfaced only later—see Chapters 3 and 6.)

The signing of this accord on September 19, 1996, in Mexico also represented the high point of the entire peace process; clearing this major hurdle stamped the process with a certain finality and irreversibility, since demilitarization had been one of the main issues underlying the negotiations. This signing was widely hailed and celebrated as the effective end of the war. Undoubtedly, it represented the profound shift that had taken place with the Arzú government. Only two years prior (summer 1994), the army and its civilian allies in the de León Carpio government had been insisting that the army would never negotiate with the URNG about its future downsizing or reduced role; rather, these issues would be determined internally and unilaterally within the army. At that point the army had still been arguing that it was "victorious" and therefore could impose its terms. Hence, with the radically different outcome represented by the September 1996 accord, there was a sense that at long last, people could begin to believe in the peace process and that once-distant visions of democracy could become realities.

No one was prepared, then, for the plunge from peace euphoria to peace backlash in response to the news in late October that a high-ranking cadre of one of the URNG organizations, the Organización del Pueblo en Armas (ORPA) was responsible for the kidnapping of eighty-six-year-old

Olga de Novella, from one of Guatemala's richest families and a personal friend of President Arzú. Kidnapping had become the most common form of crime in Guatemala, but this was different: a high-level kidnapping by the URNG—especially by ORPA, which had always been considered the most pro-negotiation of the URNG organizations—coming precisely when the end of the peace negotiation was in sight. This was followed by the equally shocking revelation that the government had negotiated a swap with the URNG (Novella for the responsible URNG cadre, Isaías). After the scandal broke, the government suspended the demobilization of the PACs that had begun; and with the backing of the UN moderator, it suspended the peace talks for several weeks, returning to the table only after ORPA's head, Gaspar Ilom (Rodrigo Asturias) had resigned from the URNG negotiating team.[27]

Aside from the virtually irreparable political damage to the URNG itself, this incident nearly jettisoned the entire process. It gave the coalition of peace resisters in the army and the private sector exactly the ammunition they needed to launch their peace backlash ("we cannot negotiate with terrorists") and raised real questions about the URNG as a negotiating partner. In many circles, peace itself became a dirty word, and it became clear how thin the support was for peace even among "modernizing" business elites (not to mention the army). CACIF stated that it would support a permanent ending of the process if the government decided to take that course. Only international pressure and the efforts by UN negotiator Arnault—and the fortunate fact that all of the substantive agreements had been signed, above all the demilitarization accord—eventually (in November) got the process back on track. By that time, however, the URNG and the pro-peace forces in the government were under widespread attack—a tendency that worsened, rather than abated, over time. The very survival of the peace process was a testament of some kind to the fact that it was solidly grounded and that the UN and the entire international community, as well as key Guatemalan players, had a considerable stake in its success.

The negotiation of the operational accords during November and December—leading up to the signing of the final peace accords in Guatemala on December 29, 1996—was significantly influenced by the changed correlation of forces, with the URNG now clearly on the defensive and making tactical (if not substantive) concessions. The European governments and Mexico took initiatives to save the process by arranging a three-week tour for the signing of these operational accords; they invited not only the negotiating team but also key representatives from Guatemalan society (ASC, CACIF, and others). The Europeans seemed to understand the crucial role they could play in making Guatemalans believe in the process—in a sense, holding up a mirror to reflect back to the

Guatemalans their accomplishments. The official cease-fire agreement was signed in Oslo in early December, followed by the accord on constitutional and electoral reforms (in Stockholm),[28] on the legal incorporation of the URNG (in Madrid), and finally, a detailed implementation *Cronograma* or Timetable (in Mexico). Of all the Friend governments, only the United States remained aloof and did not insist on claiming its share of the credit—an indirect sign, perhaps, of where Guatemala stood on Washington's priority list, once the threat from armed insurgents was gone.

The last major crisis came over the accord on legal incorporation of the URNG, because it raised the (always latent but unresolved) issue of amnesty—for whom and under what conditions. Clearly, the war could not be ended without pardoning URNG insurgents whose only crime had been to take up arms against the state. But the issue remained as to whether human rights criminals in the army would be amnestied under the same terms as URNG insurgents. Human rights groups had been mobilizing for months to prevent such an amnesty. The accord itself, signed after a three-day marathon negotiation in Madrid, contained more limited provisions to amnesty army officers (see Chapter 3). But the conservative-dominated Congress immediately rushed through a law that considerably widened the amnesty. In its final form, the partial amnesty would cover war-related crimes—excluding genocide, torture, and forced disappearances, but not extrajudicial killings. Essentially, it kicked the ball back to the courts; but the judicial system was still operating within a context of impunity and threats from the military.

Human rights groups had already greeted the watered-down Truth Commission accord of 1994 with howls of protest; now some of them immediately threatened to take the new amnesty law to court and to challenge it in every way possible. (Several of those groups had also taken initiatives to compensate for the weakness of the peace accords on the issue of justice for victims of the army's crimes, by setting up their own entities and coalitions for investigating war crimes—see Chapter 6.) The tensions on the eve of the signing of the final peace accord left no doubt that the struggle against impunity would continue well into the postwar situation.

Despite this unhappy final scene in the drama of the peace negotiations, the return of the URNG leadership (minus Gaspar Ilom) on December 28, 1996, and the actual signing of the final accords on December 29 were a momentous occasion, a turning point in Guatemalan twentieth-century history. Because it ended not only Guatemala's thirty-six-year civil war but also the whole cycle of Cold War counterinsurgency wars fought in Latin America since the 1960s, the signing of Guatemala's peace accords was an event of great importance for Latin America as a whole, as is argued in the Conclusion.

SOURCE: Mario Minera, 1996. By permission.

SOURCE: Jonathan Moller, 1996. By permission.

Above and on the following page, scenes from the massive celebration of the signing of peace on December 29, 1996.

SOURCE: Jonathan Moller, 1996. By permission.

Guatemalan Peace in the International Limelight

To return to issues of UN peacemaking: As outlined above, by the beginning of 1994, both parties to the Guatemalan conflict had become convinced that a high-level UN role was essential to the success of the negotiations. UN moderation of the peace process dramatically raised the stakes for all concerned and made the entire process much less reversible. At the same time, the UN became convinced that it should become seriously involved in Guatemala. (This was still something of a gamble, since it was by no means clear that Guatemala could be a peacemaking "success.") Yet by this time, Guatemala had become important to the international community, despite its small size—partly for symbolic reasons, including the magnitude of the human rights atrocities there, and partly for practical reasons: A "success" in Guatemala could contribute to larger goals of leaving Central America a zone of peace and stabilizing the situation in southern Mexico (i.e., Chiapas).

By 1994, then, the need for UN involvement in Guatemala seemed clear to almost everyone; however, there were currents that had to be carefully navigated. The first of these was the articulation between domestic and international players. The wisdom of the January 1994 Acuerdo Marco, which marked the transition from internally to internationally moderated negotiations, was the simultaneous creation of the ASC and the formalization of its role—if not specifically at the negotiating table, at least in making proposals to be taken seriously. Indeed, if the UN had been perceived as displacing this important Guatemalan player, the entire process could have been derailed. Structurally, the accord created a mechanism for articulation between the ethnically, culturally, and politically diverse world of Guatemala and the larger world of the international community. To build on the plurality of forces in Guatemalan civil society was an (often underrecognized) innovation, an element that had not been part of the Salvadoran experience.

The most difficult issue surrounding the role of the UN and the international community (some of the Friend governments) in 1994–1995 was the recurring theme of artificial timetables and deadlines appearing to be imposed upon the process. One example occurred in June 1994, when the URNG was generally believed to have been forced to accept an unacceptably weak Truth Commission as a sign of "progress" (see Note 10). Ironically, despite generalized dissatisfaction with the Truth Commission accord, structurally the agreement may have helped clear the way for the international community to begin taking the Guatemalan peace process seriously. On various occasions subsequent to MINUGUA's arrival, there were subtle (and not-so-subtle) hints that its mandate might not be renewed without concrete advances in the negotiations. The crisis of late 1994 to early 1995 had overtones of an international ultimatum, particularly to the URNG (see Note 12); once this crisis was resolved in February 1995, there was a palpable easing of international pressure. Analytically, these examples reveal the contradictory nature of proactive international involvement: The added leverage it brings is necessary to overcome internal resistances; but unless handled with great care and intelligence, it can generate new resistances.

In the end, peace depended on the political will of the internal players. But structurally, extensive UN involvement (and that of the international community as a whole) made a decisive difference, by taking the process out of the circumscribed world of Guatemala, opening the door for the country to enter the world of the twenty-first century. International pressure and presence was required to overcome the convoluted, ideologically overdetermined logic of Guatemalan politics, the legacy of a thirty-six-year Cold War civil war. As one URNG leader acknowledged (*New York Times*, Mar. 27, 1996), "We couldn't have kept it alive among Guatemalans. Without the persistence of the UN, the peace process would have been impossible."

At another level, UN involvement was the best guarantee against a peace that changed nothing, which would be an unstable peace and could not last. The Guatemalan accords between the government and the insurgents were designed to be internationally endorsed as well as internationally verified—a very different proposition than some of the Southern Cone "pacted transitions" among elites. (This argument is developed in more detail in Chapter 4.) To put it another way, UN involvement was the best guarantee that Guatemala would not end up fifteen to twenty years later like Chile, where General Pinochet retained important veto powers.

Yet the centrality of the UN in the Guatemalan peace process was never a given; it was always a struggle to establish and preserve and came under constant challenge from high quarters in Guatemala (and at times in Washington as well). We have seen the resistances to UN involvement by the Guatemalan elites—often disguised forms of resistance to the peace process as a whole. These dynamics emerged once again from the Arzú government, even in the afterglow of the signing of the final peace accords, in January 1997.[29] The challenge to UN authority in Guatemala also had a more structural basis. Whereas the UN had been at the height of its influence during the Salvadoran peace negotiations, it was under considerable political and financial attack during the years of the Guatemalan negotiation, especially from the United States (see Note 19).

Furthermore, at various points during the process—and increasingly as the Guatemalan process moved toward its conclusion—opinions began to circulate in Washington (doubtless, with support from some U.S. officials) that perhaps the Organization of American States (OAS) should play a more "equal" role with the UN in the tasks of verification. This scenario did not materialize, but it remained "in the air" as a possibility.[30] Perhaps this should come as no surprise, if we remember that central UN involvement in the historic "backyard" of the United States has been perceived as posing a challenge to U.S. domination in the hemisphere. In 1954, when laying the diplomatic groundwork for the overthrow of Arbenz, Washington went to great lengths to steer the resolutions condemning Guatemala as "pro-Communist" out of the UN and into the far more compliant OAS. Today the Cold War has ended, and the OAS is more autonomous, but old habits and headsets die hard.

Preliminary Lessons and Mines in the Road Ahead

The Salvadoran accords of 1992 revealed how much could be gained by an insurgent force that, although unable to win state power outright, remained militarily strong enough to be invincible. Hence, after pouring $6 billion into the war against the FMLN during the 1980s, even the United States was eventually forced to admit the need to negotiate with the FMLN. But the correlation of forces was quite different in Guatemala— that is, the lesser military strength of the URNG vis-à-vis the Guatemalan army. This led to great skepticism all along as to whether the URNG could negotiate a good settlement. The fact that it was able to do so was clearly a result more of the political than the military correlation of forces. The Guatemala experience serves as a reminder of the particularity of each case. As discussed in detail in the Conclusion, despite the lessons to be learned from other experiences (for example, El Salvador), these should not be turned into formulas.

What, then, made possible the relative success in Guatemala, if the military situation in itself was not precisely a stalemate/impasse and the intensity of the war was low enough to permit many sectors of society, especially in the capital, to deny its centrality? First, although weaker than the FMLN in El Salvador, the URNG was by no means a "defeated force," as the army liked to boast; and what the war lacked in military intensity, it more than made up for in "political weight" of a sui generis nature. For example, the URNG gained a certain moral stature by refusing to submit to Latin America's most brutal and despised counterinsurgency army. Second, even though many of the organizations within the ASC were quite critical of the URNG, in the end, the URNG's agenda coincided with the agenda of most organized forces in civil society (other than CACIF), as became clear when the ASC became a player. The URNG recognized this as strengthening its hand at the negotiating table—perhaps even more so because the ASC included many sectors and organizations that did not support the URNG per se. Third, the URNG showed considerable intelligence at the negotiating table, with a few notable exceptions (which mostly surfaced later). In addition, despite tactical differences among its organizations, and even in the face of the severe strains during the "October (1996) Surprise" (the Novella kidnapping), the URNG maintained its unity, which increased its credibility as a negotiating partner.

Fourth, at a certain point (beginning with the *Serranazo*), modernizing elements within the private sector recognized their own interests in and reasons for supporting the peace process: first, to end the war, which was negatively affecting them; second, to gain access to free trade arrangements such as NAFTA, to foreign investment, and to international funding promised to Guatemala after the signing of the peace accords; and finally, to increase their advantage over the more reactionary anti-negotiation oligarchical forces, without sacrificing their essential privileges.

Finally, even in the army, there were a (very) few high-level officials—by no means the bulk of the "institutionalists"—who had a more modern and pragmatic view of the future. They acknowledged that the army had not "won the war" after all and that the army would have to be drastically altered for a peacetime future.[31] The Arzú government put members of this small group into key positions (e.g., minister of defense, army representative to COPAZ) in order to bring the negotiations to a successful conclusion—although, as is described in Chapter 6, the struggle among factions in the army continued into the postwar period.

Looking toward the postwar future, the same factors that made the peace negotiations so difficult and protracted could be expected to affect the second round of negotiations, that is, for the implementation of the accords. Even as the final peace accords were signed, the contours of fierce upcoming battles over government compliance were already visible. The Guatemalan Congress (including a strong but not decisive contingent from Ríos Montt's FRG) would have to pass legislation implementing the accords; and a two-thirds majority would be needed to make the crucial constitutional reforms. Furthermore, there remained a very high level of resistance from far Right forces, especially in the army and CACIF (those who believed that too much was "given away" to the URNG), and a high potential for them to engage in destabilizing activities. And from the side of the URNG, compounding the predictable difficulties of transforming a guerrilla movement into an effective political force, the "October Surprise" and its ongoing repercussions in the postwar period left some previously unrecognized questions (see Note 27). Overall, then, nothing could be taken for granted in Guatemala, and there remained many mines on the road ahead.

Hence, although the organized forces in Guatemalan civil society prepared to monitor compliance with agreements reached, it was clear that they would need continual support from the international community, including citizens' movements and international NGOs as well as governments and the UN. In part, it remained a question of financial support for UN peacekeeping and for implementation of the peace accords. But even more important, as outlined in Chapters 6 through 8, would be the role of the international community (the donor countries and the international financial institutions—the International Monetary Fund, the World Bank, the Inter-American Development Bank) in conditioning financial support upon compliance with the accords.

Notes

1. Fortunately, some of those versions, by primary actors, are or will be available in written form (e.g., de Zarco 1996; Rosada 1996, 1997b; Gobierno de Guatemala [GG] 1997c). Also exceptionally revealing was FLACSO's (January 1998) first anniversary forum, *A un año de la firma de la paz en Guatemala*, which FLACSO graciously made available to me on videotapes; this forum brought together all of the successive heads of COPAZ (government negotiating team) as well as the URNG's Rolando Morán, Msgr. Rodolfo Quezada Toruño, Gen. Julio Balconi, UN moderator Jean Arnault, and several other key players in and observers of the peace process. I shall cite from presentations made at this forum, as its proceedings are public (although, unfortunately, not published).

2. In addition to the Catholic Church, other domestic religious players played an important role in the Guatemalan process—among them, a coalition of progressive Protestant denominations. Internationally, since the beginning of the peace process and throughout the negotiation years, the Lutheran World Federation office in Norway—which had close ties to Jorge Serrano (who became president in 1991) as well as to leading actors in the Norwegian government—was active at various levels of the process. In particular, at many crucial moments, it organized a series of *Consultas Ecuménicas* for informal multisector exchanges of opinion among the Guatemalans in other venues—exchanges that would have been impossible inside Guatemala.

3. Earlier in August 1992, during negotiations on the future of the PACs, the URNG had made significant concessions (as detailed in Chapter 3), accepting a temporary situation that fell far short of abolition of the PACs, as all international institutions and human rights organizations were demanding. The URNG's compromise on this issue was interpreted by the government to mean that the URNG would continue to make concessions on all issues. This assumption was abruptly dispelled only weeks later in late August, when the URNG dug in its heels; the talks in Mexico ended with no agreement. The worst-case scenario of an open rupture of the process (which would have meant a return to all-out war) was avoided—probably because the initial terms of the negotiation included a mutual agreement not to abandon the negotiating table unilaterally. However, the talks remained at a virtual impasse for months.

4. Some of the top URNG leaders later acknowledged (in interviews) that at the beginning (1986–1987), they had seen the peace process "tactically"—i.e., they viewed it primarily as a way to open up space for the popular movement, within a context dominated by counterinsurgency structures; at that time, they did not fully see how Guatemala could be transformed through a peace process. Early on, as they found great receptivity to a peace process in Guatemalan society, their view began to evolve. And as it unfolded—certainly by 1994—"the process itself," as one of them put it, and the arrival of MINUGUA convinced them to believe in it. Other URNG leaders had been less skeptical about the peace process from the beginning.

It is important to clarify that for most of the URNG leadership, their early view was "tactical" *not* (as some critics have suggested) in the sense of holding out for a military victory. Rather, it was "tactical" in the literal sense of being instrumental to some other goal—in this case, gaining time in order to strengthen the popular and indigenous movements, which would overall weaken the government/army side and particularly its peace resisters. The overall URNG goal was to negotiate substantive agreements with a government that was serious about the whole enterprise. (Interviews with multiple actors; see also Arnault in Arnson 1999, 292–293.)

None of this meant that the URNG organizations in their entirety were totally "convinced" by 1994. It was well known that there were differences among the URNG organizations and their leaders (and within each organization, among top leadership, middle-level leadership, field commanders, and rank-and-file membership) regarding the value of the negotiations and the likelihood of reaching satisfactory agreements. More significant, however, is that these differences never took precedence over the commitment to resolve them and to maintain unity at the negotiating table.

5. Underlying Quezada Toruño's protagonism and outstanding contribution (dating back to the years when he was president of the CNR) was that of the Catholic Bishops' Conference as a whole. Since the very beginning, in fact, the Catholic Church played a central role in paving the road to peace negotiations. It was the only institution as omnipresent throughout the country as the army (and the latter's arch rival since the mid-1980s). As an important player in the 1989-1990 dialogue process, the Church had the moral authority to pull together a broad national consensus in support of peace talks. Even after the UN began moderating formal negotiations, the Church remained central (e.g., the early 1996 informal diplomacy in Rome, and pro-peace emphases in relation to the Pope's 1996 visit to Guatemala).

6. According to one UN source, the reason for Vendrell's replacement was his role in arranging a meeting between Serrano and the URNG leadership; when this became public, he was accused of having overstepped his mandate as observer (Whitfield 1999, 270).

7. The interest of several key Norwegian individuals dated back to the 1970s, and some of them became involved at the time of Guatemala's 1976 earthquake. They subsequently rose to positions of power, respectively in the Norwegian Foreign Ministry (Jan Egeland), in Norway Church Aid (Petter Skauen), and in the Lutheran World Federation (Gunnar Stålsett). Hence, it was not coincidental that Oslo was the site of the March 1990 meeting that launched the formal peace

process (and was attended by Jorge Serrano as a CNR member). It was also in Norway that Rigoberta Menchú was awarded the Nobel Peace Prize in 1992. Some of the Norwegian individuals and entities mentioned above became involved in the ongoing informal *Consultas Ecuménicas* during the early 1990s involving sectors of Guatemalan civil society (see Note 2).

8. The Group of Friends was somewhat different in its origins and functioning in the Guatemalan case than in the Salvadoran process. For one thing, in the Guatemalan case, some of the Friend governments had been actively engaged with the process in its earlier, pre-UN stages; and even after their role was redefined in the 1994 Acuerdo Marco, the Friends remained substantially more autonomous vis-à-vis the UN Secretariat than in El Salvador. As one high-level UN functionary put it, in El Salvador, the UN secretary general convened the Friends; in Guatemala, by contrast, they came together at the request of the negotiating parties. Of the four main Friends, each had its own particular role, interests, and agenda:

- Mexico (the lead Friend, "voice" of the Latin Americans): Aside from its crucial functions as host country for most of the negotiations since 1991 and the "home base" of the URNG leadership, Mexico was generally the Group's convener. Mexico also had the advantage of having close ties to both of the Guatemalan parties and, hence, mechanisms for pressuring both sides at key moments. Mexican officials, who have always had good reasons (business, immigration, national security) to be concerned about what happens on Mexico's southern border, consistently recognized the need for lasting solutions in Guatemala, as opposed to a minimalist peace—all the more so after the beginning of the Chiapas uprising in January 1994.
- Norway (the "honest broker"): As described in Note 7 above, Norway took many initiatives in the Guatemalan case (as in the Middle East), going back to the days of the National Dialogue (1989–1990), the 1990 Oslo agreement, and the 1992 Nobel Peace Prize for Rigoberta Menchú. Oslo was also the site of the troubled June 1994 accords. Norway remained deeply involved in the informal diplomacy of the Guatemalan peace process at difficult moments, including the crises of the last months in late 1996.
- Spain (the "voice of the European Community"): Spain served as the liaison to Western Europe in a variety of settings, as well as the site of some informal peace talks, including the fruitless first encounter between the government and the URNG in 1987 and the more productive URNG meeting with the political parties in 1990. Spain also played a leading role when the process was in serious trouble in late 1996.
- the United States (the "500-pound gorilla" or "heavy-weight," as one diplomat put it): Although its role was less direct than in El Salvador, the United States remained the only superpower involved and the principal external player influential with the Guatemalan elites. Particularly because of its long-standing ties to the Guatemalan army, the United States was the only player that had the power to pressure the

army to accept full civilian control and demilitarization in the peace accords—although it was never clear to what extent Washington used that power, as is discussed in Chapter 5. The Guatemalan peace process was never as important a priority for Washington as for the other three major Friends—an irony, given that Guatemala is in the U.S. sphere of influence.

9. In the words of UN mediator Alvaro de Soto, the Salvadoran negotiations were conducted "almost in laboratory conditions" (cited in Whitfield 1999, 258). In this relatively insulated trio, moreover, the UN often took the initiative in ways that would never have fit with the dynamics of the Guatemalan process (Whitfield 1999, 262 ff.).

10. In regard to the Truth Commission battle: The URNG had arrived in Oslo pushing for a Salvadoran-style commission; hard-line forces within the government/army delegation came determined to agree to no commission whatsoever. A two-week impasse was broken through heavy international pressure from Friend diplomats, particularly on the URNG. The agreement finally forged under these pressures established a commission to shed light on (esclarecer) past human rights crimes, but without naming the names of the individuals responsible or having any faculties to prosecute them. The reverberations of this agreement for an emasculated Truth Commission paralyzed the peace talks and raised the tension level during the summer of 1994. Within the Guatemalan Right, the very idea of a Truth Commission was enough to provoke threats of a coup. On the side of the popular organizations, there was great discontent with a Truth Commission viewed as ineffective and morally inadequate. Many people blamed the URNG for having agreed to it—or alternatively, the international community for pressuring the URNG to accept an unacceptable arrangement, in essence "imposing" the agreement. Some have suggested that this was made a condition for deployment of MINUGUA and/or for postwar financial assistance. (Information based on interviews; see also Baranyi 1995, 9; Padilla 1995a, 52–54.)

11. There are various explanations for these delays, most of them concerning the UN rather than the Guatemalan peace process. One was the question of whether MINUGUA (as a human rights verification mission rather than a full-fledged peacekeeping mission) would fall under the jurisdiction of the Security Council (as proposed by the UN Secretariat) or the General Assembly (as several members of the Group of Friends were insisting). The latter position prevailed. The Latin American Friends, led by Mexico, did not want to establish the precedent of Security Council monitoring of human rights within a country; the United States favored the General Assembly primarily for financial reasons.

12. The deeper tensions over the time line for the negotiations came to a head in December 1994 and January–February 1995. The URNG was resisting extremely strong international pressures for a deadline; according to some observers, they were also undergoing internal reassessments of the peace process as a whole. While the government and the URNG traded pseudo-proposals certain to be unacceptable to the other side in January 1995, the UN Secretariat tried to break the deadlock. An initial UN letter proposed a cease-fire during the rest of the talks, simultaneous discussions of substantive and operative themes, and a "fast-track"

schedule—all of which was rejected by the URNG. Following shuttle diplomacy by Marrack Goulding, UN Under-Secretary General for Political Affairs, a second UN proposal returned to the original negotiation format (substantive before operative themes) and extended the time frame; this proposal—in reality, an ultimatum from the UN—was accepted by both sides. By this time, the URNG was beginning to make clear its intention to participate in the 1995 electoral process. (Information based on interviews; for different interpretations, see Whitfield 1999, 272–273; Baranyi 1995, 20; and Padilla 1995a, 55–56.)

13. In fact, the scandal may have had a more immediate positive effect. Just the week before the scandal broke, the government representative had angrily threatened to leave the negotiating table in Mexico, vowing never to sign an accord involving constitutional reforms on indigenous rights. But within a few days after the scandal broke, the government signed the far-reaching indigenous accord, including the provision for constitutional reforms. Although there is no proof of a connection, I have always suspected—and a number of interviewees involved in the negotiations agree—that the government's sudden flexibility was more than a mere coincidence. (See also *Inforpress Centroamericana*, Mar. 23, 1995, Mar. 30, 1995, April 4, 1995.) In any case, it belies the argument being made by U.S. officials at the time that human rights pressures were interfering with the peace process.

14. During the second half of 1995, the most recalcitrant wing of the private sector launched a lawsuit against COPAZ coordinator Hector Rosada for engaging in "illegal" negotiations with the URNG. Throughout 1995 as well, there was the specter of an electoral victory by Ríos Montt's party, which (despite having signed the August Contadora agreement) had never given clear assurances of its commitment to continuing the peace process.

15. At the FLACSO forum mentioned in Note 1 above, Rosada gave a most revealing presentation about the challenges he faced as COPAZ coordinator: "We were not negotiating only with the URNG," but with all sectors of Guatemalan society. Within COPAZ, he had to negotiate the government's position with all the different factions of the army—and then also with CACIF (41 meetings with CACIF versus 26 with the URNG in 1995), with the ASC, with all of the political parties and their 1995 presidential candidates, with the ambassadors from the Friend countries and other governments, and with the UN. In regard to the URNG, COPAZ met not only with the leadership but also with its field commanders, and ex-URNG dissidents. The need to engage in such extensive negotiations with even its allies suggests the fundamentally weak position of that government.

16. Actually, in making this decision, the URNG was taking a calculated but high-stakes risk, since the runoff election for the presidency had not yet taken place. (Some individuals from Friend countries close to the URNG had advised them not to take that risk.) If the runoff election had gone the other way, the entire peace process might have been halted; see Note 22 below.

17. For an institutional analysis, see Baranyi 1995.

18. Even within the limitations of its mandate, MINUGUA slowly expanded its functions in several directions. Despite government challenges of its right to do so, MINUGUA became involved in the Bámaca case—not in regard to the circumstances surrounding his death, but in regard to the conduct of 1995–1996 investigations. MINUGUA also began to work on implementation of the human rights

aspects of the indigenous accord—although it was limited by the absence of mechanisms or standards for "verifying" long-standing structural problems of injustice and discrimination against Guatemala's indigenous population.

19. MINUGUA was supposed to be an expression of the international community's commitment to Guatemala, and the Friend governments took the lead in mobilizing support for MINUGUA mandates and funding at the UN General Assembly. But in the context of the UN's financial crisis, the anti-UN mood in the U.S. Congress (including nonpayment of U.S. dues to the UN), and the U.S. campaign to replace UN secretary general Boutros Boutros-Ghali, Washington was insisting that MINUGUA be funded out of "existing resources" or voluntary contributions, as opposed to special (additional) budget allocations for the mission. The UN secretary general responded that it was not possible to authorize new missions and at the same time deny them the necessary funding. The impasse was partially resolved by the MINUGUA mission being given "commitment authority" to spend funds through September 30, 1996; but this precedent cast a shadow for the postwar future, when MINUGUA would need to be expanded into a full-fledged peacekeeping mission.

This budget crisis cast the spotlight on larger issues. In the words of the UN secretary general, the struggle over funding for MINUGUA "goes to the heart of the purposes for which [the UN] was created"; it was this widely shared perception that led the UN and the international community to commit resources to Guatemala prior to a final peace accord.

20. All of the above is based on extensive interviews, and examples are chronicled in the Guatemalan press; see also Americas Watch 1996.

21. For example, after its first report, which was extremely critical of the government, MINUGUA came under pressure to appear "even-handed" (although the magnitude of human rights violations was by no means equal on both sides). Hence, its second report had to establish its "objectivity and professionalism," i.e., a basis for acceptance by government and conservative sectors, by highlighting criticisms of the URNG. To take another example, many MINUGUA functionaries acknowledged the need to use "diplomatic language" in their criticisms.

22. For one thing, the FRG made public statements about not feeling bound to honor the 1995 Contadora agreement and not viewing the previously negotiated accords as "accords of state," i.e., binding on any government. According to one inside source, had the FRG won the presidency in 1995–1996, it might well have continued the peace negotiations formally, but without any fundamental commitment to making concessions or reaching final agreements. At the very best, it would have continued the grudging, pro-army stance of COPAZ during much of the de León Carpio era. In any case, the URNG might not have been willing to negotiate with a government run from behind the scenes by Ríos Montt.

23. Face-to-face meetings by Arzú and his representatives with the URNG leadership, under the auspices of the Vatican-sponsored Community of San Egidio, had taken place beginning in December 1995 (before Arzú's runoff victory) in several different locations, including Italy, El Salvador, and Mexico. These secret meetings were made public in February 1996 in a joint government/URNG communiqué delivered in Rome. The Community of San Egidio has played a role in international conflict resolution and "track-two" diplomacy in several other situations.

24. This kind of "chemistry" has proven to be critically important for building confidence and turning negotiating antagonists into partners in other difficult peace processes, as well. The best-known example is the Mideast process, during the era of Yitzhak Rabin and Shimon Peres in Israel (see Bruck 1996).

In the Guatemalan case, some of the antecedents for Arzú personally and for members of his negotiating team dated back to contacts established in informal multisectoral encounters, conferences, and so forth. One important conference of this kind took place in San Francisco, California, in October 1994. The three-day roundtable conference, "Imagining a Post-War Guatemala," was sponsored by the Arias Foundation (headed by former Costa Rican President Oscar Arias, who won the 1987 Nobel Peace Prize for the Central American Peace Accords), together with the Vesper Society. As mentioned in the Prologue to this book, that conference provided numerous opportunities for key players—ranging from CACIF to trade union and indigenous leaders, from established political party leaders and top army officials to top URNG leaders—to talk informally and, quite literally, to begin to know each other in ways that later proved crucial. I was particularly struck by Arzú's openness to dialogue with political/ideological opponents. It was here as well that Gustavo Porras, who was already close to Arzú and who was later to head Arzú's COPAZ, reencountered top URNG leader Rolando Morán—for the first time since having left the URNG as part of the mid-1980s split within the EGP.

25. Aside from my interview information, this tendency during the spring of 1996 is described in *Inforpress Centroamericana* Mar. 21, 1996 and Mar. 28, 1996. It is also confirmed in *Crónica de la paz 1996* (GG 1997c, 23), a document that presents the government's view of the dynamics throughout 1996.

26. Obviously, given the divisions in CACIF and the fact that its right-wing fringe was filing lawsuits against the government for negotiating with the URNG at all, the "embrace" was not unanimous. Interestingly, the final socioeconomic accord was more favorable to CACIF's interests than an accord signed with the previous government might have been, according to an interim working document that circulated informally during the winter of 1995–1996 *(Documento Consolidado no. 2)* (see Rosada 1996, 25). However, it seems unlikely that it would have received the necessary support from CACIF.

27. The entire affair, and its spring 1997 sequel, which threatened to disrupt the implementation process (see Chapter 6), put a severe strain on the unity among the URNG organizations and left questions with no answers: Why had ORPA—generally regarded as much more pro-negotiation than its harder-line partners, EGP and FAR—been willing to risk everything to resolve its financial problem? (ORPA and the URNG generally had greatly diminished funds, because the URNG had agreed to stop collecting "war taxes" after signing the socioeconomic accord.) Who within ORPA had authorized the action? And on a different note pointed out by a former COPAZ negotiator and adviser, why did Arzú violate an unwritten cardinal rule of the peace talks that outside events, no matter how terrible—even the October 1995 Xamán massacre—should not be allowed to "contaminate" the negotiation table (but rather, should be worked out in a more informal setting)?

28. Although never one of the formal Friend governments, Sweden had been actively following the peace negotiations, at times acting in cooperation with Norway.

29. During and immediately following the final Peace Accord signing, Guatemalan government officials, including President Arzú, went so far as to suggest that verification would be "unnecessary" or could be carried out by the OAS. For more examples, see Chapter 6.

30. For an extremely interesting and sophisticated discussion of UN-OAS dynamics, see de Soto 2000.

31. The clearest example is General Julio Balconi, who served as part of the army's team on COPAZ from 1991 to 1995 and as Arzú's minister of defense from January 1996 through July 1997. As early as the summer of 1994, when the civilian leadership of COPAZ was still talking about imposing the terms of peace on the URNG, Balconi put it very clearly to me in an interview: "We can't oblige the URNG to sign anything. Even if they are militarily weak, it takes two to sign an agreement; so at the negotiating table, they are our equals." (That was the first time I had heard this from any government official.) Interviewed by an Univisión television reporter at the time of the peace signing in December 1996, Balconi said the settlement showed that neither side had won the war; the army had accomplished its goal, which was "to not lose the war" with the URNG. After the signing of peace, he also revealed that a few army officers and URNG leaders had been meeting secretly after the formal negotiations began in 1991 (not even the civilian members of COPAZ were informed); later, this was extended to lower-level field commanders on both sides (in Arnson 1999, 127–128). In another interview, he confirmed this, while clarifying that the hard-liners remained the predominant voice within the army even as peace was signed (see Dirk Kruijt's introduction to Arévalo 1998a, 26–28).

The Terms of Peace

This chapter summarizes the contents of the accords as signed; it will serve as a basis for interpreting (here and in subsequent chapters) their strengths and limitations, both individually and as an overall package. This account of what was and was not achieved, at least on paper, addresses the accords in the order signed over the course of the six-year process. This summary reveals the complexity and level of detail of the accords on some issues, as contrasted with the gaping holes on others.[1]

The architecture of the accords is also important. The initial framework agreement of Mexico (April 24–26, 1991) set an agenda of eleven issues to be negotiated. Most significantly, it distinguished substantive from operational themes and established that substantive themes were to be resolved prior to operational—in itself a major issue, since the Serrano government had initially hoped to negotiate them simultaneously. The previous government had insisted it would negotiate substance only after the operational cease-fire and disarming of the URNG—a position totally unacceptable to the URNG. Although government negotiators periodically tried after 1991 to put cease-fire before substance (e.g., after de León Carpio first took office in 1993), the URNG insisted on maintaining the basic framework established at the beginning, and this became the pillar of the peace process. Within the substantive agreements, the first three major accords during 1994 (human rights, resettlement, and Truth Commission) dealt with the effects of the war; the three substantive accords of 1995–1996 (indigenous rights, socioeconomic issues, and demilitarization) addressed the more difficult issues embedded in the causes of the war (Aguilera 1997).

Democratization (July 1991)

The parties held their first substantive meeting on democratization in Querétaro, Mexico, July 22–25, 1991. Initially, the idea had been to combine the themes of democratization and human rights in the same accord.

This proved impossible, as a result of the profound disagreements about human rights. Hence, the first accord was a general statement of principles: It accepted the existing constitutional order as legitimate but emphasized the establishment of a functional and participatory democracy, as well as the strengthening of civil society and of an effective *estado de derecho* (rule of law). This agreement was easy to achieve because it stated little beyond what was already in the 1985 Constitution on paper (which the government posited as the existing political reality but the URNG viewed as a goal) and required no concrete changes. Its main significance was the URNG's acceptance of the constitutional order, although with the perspective of negotiating reforms to the constitution.

The difficult issues that were supposed to have been discussed within the same agenda item (human rights) were postponed; hence, in a sense, the real negotiations began only after Querétaro and lasted nearly three years, as detailed in Chapter 2. Partial accords were reached during the first half of 1992. In February 1992, a general agreement was signed on the government's acceptance of its human rights obligations in principle. More concrete was an early August 1992 partial accord on one of the most controversial issues, the future of the "civilian self-defense patrols" or PACs: The Human Rights Ombudsman would be permitted to verify that the PACs were truly voluntary, as was supposedly guaranteed in the 1985 Constitution. The government/army also made the commitment not to form new PACs, except in particular areas where it saw a "specific need" (i.e., increased guerrilla activity). On the more difficult question of dissolving the PACs—as was being recommended by the United Nations and virtually all other international and human rights organizations— the parties deliberately agreed to postpone discussions until other, more substantive agreements were reached. In any case, neither of these partial accords was to take effect until the signing of a global human rights accord.

Acuerdo Marco/Framework Accord
(January 1994)

There were no further agreements on human rights or any other issue during the rest of 1992 and 1993. Serious negotiations were resumed with the signing of a new Acuerdo Marco (Framework Accord for the Resumption of the Negotiating Process) in January 1994. Beyond reaffirming the validity of the agreements already signed (which the de León Carpio government had initially tried to overturn during the second half of 1993), it established new mechanisms for the negotiating process. Most importantly, the Framework Accord elevated the role of the United Nations to "moderator." It also formalized a function for the Group of Friends governments. Finally, it established the Asamblea de la Sociedad Civil (ASC) and specified mechanisms for its participation in the process: making (nonbinding) consensus proposals to the negotiating parties, and deciding whether to endorse accords once they were signed. As discussed in Chapter 2, beyond getting the process back on track after a long and difficult hiatus, the Framework Accord also raised the stakes by involving the UN directly. In March 1994, a "timetable" was adopted as a guide to the schedule for the rest of the negotiations; however, its projection of completing the negotiations by the end of 1994 proved totally unrealistic.

Comprehensive Accord on Human Rights (March 1994)

In March 1994, the first major substantive accord was signed, addressing significant human rights issues, although the particularly sensitive issue of the Truth Commission was postponed for a separate agreement. This accord was crucial because it was designed to enter into immediate effect—unlike the other accords, which would be implemented only at the end of the entire negotiation process, with the signing of the final peace accords.

The main provisions of the human rights accord fell into several categories:

- Both the government and the URNG would respect human rights established in the Constitution and the treaties to which Guatemala was a party.
- Both the government and the URNG promised to fulfill their obligations under international humanitarian law regarding conduct of the war—in particular, to eliminate the suffering of the civilian population and to observe international norms regarding prisoners captured in combat.
- The government would respect the independence of national institutions concerned with human rights protections and strengthen them. Among these institutions were those of the judicial system, the Ministerio Público (Public Prosecutor), and the Human Rights Ombudsman's Office. The government would also protect officials of those institutions, as well as of nongovernmental organizations working for human rights protection. Finally, the government would aid and/or compensate victims of human rights violations (although no concrete programs were spelled out).

- The government agreed to eliminate secret or illegal security units and to professionalize and purge existing security forces. Furthermore, the government would work to end impunity, that is, to bring human rights violators to justice.
- The government would guarantee freedom of association, movement, and organization—essentially a ratification of the earlier partial accord on PACs, regarding their voluntary nature, as verified by the Human Rights Ombudsman. The government would also ensure that PAC activities did not violate human rights. Further, it would initiate new laws to ensure that military conscription was carried out in a legal, noncoercive, and nondiscriminatory manner.

Most important of all, this accord invited the United Nations to send a human rights verification mission to operate inside Guatemala, paying particular attention to basic civil and political rights and to the situation of the "most vulnerable groups of society" and those most directly affected by the war (the displaced, refugees, and returnees). The UN mission would have the following functions:

- to receive, "consider" (assess), and follow up on accusations of human rights violations;
- to issue periodic reports assessing the human rights situation in general, as well as specific cases. These reports were to be disseminated through the mass media. In order to prepare such reports, the mission would be permitted to move freely around the entire country, to interview individuals or groups freely and privately, and to make visits without previous notification when necessary (to state institutions or URNG camps);
- through these reports, to make recommendations to the parties regarding measures necessary to promote human rights and guarantee compliance with the accord;
- to assure that national organisms charged with investigating human rights violations were autonomous and strong enough to function effectively. Furthermore, the mission would work with these organisms (both governmental and nongovernmental) through institutional strengthening programs (the UN term is "institution-building") and promote international financing and technical support to achieve these ends.

In keeping with the idea that this agreement was to take immediate effect, the UN was mandated to send a preliminary mission to Guatemala to prepare for deployment of a full-fledged human rights verification mission (MINUGUA) as soon as possible. Aside from disagreements that arose between the government and the UN over the mandate of this mission and the scope of its activities, a major limitation was built into the accord: The UN mission's investigations could include only violations arising subsequent to its installation. On balance, however, the presence of the UN mission after it finally arrived, and the signing of the human rights accord overall did make a decisive difference—not in eliminating human rights violations, much less eradicating impunity, but in less direct ways, as spelled out in Chapter 2.

Resettlement of Population Groups Uprooted by Armed Conflict (June 1994)

This agreement, signed in Oslo in June 1994, established the basic principles of a long-range program for resettlement of and guarantees to populations uprooted by the war—both the displaced within Guatemala and refugees returning from Mexico. According to its main provisions, the government would guarantee the existence of conditions for the voluntary return of those who had been uprooted to their original homes or to another site of their choice. The return process would take place within a broader context of full respect for their human rights; furthermore, representatives of the uprooted populations were to participate in decision-making regarding the general and specific plans for their resettlement. In addition, this process was to take place within the context of sustainable and equitable development of the resettlement areas; the government would invest in infrastructure for those areas.

Within the context of "productive integration of the displaced populations and development of resettlement zones," the accord recognized land and land tenure as a basic factor in the reintegration and resettlement of the uprooted but left concrete solutions for the posterior socioeconomic accord. More specifically, the government was to return land abandoned by refugees fleeing war violence to those refugees or arrange for their compensation; the government would also identify state or other lands that could be made available. The accord also established the principle of reconciling the interests of those who were now living in resettlement areas and those who had fled and would be returning. Finally, the accord mentioned a "gender-based approach" and committed the government to eliminating all forms of discrimination against women in gaining access to the benefits specified in the accord.

The entire process of resettlement was to be verified by the UN mission; to complement its own public expenditures and investments, the government would actively seek financing from international agencies and donor countries.

In addition to the practical elements of resettling the uprooted, the accord contained several indirect political messages—among these, implicit governmental recognition of the Comunidades de Población en Resistencia (CPRs) as a sector of the civilian noncombatant population. Previously the CPRs had been treated as appendages of the URNG. In addition, the accord signified the government's recognition of the "dispersed refugees" in Mexico (those living outside the official UN refugee camps) with whom it had previously refused to negotiate.

Despite its positive potential for an (unspecified postwar) future, the resettlement accord was the subject of skepticism and criticism from representatives of the refugee committees because it would not take immediate effect. The only immediate measure was the creation of a technical commission to identify the needs of the displaced populations and the establishment of a fund for (future) implementation of the accord. For these reasons, many regarded it as one of the weaker agreements.

Historical Clarification Commission
(June 1994)

This accord called for the establishment of Guatemala's Historical Clarification Commission (CEH—formally, the Commission to Clarify Past Human Rights Violations and Acts of Violence That Have Caused the Guatemalan Population to Suffer), to begin functioning when the final peace accord was signed. The commission (in reality, Guatemala's Truth Commission) would be composed of three members, one being the UN moderator of the peace negotiations, the other two being distinguished Guatemalan citizens. The Truth Commission's work would last an initial six months, with a possible six-month renewal. At the end of that time, it was mandated to issue a report (to cover the entire period of the armed conflict—that is, since 1960) containing the results of its investigations and its recommendations for national reconciliation and promotion of a culture of tolerance. The report and recommendations issued by the commission would not individualize responsibilities for specific human rights violations or have judicial objectives or consequences.

This accord was reached only as a result of extreme pressure from several of the Friend governments, as detailed in Chapter 2. Hence, it was the accord that satisfied almost no one in Guatemala. The government/army side had to accede to the existence of such a commission (which it had opposed); from the other side, the CEH was perceived as a watered-down commission, since it would not individualize responsibilities nor would its report/recommendations have judicial consequences. Hence, it protected army human rights criminals from prosecution—at least under the mandate of the commission itself. (It did not prohibit the initiation of legal proceedings through other mechanisms.) The provision for not individualizing responsibilities received the most criticism;[2] it led the entire accord to be compared unfavorably with the Salvadoran Truth Commission—although the efficacy of the latter was vitiated when, within days of its March 1993 report that did name names, the rightist-dominated Salvadoran Congress passed a general amnesty that spared all those named from going to jail.

Identity and Rights of Indigenous Peoples (March 1995)

This accord, one of the most far-reaching, incorporated many of the demands of the Mayan groups participating in the ASC and took nine long months to negotiate. It proposed to formally define Guatemala as a multiethnic, multicultural, and multilingual nation; further, it recognized that the identities of the indigenous peoples (Maya, Xinca, and Garifuna—including diversity among the Maya groupings) are fundamental to the construction of national unity. On this basis, the government took on the commitment to promote in Congress a constitutional reform redefining the Guatemalan nation "as being of national unity, multiethnic, multicultural, and multilingual."

The accord contained many specific provisions to overcome the historic discrimination, exploitation, and injustice suffered by indigenous peoples. It proposed to make ethnic discrimination a crime, requiring legislative reforms to eliminate discriminatory laws. Further, the rights of indigenous peoples were to be protected through the educational system and the mass media and through legal aid to the poor. The rights of indigenous women, who have suffered dual discrimination (on both ethnic and gender grounds), were to be protected through creation of special mechanisms for their defense. The accord also called for ratification of the 1989 International Convention for the Elimination of all Racial Discrimination and the International Labor Organization (ILO) Convention 169 on Indigenous and Tribal Peoples.

In another specific area, the accord called for protection of the cultural rights and institutions of indigenous communities—language, names, ceremonial centers and sacred places, spirituality, use of native dress or *traje*. In this area, it laid out in significant detail the necessary educational reforms, which would decentralize the educational system in accordance with the needs of indigenous peoples, promote multilingual and multicultural education, and incorporate those elements into the entire educational system (i.e., also for the ladino population). Support would be

given for creation of a Mayan university. The accord provided for constitutional recognition (and official promotion) of indigenous languages in
schools, social services, official communications, and mass media (including access to those media), as well as legal proceedings. Special mention
was made of Mayan spirituality, the importance of ceremonial centers,
and the value of indigenous scientific knowledge and technologies,
which were to be disseminated nationwide.

Additionally, the accord contained provisions to reform the Municipal
Code, in order to respect, recognize, and promote the forms of organization of indigenous communities based on customary law (*derecho consuetudinario*). One entire section of the accord dealt with the incorporation of
customary law, which had never before been acknowledged or incorporated into national legislation. It also recognized the right of these communities and their authorities (leaders), in accordance with the norms of
municipal autonomy and customary law, to decide their own development priorities in regard to education, health, culture, and infrastructure.

In regard to civil and political rights, in addition to promoting the constitutional redefinition of the Guatemalan nation as multiethnic, multicultural, and multilingual, the government made a commitment to guarantee
indigenous rights to their diverse cultures, languages, and ideologies—
hence ending five hundred years of a monolithic, ladino-based notion of
the "Guatemalan nation" that had been imposed on the indigenous peoples. Furthermore, in recognition of the past systematic exclusion of indigenous peoples from decisionmaking in Guatemalan political life, the
government promised to promote legal reforms institutionalizing the representation of indigenous peoples at the local, regional, and national levels
and to assure their free participation in decisionmaking at all of these levels. Additionally, indigenous representatives were to be included in administrative units, and their communities were to be consulted regarding
national measures affecting them. The accord recognized that indigenous
people involved in court proceedings had a right to have such proceedings
conducted in (or translated into) their own language.

On the thorny issue of land rights, the accord recognized communal
and collective land ownership as well as individual. Furthermore, communities were to have the right to gain title to and manage those lands according to local norms and for the benefit of those communities; mechanisms for consultation and coordination with the communities
themselves were specified. These rights would include access to, use, and
administration of natural resources, as well as restitution of communal
lands, compensation for lands seized by others, and acquisition of land
for development of indigenous communities. There were also provisions
for judicial protection of these communities. Special provisions would be

made to eliminate discrimination against indigenous women as land-holders.

Finally, the accord provided for the creation of several joint commissions *(comisiones paritarias)*, composed of an equal number of governmental representatives and representatives of indigenous organizations, to guide implementation of educational reforms, other state reforms (including the judiciary), and land tenure arrangements. As with the other accords, verification would be conducted by the UN, which would take into account the opinions of indigenous organizations in designing verification mechanisms.

Those elements requiring constitutional reforms, new legislation, or institutions would not take effect until a final peace accord was signed; however, those having a basis in national or international laws already in force in Guatemala, particularly concerning human rights, were to take immediate effect, and their implementation was to be verified by MINUGUA. In practice the immediate implementation efforts focused on dissemination of the accord in indigenous languages and on antidiscrimination provisions. MINUGUA began to carry out preliminary verification within the limits of its mandate (human rights) and gradually moved toward expanding its activities in verifying this accord.

While stopping short of full regional/territorial or administrative/political autonomy and full regionalization of the state in conformity with Convention 169, the accord did regionalize educational, health, and cultural services "in accordance with linguistic criteria." Even those who were critical of its limitations agreed that the accord was a crucial starting point for future expansions of indigenous rights. Beyond its own provisions, the accord mandated ratification of the ILO Convention 169, guaranteeing the rights of a people to have its own language, territory, kinship, and political institutions; after considerable additional debate and struggle, the convention was ratified by the Guatemalan Congress in 1996, although with an amendment subordinating it to the Guatemalan Constitution, which left open the likelihood of future legal battles. In any case, the accord's provision for constitutional redefinition of the entire Guatemalan nation and its identity complemented demands for forms of regional autonomy. Its provisions were particularly appropriate because Guatemala's Maya populations are not a minority and are no longer concentrated solely in the highlands but now live all over the country.

Going far beyond antidiscrimination measures, then, this accord promised a profound transformation from the previous five hundred years of a ladino state imposed monolithically upon the indigenous majority of Guatemala's population. Taken as a whole, it paved the way for building a more inclusive and participatory, less exclusionary nation. If fully implemented, it also had the potential to make Guatemala a useful example to other countries or regions characterized by ethnic diversity.

Social and Economic Aspects and Agrarian Situation (May 1996)

The socioeconomic accord, signed in May 1996 after more than a year of negotiations, established a series of basic (although minimal) reforms that could open the door to possible future longer-range changes in the direction of modernizing the state and the landholding structure. While making no immediate structural transformations, it envisioned a more just and humane development model, with a stronger social orientation and a general goal of closing the huge gap between rich and poor in Guatemala. It was composed of five sections: democratization and participatory democracy; social development; agrarian situation and rural development; modernization of public management and fiscal policy; and final dispositions.

The first section of the accord put great emphasis on mechanisms for broader citizen participation in development, "consensus-building and dialogue among agents of socioeconomic development." More concretely, planning and implementation of development projects were to be decentralized through urban and rural "development councils," which would be reformed/reinvented from their past forms during the late 1980s (see Jonas 1991, 165–166) to broaden the range of sectors participating. There was also a commitment to encourage the formation and legal recognition of grassroots organizations; but the statements of intention were stronger than the actual mechanisms laid out, and some of the proposed reforms required new legislation. The accord also included a section on the particular mechanisms needed to assure the participation of women in economic and social development and to eliminate all forms of discrimination against women embedded in existing laws.

In the area of social development, which the accord committed the government to prioritize, there were detailed sections setting targets for increased state spending on education, health, social security, and housing. Specifically, the government would increase gross domestic product (GDP) by at least 6 percent annually and, by the year 2000, would increase the proportion of spending on education and health in relation to GDP by at least 50 percent over 1995 levels. Further, the government committed itself to ensuring that the literacy rate would be increased to 70 percent (up from 55.7 percent, the second lowest in Latin America) by the year 2000, and all children between the ages of seven and twelve would receive at least three years of schooling—bilingual education, where appropriate. A section on work emphasized reduction of structural unemployment and access to jobs paying increased real wages (although without setting spending targets for job creation or specifying wage goals); it promised vocational training to at least 200,000 workers by the year 2000. A subsection on labor protections committed the government to enforce existing labor laws, with particular emphasis on rural workers, and to facilitate legal recognition of new unions.

On the ever-elusive and complex issue of land ("the agrarian situation"), the accord did not mandate a full-fledged land reform, which was politically infeasible (unacceptable to CACIF), or a reform of articles 39–40 of the Constitution to stipulate the "social function of property," a long-standing demand of the Left and popular movements. Such a constitutional reform would have required a Constituent Assembly, opening up a nightmarish Pandora's box and, in any case, would have also been unacceptable to CACIF. Rather, the accord took the approach of agrarian modernization: market-assisted land redistribution, with commitments to promoting peasants' access to land ownership and sustainable use of land resources.

Concretely, the accord provided for creation of a land trust fund, from which land would be acquired by the government and made available to landless peasants at low prices—initially focusing on (1) lands in colonization zones that had been given out or held "irregularly" (by army generals) during the war years; the government promised to get back these lands through legal actions; (2) uncultivated state land and state-owned farms; (3) land acquired through government resources for the National Land Fund and the National Peace Fund; (4) (very limited) unused lands, available to be expropriated in accordance with the existing constitution; (5) land acquired through loans from international financial agencies.

Additionally, the accord provided for protection of municipal and communal lands and limited their alienability. It introduced the concept of rural development with emphasis on social capital (infrastructure) requiring government investments. Finally, it provided for a national land survey and a national land registry, to begin in January 1997, to determine legal ownership of all properties (rural and real estate) in the country and to identify idle or underutilized lands that could be acquired by the land trust fund or taxed at a higher rate. All of the above would be evaluated in 1999 to see if these mechanisms for getting land into the hands of small and medium peasants proved adequate. Certainly it was a far cry from comprehensive land reform, and it made no mention of reforming the constitution to limit the absolute right of private property or to establish a "social function of property"; but it outlined incipient steps toward modernizing the landholding system.

But even the sensitive land issues took second place to the most important, and ultimately the most contested, element in the accord: taxes and fiscal policy. Within an overall goal of 6 percent annual growth at the macroeconomic level, the accord committed the government to raising the ratio of taxes to GDP by 50 percent (i.e., from under 8 percent—the lowest tax to GDP ratio in Latin America—to at least 12 percent) by the year 2000, with specific targets for each intervening year. Although specific tax measures were not mandated, the principle was established that the tax system should be "fair, equitable, and on the whole progressive, in keeping with the constitutional principle of ability to pay." In addition, the government would take measures to close tax loopholes, impose stiffer penalties for tax evasion, and in other ways improve the administration of tax collection. As is described in Chapter 7, this was to become one of the major battles in the early years of peace accord implementation.

Immediately after its signing, this accord sparked major debate over whether the glass was half empty or half full. CACIF embraced it enthusiastically, leaving the impression that the traditional business elites had given up almost nothing. (They subsequently balked at meeting even the minimal commitments in the accord.) But among the popular sectors and even within the URNG, this accord became the most controversial since the watered-down Truth Commission accord of June 1994. There was a widespread perception of the accord as nothing more than the PAN government's neoliberal economic program. In addition, the mechanisms for meeting even the limited goals laid out were not well specified. Peasant organizations were so skeptical that they carried out land occupations immediately following the signing of the accord. Furthermore, it fell far short of the kind of job creation programs that were needed, although it did provide for job training and did include a more labor-intensive view of development. Finally, it provided no protection for public sector workers against neoliberal privatization measures. The ASC was not convinced to endorse the accord until two months after it was signed.

But for those with a more positive interpretation, especially UN and other international officials, the glass was more than half full. From their perspective, the accord embodied a comprehensive approach that everyone could live with; it was acceptable not only to CACIF but also to the international financial institutions (IFIs) in Washington. The final accord contained targets and a philosophy that was "an alternative to neoliberalism" and proposed to strengthen the role of the government in relation to taxation and other socioeconomic matters; at least it had a core concept, which constituted a vast improvement over the Salvadoran accords. In addition, it established the principles of political empowerment and conflict resolution and presented opportunities to resolve social conflicts and initiate minidialogues among different sectors that had never engaged in such dialogues.

On balance, both of the above interpretations appear somewhat exaggerated. Objectively, this accord was one of the weaker or "softer" accords: Certainly it did not resolve the massive structural inequities giving rise to the war. But in combination with other accords, it did provide the space for political forces to put those issues on the agenda. In this respect, the accord could be most positively understood not by itself but in conjunction with the rest of the accords—particularly the Accord on Indigenous Identity and Rights. In reality, this was about the best that could be expected, given the privatizing, pro-business orientation of the Arzú government and the need to have CACIF and the IFIs on board for the entire peace process. And certainly the accord did provide an opportunity to begin addressing the massive problems of poverty affecting 90 percent of the Guatemalan population.

Strengthening of Civilian Power and Role of the Armed Forces in a Democratic Society (September 1996)

For Guatemala, this accord—the last of the substantive agreements—was central to the entire peace process, and its signing in Mexico on September 19, 1996, was regarded as the effective end of the war. If implemented, it held the potential for a far-reaching and comprehensive transformation of the counterinsurgency state that had dominated Guatemala since the 1960s through the army's control over internal security matters. The accord's most essential provisions reduced the many functions of the previously omnipresent army to defense of national sovereignty and the country's territorial integrity (i.e., guarding the borders against external armed threats).

Within the context of modernization and strengthening of the state, the accord established a new, broader concept of integral security (citizen security as well as state security), linked to citizens' exercise of political, economic, social, and cultural rights and duties. Its participatory provision mandated the president to establish an advisory security council made up of distinguished representatives of diverse sectors of the population.

The accord established a professional and autonomous National Civilian Police (PNC) as the only police body to handle matters of public order and internal security. It required the restructuring of all existing police units, as well as private security forces, under the control of the new PNC. The PNC was to function under norms of respect for human rights and would be controlled by civilian authorities; to this end, the government promised to promote the necessary constitutional reforms and new security laws to govern the functioning of the police, as well as a new Law of Public Order prohibiting infringement on other (citizen) rights in the name of maintaining public order.

The new police force, which would function under the jurisdiction of the Ministry of the Interior and would be hierarchically structured (i.e., autonomous from any other entity such as the army), was slated to be fully in place by the end of 1999, with at least 20,000 agents—although there were some provisions for functioning during the transition period (see below). In its final form, the PNC was to reflect the multiethnic and multicultural composition of the Guatemalan population in its recruitment and selection of personnel. All members would be professionally trained in a new police academy. The functioning of the new police was to meet international standards; special training was to be given in criminal investigation and other particular areas to end the pervasive impunity. In order to meet all of these goals, an appeal would be made for technical and financial assistance from the international community.

The army's mission would undergo a fundamental redefinition, limited to defense of the country's sovereignty and the integrity of its territory; it would have no other assigned functions, and its participation in other areas would be limited to "cooperation." To this end, the government made a commitment to promote constitutional reforms regarding (1) integration, organization, and functions of the army; (2) limiting the competency of military tribunals to violations of the military code (not common crimes); (3) primacy of the president as commander-in-chief of the army over the defense minister (whether the latter be civilian or military). In the spirit of these changes, the army doctrine would be reformed to meet principles of human rights and a culture of peace. Further, all institutions under army control would function under the same rules as any other nonprofit institution, and its television station would be brought under civilian control. Recruitment was to be voluntary, universal, and nondiscriminatory under a new Civic Service Law covering both military and community (social) service—that is, permitting citizens to choose their form of service. The law to this effect was to be drafted by an *equipo paritario* (i.e., joint team or working group, with representatives from various sectors).

A further constitutional reform to be promoted by the government provided for exceptional situations: When the ordinary means for maintaining public order have been exhausted, the president would be empowered, by exception, to call upon the army for temporary service, under civilian

authority, without any limitation on citizens' constitutional rights—
hence, not involving the traditionally common "state of siege" (or "emer-
gency") in which such rights were suspended. The president would be
accountable to Congress for all such exceptional situations, and Congress
would be empowered to end them.

In terms of the much-feared special military units, the accord provided
for elimination of the Estado Mayor Presidencial (EMP—literally, Presidential Chief of Staff, with the functions of a presidential military guard)
and its replacement by a civilian-controlled entity charged with protecting
the president and vice president. The military intelligence apparatus
would be limited to the areas falling under the army's jurisdiction as specified in the accord; all other matters were to be investigated by a new civilian department of intelligence under the Interior Ministry, oriented toward organized crime and delinquency. Previously existing intelligence
files in the *Archivo* unit of army intelligence (except those relating to external defense) were to be transferred to the Interior Ministry, and it would
become a crime to possess illegal records or files containing political information on Guatemalan citizens. The accord also provided for creation of a
civilian strategic analysis secretariat reporting directly to the president.

Other, more operational aspects of the accord stipulated the following:

- demobilization and disarming of the PACs within thirty days of
  signing of final peace accords;
- demobilization and dissolution of the Policia Militar Ambulante
  (Mobile Military Police) that had controlled Guatemala's countryside for decades;
- 33 percent reduction in army troops by the end of 1997 (as opposed to 50 percent, the initial URNG demand) and redeployment of the military forces to meet only external defense needs;
- 33 percent reduction in the military budget in relation to GDP by
  1999 (relative to 1995), hence freeing up funds for social and citizen security programs;
- reorientation of military training, adaptation of courses away
  from their counterinsurgency orientation to the new values expressed in the accord, such as human rights;
- programs for reincorporation of army members demobilized by
  the accord into the productive life of the country.

Reaching beyond the security and military issues that were at its core,
the accord also contained detailed reforms designed to modernize and
strengthen all branches of the state: the executive, the Congress, and the
judicial system. Among the most important reforms were the following:

- professionalization of civil service;
- improvements in the (long-discredited) Congress, including reforms designed to improve its legitimacy and transparency and
  to assure congressional cooperation in implementation of the
  peace accords;
- constitutional reforms of the judicial system (under widespread
  criticism for decades of impunity, corruption, and inefficiency).
  These reforms would be designed to significantly improve the administration of justice and eliminate the pervasive impunity, to facilitate access to the judicial system by those speaking indigenous
  languages (in accordance with the indigenous rights accord), to
  streamline and professionalize judicial processes, and to include
  representatives of civil society within the reform process. In addition, the accord provided for establishment of a special commission for strengthening the justice system, with a broad six-month
  mandate to make recommendations for other needed changes.

Finally, separate articles within the accord provided for social and community participation within a context of ideological pluralism. A special
section of the accord dealt with women's participation in strengthening
civilian authority and the involvement of women's organizations in the
implementation of this and other accords.

The breadth and depth of the reforms mandated in this accord made it
the linchpin of the peace process. It went well beyond what might have
been expected, given the decades of military domination in Guatemalan
state and society. Observers present at the jubilant signing ceremony in
Mexico City characterized it as "an entire revolution, given Guatemala's
recent history." Indeed, every phrase of this accord expressed an important subtext of the peace process: the great desire to make a break from
the past. More globally, this accord could be interpreted as a blueprint for
dismantling Latin America's most brutal Cold War counterinsurgency apparatus. Combined with a commitment to full ideological pluralism and
cultural pluralism (as reflected both in this accord and in the accords on
indigenous rights and human rights), it consummated the commitment to
the de-centaurization and democratization of Guatemala (see Chapter 4).
It also laid the basis for fulfillment of the basic rights that had existed on
paper since the 1985 Constitution and, in this sense, was the necessary
counterpart to that constitution. As MINUGUA director David Stephen
later put it, Guatemala was being transformed *"del estado contrainsurgente
al estado de derecho"*—from a counterinsurgency state to a state under the
rule of law.

Despite all of the above, the accord did contain certain ambiguities,
loopholes, and omissions that were to become more apparent during the

first year of implementation of the accords (see Chapter 6). Among the most important of these were the following:

- Although the new PNC was to be under the civilian leadership of the Interior Ministry, the accord was vague about whether ex-army (or security force) members or ex-URNG combatants would be eligible to serve; it did not expressly prohibit members of the existing police forces, assuming that they would go through a re-education process. (In this respect, it compared unfavorably to the Salvadoran accord, which spelled out all these details.)
- Although the URNG had initially demanded that the accord dissolve the Kaibil military unit (the elite counterinsurgency force) and its training facilities, this was not accepted by the government/army (GG 1997c, 47).
- The accord did not explicitly prohibit military officials from inclusion in the new Department of Civilian Intelligence or the Secretariat of Strategic Analysis, whose members were to be named by the president.
- The accord contained no mechanisms for purging human rights violators within the army.
- More generally, in accordance with a major government/army objective, it included nothing that would impugn the army's institutional "dignity" (GG 1997c, 44).
- Overall, the accord transferred a great deal of power into the hands of the president (e.g., to call on the army "as needed" for internal security purposes)—which could undermine the entire arrangement, if the next president were an ally of (or part of) the old counterinsurgency network.
- Postponing the reduction in the army's budget to 1999 did not prohibit the army from increasing its budget during the interim, and it gave the army considerable time to consolidate its own projects for financing its operations.
- Most ominous of all, the accord was not clear about what arrangements for internal security would be made for the transition period between 1997 and 1999, that is, before the 20,000 professional police agents were in place; nor did it specify how to ensure the subordination of the military to civilian authorities during this transition.
- Finally, all of the significant changes required constitutional and legislative reforms in Congress, with constitutional reforms needing a two-thirds congressional majority and a subsequent national referendum—hence leaving the possibility of weaken-

ing the actual laws or, in the worst case, of postponing or never making the needed reforms.

In short, despite its transformatory potential, this accord—like the others—was to be subject to the second round of "negotiations," the battle for implementation.

A Missing Accord: Women's Rights

Largely because of the long-standing lack of attention to gender issues by both negotiating parties and the late development of the women's movement in Guatemala (not until the 1990s—it was only after the formation of the ASC that the Women's Sector was created within it), the negotiation agenda never included a separate accord on women's rights. As the process continued, however, special provisions concerning women were introduced into the accords; those provisions increasingly brought a gender perspective into the definition of public policy. Additionally, the very process of introducing and insisting on that perspective became an important factor in consolidating the ability of diverse women's organizations to work together to generate consensus, as well as strengthening them to carry out their own campaigns.

A few of the most important provisions in the accords concerning women include the following (for details, see Gaitán 1997; Escobedo 1997):

* The resettlement accord emphasized that special attention must be given to displaced families headed by women and/or those widowed by war violence. Furthermore, the government would be obligated to combat any and all forms of discrimination against women and specifically to promote gender equality in its resettlement projects.
* The accord on indigenous rights recognized the double discrimination that indigenous women have suffered. Hence, the government would be committed to penalize any crimes against indigenous women; create a Defensoría de la Mujer Indígena, formed by Mayan women in various organizations; correct discriminatory content (or "invisibilizing" content) in educational texts and materials; and (beyond combating discrimination) promote women's access to land, including land titles, housing, credit, and participation in development projects. The government would also have to comply with the Convention on the Elimination of All Forms of Discrimination Against Women. All of the

above objectives were to be supported and disseminated by the mass media, as well as rights organizations.

- The socioeconomic accord recognized equal opportunity for women as a basic premise of development, as well as the contribution of women to community improvement and other areas of economic and social development. Specifically, public policy was to include gender considerations and state employees were to be trained to that effect; women were to be given equal treatment with men in the (public) sphere of production as well as in the (private) sphere of the household; women should have equal access to land, credit, and technological resources, as well as to training and education. Educational texts were to be revised to eliminate discriminatory material; women were to have equal access to housing and to integral health care—including all necessary information for making decisions about having children. In the area of work opportunities, women were to have legal equality, equal training, protection for domestic labor (including decent salaries and working conditions), equal access to public sector jobs and policymaking, equal participation in the "development councils" at all levels, and equal treatment in the countryside, whether as workers or owners of land, and in decision-making about rural development issues.
- The accord on strengthening civilian power recognized the importance of women's participation—and the work of women's organizations—in such strengthening. To this end, the government promised to undertake educational campaigns against the previously existing limitations on women's roles and to strengthen women's participation in all organizations of civil society, as well as to promote organizations specifically concerning women's issues.

Finally, the Timetable accord (see below) provided for creation of a Women's Forum on the commitments concerning women's rights and participation set out in the peace accords; this was to occur during the first three months after the signing of peace. The final peace accord itself made reference to the need for full participation of *ciudadanos y ciudadanas* (citizens, both men and women) in achieving the goals of the accords.

The Operational Accords (December 1996)

After considerable struggles (from the beginning of the process through at least 1993) to establish this principle, the peace process had postponed the "operational" agreements until after all of the substantive themes had been negotiated. However, the line between substantive and operational turned out to be less clear-cut than the formal distinction might suggest; in addition to finalizing the cease-fire, the latter also included significant matters of substance in the accords on constitutional and electoral reforms, reinsertion of the URNG and amnesty issues, and the (extremely substantive) *Cronograma* or Timetable for implementation of the accords.

It should also be recalled that the negotiation of these final agreements was heavily impacted by the Novella kidnapping scandal of October-November 1996, which led to the suspension of talks until the head of the responsible organization (ORPA) resigned from the URNG's negotiating team. In short, the URNG went into the final round of negotiations from a position of weakness; even the government team itself was under heavy attack from right-wing peace resisters who had always opposed the peace process and now saw an opportunity to abort it. One of the most concrete effects of this changed climate of opinion and correlation of forces was the URNG's offer to alter the order of the operational accords, formalizing the cease-fire first. So imperiled was the process that several of the Friend governments (Norway and [unofficial Friend] Sweden, Spain and Mexico) intervened proactively: In order to revive the process and assure its completion, they arranged for the signing of these last accords in their own capital cities, bringing along (and paying for) a sizable delegation from Guatemalan civil society as well as the formal negotiators.

Definitive Cease-Fire

Of all the accords, this one, signed in Oslo on December 4, was the only strictly operational one, establishing the specific conditions of a definitive cease-fire (as contrasted with the de facto cease-fire that had been in effect since March 1996). The definitive cessation of all insurgent and counterinsurgent actions was to take place on a specified date, when the UN verification mission was to be in place, and was to last sixty days during which time the URNG was to be completely demobilized. It also provided for the separation of forces—the redeployment of Guatemalan army units and their withdrawal from areas around the camps in which the URNG was concentrating, demobilizing and disarming, and turning in information about weapons, as well as the weapons themselves.

Limited operations of certain Guatemalan army units were also to be verified by the UN mission. Nevertheless, it should be noted that Guatemala's cease-fire accord, unlike that of El Salvador, did not make the URNG's demobilization contingent upon the equivalent reductions and other changes in the Guatemalan army—nor upon the government's compliance with other accords. Therefore the URNG would not be able to use its own demobilization as leverage for pressuring the government and army.

Constitutional Reforms and the Electoral Regime

Signed in Stockholm on December 7, this crucial accord specified the constitutional reforms that the government was committed to sponsor in Congress, within sixty days of the signing of the final accord. The specifics were based on previous (substantive) accords on indigenous peoples' identity and rights and on strengthening civilian power, the latter to include redefining the role of the armed forces, creating the National Civilian Police, and guaranteeing the improved administration of justice. The constitutional reforms from both accords involved profound changes in the state apparatus and its relation to Guatemalan society. However, guaranteeing that these constitutional reforms would be fully made was beyond the scope of this accord: After the government submitted them to Congress, they would have to be approved by a two-thirds majority in Congress and subsequently approved in a national referendum.

The other significant provision of this accord was its call for creation of an Electoral Reform Commission to "consolidate a pluralist and representative democracy in Guatemala"—specifically, to guarantee transparency of future elections, overcome the widespread abstentionism, and reform campaign financing and voter documentation.

Basis for the Legal Integration of the URNG

This accord, signed in Madrid on December 12, detonated the most explosive controversy of the entire process. Because it established the terms for legal integration or incorporation of the URNG—the necessary last step in ending the thirty-six-year civil war—it also dealt with the issues of amnesty, and this was interpreted as applying to both parties to the civil war, the army as well as the URNG. Hence it was bound to reopen the wounds from the previous battles over the mandate of the Truth Commission, in regard to justice for victims of human rights atrocities, committed overwhelmingly by the army.

The provisions for the URNG's incorporation laid out detailed plans for the phased demobilization and subsequent reinsertion of the URNG and its members into the legal political, social, economic, and cultural life of the nation. A special commission was to be created, composed of members of the government and URNG, and international donor representatives in a consultative capacity. As one component of the incorporation program, the accord included provisions for a National Reconciliation Act, to be passed in Congress. Such a law would be designed to avert all forms of revenge while protecting the rights of victims and of the society as a whole—above all, the right, through the Truth Commission, to know the truth about human rights crimes. The accord also contained provisions for compensation to victims having suffered these crimes.

Other provisions of the accord were designed "to promote national reconciliation without neglecting the need to combat impunity," by including within the Reconciliation Act a mechanism for legalizing URNG members, previously "outlaws." This provision, "extinguishing criminal liability" for "political crimes," was necessary to cover URNG members' political crime of having taken up arms against the government and having violated "state security" and the institutional order. It was further extended to "related" common crimes committed during the course of the armed conflict—meaning those crimes that were "directly, objectively, intentionally, and causally related to the commission of the political crimes" mentioned above and "which cannot be shown to be motivated by personal goals."

The bombshell was the further provision that the amnesty would also cover "common crimes" that could be objectively proven to have been committed by state security forces in their combat against the insurgents—"where such crimes were directly, objectively, intentionally, and causally related" to counterinsurgency aims, "unless it is demonstrated that there is no relationship between the criminal act and the stated aim." The amnesty provisions could "under no circumstances extend to crimes which, under domestic law or the international treaties ratified or signed by Guatemala, are imprescriptible"—meaning not subject to any statute of limitations (e.g., the undue use of force against persons detained or held prisoner)—or those "which are not subject to an extinction of criminal liability," that is, which are incapable of being forgiven, and which hence must be prosecuted.

Within days of the signing of this convoluted but carefully crafted and worded accord, the Guatemalan Congress rushed to pass a National Reconciliation Law. It was the congressional law, passed in final form on December 18, that provoked an explosion of the long-building tensions over a perceived "general amnesty." The conservative/rightist-dominated Congress was far more disposed than the negotiating teams to amnesty virtually all crimes committed by the army. Only the FDNG and the Unión del Centro Nacional (UCN), the party of assassinated journalist/politician Jorge Carpio, voted against it. Under extreme pressure from domestic and international human rights organizations, Congress incorporated into the final version of the law exemptions from amnesty covering the crimes of genocide, torture, and forced disappearances, as well as for crimes involving the undue use of force against persons being held in custody of the armed forces. Not exempted from amnesty were extrajudicial executions that did not fall under the previous categories; this became the main issue for ongoing protests and challenges to the law, including its constitutionality.

On paper, even the congressional law, whose amnesty provisions were considerably broader than the accord, did not amount to a blanket amnesty law, as was charged by less careful critics. More precise analyses were issued by MINUGUA and the Robert F. Kennedy Center in Washington (see Popkin 1996). (And regardless of what the accord might have said, pre-1986 crimes were already off limits, as a result of the army's "self-amnesty" just before handing over power to civilian president Cerezo in 1986.) Nevertheless, all concerned knew full well that in practice, the law contained issues of interpretation that would have to be resolved in the courts; in essence, it kicked the ball back to the judicial system, with all its institutional weaknesses, susceptibilities to threats, and traditions of impunity—but a judicial system that was also slated for total overhaul under the accords. In short, the law opened up what was to become one of the major ongoing battles during the years of accord implementation (see Chapter 6).

Timetable for the Peace Accords

The *Cronograma* or Timetable accord (formally, Implementation, Compliance, and Verification Timetable), negotiated in Mexico in the days just preceding the final accord but formally signed in Guatemala on December 29, 1996, laid out the Timetable for the phased implementation and verification of the commitments in all of the previous accords whose timing could be reliably scheduled. For those which were ongoing (the Comprehensive Human Rights Accord) or whose timing depended on other political forces (primarily Congress and the *comisiones paritarias*—and, in the case of constitutional reforms, a referendum), the accord established a Commission to "Follow Up" or Accompany the Peace Process. This commission was to be composed of an equal number of representatives of the government and the URNG, plus four "notable citizens," one congressional representative, and the head of MINUGUA as observer. The commission's functions were to facilitate implementation of the accords, screen and approve governmental proposals stemming from the accords before they were sent to Congress, work out problems and reschedule targets, as needed, and issue periodic reports on the progress and problems of implementation. Finally, the accord established the mandate and functions of the international (UN) verification mission for the duration of the implementation process.

The Timetable was divided into three phases: the first covering a ninety-day period beginning January 15, 1997; the second covering the rest of 1997; and the third covering 1998, 1999, and the year 2000. Special provision was made in an appendix for fixing tax reform targets to be met during each year for the period 1997–2000. The first ninety days were primarily for the demobilization of the URNG, the sending of proposals for constitutional reforms to Congress, the creation of the new National Civilian Police, and the establishment of all of the commissions and other institutional arrangements necessary for implementation during the following four years. The Timetable also spelled out in great detail the schedule for compliance with accord commitments for the subsequent two phases (the rest of 1997 and 1998–2000). The actual progress of compliance and implementation is assessed in Chapters 6, 7, and 8.

A Firm and Lasting Peace

The final accord, signed amid great ceremony in Guatemala City's National Palace on December 29, 1996 (see the Prologue), was the culmination of the entire process. It officially ended Guatemala's thirty-six-year civil war and formally initiated the process of implementation of all of the accords except the already-in-effect human rights accord.

Notes

1. This summary is based on the United Nations texts of the accords as published in Spanish and translated into English. I have used the official UN translations, except as specifically noted in the text, and except for using the word "accord" instead of "agreement."

2. Despite the furor over this last point, it is worth noting Msgr. Quezada Toruño's reaction (in the press) that not individualizing responsibilities for judicial purposes was not the same as not naming names (cited in Padilla 1995a, 53–54). In any case, because of the limitations in the June 1994 accord and because the CEH was not to be set up until after the signing of the final peace accord, the Bishops' Conference of the Catholic Church initiated its own project, "Recovery of the Historical Memory" (see Chapter 6). Of course, final judgments about the mandate of the CEH could not be established until after the closely related reinsertion/amnesty arrangements had been negotiated—an "operational" theme, hence one of the last on the negotiation agenda.

4

Can Peace Bring Democracy or Social Justice?

The Guatemalan peace process provides an excellent opportunity to address a number of ongoing discussions about political democratization and social justice in Latin America.* The first part of this chapter briefly summarizes how, beyond ending the war, this peace process contributed significantly to the democratization of Guatemala; it highlights both how the process opened up political space and what gains have (and have not) been achieved in the content of the accords signed. The rest of this chapter analyzes the Guatemalan experience from the early 1980s to the present and uses that experience to address some broad theoretical debates about democratization and social justice in Latin America.[1]

In engaging the conceptual debates about political democracy and its relation to socioeconomic equity, I make no pretense of "settling" those debates. Rather, my primary goal is to interpret Guatemala's political evolution during recent decades. In such an interpretation, I believe, there should be no disjuncture between the analytical use of terminology about democracy and public discourse about actually lived experience. Hence, we should not assign the label of "democracy" or "democratic transition" to situations and time periods that were not experienced as such by large numbers of Guatemalans. When and how did a genuine democratic transition begin in Guatemala? Can we characterize as a "democratic" transition the period (early 1980s to early 1990s) when the political/electoral transition had begun but prior to the peace process? The

*This chapter was written and revised several times during the course of 1997–1998. Despite the changes that may develop after the May 1999 referendum on constitutional reforms (analyzed in Chapter 8), I have not substantially altered this chapter, since its focus is the *democratic project* of the peace process, rather than its vicissitudes. Some of the issues raised here are revisited in the Conclusion.

answers to these questions rest on an analysis of the interaction between elections and the peace process in opening up Guatemala's exclusionary political system.

From this follows my broader question: What does the Guatemalan experience add to the ongoing debates among different paradigms or schools of analysis about political democracy in Latin America? The most commonly accepted definition in the contemporary political science literature is one or another version of the "procedural minimum." I shall argue here that experiences such as that of Guatemala, involving societal ruptures and decades-long civil wars, cannot be fully understood simply within the context of one (useful but limited) body of literature about democratic transitions. That perspective, which was developed mainly to deal with transitions from authoritarian to democratic rule in southern Europe and the Southern Cone of Latin America, provides partial insight. Nevertheless, for the cases of the Central American countries that underwent revolutionary turmoil during the 1980s, it must be complemented by other bodies of literature that highlight the participatory dimensions of democratization. In particular, key elements of the Guatemalan experience are best captured through the lens of the classical tradition that emphasizes participatory as well as procedural elements of democracy.

In addition, because 60 percent of its population is indigenous, the quality of political democracy in Guatemala will be profoundly affected by issues of cultural diversity *(pluriculturalidad)* and intercultural dialogue. Finally, beyond the debates about the nature of political democracy lies the highly contested and still unresolved issue of its relation to socioeconomic equity or justice—especially in this era of neoliberal economic policies. This issue as well can be reexamined in the light of the Guatemalan peace process experience. In sum, my purpose in this chapter is to theorize the experience of Guatemala from the early 1980s to the present and hopefully to enrich the broader debates.

"De-Centaurization" and Other Gains for Democracy

In this section I highlight the democratizing elements of the Guatemalan peace process and the accords signed in December 1996. In Guatemala, as elsewhere, a peace negotiation is, in the end, a political settlement, and much of what it is able to deliver in the short range concerns postwar political arrangements. Particularly striking in the Guatemalan case are the democratizing elements of both the negotiation process, with its provisions for broad input and participation, and the content of the accords as signed.

It is important to remember that as recently as 1992–1993, hard-line forces in Guatemala's military and civilian elites were determined not to negotiate a settlement permitting a legal presence or political participation by the URNG or its allies in Guatemala; and they regarded virtually all of the organizations of civil society as URNG allies or "facades." Furthermore, particularly after the signing of a negotiated peace in neighboring El Salvador, these elites vowed "never" to tolerate such an outcome in Guatemala. The extraordinary story of how and why, from 1994 to 1996, the Guatemalan army and government found themselves involved in very much the same kind of process as the Salvadoran, with the United Nations as moderator and verifier of the process, has been chronicled in detail in Chapter 2. Slowly but surely, despite fierce resistances and significant delays, the peace process acquired credibility in Guatemala. With all its difficulties, it created a space for the discussion and negotiation of issues that had been taboo for decades and remained taboo in the still-restricted electoral arena prior to 1995.

In addition, the formal electoral arena was paralleled by the "informal political arena" that evolved after the 1993 *Serranazo* and coalesced in 1994 as the ASC in the context of the peace negotiations. As discussed in Chapter 2, the broad-based multisector ASC included virtually all organized sectors of civil society (even, for the first time, women's organizations), as well as the major political parties. Only the big-business sectors represented in CACIF decided not to participate. Having gained new experience during the *Serranazo*, these grassroots organizations had become increasingly vocal in demanding participation in the peace process. The ASC was also striking for the diversity and plurality of political/ideological positions represented within its ranks; unlike the popular organizations in El Salvador, the ASC was by no means a simple instrument of the URNG. In particular, the indigenous organizations demonstrated considerable autonomy. As the main peace agreements were being hammered out, the ASC—after engaging in a fascinating process of consensus-building among widely divergent positions—offered proposals to the negotiating parties on each issue. Though not binding, their positions had to be taken into account by the negotiating parties, and the URNG adopted many of the ASC proposals as its own negotiating positions.

Furthermore, the formation of the ASC gave Guatemala's organized popular sectors their first sustained experience of participating in and considering themselves part of the political process. This was particularly important for sectors that had always rejected electoral participation and prided themselves on their anti-system political culture of *denuncia* (accusations) as a manifestation of political resistance. In the particular unfolding of Guatemalan history, the ASC experience was the precursor to the eventual participation by many of those sectors in the 1995 election. In these respects, the peace process came to offer Guatemalan civil society its best opportunity to democratize an exclusionary system and to make some changes that would have been impossible or highly unlikely under any other circumstances.

Seen in its totality, the negotiation process was a great step forward for Guatemalan democracy. The accords constituted a truly negotiated settlement, much like El Salvador's of 1992. Rather than being imposed by victors upon vanquished, they represented a splitting of differences between radically opposed forces, with major concessions from both sides. This exercise in the culture of compromise was a real novelty in Guatemala.

Additional process-related gains for democracy have accumulated since the signing of the peace accords. Most of the accords contain important provisions for participation in decisionmaking—including *comisiones paritarias* (with equal representation from the government and indigenous organizations) and a host of other multisectoral commissions. In addition, the implementation of the accords has given rise to a far-reaching culture and practice of *consultas,* involving some (not all) policymakers in direct interchanges with citizens and social organizations—some of them outside the capital city (also a novelty); this was the methodology followed, for example, by the Commission on Strengthening the Justice System. Finally, the accords provide innovative mechanisms (such as the Foro de Mujeres, or Women's Forum) for training and capacity-building among those who have never had such opportunities.

Substantively, whatever else the accords do or do not accomplish, they provide the framework for institutionalizing full political democracy in a country that has not enjoyed such democracy since 1954. (The question of the early and mid-1980s through early 1990s is addressed below.) First, as described in Chapter 2, the human rights accord (March 1994) was important not so much for any new concept of human rights; these were already guaranteed on paper in the 1985 Constitution. The genuine novelty was to bring the UN verification mission, MINUGUA, into the country, which contributed significantly to ending the systematic violation of those rights in practice.

Second, at the heart of the entire arrangement is the September 1996 demilitarization accord (Strengthening of Civilian Power and Role of the Armed Forces in a Democratic Society). As described in Chapter 3, this accord mandates far-reaching constitutional reforms to limit the functions of the army—which since the 1960s has considered itself the "spinal column" of the Guatemalan state and has involved itself in everything from counterinsurgency and internal security to civic action and vaccinating babies. Henceforth, the accord stipulates, the army will have one single function: defense of the borders and of Guatemala's territorial integrity.

The accord also eliminates the dreaded paramilitary Civilian Self-Defense Patrols (PACs) and other counterinsurgency security units, reduces the size and budget of the army by a third, and creates a new civilian police force to guarantee citizen security. Finally, it mandates necessary reforms of the judicial system to eliminate the pervasive impunity.

As introduced in the Prologue to explain the title of this book, the best metaphor for understanding the essence of Guatemala's repressive political system of the 1960s, 1970s, and 1980s has been Figueroa's (1986) image of the "centaurization" of the Guatemalan state, that is, its conversion into a counterinsurgency apparatus that was half-beast, half-human—a mix of civilian and military power, with the military component predominating. Following the implosion of this model in the 1993 *Serranazo* (see below), the 1996 demilitarization accord mandates the "de-centaurization" of the state, as the precondition for strengthening civilian power and genuine democratization. It is also the precondition for Guatemala's governability and viability for the twenty-first century.

If the battle for full implementation is won—which cannot be taken for granted in Guatemala—this accord will stand out as marking profound changes in the rules and the principal players of Guatemalan politics—what Booth (2000b, 2) denominates a "regime change." For those who have lived under Guatemala's militarized and exclusionary political system all these years and have experienced the fear that permeated human and social interactions, ideological pluralism is a significant achievement. Strange as it sounds, people can celebrate the fact that Guatemala is becoming a "normal" country because they have been living in a virtual state of exception for decades.

The other significant gain is the 1995 Accord on Identity and Rights of Indigenous Peoples. This accord goes far beyond antidiscrimination protections for Guatemala's indigenous majority—60 percent of the population—to mandate a constitutional reform redefining Guatemala as a multiethnic, multicultural, and multilingual nation. If fully implemented, this agreement will require profound reforms in the country's educational, judicial, and political systems. It lays the formal basis for a new entitlement of Guatemala's indigenous majority and establishes their right to make claims upon the state. In a country such as Guatemala, democracy and genuine pluralism cannot be divorced from the construction of a multiethnic, multicultural nation, as envisioned in the accord. Overcoming the historic polarization of Guatemalan politics requires recognition of the diversity that *is* Guatemala and of the strong indigenous component of Guatemala's national identity. As is discussed below, this accord, together with independent initiatives by indigenous organizations, also creates a basis for new social and political interactions and for a more democratic political culture.

The most important elements of the peace accords in democratizing Guatemala require changes in the 1985 Constitution. Although it contains a Bill of Rights on paper, it simultaneously legalizes functions and powers for the army that make political democratization almost impossible to achieve in practice. Furthermore, the 1985 Constitution does very little to address the principal issues of indigenous peoples' rights. Hence, the major democratic gains from the peace process cannot be consolidated until the constitutional reforms are in place (see Chapter 8).

To summarize: On the positive side of the balance sheet, the peace process and the accords have changed many rules of the political game and created a new political scenario, including the legalization of the formerly "subversive" URNG. If the forces of the Left are coherent and intelligent enough to use it well, they now have the space to fight for many of the goals not achieved in the accords themselves.

On the negative side, there are serious limitations and flaws in some of the accords and important issues that were left unaddressed. Unless they are addressed directly, some of these flaws and omissions are serious enough to eventually undermine democratic gains. One immediately visible area is the weakness on issues of justice to victims of the war, expressed mainly in the limited mandate of the Truth Commission and the partial amnesty covering some (not all) army war crimes. Rather than directly punishing the perpetrators, these accords leave major human rights cases in the hands of the courts, which still operate within a generalized framework of impunity and threats; this is unlikely to change until the judicial system reforms are implemented.

Equally or more serious in the long run are the shortcomings on socioeconomic issues in the accord, which does almost nothing to improve daily life for the majority of Guatemalans. The steady deterioration of social conditions in El Salvador since the 1992 peace accords is an ominous precedent. Despite attempts to learn from the Salvadoran experience and to avoid a direct conflict between the peace agenda and a neoliberal economic agenda, Guatemala's accords do not contain measures for land reform or job creation. Furthermore, the resistances to tax reform and socioeconomic redistribution could become the Achilles' heel of Guatemala's peace accords and eventually undermine democratic gains. For example, ongoing and worsening poverty is one of the major factors contributing to an increase in social violence and common crime; this in turn has sparked calls for maintaining army involvement in internal security—a most definite threat to democratic gains.

Moreover, as suggested above, the democratic reforms are not automatically in place but require additional battles. With the signing of the accords, Guatemala's "peace resisters" and defenders of the old order immediately began sharpening their knives. Just getting the entire complex of constitutional reforms and new laws through the Guatemalan Congress has entailed a series of battles on many fronts, as is detailed in Chapters 6–8. Until these fundamental battles of the second (implementation) phase of the peace process are won, Guatemalan democracy will remain fragile and unconsolidated.

Democracy Without Adjectives

It is the premise of the rest of this chapter that fulfillment of the peace accords, particularly on demilitarization, is the necessary precondition for full development of political democracy. The quality of that democracy will also be affected by the degree of citizen participation (both individual and collective) in using democratic institutions to improve their lives. Below, I develop a series of arguments about interpretations of the Guatemalan experience and implications for the broader debates in Latin America. First, after examining the Guatemalan transition experiences from the early 1980s through the mid-1990s, I argue that the transition literature, developed primarily to explain events in the Southern Cone, does not by itself capture the essentials of the democratization process as it actually occurred in Guatemala. In order to fully comprehend experiences such as the Guatemalan (and others in Central America), we must also draw on other paradigms of democracy. The Schumpeterian/representational tradition, which emphasizes only procedural/institutional democracy, is not "wrong"; but for situations such as Guatemala's, it includes too much and, at the same time, describes too little. If that procedural definition is complemented by other theoretical frameworks (both classical and contemporary) that emphasize political participation, we can gain a better perspective on how much political democratization can mean after a long anti-democratic period. Finally, I address the recurrent issue of socioeconomic equity and its relation to political democracy. This has been one of the major battles over interpretations of societal upheavals since the French Revolution. I make no pretense of resolving this monumental issue, but its ongoing relevance should be highlighted.

How Democratic Was
Guatemala's "Pacted Transition"?

As seen above, the peace process has been a broadly democratizing experience for Guatemala. But how does its contribution compare to that of the electoral democracy restored during the mid-1980s through an inter-elite pact? This question presupposes another: How shall we characterize the "pacted transition" period from the early 1980s through the early

1990s, before the peace process was fully under way (although it had begun)? By what criteria shall we judge the quality of democracy during that previous period? It was certainly a political transition, but can it be considered a "democratic transition"? And if not, how and when did the transition become more democratic?

During the period from the early 1980s through the early 1990s, Guatemala did experience a transition pacted between civilian and military elites and did hold elections that were considered "free and fair" (nonfraudulent) as well as competitive. However, those elections were restricted, that is, not representative of all political tendencies (see below). Furthermore, as described more empirically in Chapter 1, at the same time a repressive/coercive counterinsurgency apparatus was effectively stifling basic freedoms (of expression, assembly, and so on) and imposing military control on entire sectors of the rural population. Only the Reagan State Department cheerfully proclaimed Guatemala a "consolidated"/"post-transitional" democracy after nothing more than the 1985 election (cited in Jonas 1989). More sober and rigorous academic analysts implicitly acknowledged the problem when they had to invent new categories of democracy (restricted, pseudo-, *tutelada*, "facade," *democradura*) in order to include Guatemala in the "democratic family." When it becomes necessary to add all those qualifiers or adjectives, the definition of democracy is being stretched beyond acceptable limits.

Within Guatemala itself, the debates about the "democratic transition" have been very sharp and contested. Officers of the Guatemalan army and some of their civilian allies generally claim that the army guided Guatemala to democracy, beginning with the 1982 coup, continuing through the period of the Constituent Assembly (1984), the writing of a new constitution (1985), and the 1985 elections that restored civilian government in 1986. Hence, according to this reading of recent Guatemalan history, farsighted army officials and their civilian allies demonstrated the clearest "democratic vocation" and should go down in Guatemalan history as the fathers of contemporary Guatemalan democracy—as one retired army general recently put it, the "democratic vanguard." Some civilian social scientists argue that the democratic transition began in the first half of the 1980s, although they do not credit the army with having "graciously" conceded real power to civilians.[2]

A second debate focuses on the period of elected, formally civilian rule beginning in 1986 (the governments of Cerezo, Serrano, and de León Carpio), which a number of Guatemalan analysts take as the starting point for contemporary Guatemalan democracy.[3] Generally, their argument is not the simplistic one based only on having civilian presidents; in addition, they maintain that despite the large quota of power held by the army (and despite its intentions to retain that power), these governments saw the gradual undermining of military power, finally to the point of the subordination of military to civilian power. Although it is true that the army lost absolute power and/or saw its power undermined, I agree with those who have challenged the idea of calling this period "democratic" without any further qualification. Torres Rivas (1989, 1996), for example, has described the entire period beginning in the early 1980s as an "authoritarian transition to democracy." No one questions the fact that there were changes beginning in 1982 or that this entire period was one of transition; one could even say that it eventually became a "transition to democracy"—although only in hindsight and largely for reasons outside its own logic. But this is quite different from characterizing it as a "democratic transition" per se, particularly the period 1982–1985.

Elsewhere (Jonas 1991, 1995), I have argued in detail that because power was not effectively transferred from the army to civilians, the transition from overt military rule to elected civilian government in Guatemala during the mid-1980s was not so much a "democratic transition" as the top-down liberalization of an authoritarian regime—a process that is generally agreed to be quite different from genuine democratization. In the Guatemalan case, the regimes of the late 1980s and early 1990s made no serious attempt to impose civilian authority over the military (with the brief exception of Serrano, at the very beginning of his government). Liberalizations can be controlled: Openings can be shut at will—as was attempted in Guatemala as recently as the 1993 *Serranazo*. The failure of the *Serranazo*, in fact, was the first real sign that a deeper, truly democratic transition was beginning.

After the necessary "recomposition" of the counterinsurgency state to resolve its internal and external crises of legitimacy (beginning in 1982–1983), what existed from 1986 through the early 1990s can be described as a civilian version of the counterinsurgency state, with its own particularities, but leaving the army with a great deal of power—although not absolute power—over civilian authorities. In essence, what did not change was the prevalence of a predominantly coercive state on an ongoing (not exceptional) basis, and of military domination as opposed to hegemony or creation of social consensus. The counterinsurgency state is a project not simply of the army but of the ruling coalition (including economic elites) as a whole. But civilian counterinsurgency states have their own contradictions, particularly in their responses to popular protest.[4] Formally, the post-1986 civilian government reestablished the rule of law, but on the ground, many Guatemalans did not feel protected by it or behave as if their rights were protected.[5] On paper, the 1985 Constitution contained basic liberal democratic guarantees, but that same constitution codified the counterinsurgency institutions (e.g., army-controlled PACs and "model villages") that violated such guarantees in practice, particularly in rural ex-conflict zones. For the most part from 1986 through the mid-1990s, civilian presidents allowed the army to rule from behind the scenes and were afraid to challenge the army's prerogatives. In short, the ruling coalition ceded and the politicians accepted very restricted spaces for autonomous action.

To be sure, the constitutional framework provided some important spaces from which citizens or popular organizations could organize to force open broader spaces. Nevertheless, as documented by virtually all human rights reports covering the period from 1986 through the mid-1990s, the levels of repression directed against those who tested the limits and the pervasive climate of fear marred the liberalization to such a degree that this could not be considered a climate favorable to citizen participation (see Note 5). In addition, the levels of impunity and arbitrariness, especially by military authorities, and the absence of due process in the judicial system were striking. As late as 1995, MINUGUA reports still identified impunity as the major obstacle to real improvements in the human rights climate.

Elections during this period—specifically, the 1985 and 1990–1991 elections—were free of fraud and certainly featured competing political parties (eighteen or nineteen of them). However, these elections could not be called "representative," as many studies have demonstrated.[6] Far from being fully pluralistic, they were ideologically restricted, with virtually all forces to the left of center excluded, as well as persecuted, until 1995.[7] As a result, many real issues were left undiscussed in the electoral arena. Many citizens were too inhibited by fear to engage in political activity of any kind. Finally, on the dimension of voter participation, these elections were characterized by ever-declining levels of participation: Abstention among registered voters rose from 31 percent in the first round of the 1985 presidential election to 44 percent in the first round of the 1990–1991 presidential election and reached the absurd extreme of around 80 percent in the 1994 congressional election.[8]

None of the above should be interpreted as dismissing the critical role of elections in any democratizing process. In particular, the 1985 election, the first serious one in two decades, awakened high hopes among the Guatemalan citizenry about the change from military to civilian rule—although these hopes were subsequently dashed. The main virtue of the 1990–1991 election was the transfer of power from one elected civilian government to another—an important advance for Guatemala, but still a "fraudulent pluralism," according to one centrist analyst (Cruz Salazar 1991). The U.S.-based National Democratic Institute (1991), which observed that election, concluded that Guatemala was consolidating an "exclusionary democracy," still lacking in basic political guarantees. In short, these elections overall (through 1994) were so exclusionary as to be insufficient grounds *by themselves* for establishing a claim to "democracy."

Underneath the surface during those years, in addition, there was an intense debate within the Right as to whether to tolerate any autonomous political actor (the URNG, once it laid down its arms, or any other leftist force). The Right was obsessed with the problem of the URNG's *aterrizaje* (landing) and legal insertion into civilian political life—and, more fundamentally, of what forces in civil society would become the social/political bases for parties of the Left. Their fears were not unfounded: Private presidential polls showed that the URNG came to enjoy a 10 percent *simpatía* in the spring of 1992, even while it was illegal. In fact, many observers agreed that any new force untarnished by the existing political crisis had the potential to gain support rapidly, once its participation was permitted. Because the peace process could potentially open up the previously exclusionary system, it became a source of tensions within the army and the private sector. There were constant pressures to end the process and thus to close the spaces that it began to open. This was the particular logic underlying human rights violations during that period: Hard-liners in the security forces were striking out against movements that might function autonomously, precisely in order to avoid a truly pluralistic politics.

To the extent that there were real democratic gains during this period, it was not simply a result of elections by themselves. The beginning of the peace negotiations opened up new spaces outside the electoral arena, and eventually a sui generis interaction developed between elections and negotiations that democratized the political transition.[9] Furthermore, as argued above, the peace process itself involved an articulation between the formal negotiations and the concurrent empowerment of forces in civil society—most notably, the organizing of autonomous indigenous movements. It was this complex dynamic that influenced electoral politics as much as the reverse. More broadly, it was precisely this interplay of forces that differentiated Guatemala's transition from one pacted simply between civilian and military elites—and that helped transform the (sub)minimalist democratic procedures of the late 1980s into a more participatory experience.

A further example of this mutual interaction came in 1995, when the peace process was directly impacted by the dynamics of the campaign for the November general election—as well as vice-versa. Early in 1995 the URNG issued an unprecedented call urging people to vote, which was interpreted as signaling an implicit shift toward political means of struggle. Meanwhile, for the first time in forty years—in no small measure as a result of the simultaneous peace process—a left-of-center coalition of popular and indigenous organizations, the FDNG (the "left flank" of the ASC), was formed to participate in the elections. Equally significant was the August 1995 agreement signed on the Panamanian island of Contadora (brokered by the Central American Parliament): The URNG agreed to suspend military actions during the last two weeks of the electoral campaign, in exchange for a commitment by the major political parties to continue the peace negotiations under a new government and honor the accords already signed. For the first time, the Guatemalan political class accepted in principle that the accords constituted "accords of state" and hence could not be jettisoned by any future government or Congress.

In the November 1995 elections, marked by a very low level of partici- pation (47 percent of registered voters), no presidential candidate re- ceived an absolute majority, requiring a January 1996 runoff (between modernizing conservative Alvaro Arzú and a stand-in for former dictator Efraín Ríos Montt).[10] In the runoff election, with only 37 percent of regis- tered voters participating, Arzú won by a scant 2 percent of the vote, hence assuring the continuity of the peace negotiations; despite the Con- tadora agreement, Ríos Montt's party had given signals in the opposite direction. The major surprise of the 1995 election was the far stronger- than-expected showing of the newly formed leftist FDNG. Despite oper- ating at great disadvantage, and weakened by the lack of resources and prior political experience, the FDNG won 8 percent of the presidential vote and six congressional seats, making it the third strongest party in Congress. Additionally, alliances between the FDNG and locally based in- digenous *comités cívicos* (civic committees) won several important may- oralties, including Xelajú (Quetzaltenango). These victories resulted from the fact that the early 1990s had also seen the spread of indigenous politi- cal movements that were autonomous from the traditional political par- ties and took electoral form in civic committees.

The more pluralistic election of 1995 was a result of this complex inter- play of forces and would not have grown simply or automatically out of the electoral system itself. Something similar, involving nonelectoral as well as electoral forces (although without the indigenous or ASC compo- nents) had taken place in El Salvador; hence, the particularity of what I call the *camino centroamericano*, the Central American path of democratiza- tion, which was simultaneously a transition from war to peace.[11] As this Central American path has unfolded, it has revealed the profound differ- ence between a true negotiation between armed leftist insurgents and civilian/military elites as two semi-equal negotiating parties and a more limited "pact" simply between civilian and military elites, as in Chile.[12] The Central American negotiation processes involved mutual compro- mises in internationally verified political agreements, not counterinsur- gent "winners" imposing a settlement on insurgent "losers." Rather than simply moving to the right, leftist and popular forces maintained consid- erable integrity on issues of democracy and (in Guatemala) indigenous rights—even though they implicitly agreed to defer social justice issues; after all, this was a negotiation, not a revolution.

There are other reasons why the Southern Cone model by itself does not "fit" Central America: Whereas the former involved "*re*-democratization," the latter had no such internal point of reference (with the exception of the brief 1944–1954 interlude in Guatemala). One can even argue that especially in light of the extremely exclusionary and retrograde nature of Central America's political systems during recent decades, the gains made in El Salvador and Guatemala are of equal or greater import than those made in some of South America's "pacted transitions"—above all, in Chile.[13] It is beyond my purpose here to develop the comparison in more detail; Southern Cone critics of the pacted transition experiences have addressed the shortcomings of those experiences in their own countries, as the basis for alternative concepts of democracy.[14]

In any case, in Central America, even nonrevolutionary demands such as participation in elections had to be won through armed revolutionary insurgencies that confronted counterinsurgency armies and exclusionary civilian elites—followed by negotiated solutions to the civil wars, centered around the dismantling of the counterinsurgency apparatus. There simply were no electoral options for many citizens until the revolutionary Left and other leftist forces created them. In El Salvador, the FMLN invented "new political practices" for consensus-building during the course of its negotiations (see Lungo 1994). In Guatemala, it was the ASC, with its plurality of forces—some sympathetic to the URNG, some not, but most of them (except the political parties) excluded from the electoral arena—that ultimately created space for the emergence in 1995 of a leftist electoral option, the FDNG, the first such force since 1954.

The above analysis of the period from the early 1980s through the mid-1990s is not meant to suggest that there was one identifiable moment when Guatemala ceased to be a counterinsurgency state and became democratic. The evolution or process of change that I have described here—in which what began as an army-controlled, top-down "authoritarian transition" eventually became a democratic transition—was very complex and contradictory. Even the three civilian presidents who subordinated themselves to the army—Cerezo, Serrano, and de León Carpio—were part of a process of liberalization or "political opening" that eventually permitted the formation of important democratic counter-institutions (e.g., Human Rights Ombudsman). The 1993 *Serranazo* was an important moment in galvanizing all of Guatemalan society for a return to the constitutional order and demonstrated the nonviability of military coups or other expressions of the state-as-centaur. If not *the* moment when a more genuinely democratic transition began, this was most certainly a key turning point, one that marked the beginning of new forms of political behavior.

Theoretically, my point is that political/electoral openings or liberalizations of right-wing authoritarian regimes do not automatically or inevitably lead to full democratization, as Jeane Kirkpatrick (1979) argued. There was no way to predict in 1986 (much less in 1982) that a genuine democratization, going beyond a liberalization or political opening, would occur in Guatemala. This process has begun now, in large measure because the negotiation of binding and internationally verifiable peace accords, as well as MINUGUA's in-country presence, extracted democratic concessions that no election could guarantee—above all, and as the precondition for all else, the demilitarization of state and society. Furthermore, in the Guatemalan case, only the force of such accords has the potential to overcome the internal resistances of an exclusionary system and hopefully to ensure the irreversibility of the democratic changes.

Dimensions of the Democratic Project

It has come to be widely accepted among students of democratic transitions that civilian control over the military is a necessary condition for functional democracy. Hence, they have included this criterion in their "expanded procedural minimum" definition of democracy. But is this a sufficient description? Does it fully capture the richness and complexity of the real experience—above all, in a country such as Guatemala, where the indigenous majority makes cultural pluralism a central issue? I shall argue that the multidimensional democratization that is occurring in Guatemala today requires broader theoretical horizons than are comprehended in the transition literature by itself.

Much of the theoretical literature on democratic transitions has taken as its starting point the Schumpeterian model, refined by Dahl's "polyarchy"—from which are derived various "procedural minimum" conceptions, ranging from very minimalist to more "expanded."[15] However, there are other traditions from which to draw for our discussions of democracy: first, the formulations based on classical conceptions of democracy, as laid out by theorists such as Pateman (1970) and Morlino (1985), and applied to Central America, for example, by Booth (1989 and 1995) and Montobbio (1997b); and second, a number of contemporary contributions to the democracy literature drawing largely on the experience of social movements (e.g., feminist, indigenous). These traditions, which fall outside the transition literature, provide a context for my broader argument about the potential for Guatemala's democratic project.

Taking the broadest of the procedural definitions, the "expanded procedural minimum" goes beyond Dahl, by adding two further conditions that are essential in the Latin American cases: The polity must be self-governing (sovereign); and there must be civilian control over the military (Karl 1990, 2), or at least the absence of a military veto.[16] But even though this formulation adds civilian control over the military, it explicitly excludes extensive "participation" as a requisite, stipulating that "all citizens may not take an active and equal part in politics, although it must be legally possible for them to do so" (Schmitter and Karl 1991, 83). Without begging the question of whether "all citizens" are active participants, there is a real issue of the relative weight given to the participatory element.

Booth (1995, 5) spells out an alternative approach to what he calls the "pluralist-elitist conception." His alternative is rooted in the classical conception as laid out by Pateman (1970), among others: "participation by the mass of people in a community in its governance (the making and carrying out of decisions)." As Montobbio (1997b, 18–21) points out in his essay about El Salvador, the classical tradition is particularly appropriate in cases (such as the Central American) involving ruptures of the social contract—that is, civil wars—as contrasted with "peaceful transitions." This tradition is based on a broad conception of citizens' rights and goes back to theorists from Aristotle through Mill; *beyond not being legally precluded, political participation lies at the heart of democracy*. Although the degrees of democracy may vary, this depends on "the amount and quality of public participation in decision-making and rule" (Booth 1995, 6). Hence, according to Booth and others,[17] electoral participation is one important aspect—but only one among others. Referring specifically to Guatemala, Poitevín (1992, 27) speaks of a concept of citizenship in which the population is more than an "occasional legitimator" of the existing power structure (through elections) and in which all sectors enjoy full freedom to organize and exercise effective power.

Why insist on the participatory element? First, even in regard to elections, it implies going beyond the absence-of-fraud measure to permit a critique of elections held in an overall context of a system that excludes certain ideological positions and retains many coercive/repressive elements. Second, starting from a broader conception of politics, it permits us to take into account participatory activity in the "informal" (extraelectoral) political arena, as well as formal electoral participation, and the interaction between these modes of political action. Third, and perhaps most important, it provides a basis for appreciating the dimensions of democracy when it finally does come to exist; these include ideological and cultural diversity, the growing effectiveness of civil society, and an expanded conception of citizenship to include rights beyond those associated with the legal status.

These points can be developed by referring to several relatively "newer" or more contemporary bodies of literature that deal with noninstitutional aspects of democracy; most of these grow out of practical social movement experiences in Latin America and elsewhere. A few examples of the themes emphasized in these newer literatures include the following: citizenship and social citizenship (including cross-border rights), civil society, indigenous peoples' rights (see below), feminism and its critiques of earlier conceptions of democracy, human rights, local power, Liberation Theology, and ecology/environmental justice. Much of the literature growing out of social movements emphasizes group rights as well as strictly individual rights.[18]

All of the above dimensions have great relevance to Guatemala in this particular period of its democratization. Many of them were expressed in the organizations that came together to form the ASC in the early 1990s, and others are taking shape in new forms of social organization today. Rather than spelling out what each of them means in Guatemala—a project for a future book—I shall highlight here the dimension most relevant to political democracy in a country that is 60 percent indigenous: the dimension of cultural rights alongside civil and human rights. Many of these are codified in the Accord on Identity and Rights of Indigenous Peoples, which mandates a constitutional reform redefining Guatemala's identity as a multiethnic, multicultural, multilingual nation. It is an implicit premise of that accord that political democracy cannot be fully achieved in Guatemala without recognizing and acting on the basis of the country's cultural diversity.

Aside from the indigenous accord, other on-the-ground advances by Mayan movements in recent years include the broader use of alternative forms of political organization. Among the most prominent of these have been the *comités cívicos*[19] that won important mayoralties in 1995, among them Guatemala's second largest city, Quetzaltenango (which is half indigenous, half ladino). As is described in Chapters 6 and 8, various other initiatives promise to profoundly enrich the content of Guatemala's democratic project by incorporating indigenous traditions of community democracy and customary law (*derecho consuetudinario*).[20]

Although some of these issues are still very much contested by ladinos as "divisive" or threats to "national unity" (see Chapter 8), they are central to the quality of democracy not only for Guatemala's indigenous peoples but also for *Guatemala as a whole*. They raise the issue of building a tolerant, pluralistic political culture among all Guatemalans, in a society that has been as exclusionary as South Africa or the slave South in the United States. Anything less than a new framework of this kind would mean electoral democracy within the context of de facto apartheid. The assertion of cultural rights in this case is not "identity politics" but a new political framework for Maya-ladino social relations. This is now being formulated in a discourse about intercultural as well as multicultural relations. From this positive perspective, *if* advances are made and consolidated in this area, they will not only have an impact internally but also be recognized as an example outside Guatemala.

The above reflections—which I shall develop further in the Conclusion—suggest that minimalist or primarily procedural conceptions of democratization, even when "expanded," often sell democracy short by not emphasizing the full ideological and cultural diversity that is central to the participatory dimensions of political democracy and by not emphasizing—indeed, often entirely missing—some of the most profound transformations in the rules of the political game. In Guatemala, the symbolic "moment" when these democratic transformations came closest to being formally "adopted" as a national project or agenda will be remembered in the signing of the peace accords more clearly than in any other moment since 1954—certainly more than in any of the elections between 1954 and 1996. (This is not to deny the obvious fact that the changes had begun several years before the signing of peace and that their realization will take many years.) To use a crude indicator, on the evening of the signing, a telephone poll by the conservative daily newspaper *Prensa Libre* elicited a 77 percent "happiness" response; and despite limited expectations, "the prevailing mood [in the Plaza Central] was of being at the ushering in of a new historical era" (Hernández Pico 1997c).

Experiences such as these also signify a potential transformation in political/cultural/social relations. As Carlos Vilas put it in a recent talk about Central America, even if a revolution fails, nothing in the country is the same as before, and people do not behave in the old ways. The redefinition of the nation as multicultural and intercultural poses the possibility of transforming the collective political culture of Guatemalan society as a whole; certainly the indigenous population is engaging in new forms of behavior, and it is to be hoped that this will eventually elicit new responses from ladinos. In Guatemala, furthermore, lifting the blanket of fear that has permeated virtually all human interactions since 1954 constitutes, if not a revolution in the old sense, at least a very profound transformation. Subjectively, it opens up space for a "revolution of rising expectations" among many previously excluded sectors, despite the fact that they still live in poverty and face deeply entrenched opposition to change from powerful elites. Guatemalans are beginning to feel entitled to nothing less than what is enjoyed by citizens in the traditional Western democracies.

Some of the above-mentioned general observations have been substantiated by the findings of at least one major empirical survey documenting the expansion of political participation and a democratic political culture in Guatemala in the mid- to late 1990s (Development Associates et al. 1998). (The working definition of "democratic political culture" measured the level of incorporation of citizens into political processes and interest

in participation in decisionmaking about issues affecting them, knowledge of their rights and obligations, and the ability to organize around
demands that public institutions fulfill their functions.) Among the survey's most important findings and conclusions were the significant increases (between 1993 and 1997) in the levels of political tolerance and of
participation in local government and, even more notably, in organizations of civil society (educational, religious, and community development). By 1997, 78 percent of the 1,200 interviewees participated in at
least one such organization. (A significant contrast was the ongoing lack
of confidence in the judicial system and in the central government more
generally—which could explain the gap between the high level of social
participation and the low level of voting.) Overall, the 1997 survey concluded that the signing of the peace accords was crucial in the changes between 1993 and 1997, that there now exist opportunities to consolidate
democracy *desde abajo* (from below), and that the stereotype of the un-
movably authoritarian Guatemalan political culture is misleading—particularly among the indigenous population.

From a historical perspective, Guatemala stands today on the threshold
of possibly completing its long-interrupted national democratic revolution of 1944–1954; but this time, having suffered the interlude of a forty-
two-year nightmare and thirty-six years of Cold War counterinsurgency
war, people are experiencing democracy in a new way. This time (unlike
1954), it is to be hoped that Guatemalans will fight to defend their gains if
those gains are threatened. Today, moreover, the incipient democratic revolution is broader than fifty years ago, as it includes new—or, more precisely, newly recognized—social protagonists, most notably, indigenous
peoples and women. It also includes new forms of organization that are
mobilizational as well as electoral. Although Guatemalan democracy remains very fragile and unconsolidated, one can begin to catch a glimpse
of a possible democratic project for the twenty-first century, in all of its
political, ideological, and cultural dimensions.

The Unresolved Question of Social Justice

One of the consistently troublesome and unresolved discussions about
political democracy is its relation to social justice. While I cannot fully address the issue here, I shall discuss some reasons for its relevance to the
case at hand. It is widely argued that without being *definitionally* part of
political democracy, social justice issues have profoundly affected the fate
of "new" democracies (and older ones) in practice—or, as some analysts
have put it, the "quality of democracy." Others have begun to take this up
as an issue of "social citizenship." Przeworski (1996) warned of the dangers of a new "monster": democracy without citizenship, that is, without

the minimal conditions necessary for citizens to exercise their rights in practice. O'Donnell (1997) has expressed similar concerns. Montobbio (1997b, 25) put it in slightly different terms for El Salvador, warning of a *congelación* (freezing up), in which "authoritarian enclaves" retain considerable power and the democratic transition is never fully consolidated, stable, or lasting. Consolidation, he continues, implies not only dealing with the elimination of military control but also addressing the country's historical problems, including massive social inequalities.

In recent Latin American experience, formal political democracy has generally been regarded as a precondition for struggles for greater social equality. But beyond that, there are two opinions about whether a fully democratic system can be sustained amid major social disparities or whether the huge socioeconomic gaps will eventually (directly or indirectly) undermine democratic gains. The experiences of the past two decades in Latin America are mixed and open to a variety of interpretations. Some situations in South America suggest the difficulties of consolidating political democracy on a lasting and stable basis while simultaneously institutionalizing neoliberal measures that increase social inequalities (see Note 14). Venezuela illustrates the complexities: Since the late 1980s, austerity policies have generated food riots, populist military coup attempts, and, in December 1998, electoral victory by the coup leader—all this in a country regarded for the last forty years as a stable, consolidated democracy.

But there are particular dynamics in countries emerging from long-standing civil wars or national liberation struggles inspired by revolutionary visions, such as Central America in recent decades—not unlike South Africa's struggle led by the African National Congress (see Wallerstein 1996) The traditional socialist revolutionary visions have clearly been modified in the last twenty years, but democratization has brought rising expectations about greater social justice. In the Central American cases, there is much discussion about whether the "structural causes" that gave rise to the revolutionary movements of the 1960s–1980s are being addressed by the peace settlements of the 1990s. Clearly these problems have not been resolved thus far; in this sense, peace did not bring social justice. But the widespread expectation or demand remains very much alive. Minimally, this means building an internal market economy, even in this age of world-market export frenzy; this presumes a concern (and state intervention) to raise wages and living standards for the majority of the population in order to create an internal consumer market. *Social equity is not part of the definition of democracy, but it is unquestionably part of the panorama of issues opened up by democratization.* If the rising expectations are frustrated and significant numbers of citizens perceive that "nothing has changed," democracy itself can be delegitimized, undermined, or destabilized.

Coming out of a thirty-six-year civil war, Guatemala is certainly experiencing this revolution of rising expectations. Yet, as discussed above, the socioeconomic accord does not directly resolve the social issues; and Guatemala is surrounded by the chilling realities of social deterioration in El Salvador and, even more, in Nicaragua. El Salvador's peace agenda has been undermined by the government's neoliberal economic agenda. (See de Soto and del Castillo 1994; Boyce 1996; Montobbio 1997b.) Guatemala faces a host of dangers that typically plague postwar societies, as well as some that are particular to Guatemala, which could undermine rather than consolidate democratic gains. One very immediate source of undermining is a rise in common crime (partly driven by poverty and the lack of jobs) and authoritarian responses to that situation—already a serious problem in Guatemala.

Few Guatemalans seriously discuss democracy without addressing these issues, because they believe that so long as nearly three-fourths of the population lives in extreme poverty, formal democracy will remain forever fragile. (In the Guatemalan case, the socioeconomic structure has been so skewed that even the World Bank recommends more state spending.) As Guatemalan analysts Poitevín (1992, 35–37) and Torres Rivas (1991) argue, social struggles have become the condition for liberal democracy: "A democratic process is not possible without a minimum basis for developing social relations of equality," without a material basis for the exercise of citizen rights.[21] Moreover, liberal democracy has arrived in Guatemala linked to a much broader national project or *imaginario* (vision) contained in the peace accords (Aguilera 1997). Torres Rivas (1995, 46 ff.) refers to something similar in the concept of "good government," which "seeks a permanent link between political freedom and social justice."[22] Gálvez (1995) and others use the concept of "governability" in a similar manner, that is, beyond formal institutionality, to refer more broadly to the relation between the state and civil society, particularly in meeting popular expectations. Hence, *without being substituted for political democracy*, the broader social dimension is linked to it time and again by a wide range of Guatemalans and Latin Americans in general; and the experience of recent years demonstrates the importance of this link in moving toward a society that is viable and stable—"governable"—as well as humane.

At the theoretical level, Wallerstein (1991) has written about the ongoing battle since the time of the French Revolution over the interpretation of its legacy, in particular between the libertarian and social emphases. Theoretically, there is not one correct answer but rather an ambivalent legacy (hence the battle over interpretations). It is one of the great ironies of history since the French Revolution that struggles for "liberty" (liberal democracy) have been led and won by revolutionaries—that is, those who also had a social justice agenda. As Vilas (1994, 99) put it, "at the root of popular acceptance of calls for revolution is an unavoidable democratic demand."[23] But although revolutionaries have been successful in winning democracy, they have generally not won the struggles for social equality. In the cases of Central America during the 1980s–1990s, we have seen a continuation of this historical tendency. Furthermore, their ability to win social justice is even more constrained in an era dominated internationally by neoliberal policy prescriptions (e.g., privatization, dismantling of the social safety net). The unanswered question for progressive and leftist forces in Guatemala and the rest of Central America today is whether they will be able to use the political space won through the peace accords to make significant social justice gains in the future. The answer to this question—which I revisit in the Conclusion, but which will also have to be revisited many times during the next ten to fifteen years—will be essential to long-range assessments of the *camino centroamericano*.

Notes

1. For this chapter, perhaps more than any other, I am grateful to numerous colleagues in Guatemala, elsewhere in Latin America, and in the United States for critical feedback on earlier drafts and presentations of the arguments developed here, as well as stimulating interchanges overall (see Acknowledgments).

2. See, for example, Padilla 1996b, 33; and Rosada in ASIES 1998a, 32. Rosada has also been quoted (*Inforpress Centroamericana*, Sept. 5, 1997) as maintaining that 1982 was the second of the two great moments (the first being 1944) when formal democracy was institutionalized in Guatemala.

3. In addition to those mentioned in Note 2, see various writings by Aguilera (e.g., 1996a, 1997), as well as Arévalo 1998a and Azpuru 1999. Some Guatemalan analysts move back and forth between the early 1980s and 1985–1986 as the starting point. An important subtext here is the issue of whom to credit as the agents of democratization—particularly since the army "institutionalists" appropriate for themselves the role of having restored Guatemala to democratic rule (e.g., Gramajo 1995).

4. For a fuller discussion of the rationale for and implications of my argument that Guatemala under civilian rule during the late 1980s remained essentially a counterinsurgency state, see Jonas 1991, 171 ff. In that same discussion, I also argued against the exaggerated versions of the "counterinsurgency state" thesis, which posit that such a state in Guatemala is "permanent," stable, unchanging, self-perpetuating, or all-controlling. On the contrary, such states are basically weak: Because of the army's coercive relation to civil society, they lack a broad social base, whether the president is military or civilian. Hinkelammert (1994) argues more broadly that a strong state is one that foments the development of all sectors of civil society, not only the bourgeoisie.

5. For examples as recent as 1994, see annual reports by Americas Watch, Amnesty International, and even the U.S. State Department's Human Rights reports; see also Jonas 1994a.

Lest this sound like academic hairsplitting, the "behavior" tests are revealing. Through the early 1990s, some of the very analysts mentioned in Notes 2 and 3 above took precautions that should not be necessary in a democratic society: One of them wore a bullet-proof vest throughout this period; another called to warn me (in 1991) not to leave my hotel room because independent journalists and writers were being targeted by military and/or paramilitary forces. Other examples are in my Prologue.

6. In addition to Jonas 1995, see both Trudeau 1989 and Jonas 1989, and a host of primary sources and election studies cited in all of these articles, including IHRLG/WOLA 1985; Castañeda 1990; and NDI 1991.

7. The very small social democratic Partido Socialista Democrática (PSD) was permitted to participate, once its politicians had accepted the "rules of the game" (which included rejection of any possible alliance with the URNG) and the unspoken limits on its platform imposed by the military; meanwhile, some of its leaders remained in exile.

8. The figures are more extreme if we take into account some additional considerations: First, over 30 percent of eligible voters were not even registered; this would bring the effective voter abstention rate to 52 percent in 1985 and 69 percent in 1990. More recent estimates of nonregistration are as high as 35–40 percent (see Chapter 8). Second, in both cases, abstention among registered voters increased significantly in the presidential *segunda vuelta* or runoff elections (from 31 percent to 35 percent in 1985, and from 44 percent to 55 percent in 1990–1991). Third, at least 12 percent of ballots, in some cases higher, were not valid (null or protest votes). (Sources: OAS 1997 and Aguilera 1996b, based on official figures from the Supreme Electoral Tribunal.)

9. Other analysts characterize that interaction in a different way. For example, Padilla (1996a, iii) argues that "democratization [i.e., elected civilian rule] made peace possible, not vice-versa." He makes the valid points that (1) the elected governments beginning with Serrano had a clear mandate from the electorate to initiate peace negotiations, and (2) the peace process could not have progressed outside the framework of elected civilian rule. In fact, the promise to negotiate was one of the reasons for Serrano's victory in the 1991 runoff election. Padilla's second point is also true, but only partial; civilian rule was a necessary but by no means a sufficient condition for the peace process (as shown clearly by the Cerezo era). Azpuru (1999) argues that peace and democratization were two parallel processes that mutually reinforced each other between 1986 and 1996.

10. In terms of voter participation/abstention in the 1995–1996 elections: In the November 1995 first round, participation was only 47 percent of registered voters (i.e., abstention was 53 percent); these figures worsened to 37 percent participation (63 percent abstention) in the January 1996 runoff. Here again, over 30 percent of eligible voters were not registered to vote, meaning that effective participation rates were substantially lower (33 percent in November, 26 percent in January).

Why did this happen despite the first-time option of a leftist party (FDNG)? Among other explanations, what stands out are the following: First, the FDNG came together very late in the game and virtually at the same time as the deadline for registration of new voters; Rigoberta Menchú had led a campaign for voter registration but also only a few weeks before that deadline. Second, political parties in general remained totally discredited by their corruption and inefficacy during the first decade after the return to civilian rule. For more detailed analyses of the obstacles to voting in the electoral system itself, see OAS 1997, Aguilera 1996b and Chapter 8 below.

A further troubling question arises in regard to the election of 1995–1996: The January 1996 presidential runoff, with participation by a bare 26 percent of those eligible to vote, came within a hair's breadth of restoring to (indirect but virtual) power an ex-dictator whose policies would have ended the peace process. If the anti-peace Ríos Montt forces had won this low-turnout runoff election, even without fraud, the victory would have been for a "democracy" of the iron fist, another *democradura*, and the peace negotiations would likely have been scuttled. Could such an outcome really have been regarded as advancing the cause of democracy in Guatemala?

11. For an excellent study of the structurally similar dynamics between democratization and demilitarization ("decolonization of the state apparatus and of everyday life" from army control) in El Salvador, see Williams and Walter 1997. Although the dynamics played out quite differently in Nicaragua during the 1980s, the positive contribution of the Sandinistas was their deliberate attempt to combine representative with participatory democracy even under wartime conditions (see Jonas and Stein 1990b).

12. This was by no means a "gift" from the Guatemalan army. As recently as 1994, that army was still trying for a Pinochet-type outcome, maintaining that it had been "victorious," and hence would not negotiate its future with the URNG, but would decide that internally and unilaterally.

13. Even in the late 1990s, Chile's General Pinochet held substantial veto power, and in November 1996, a leading Communist Party politician was jailed for verbally insulting him. According to the constitution written under his dictatorship, the military retained four reserved seats in the Senate, as well as half of the seats on the National Security Council (*New York Times*, Nov. 10, 1996). In 1998, Pinochet refused to resign as defense minister unless he was guaranteed a seat as Senator-for-Life—which he subsequently obtained. Finally, it took international initiatives in the fall of 1998—by European judges and governments—to finally raise the issue of holding Pinochet accountable for crimes against humanity; even then, the democratically elected civilian government of Chile opposed those initiatives and sided with Pinochet in resisting them.

14. To give a few examples of Southern Cone analysts who have argued that participatory democracy is essential to representative democracy and have associated participatory democracy with a commitment to reducing socioeconomic inequality: Argentine sociologist Nun (1993, 19) follows up his remarks that participatory democracy is necessary to the consolidation of representative government in "precarious contexts" (such as those of Latin America) by quoting Robert Dahl's 1985 statement: Modern capitalism tends "to produce inequalities in social and economic resources so great as to bring about severe violations of political equality and hence of the democratic process." Therefore, Nun continues, "his basic proposal finally entails a return to Mill: to protect freedom, it is necessary to extend the democratic principles even to the economic enterprise itself." He notes

that this is the case not only in advanced capitalist societies; it is all the more "necessary and urgent" in Latin America. Brazilian analyst Weffort (1992, 31–32, 56), adding interpretation to strict definition of political democracy, argues that although democracy is theoretically possible in highly unequal societies such as Guatemala and Brazil (or even those with growing inequality), it will be greatly constrained and permanently unstable, and cannot be consolidated.

Argentine analyst Borón (1993, 1998) raises these questions more sharply, viewing the "minimalist concept" of democracy as a "radical departure" from classical writings about democracy. He notes Dahl's distinction between democracy and polyarchy and argues (1998, 44–45) that democracy requires two "social conditions": "a minimum level of fundamental equality must be widespread"; and "the citizenry must have the effective enjoyment of freedom . . . as a living and practical day-to-day experience," i.e., participation. According to French sociologist Alain Touraine (1991), "it is difficult to consider a political system democratic when it leads to or does not impede [growing inequality]." All of these conceptualizations clearly suggest that democracy is inconsistent with what Peeler, speaking of Central America (1995, note 17), has called "predatory class relations."

15. In her pioneering treatment of the subject, Pateman (1970) suggested that the initial antipathy to including participation and mobilization emphases in discussions of democracy in U.S. political science models was in part a function of the Cold War ideological bias against "the other model" (that of Soviet/Third World socialism). Some even suggested that too much participation could be dangerous to democratic stability (see Pateman 1970, 10).

Looking at the recent literature regarding Latin America, the most careful constructions of the "expanded procedural minimum" can be found in Karl 1990; and Schmitter and Karl 1991. For a survey of the literature on this topic, see Collier and Levitsky 1997. It should be noted that recently a number of the most prominent "transitologists" have been moving back in the direction of discussing the importance of nonformal criteria and even some social issues as they affect political democracy. This can be seen in recent presentations by O'Donnell, Przeworski, Schmitter, and Karl, among others.

16. According to Schmitter and Karl (1991), "popularly elected officials must be able to exercise their constitutional powers without being subjected to overriding (albeit informal) opposition from unelected officials"—in Central America, above all, the military.

17. In addition, see Fagen's (1986, 258) "working definition" of the "constituent elements" of democracy, which include "effective participation by individuals and groups in the decisions that most affect their lives" along with classical individual rights and equality before the law. Similar emphases can be found in various writings by González Casanova, Vilas, and other Latin American analysts (see listings in References).

18. A few examples of these participatory social movements and themes, as described and theorized in recent literature, include the following: citizenship and social citizenship—some but not all of it developed out of feminist critiques of older models, both left and right (e.g., Dagnino 1993; Jelin 1990 and 1995; for Guatemala, Rodríguez 1998; see also Falk 1993); on civil society and its relation to formal politics (e.g., Fox 1996; Foley 1996; Lungo 1994; for Guatemala, Pearce

1998a and 1998b); on local power (e.g., Sader 1992; Bittar 1992; NACLA 1995; for Guatemala, Gálvez et al. 1998); on Liberation Theology (e.g., Boff 1981, 1986; Richard 1995); on ecological and environmental justice movements and other new social movements (e.g., articles in Escobar and Alvarez 1992); on group rights, as opposed to strictly individual rights (e.g., Falk 1989; Felice 1996). Many of the above themes are also illustrated in Jonas and McCaughan 1994; Alvarez et al. 1998; Jelin and Hershberg 1996. Regarding the growing literature on indigenous rights and democracy in Guatemala, see Notes 19 and 20 below.

19. In addition to interviews, written sources on *comités cívicos* include, among others, Ochoa et al. 1995; Gálvez et al. 1997; ASIES 1998a.

20. See Cojti 1991 and 1998; Poitevín 1991 and 1992; Solares 1992; Bastos and Camus 1993; Esquit and Gálvez 1997; Adams 1994 and 1995; Warren 1998a; Plant 1998; on the contributions of *derecho consuetudinario*, see Rojas Lima 1995; Sieder 1996a.

21. As Vilas (1996b, 502) put it, "the challenge of democratisation in Central America is . . . how to combine institutionalisation of conflict management and the capacity of the political system to transform socioeconomic structures and overcome cultural rigidities." If such a process is understood to be medium- or long-range, he continued, the Guatemalan peace process appeared "promising" in its ability to combine both of these two elements.

22. Torres Rivas's (1995) concept of good government is "a metaphor for the democratic search to put public order in the service of addressing the problems of the majority." Furthermore, he continues, the link between democracy and social justice is necessary "to avoid discrediting the electoral system, the democratic premise, civilian governments chosen for their promises and programs, or politics itself."

23. Wallerstein (1995, 250) makes a similar point about the potentially revolutionary character of pushing for complete fulfillment of the democratic demand—as follows:

A multi-front strategy by a multiplicity of groups, each complex and internally democratic, will have one tactical weapon at its disposal which may be overwhelming for the defenders of the status quo. It is the weapon of taking the old liberal ideology literally and demanding its universal fulfillment. . . . One can push on every front for the increased democratisation of decision-making as well as the elimination of all the pockets of informal and unacknowledged privilege. What I am talking about here is the tactic of overloading the system by taking its pretensions and its claims more seriously than the dominant forces wish them to be taken.

In discussing the two faces of the French Revolution (social peasant revolution and political bourgeois revolution), Amin (1991, 36 ff.) points out that the Anglo-American tradition has tended to deny the role of the revolutionary in establishing the democratic.

5

The U.S. Role:
The Cold War and Beyond

As seen in Chapter 2, the United States was one of the Friend governments during Guatemala's peace process; however, it was a very different kind of Friend than the others because it had been a major player in Guatemala during the thirty-six-year civil war, and even before that, in the events that set the stage for the civil war. In fact, it was the U.S. role that made it a *Cold War civil war*, with all of the ideological and political overtones of an East-West confrontation. Hence, the signing of Guatemala's final peace accords ended more than just the Guatemalan internal conflict; in reality, it ended the last of the Cold War civil wars in Latin America. Even in the post–Cold War era, the United States is the superpower that retains significant influence there; the United States continues to have a strong bilateral agenda for Guatemala, which at times does and at times does not coincide with the agenda of Guatemala's peace accords. For these reasons, I turn here to a brief examination of the U.S. role in Guatemala and the continuities and changes in the bilateral relationship that affect the peace process.

Dangerous Liaisons:
U.S. Involvement in Guatemala's War

Guatemala's civil war began in 1960, only six years after the 1954 U.S.-orchestrated ouster of the popularly elected government of Jacobo Arbenz (see Chapter 1). At the height of the Cold War, the U.S. government was unwilling to tolerate a moderately progressive and nationalistic government that sought to pursue a reform agenda and regulate U.S. interests in the country, and it branded Guatemala a "Soviet beachhead" in the Western Hemisphere. The reversal of the 1944–1954 Revolution and its land reform set the stage for more than forty years of turbulent, polarized history. Many Guatemalans, correctly reading the message of 1954, concluded that moderate change would not be permitted. Not surprisingly, then, by 1960, shortly after the Cuban Revolution, an armed insurgent movement was formed in Guatemala, one of the earliest in Latin America. Its political influence grew during the early and mid-1960s, as Guatemalan politics offered virtually no legal channel for the expression of social demands. From 1966 to 1968, the United States became directly involved in counterinsurgency operations in order to keep Guatemala from becoming a "second Cuba"—a danger that appeared very real to both the U.S. and Guatemalan governments during the 1960s (see Jonas 1991, 69). The United States sent hundreds of Green Berets to Guatemala and played a crucial role in "professionalizing," training, and reorganizing what it viewed as an inefficient army; the goal was to transform it into a disciplined counterinsurgency force, driven by a Manichaean anticommunist "national security" logic. This was the origin of the killing machine known as the Guatemalan counterinsurgency army.

It was in Guatemala that Latin America first saw such phenomena as death squads and "disappearances," which subsequently became standard operating procedure in counterinsurgency wars throughout the hemisphere. U.S. military advisers were involved in the formation of the death squads, and the head of the U.S. military mission publicly justified their operations. (For details, see Sharckman 1974.) Working directly with U.S. advisers, the Guatemalan army temporarily defeated the rebels by 1968. Since the army's objective was to eliminate the social support base of the guerrillas, the price was paid in civilian lives (around 8,000) in the conflict area and among center-leftist forces in the capital—a pattern repeated on a much larger scale during subsequent phases of the war.

The second phase of the war, in the late 1970s and early 1980s, saw a resurgence of the guerrilla movement, this time with a large social base in the indigenous highlands; the army responded with a scorched-earth counterinsurgency campaign (see Chapter 1). By this time, however, the U.S. relationship with the Guatemalan army had undergone some important modifications. During the 1970s, the Vietnam Syndrome and the rise of human rights politics began to influence U.S. foreign policy. Given the Guatemalan army's reputation for brutality unsurpassed in Latin America, it became politically infeasible for Washington to openly support the army's counterinsurgency campaign of 1981–1983. Strains had first emerged between the United States and Guatemala in the late 1970s, when human rights pressures led the Carter administration to impose conditions on U.S. aid, and the Guatemalan government rejected aid under those conditions. Congress subsequently cut direct security assistance during the period from 1977 to 1983. During those years, Guatemala's military dictatorships were armed, trained, and assisted by other countries: Israel, Taiwan, and Argentina.

Nevertheless, the Reagan administration found indirect ways to signal its approval for the Guatemalan army's "dirty war" of the early 1980s—for example, through visits by U.S. officials, collaboration on counterinsurgency plans, and covert CIA assistance (Jonas 1991, 197–199 and sources cited there). Meanwhile, the Reagan administration battled with Congress to restore open military aid to Guatemala. This difficult situation gave rise to a two-track double-message policy toward Guatemala throughout the 1980s and into the 1990s. Publicly, U.S. policymakers paid lip service to human rights concerns and pushed the Guatemalan government to liberalize—eventually coming to believe that a civilian government backed by a strong army was preferable to outright military rule. But behind the scenes, the United States continued to view the Guatemalan army as a problematic but strategic and "reliable" ally in Central America, and the underlying ties were never broken, even during the most difficult period. (The details, as they have emerged in newly declassified documents, paint a much more appalling picture—see Note 5.)

From the Guatemalan side, meanwhile, both military and civilian governments during the 1980s began to distance themselves *publicly* from the Reagan administration's obsession with overthrowing the Sandinista government in Nicaragua through the Contras (although covertly helping the United States in this effort—see Note 5). As one manifestation of the contradictions growing out of Washington's Contra war, the Guatemalan government developed the policy that subsequently became known as "Active Neutrality." In fact, the Cerezo government (1986–1990) played a decisive role in the events leading up to the signing of the Central American Peace Accords of 1987 (Esquipulas II) and the broader development of Central America's "relative autonomy" from the United States. (For details, see Jonas 1991, chapter 13; Jonas 1990, and sources cited there.) The point is worth emphasizing because the rise of "relative autonomy" in the Central American region—specifically, the Central American presidents' unanimous rejection of the Reagan administration's Contra war (because it harmed their own stability and interests)—had another effect: These events indirectly opened the door for subsequent United Nations involvement in peacemaking and peacekeeping in both El Salvador and Guatemala, in the heart of the United States' traditional sphere of influence.

The Guatemalan government's manifestation of a certain degree of relative autonomy never went so far as to openly challenge the strategic alliance between the United States and the Guatemalan army. Nor did the United States ever cease to support that army's counterinsurgency war, at least indirectly when it could not do so directly. Nevertheless, at times during the 1980s, the contradictions of Washington's two-track policy and Guatemala's relative autonomy strained relations between the two allies.

Washington's mixed-message policy intensified after the 1985 election of a civilian government, led by Christian Democrat Vinicio Cerezo and the restoration of formal civilian rule on terms that left the army's power nearly intact. Democrats in Congress now took the lead in promoting aid to the army (including the full Military Assistance Program), arguing that such contact would "civilize" the Guatemalan security forces and that the army should be "rewarded" for permitting a civilian government. After 1987, direct U.S. military collaboration with the army increased, as it became clear that the URNG had been weakened but not defeated, and the war heated up again, though never to the levels reached in El Salvador in the late 1980s. While overt military aid remained at modest levels, hundreds of millions of dollars were channeled to the Guatemalan government through Economic Support Funds—disguised security assistance insofar as it freed up local funds for counterinsurgency. Even with the emphasis by the Bush administration (1989–1992) on curtailing human rights abuses and its suspension of military aid in December 1990, after the killing of U.S. citizen Michael DeVine, U.S. officials continued to regard the Guatemalan army as a strategic ally in the region—and, as was later revealed, secretly substituted CIA funds for overt military aid. As one U.S. official summarized a view widely held in Washington, "No matter what happens, the army is still the most important institution and will have to be the conduit for Guatemala's development" (*Christian Science Monitor,* Dec. 11, 1990).

Mixed Messages from Washington During the Peace Process

By the early 1990s, for a variety of tactical reasons—new human rights pressures from religious organizations and Congress within the United States, budget pressures at a time of economic recession, a desire to get Central America "off the agenda" in the post–Cold War era and to isolate Cuba as the only "human rights violator" in the hemisphere—U.S. policy reflected some shifts toward Guatemala. The United States became more publicly critical of the Guatemalan government and slowly began using security assistance as a lever. In addition, the opening up of peace negotiations in Guatemala during the early 1990s caused other adjustments in U.S.-Guatemalan relations.

Beginning in 1994, the U.S. government became a member of the "Group of Friends" whose purpose was to facilitate the peace process and support the UN as its moderator. The very fact that the United States was one of the Friend governments—according to some accounts, at the initiative of the URNG—was an important contribution to the peace process, insofar as it implicitly recognized the URNG as a legitimate negotiating partner. It was also an advance over the U.S. role in the Salvadoran peace talks, in which the United States was so totally identified with the government side that it could not have been a Friend of the peace process. Its role as a Friend in Guatemala presumed a neutral U.S. stance, but the reality was often more complex. In practice, for example, Washington favored the position of the Guatemalan government/army, in that it supported their goal of reaching a cease-fire quickly, without first having negotiated the substantive issues, as was stipulated in the Oslo process.

By virtue of its long relationship with the Guatemalan army—despite the restructuring of that relationship and the greater autonomy of the Guatemalan army after the late 1970s—the United States remained the only international player with the leverage to pressure for demilitarization. Diplomats close to the peace process and even some U.S. officials recognized this reality. Yet Washington continued to send mixed messages. Although the U.S. Congress pressured for the demilitarization of Guatemala, many U.S. policymakers still viewed the army as the country's most (or only) efficient institution. Furthermore, the United States never really supported the efforts to "civilianize" the Interior Ministry, that is, to assure its independence from the army, according to a Guatemalan civilian official who was deeply involved in security matters in Guatemala during the mid-1990s .

While strongly criticizing the most outrageous human rights abuses, Washington maintained close working relations with the army during the early and mid-1990s. For example, the United States supported a continued role for the army and its intelligence unit in antidrug operations—even while identifying some top military officers as drug traffickers—as well as an expanded role in civic action and development-related tasks. The Pentagon's "Humanitarian and Civic Assistance" exercises in Guatemala conveyed an image of U.S. cooperation with the army and suggested that the army was the appropriate institution for meeting the needs of the local population and carrying out nonmilitary tasks, such as building roads, schools, and clinics, and providing medical services. Even after Congress cut off aid to the Guatemalan army and security forces in the fall of 1995 after the CIA scandal broke (see below), the Pentagon's "assistance" program and CIA "liaison" funds for counternarcotics operations continued.

While the UN, the OAS, and the Europeans repeatedly called for immediate abolition of the army-controlled PACs during the mid-1990s, Washington never did so; at least implicitly, it supported Guatemalan government proposals to convert them into "peace and development committees"—units of local power that could continue to dominate their communities in new ways. Furthermore, unlike the Europeans, the United

States consistently favored sparing Guatemala from the harshest condemnation at the annual UN Human Rights Commission meetings in Geneva. These actions raised questions about Washington's political will to help demilitarize Guatemala.

"Guategate": The 1995 CIA Scandal

Prior to the 1990s, criticisms of the U.S. stance had been primarily on moral grounds. But in the 1990s, Washington's wavering came to be counterproductive as well; the decades-old alliance increasingly came to resemble a deteriorating and dysfunctional marriage. On one occasion, during Serrano's attempted 1993 *auto-golpe,* the Clinton administration threatened to break the bond (through trade sanctions) unless the army backed a return to constitutional rule—which it then did. The 1993 accession to power of the former Human Rights Ombudsman, Ramiro de León Carpio, left Washington once again "feeling good" about supporting the Guatemalan government. But as it became evident that this new government was presiding over a worsening human rights situation, the Clinton administration (1992–1996 and 1997–2000) was obliged to criticize the Guatemalan army more sharply, even as it continued close cooperation.

These tensions were a mere prelude, however, to the fissures opened up after news broke on March 23, 1995, that a high-ranking Guatemalan military officer on the CIA payroll (Colonel Julio Alpírez) had been involved in the early 1990s murders of an American citizen, Michael DeVine, and a guerrilla commander, Efraín Bámaca, who was married to American lawyer Jennifer Harbury. The revelations were provoked by Harbury's hunger strike outside the White House. Although some in the U.S. government tried to prevent the airing of these dirty secrets, at least one government official—Richard Nuccio, previously the U.S. representative to the Guatemalan peace talks and a staunch defender of U.S. policy—helped bring the truth to light by taking the Harbury/DeVine story to Representative Robert Torricelli (D-New Jersey), who divulged it to the media.[1]

As more details emerged in the U.S. press, it became clear that this case was just the tip of the iceberg. The iceberg itself was the complex web of relations between various agencies of the U.S. government and the Guatemalan military during the previous forty years. Even after the extraordinary revelations, most of the iceberg remained submerged from public view. After the scandal broke, the administration came under public and congressional pressure to fully declassify and disclose its information on Guatemalan human rights criminals and their relation to the CIA and other U.S. government agencies. Even the conservative Republican-led Congress seemed unwilling to settle for a purely cosmetic damage-control operation. In September 1995, the CIA dismissed two high-level officials and disciplined nine others whose involvement and/or attempts at cover-up broke the law. In June 1996, the president's Intelligence Oversight Board (IOB), mandated to investigate CIA ties in cases involving U.S. citizens—in itself a narrow mandate, given the magnitude of human rights crimes and CIA operations in Guatemala—issued its report. The report concluded that the CIA "assets" in the Guatemalan military had committed serious human rights abuses while working for the agency and that the CIA had failed to keep congressional oversight committees fully informed about those human rights abuses. The latter violated U.S. law but was not found to be a "criminal" violation. In any case, these initial responses to the scandal left pending many broader issues of full disclosure about the past and overhaul for the future.

Meanwhile, although the scandal did not entirely break through the "business-as-usual" atmosphere that characterized U.S. relations with the Guatemalan army, it did aggravate an already deteriorating relationship. The Guatemalan army and its civilian partners were infuriated by U.S. pressures for an in-depth investigation of CIA-linked army officers. As they saw it, the scandal was Washington's problem, not theirs, and any investigation represented U.S. meddling in Guatemala's sovereign affairs. Behind their rhetoric, some Guatemalan officials truly could not understand why the Clinton administration did not simply ignore (or silence) annoying public opinion pressures—or why the U.S. embassy in Guatemala City was indulging the demands of the wife of a deceased URNG "terrorist." Washington, they concluded, must be trying to embarrass them.

By the late 1990s, it seemed likely that the loss of trust in the once-warm relationship between the United States and the Guatemalan army could be permanent. One underlying reason was that the Guatemalan army was increasingly on the defensive both at home and abroad. In addition, the end of the Cold War and the negotiated settlements of all of Central America's civil wars left Washington little justification for a strategic alliance with the Guatemalan army. Both post–Cold War U.S. administrations claimed to promote democracy, demilitarization, and human rights in Latin America, but in Guatemala their strategic ally was the main obstacle to those goals. Under the Clinton administration, the United States no longer seemed ideologically committed to the Guatemalan army, as during the 1980s, and was increasingly uncomfortable about the alliance. But without a coherent policy, old thinking dies hard: As recently as 1996, U.S. officials still offered a variety of arguments for sending mixed messages and for changing policy as little and as slowly as possible.[2]

Washington's Agendas in Postwar Guatemala

At the momentous signing of Guatemala's final peace accord in December 1996, the United States distinguished itself in two ways: First, at a historical moment when many Guatemalans were speaking publicly about the errors that had caused so much pain and suffering, the U.S. delegation did not say one word about U.S. responsibility for the events leading to or occurring during the war. Many other observers and participants were taken aback by this deliberate silence; but U.S. officials, when asked, explained it simply as "focusing on the future, not the past."

Second, and even more astonishing, the ink was not yet dry on the peace accords that would strip the Guatemalan army of all functions other than external defense, when U.S. officials were holding discussions with President Arzú, right then and there, proposing to give the Guatemalan army a "new mission" in counternarcotics control. According to one report (*New York Times*, Jan. 5, 1997), "Guatemalan officials say they are now being pressed to play a more active role in the U.S.' war on narcotics"—to accept U.S. equipment and training for the Guatemalan army in the war against drugs. (Arzú himself seemed to agree with the idea.) Subsequent reports in April 1997, when the head of the U.S. Southern Command visited Guatemala, explicitly confirmed U.S. plans to send four hundred troops for antidrug training to the army, as part of "cooperation to consolidate peace." When pushed, some U.S. officials justified this as part of the military's mission of "defending the borders." Others insisted that the antinarcotics unit of the civilian police force would be the lead Guatemalan agency, but with collaboration from army intelligence. Although the idea of direct U.S. assistance to the army for the war on drugs has continued to crop up, it could end up being a trial balloon that doesn't fly—in part because even some Guatemalan military officers have had doubts about it.[3]

Aside from the drug war, the U.S. also sought to reinitiate U.S. military training and aid to the Guatemalan army in this peacetime era in order to establish "closer relations" between the two armies (*Prensa Libre*, Apr. 22, 1997, and Apr. 24, 1997; *Inforpress Centroamericana*, May 2, 1997)—as if the transformation of Guatemala's army had been completed and civilian control established. The only brake on these plans has been opposition from the U.S. Congress, which stopped them in 1997 (with the exception of "Expanded IMET," military training specifically for human rights). In the spring of 1998 once again, the administration asked Congress to restore the regular military training program (IMET)—the very week after the assassination of Msgr. Juan Gerardi, and at a time when Guatemala's constitutional reforms, limiting the army's functions to external defense, were by no means assured. The request for full military training was repeated in the spring of 1999 (and was again rejected by Congress)—even *after* the historic Clinton apology (see below).

The other major issue on Washington's bilateral agenda with Guatemala in the postwar era has been U.S. concern about Guatemalan migration to the United States, which has continued after the end of the war, although now for economic more than political reasons. With Guatemala, as with other Latin American countries, Washington has focused on stopping undocumented migration and on deporting undocumented migrants rather than addressing the root problems in the home country—above all, the lack of decent jobs there. This issue surfaced as one of the major controversies during President Clinton's March 1999 "goodwill" trip to Central America (see below).

In contrast to its persistence regarding counternarcotics and immigration, Washington has generally been somewhat flexible regarding Guatemalan compliance with the peace accords, with the exception of tax reform (see Chapter 7). Unlike some of the European governments, the United States did not, for example, threaten to condition postwar assistance (even military) on passage of the constitutional reforms that would guarantee a lasting demilitarization. Perhaps it should come as no surprise that the United States prioritizes its bilateral agenda: While the Europeans, thousands of miles away, can afford to take a principled stance on Guatemalan peace, the United States is dealing with a country within its sphere of influence and hence is bound to emphasize its interests. As one U.S. diplomat explained, "It is our job to figure out who in Guatemala can advance U.S. policy interests." The question for the future, then, is whether the United States will adjust its definition of "interests" to new realities within Guatemala and the hemisphere.

All of the above notwithstanding, it is important to point to some indicators that such an adjustment or redefinition of interests has begun and to some significant countertendencies to Washington's "business-as-usual" approach to Guatemala. In general, the U.S. Agency for International Development (AID) programs have demonstrated a genuine comprehension of what the peace accords are all about and are oriented toward the spirit and priorities of the accords. Some examples from the ambitious postwar U.S. assistance program ($260 million over four years), as laid out in interviews and documents (e.g., U.S. AID 1997 and 1999), include the following: immediate funds for demobilization/reintegration and vocational training of URNG ex-combatants; $1.5 million to the Truth Commission (and special attention in assistance programs to war widows and orphans and communities impacted by the war); crucial programs supporting reform of the justice system, a top priority in the peace agenda; and basic education (including bilingual education) and advocacy training for some of the most disenfranchised sectors of the population. In addition, the United States has sponsored seminars that train both civilians and military personnel in Guatemala for a future in which the army is slated to come under civilian control. Finally, it is worth noting that AID officials have gone out of their way to support the overall process of implementing the peace accords, even at the most difficult moments in that process. This marks a significant evolution from past U.S. government policies and practices.

Truth and Consequences

March 1999: The Clinton Apology

> For the United States, it is important that I state clearly that support for military forces or intelligence units which engaged in violent and widespread repression of the kind described in the [Truth Commission] report was wrong, and the United States must not repeat that mistake. We must, and we will, instead, continue to support the peace and reconciliation process in Guatemala. (Clinton 1999)

These were words that no one could have imagined hearing from a U.S. president. Yet President Clinton spoke them in a historic meeting with representatives of Guatemalan civil society, held during his March 10–11, 1999, visit to Guatemala, barely two weeks after the release of the Truth Commission report (see Chapter 6). Beyond its startling findings about the role of the Guatemalan army, that report was quite severe in its characterization of U.S. responsibilities for and during the war (including its support for some illegal operations by Guatemalan government security forces). Although many groups and individuals in the United States had been urging Clinton (through intense lobbying, op-ed articles, and congressional pressures) to finally take responsibility for a half century of U.S. actions in Guatemala, they were stunned when he did so. Guatemalans who had called for a U.S. acknowledgment of this kind were equally surprised and viewed the statement as "historic."

The surprise was even greater because the initial U.S. reaction to the Truth Commission's report when it was presented on February 25 had been very defensive, in essence, a repetition of past habits of denial. U.S. Ambassador Donald Planty, described as "seething" during the presentation, reacted afterward by referring to the war as simply an internal matter among Guatemalans and characterized the report as a "wrong interpretation." Top State Department official Peter Romero criticized the report as "an exaggeration."

How and why, then, was the decision made to reverse forty-plus years of disinformation, plausible denials, and cover-ups by the United States in regard to Guatemala? The Truth Commission report—combined with the fortunate coincidence of President Clinton's Central America trip, the first by a U.S. president since Lyndon Johnson in the mid-1960s—provided the logical occasion for such an action, and there was very intense public and congressional pressure (as well as the legacy of the 1995 CIA scandal). But some in the State Department and other agencies remained reluctant to acknowledge the U.S. role in direct terms, and a White House spokesman initially said he "didn't expect the issue to come up" during Clinton's trip. Discussions within the administration continued for days, right up until Clinton's departure. In the end, although there was a general decision that Clinton should say something, the wording was not worked out in advance, and in the Guatemala meeting, Clinton spoke from handwritten notes.[4]

One could argue that it was a relatively painless gesture by Clinton, since he was apologizing basically for deeds committed prior to his presidency. But in that case, why didn't his emissaries make some kind of statement at the 1996 peace signing? And if it was so easy, why did it strike such a raw nerve in Washington (see Note 4)? Most likely, the answer as to "why now" lies in the force of the Truth Commission report, combined with the circumstance of Clinton himself being in Guatemala, at a face-to-face meeting with Guatemalan civil society representatives that included war victims and their organizations. In addition, the accumulated internal pressures within the United States may have had some impact. And finally, it is possible that Clinton and other U.S. officials were influenced by having to confront the enormity of U.S. responsibility in Guatemala, as revealed in a mass of documents declassified for the Truth Commission by various U.S. government agencies (see below).

In any case, for whatever reasons, whether it was easy or difficult, U.S. officials can henceforth view that moment in March 1999 as an opportunity, not a burden; for the first time in decades, they will be able to speak honestly about Guatemala. Clinton's words of acknowledgment/apology will be part of the historical record of the United States in Guatemala.

Declassification: The Devil in the Details

Even before Clinton's trip to Guatemala, the United States had been drawn into the imbroglio of historical clarification in Guatemala. Shortly after it was constituted in July 1997, Guatemala's Truth Commission (whose general functioning and impact is discussed in Chapter 6) had requested that U.S. government agencies open up their files. Aside from the well-known fact that after a half century of intense involvement in

Guatemala's internal affairs, the CIA and other U.S. government agencies had detailed information (most of it secret), the Guatemalan army's non-cooperation with the commission made U.S. declassification even more essential. And given the decades-long U.S. ties with the Guatemalan army, the United States had a prima facie obligation, both to Guatemalan citizens and to U.S. citizens/taxpayers, to carry out a massive declassification.

This time, the request for information went far beyond specific cases affecting U.S. citizens (as in the 1996 IOB report—see above). The Truth Commission's mandate included Guatemalan policies and structures of repression as well as specific cases and massacres, and that necessarily involved U.S. policies and U.S. training of Guatemala's security forces. As the Truth Commission's letter of September 1997 argued, "Information in possession of the U.S. Government is essential for obtaining a comprehensive and objective picture of the armed conflict," since the United States was likely to have much more systematic records than either of the two parties to the Guatemalan civil war. By this time as well, the Clinton administration was coming under strong pressures from within the United States—both from Congress (the Human Rights Information bill, proposing to require U.S. foreign policy and intelligence agencies to release, within 150 days, all human rights records regarding Guatemala and Honduras) and from the National Security Archive and other Washington-based organizations making requests under the Freedom of Information Act (see Doyle 1998).

Overall, the U.S. government's response to the various requests and pressures for declassification of information was much more positive than had been expected—although some agencies were far less cooperative than others. The most forthcoming were the State Department (although most of the documents it released were routine and unclassified), AID (whose Office of Public Safety had run an infamous police training program from 1957 to 1974), and, surprisingly, the CIA, which released a substantial amount of "raw" intelligence material from its Guatemala City station. By contrast, the Defense Department and the National Security Council released nothing of value, even though the former was the lead agency during such crucial periods of the war as 1966–1968 and even though those documents should be in the public domain according to general guidelines of declassification after twenty-five years.

The documents make clear that in addition to the period during the 1960s when the United States set up Guatemala's counterinsurgency apparatus (see above), U.S. officials knew virtually *everything* that the Guatemalan army and its paramilitary units were doing throughout the entire period of the war. Numerous documents (reports from embassy-based officials to their superiors in Washington) covering the period of the early to mid-1980s confirm that U.S. government agencies were fully aware of the atrocities by the Guatemalan army—including the torture, the genocidal massacres, the extrajudicial killings—and chose to look the other way. Subsequently, during the late 1980s, whenever possible, the United States sought opportunities to support the Guatemalan government and to fund and train its military, even as embassy-based officials were describing the human rights violations in full detail.

Indeed, it is those *details* that have been so shocking even to those of us who had previously understood the general parameters of U.S. complicity with the Guatemalan army.[5] On the basis of the detailed information that has emerged thus far from the declassified documents, we will be able to write more precisely about the history of the United States in Guatemala. Far more important, particularly in the absence of information directly from the Guatemalan army, the material from documents declassified by U.S. government agencies will be crucial in enabling Guatemalans to reconstruct and confront their own history. For these reasons, the declassification process is far too important to be seen as completed, and it is essential that the U.S. government respond positively to new and ongoing requests for information.

Broader Questions About "U.S. Interests"

Following the extraordinary departures from routine U.S. policy described above, U.S. policymakers gave out a new round of mixed messages. On the more positive side were several indicators of a more open attitude—for example, U.S. criticisms of the Guatemalan government for not responding more positively to the Truth Commission report, and pressures on the Guatemalan government to resolve the Gerardi assassination (for the very first time since the assassination—see Chapter 6). But at the same time, in a tired reminder of the past, Defense Department officials tried to convince Congress to restore full military training to the Guatemalan army—despite the latter's total lack of cooperation with the Truth Commission and its resistance to making other changes required by the peace accords.

On balance, then, we are left with some disturbing questions: How much progress has the U.S. policy establishment made in adjusting its priorities to a postwar Guatemala? Why is it that many Washington officials appear not to fully grasp the significance of the Guatemalan peace process and the changes it requires? Why are they continuing to send mixed messages and seeking new missions for the Guatemalan army—especially now that the excuse of "internal subversion" no longer exists?

And to the extent that U.S. policy is driven by economic interests (both public and private, trade and investment), why do they sometimes only half-understand that the scenarios for protecting those interests have changed?

Perhaps it is because Washington views Latin America as its sphere of influence that U.S. policy seems to change one millimeter at a time. Perhaps this reflects the ingrown political culture of superpower bureaucracies trained during the Cold War, and now groping to redefine their mission in the world. Perhaps, as some have suggested, the United States is particularly slow to change in the Guatemalan case, as a result of its intervention there in 1954 and its very long history of supporting dirty wars there, directly or indirectly, since 1960. Perhaps, as well, this is why, until the remarkable Clinton apology, U.S. officials have never wanted to say very much about Guatemala or the U.S. role there. In that case, the question today is whether they will use this opportunity to shed the baggage of the Cold War.

There is also a larger issue: Washington's relationship to UN peace-keeping in Guatemala and to the UN more broadly. As discussed in Chapter 2, the U.S. stance on financing MINUGUA (insisting that the funds for MINUGUA be taken out of cuts from elsewhere in the UN operating budget) caused serious problems for MINUGUA. Behind the argument over MINUGUA has been the much larger issue of the $1.5 billion that the United States owes the UN in unpaid back dues (the United States claims it is much less). And underlying the financial issues is the question of how much official Washington politically supports the UN as an institution.[6]

Particularly when it comes to Latin America, the United States has generally felt uncomfortable about permitting issues "vital to U.S. security" to be handled in the UN; certainly this was the case during the Cold War. When preparing its intervention against Arbenz in 1954, Washington went to great lengths to remove the issue from a UN vote and steer it into the OAS, where at that time it was much easier to get the vote Washington wanted. Indeed, within a narrow construction of "U.S. interests," the UN can be seen as a "problematic" forum: U.S. control is not always fully guaranteed, even in regard to its own sphere of influence. As one senior and experienced international diplomat observed, the last decade's developments in Central America have a very particular significance both to the United States and to the hemisphere as a whole: It was after the 1987 Central American Peace Accords (Esquipulas II) and the Central American presidents' rejection of the U.S. Contra war that the UN Security Council adopted its first resolution (in 1989) authorizing the UN to offer/exercise "good offices" in the region. This was the UN's first involvement in internal peacekeeping in Central America, the traditional "backyard" of the United States; such involvement can be seen as signifying, ultimately, a challenge to the Monroe Doctrine and as altering the relationship between the United States and Latin America as a whole.

The CIA's 1954 intervention in Guatemala brought the Cold War to the hemisphere. In the 1960s the United States fought its first Latin American counterinsurgency war in Guatemala, with the Guatemalan army serving as its proxy. Until its civil war was ended, Guatemala (together with Cuba) remained one of the last preserves of U.S. Cold War policies. Today, Guatemala presents a test of whether U.S. policymakers really understand that the Cold War is over in Latin America.

Notes

1. Nuccio was subsequently punished (by being stripped of his high-level security clearance) for the crime of rectifying his previous behavior (misleading Congress about the Harbury case). The justification for punishing him was that he had taken the information to Rep. Torricelli without having secured official State Department approval.

2. At issue are two misconceptions, one concerning the U.S. view of the army as the "most important institution" in Guatemala and the second concerning U.S. leverage. Even though the war is now over and conditions have changed, it is worth summarizing briefly these arguments (discussed more fully in Jonas 1996a) because remnants of these logics remain alive in the thinking of many U.S. officials. Although I wrote that article before having access to the recently declassified documents, those documents confirm and amply illustrate the arguments used by U.S. officials and described here.

1) For years, Washington policymakers tended to accept the Guatemalan army's version of Guatemala's realities, leading to minimalist expectations about the prospects for significant change. The Guatemalan armed forces were seen as so strong that the United States could not afford to antagonize them. The URNG was considered militarily weak; hence, the army had no reason to make major concessions, and the URNG and the popular sectors would have to settle quickly for a minimal peace agreement focusing primarily on a cease-fire. Furthermore, in the absence of strong civilian institutions, the army would be needed to carry out antidrug operations, civic action projects, reforestation, road building, vaccinations, and even internal security (police) functions.

This view was—and is, even more so today—based on appearances, half-truths, and jumps in logic; it reflected a watered-down version of the Guatemalan army's public-relations campaign. Of course, there were elements of half-truth mixed in with the army's presentation. However, it was a gross distortion and oversimplification to focus only on those aspects and ignore the significant changes in Guatemalan society: the strengthening of actors and institutions independent of (and antagonistic to) the army; divisions within Guatemala's elites, even the army itself, with modernizing elements that could be pressured to tip the balance against the status quo; the real loss of political credibility by the army, as well as its anachronistic character, which made it inappropriate for carrying out tasks other than external defense. In short, the army is no longer the "most important institution" and does not merit treatment as such.

2) The second cluster of arguments concerned U.S. leverage in Guatemala. U.S. officials argued that Washington lost leverage over the Guatemalan army after cutting off military aid; further measures would cause the United States to lose all remaining influence. For example, according to a recently declassified document (see Note 5), when Marilyn McAfee was about to go to Guatemala as ambassador in 1993, she expressed concern that U.S. human rights pressures would alienate the Guatemalan army: "We must try and calibrate our actions to build and retain the confidence of the army." In short, the U.S. should reward the army's "good behavior" (support for civilian government), regardless of its continuing human rights abuses during civilian rule—rather a low standard for "democracy." Finally, since the army was said to be reforming itself from the inside, and even "cleansing" its ranks of human rights violators, outside pressure was seen as unnecessary. This last argument was disproven time and again by all human rights organizations and verification organisms of the UN and OAS.

The result of this convoluted logic was to suggest that the United States could best promote democracy by tolerating undemocratic behavior; any other course would lead the Guatemalan army to dig in its heels. In the end, arguments over leverage came down to how seriously Washington intended to press for major institutional changes in the army.

3. In one example of how the U.S. prioritizes its antidrug agenda, the March 1997 "International Narcotics Control Strategy Report" of the State Department's Narcotics Bureau complained that "counternarcotics programs will have to compete with pressure to commit scarce resources to peace initiatives and public sector social programs." But some U.S. initiatives to use Guatemala to launch its antidrug operations have been quite controversial in Guatemala—e.g., President Arzú's decision in the fall of 1997 to accept aid from U.S. special forces (to either the police or the army) to combat drug trafficking and organized crime and to permit U.S. artillery ships to patrol Guatemalan waters (and air space) (*Prensa Libre*, Nov. 1, 1997).

4. Not surprisingly, Clinton's apology unleashed a major inside-the-Beltway controversy. While the *Washington Post* (Mar. 1, 1999) suggested that the U.S. needs "our own Truth Commission," Oliver North, veteran of the Reagan Doctrine and the Iran-Contra scandal, was infuriated: "What we were doing [in Guatemala] was a noble fight in support of democracy and . . . self-determination. For Clinton to imply otherwise is outrageous, bordering on criminal." His former (Reagan administration) colleagues Elliott Abrams and Otto Reich agreed. The neoconservative *New Republic* also criticized the apology (Lane 1999).

5. To mention only a few of the damning details that have emerged, primarily through declassified documents:

1) The documents "place a CIA officer in the room where Guatemalan intelligence officers—men responsible for death squad killings—planned their covert operations in 1965. They show that CIA and other American officials played a key role in the latter 1960s in centralizing command structures and communications of agencies that would be involved in death squad killings for years" (*New York Times*, Mar. 7, 1999). In a 1966 memo, a State Department security official said he

had established a "safe house" inside Guatemala's National Palace where local se-curity agents could meet their contacts; this became the headquarters for officers waging Guatemala's dirty war (*Montreal Gazette*, Mar. 12, 1999)

2) In March 1968, just after ending his term as deputy chief of mission (second to the ambassador) in Guatemala, Viron Vaky wrote a memo to the State Depart-ment calling on the United States to condemn the Guatemalan government's "counter-terror" rather than encouraging and blessing it. "Is it conceivable that we are so obsessed with insurgency that we are prepared to rationalize murder as an acceptable counterinsurgency weapon?" (*Inter-Press Service*, Mar. 14, 1999). "My deepest regret," he continued," is that I did not fight harder within embassy councils when I was there to press these views" (*Washington Post*, Mar. 12, 1999).

3) During the scorched-earth war of the 1980s, the CIA station in Guatemala "knew that the Guatemalan army was massacring entire Mayan villages, while Reagan administration officials publicly supported the military regime's human rights record" and called for a restoration of U.S. military aid (*New York Times*, Mar. 7, 1999).

4) In the course of excoriating Clinton's apology, Oliver North revealed that he got help from the Guatemalan government and army to funnel surface-to-air mis-siles to the Nicaraguan Contras (*Washington Times*, Mar. 12, 1999).

6. Unlike the U.S. public, which has demonstrated a very positive attitude to-ward the UN in poll after poll and favors increased involvement in and strength-ening of the UN (*New York Times*, June 15, 1996, Sept. 23, 1996, Dec. 28, 1997), offi-cial Washington under both Republican and Democratic administrations has championed unilateral decisionmaking (particularly on issues involving the use of force) and has challenged UN authority on every issue from UN finances to its secretary general to its international peacekeeping missions. The Clinton adminis-tration has also established a record of capitulating to Republican right-wing anti-UN sentiments in Congress.

Implementation Wars

The following chapters—6, 7 and 8—cover peace accord implementation during the first two and a half years after its signing. Rather than presenting a "report" that presumes to be comprehensive or definitive (neither of which would be possible at this stage), I describe the dynamics of postwar Guatemala and sketch the broad outlines of accord implementation (Chapter 6). Then I recount (or more accurately, construct) in more detail the stories of the principal struggles—over tax reform (Chapter 7) and the constitutional reforms (Chapter 8). The (mostly sad) endings of these paradigmatic tales, together with some broader structural, comparative, and imaginary perspectives, form the basis for the Conclusion—itself an interim "conclusion," since we are dealing here with an unfinished history.

One set of questions underlies the remainder of this book: Will the promise inherent in the peace accords of a "new Guatemala" be realized—or more precisely, to what extent and in what respects will it be realized? Is Guatemala moving toward reinventing itself for the twenty-first century? Or is a unique historical opportunity about to be lost? The nuances of interpretation vary depending on the question, Compared to what? To Guatemala's own (pre-peace) past—forty-two years of repression and thirty-six years of Cold War civil war? To the utopian hopes expressed at the time of the peace signing, when Guatemala was being seen by some optimists as a possible example for other countries? Or, on the contrary, to widespread skepticism about whether anything ever changes in Guatemala? What can realistically be expected from the peace accords? To what extent are the implementation problems typical of postwar reconstruction eras, and to what extent are they specific to Guatemala? Or, more precisely, *which* of the problems are specific to Guatemala? Additionally, which of these problems were predictable, even structural, and which have arisen or intensified along the way?

My starting point is that the accords, as signed, opened up the possibility for significant changes. Though not transforming Guatemala, they sought to modernize, rationalize, demilitarize, democratize, normalize—and lay the basis for possible more profound transformations in the future. Other observers view the accords themselves less favorably, because they fell so far short of resolving Guatemala's basic structural problems. Although this is true, I believe the accords represented a far better starting point than had been previously expected. Beyond ending the civil war, they reached very high in their vision of a new society. This is particularly noteworthy since the accords resulted from a political negotiation, a compromise among many different actors, including those not formally at the negotiating table (e.g., CACIF and ASC). The fact that some of Guatemala's traditional elites continued to see the accords as little more than a cease-fire and demobilization of the URNG did not negate the reality of what had been signed. It did mean, however, that the battle for implementation of the accords would be a second, even more difficult stage of the ongoing peace process.

By the time the accords were signed in December 1996, there was a general consensus in favor of a negotiated end to the civil war—although, as described in Chapter 2, establishing such a consensus had been in itself a very prolonged and difficult process. The signing of the accords was viewed positively but with skepticism about the possibilities for real change and with very little knowledge among unorganized and less-involved social sectors. Open resistance to this process (i.e., to the idea of having seriously negotiated with the URNG) had been reduced to the more extreme elements of the private sector, some former and current army officers, and congressional representatives of the FRG, the party of former dictator Ríos Montt. Clearly, the ranks of the open "peace resisters" included powerful forces, hence giving them more weight than their numbers warranted; nevertheless, by 1996, they were more isolated from the mainstream than in previous years. An important factor favoring Guatemala's peace process was the unexpected level of goodwill and generosity from the international community, mainly because Guatemala was perceived as one of the best cases for international conflict resolution in the mid- to late 1990s.

However, following the signing of the peace accords, the underlying balance of forces shifted in such a way as to bring out the obstacles more than the achievements, even as many formal obligations of the accords were being met. The peace resisters gained ground at the expense of active pro-peace forces to such an extent that on several occasions, the historical opportunity presented by the peace accords was (or appeared to be) on the brink of being lost. I do not agree with those who insist that it was definitively lost or that the potential never existed at all. However, the dangers of noncompliance or compliance *a medias* (halfway/proforma compliance) were very real. This, in turn, contributed to a widespread erosion of faith in the potential of the peace process; indifference and skepticism were based on the (largely accurate) perception that nothing in people's daily lives was improving—although these feelings varied from region to region, depending in part on the prior involvement of the population in the war itself. Finally, for both domestic reasons (1999 elections, bringing in an unknown new government) and international reasons (a predictable disappearance of Guatemala as a focal point of interest for the international community), the window of opportunity for consolidating gains was small.

Although the following assessments cover major areas addressed in the accords, they make no attempt to be comprehensive. Rather, I am emphasizing the most central issues—which also sparked the most resistance from those who never accepted the ideas at the heart of the peace accords. The first set of priority issues, those of a political-cultural nature, are considered in this chapter: demilitarization, formation and functioning of the civilian police, reforms of the justice system and the combat against impunity, the Truth Commission, and indigenous rights. But the key to many of the above (except the Truth Commission) was the dramatic two-and-a-half-year struggle over the constitutional reforms that were designed to legally establish the peace accords as irreversible "accords of state." That story, told in Chapter 8, illuminates just how long was the distance and how dangerous the minefields in the road to compliance. Chapter 7 focuses on the struggles over the other landmark issue, the tax reform needed to provide internal financing for implementation of all the accords and hence to guarantee their financial viability. But the backdrop for all of the above is a sketch of the general situation and the changing balance of forces from 1997 through mid-1999.

Backdrop:
Peace and Its Discontents

The internationally supervised process of demobilization of the URNG (February–May 1997) went smoothly and without incident. The reincorporation of former URNG combatants and militants into productive economic activity was only partially successful and remained an ongoing task for the future. But even the relatively easy process of URNG demobilization carried a hint of underlying problems that could turn into future obstacles. Whether by design or by diplomatic ineptitude, the Guatemalan government came close to torpedoing the entire arrangement for UN oversight of the demobilization: In January 1997, through its support for Taiwanese representation in the UN, the government provoked mainland China into a Security Council veto of the peacekeeping operation. Although this knot was untied after several weeks of diplomatic maneuvering, it left a disturbing question of whether the Guatemalan government was once again resisting international (especially UN) oversight of the peace process.

During the early months of 1997, a number of the structures for implementation and monitoring of the accords were established. Beyond the governmental Secretariat of Peace (SEPAZ) and its technical commission, the most notable was the top-level Comisión de Acompañamiento, the internal commission to follow up the implementation of the peace accords. This commission was designed to facilitate compliance by working out consensus among the various political actors; it was composed of two representatives each from the government and the URNG, one from Congress, four distinguished citizens, and the director of MINUGUA as an observer. Equally significant, several official commissions were set up (e.g., on reform of the judicial system and electoral reform); part of their mandate was to initiate a series of multisector *consultas* (consultations), including social sectors that had never been involved in political decisionmaking at any level. Although the actual weight of the input from these consultations varied considerably from case to case, the very existence and proliferation of such mechanisms—together with the *comisiones paritarias* established in the indigenous accord (see below)—was crucial in expanding participation in a hitherto exclusionary system.

Although the demands for civil society participation increased after the signing of the accords, the particular organizational channels for those demands changed. The Asamblea de la Sociedad Civil (ASC), which had played such a critical role during the negotiation phase, was sidelined (in reality, after 1995), as many of its leftist organizations put their energy into the FDNG campaign, and the ASC as such had no formal role in accord implementation. Beginning in 1996, the energy and demand for participation came from particular sectors—by far the most active being the indigenous organizations, whose agenda included dozens of commitments from the accords that had to be translated into realities (see below). The other notably active sector was the one that had seldom been previously included: Women's organizations were now negotiating their way into the arenas of social and political action and, in the process, proposing new (gendered) ways of conducting politics (see Rodríguez 1998; ONAM 1997). One visible expression of this was the Foro de Mujeres (Women's Forum); created in the fall of 1997, it became an arena for training and empowering women at the local, regional, and national levels and for coordinating the work of women's organizations with indigenous and other social groupings. By late 1998 it had organized 25,000 women in all linguistic regions of the country. Particularly striking was the diversity of its working groups, with each group deciding its own methodologies for discussion and participation.

Finally, in the area of democratization, the URNG began its complicated process of legalization as a political party; broader spaces were also opened up to other leftist forces, signifying finally the beginning of a more pluralistic political system. As discussed in Chapter 4, this advance for ideological pluralism could not be taken for granted: It had required an extremely long struggle and had not been resolved in Guatemala simply by the return to civilian rule. Hence, its beginning in the mid-1990s represented a qualitative advance toward overcoming counterinsurgency politics and making Guatemala a "normal" country.

However, it did not take long to remind everyone that in Guatemala any *apertura,* or opening, was almost certain to generate counterpressures or resistances. An early sign of the problems and battles to come was the February 1997 crisis over the law creating the new National Civilian Police (PNC): The government drafted and sent the law to Congress, where it was passed, before the Comisión de Acompañamiento mandated to approve it had even been constituted. The law itself contained a number of provisions (e.g., about eligibility for service in the PNC) that clearly violated the spirit and letter of the accords and threatened to leave the country with a militarized police force.

Equally ominous was the late January 1997 uprising by the Policia Militar Ambulante (PMA), one of the longtime units of the military, in opposition to its projected demobilization. The incident left clear that the army as a whole remained far from convinced about the limitations on its mission, as specified in the demilitarization accord. Concretely, the uprising resulted not only in postponement of the PMA's demobilization but also in permitting incorporation of PMA officers into the new civilian police force—a clear violation of the intent of the accord. There were subsequent incidents as well: Ex-military forces engaged overtly in destabilizing activities (such as occupations of public offices) to press their demands in ways that made them a serious public security problem. In early 1997, for example, ex-soldiers wounded in combat and ex-PAC members became very aggressive in pressing their demands for compensation—very much like organizations of ex-army soldiers in El Salvador. In short, the ink was barely dry on the accords when early warning signs of resistance to demilitarization first emerged and of government compromises in the face of such pressures.

"Mincho" and the Balance of Forces in 1997

If some of the above resistances could have been predicted, what followed was a free gift to the coalition of peace resisters. This was the "Mincho Affair," which emerged in early April 1997, re-raising once again the most sensitive issue during the last months of the peace negotiations, the Novella kidnapping (see Chapter 2). "Mincho" was a second ORPA cadre involved in the Novella kidnapping, who (unlike Isaías) was tortured, killed, and "disappeared" by government security forces. When press reports first revealed the previously secret "disappearance" and his family demanded the return of his body and investigation of his death, the ensu-

ing scandal threatened to compromise virtually all of the key protagonists of the peace process—the URNG, MINUGUA, and the "Peace Cabinet" of the Arzú government. (The most detailed investigation/summary
of the "Mincho Affair" is in Hemisphere Initiatives [HI] 1998, 25 ff. and
appendix.)

In large part because of this affair, the URNG found itself on the defensive, even after the return of its top leaders and legal incorporation of its
militants.[1] At the same time, the URNG was being swamped by multiple
demands on its energies—to provide for its militants economically as
well as politically, maintain its internal unity, legalize itself as a political
party and build relations/alliances with other leftist forces (mainly the
FDNG) in preparation for the 1999 elections—all this at the same time as
its priority task of monitoring and functioning as the "Left guarantor" of
peace accord compliance through its role on the Comisión de Acompañamiento.[2] In practice, the politically delicate challenge for the URNG
was to fully use its leverage for compliance with the peace accords (i.e.,
working with the government) while at the same time becoming an opposition party to the PAN. Instead of blowing the whistle and calling in the
UN on every instance of governmental noncompliance or halfway compliance, during 1997 the URNG leadership adopted a relatively pragmatic
strategy in its responses to governmental foot-dragging and left harsher
public criticisms to other forces. For these reasons, some human rights
NGOs came to view themselves as the "true" defenders of human rights
and social justice and criticized the URNG for making too many compromises. But by mid-1998 the URNG became much sharper and more direct
in publicly criticizing the government for noncompliance.

A second party that suffered heavy damage from the Mincho Affair
during 1997 was MINUGUA and, in particular, its new head of mission,
Jean Arnault, previously the UN moderator of the peace process (and
functioning in that capacity at the time of the Novella kidnapping). Press
articles and some public figures accused Arnault of orchestrating a cover-
up by MINUGUA—a charge found to be unsubstantiated (HI 1998,
59–62). The mission, under Arnault's leadership, issued a May 1997 report naming the Estado Mayor Presidencial (EMP), or presidential military guard, as responsible for the assassination. This, in turn, unleashed a
crisis between MINUGUA and the government that sent top government
officials scurrying to New York to complain that MINUGUA was *so-
brepasando* or *extralimitando* (exceeding) its mandate. Throughout 1997,
whenever MINUGUA criticized the government and in particular the illegal activities of the EMP and military intelligence, the government
struck back (in New York as well as in Guatemala) with rhetorical threats
to "revise" (restrict) the mission's mandate.[3] The government refused to
give MINUGUA access to material needed for its investigation of this first
case of state repression under Arzú. Of course, the entire Mincho Affair

implicated the EMP, and few seriously doubted its responsibility; but this was so much in keeping with the EMP's prior history that the actual political damage to the EMP was minimal.

The above dynamics compounded the situation of the UN's in-country mission: After the government's trip to New York in May 1997, a perception began to circulate among some human rights NGOs that MINUGUA was softening its criticisms of government human rights violations and slow compliance with the accords. Both in Guatemala and internationally, some of these groups made exaggerated charges that MINUGUA was accepting a simple role as facilitator rather than *fiscalizador*, accompaniment rather than verification—even after MINUGUA named the EMP as responsible in the Mincho case.[4] From April throughout much of 1997, MINUGUA was besieged by sharp criticisms from all sides; even though many of these criticisms were unjustified, they temporarily weakened a key player. And long after the Mincho scandal died down, the right-wing peace resisters maintained a permanent campaign against MINUGUA and responded vitriolically to its verification and human rights reports.

Despite these problems, objectively, MINUGUA's presence and its role in strengthening institutions as well as verification of compliance remained irreplaceable. Just the technical expertise that MINUGUA (together with other international agencies and donor governments) was able to introduce into a system as closed as Guatemala's contributed significantly toward bringing Guatemala into the twenty-first century. In addition, despite the fiercest of resistances by the Guatemalan elites, MINUGUA's presence and its periodic reports on human rights and on compliance with the accords remained key to keeping Guatemala in the international spotlight. Furthermore, Guatemala benefited enormously from the in-country presence of other agencies of the UN system. In particular, the Guatemala office of the UN Development Program (UNDP) stands out for its energy, creativity, and belief in the possibilities of bringing together different sectors of Guatemalan society to resolve conflicts, build consensus, and improve the country's living conditions.

The Arzú government, meanwhile, was running into walls of criticism on a variety of fronts, which quickly became more important than its success in the peace negotiations. Above all, it was seen as unable to resolve Guatemala's two main problems, chronic socioeconomic crisis and *la delincuencia*, the soaring rate of common crime—daily-life issues on which the accords did not provide adequate solutions or even partial relief. In fact, these very real problems were not fully resolvable within the framework of the accords; but they were used to undermine the accords and the government's credibility in general. An additional problem stemmed from profound divisions within the Arzú government and the ruling party. In the executive branch, the "Peace Cabinet" was counterbalanced by cabinet ministers who had other (non-peace) priorities. In

Congress, the PAN was so divided that crucial issues such as the constitutional reforms had to be negotiated within the president's own party as well as with opposition parties (see Chapter 8).[5]

Furthermore, in the government's relations with the private sector, its natural "base," on numerous occasions CACIF leaders manifested a decorous fury toward government (SEPAZ) officials responsible for implementing the accords—as if those officials were betraying their class interests. During the negotiations, most of CACIF, minus the extremists among the landed oligarchy (who had filed suit against the government for negotiating with the URNG), seemed to have understood the need to modernize, and played an important role in crafting the socioeconomic accord so as to minimize the damage to their interests. Subsequent to the signing, however, there was considerable backsliding toward more traditional stances of resistance and throwing up obstacles. In addition to resisting tax reforms that would affect them (see Chapter 7), they supported maintaining internal security functions for the army—though at this point probably less out of ideological sympathy for the army than out of a practical interest in protecting their property.

Equally problematic for the government was the widespread criticism of Arzú's "governing style" as arrogant and exclusionary, despite formal efforts to engage in dialogue. This became evident in the government-initiated multisector "forums"; soon after this process began in the spring of 1997, important political parties and sectors pulled out, alleging government manipulation. (Obviously, some of them did so more out of political self-interest than principle.) An escalating battle with the press also plagued the government during 1997–1998. Meanwhile, the peace resisters used every available opportunity, including their considerable influence over some sectors of the press, to destabilize the already fragile situation and to criticize the government for the necessary trade-offs involved when it did attempt to implement the accords. For all of the above reasons, the government increasingly fell hostage to the peace resisters, including those within its own party. The government also displayed a serious weakness, timidity, lack of vision, and/or premature preoccupation with the 1999 election in not countering those pressures through greater reliance on social forces that were fully committed to the peace accords. Rather than mobilizing support from those forces, in fact, the government made them feel excluded.

Finally, in regard to peace accord implementation itself, a pattern emerged of foot-dragging by a number of government officials, leading some observers to believe that the Arzú government had been ideal for negotiating the peace, but not for carrying out its provisions. In particular, there was a growing perception that the government was cutting corners and looking for loopholes, leading critics to accuse the government of lacking political will (or ability) to implement the accords or to counter the strong pressures coming from peace resisters. There was also a kind of "peace opportunism" in some government circles, that is, a tendency to favor accord implementation unless there was a political cost. Finally, in the two years leading up to the November 1999 election (rather a long pre-election period), the PAN leadership appeared willing to sacrifice everything on the altar of political expediency—a stance that could always be explained to the international donors by holding up the specter of Ríos Montt as the alternative.

Doubts about the government's commitment to the peace process were reinforced by its continual attempts, in the name of preserving "national sovereignty," to downplay or negate MINUGUA's function, that is, *independent* verification of governmental compliance with the accords. This only served to feed the ongoing anti-MINUGUA campaign. (The government even used the spurious argument that it had such good working relations with the URNG as to make international verification unnecessary; all that was needed from the UN, it argued, was international support and "accompaniment.") Within the government, in short, there developed a peculiar dynamic in which the anti-peace forces gained ground as the pro-peace forces lost ground—to such an extent that at times it appeared that in order to preserve their place in the government, some principal protagonists of the peace process, such as foreign minister Eduardo Stein, were now having to convey messages of resistance or foot-dragging (e.g., at the UN).

The most startling government move affecting the climate for accord implementation was Arzú's shake-up in the army top command in early July 1997. These sudden and unexpected changes included the removal of the pro-peace defense minister Julio Balconi, as well as his rival, the hardline chief of staff of the armed forces, Sergio Camargo; former army peace negotiator Otto Pérez Molina was "exiled" to Washington; and EMP chief Marco Tulio Espinosa, allegedly responsible for the Mincho assassination, was named to replace Camargo, while the less controversial Hector Barrios replaced Balconi.[6] These changes in the army high command raised questions as to whether the move was Arzú's way of imposing civilian authority on the army or vice versa. Whatever the reasons, these changes had the effect of making peace accord implementation a much lower priority (if not a counter-priority) for the army. The new command seemed to be taking the accords as a formality more than as a binding commitment. Their subsequent conduct was a reminder that the vast majority of the army high command, including the "institutionalists," had never really united with the project of the peace accords. (This was confirmed by their statements in interviews; see also Arévalo 1998a, 26 and 131.) One had the sense that the army's goal was to maintain a low profile and mouth the right discourse while doing the minimum necessary toward compliance with the accords—essentially waiting for the interest in peace to blow over, trying to "survive" or outlast the peace.

Subtext of the Gerardi Assassination:
Return of Political Violence in 1998?

Throughout the second half of 1997 and the first months of 1998, there was an eerie *compás de espera* (interval, hiatus, waiting period) on the peace front, a dynamic of one step forward, two steps backward, against a societal backdrop of dramatically increasing *delincuencia* (common crime) and deteriorating social conditions. By early 1998, the shadow of the 1999 general elections already loomed over virtually every political move by every political actor. All of these dynamics came into sharp relief in February 1998, with the government's disastrous retreat on tax re- form—a political setback for the peace process as a whole (see Chapter 7). More generally, as MINUGUA (1998a, 16) noted in its verification report covering the first half of 1998, there was a "noticeable slowing down" of the peace process after the beginning of 1998 as compared with 1997.

But nothing in that panorama—rather typical for Guatemala and per- haps, more generally, for post-conflict societies attempting to make con- troversial reforms—prepared Guatemalans to wake up on the morning of April 27, 1998, to the televised images of Msgr. Juan Gerardi's bloodied skull, crushed by a cement block and spread across the floor of his garage the previous night. The corpse of Gerardi, Auxiliary Bishop and one of the leading figures of the Catholic Church's Bishops Conference, could be identified only by the ring on his finger, the only object of value. The method of assassination was designed to be grotesque, the message an unmistakable reminder of the worst atrocities of the war. But the war was over; this was the kind of political crime that was supposed to have ended forever with the signing of peace. At the time, no one could prove a political motive; but the assassination just happened to occur two nights after Gerardi's high-profile presentation of the monumental report on the war's human rights crimes. The report had been prepared by the Arch- bishop's Human Rights Office (ODHA) that Gerardi headed. Based on testimony taken from 6,000 civilians nationwide during three years, the report, ironically titled *Nunca Más ("Never Again")*, made clear that the overwhelming majority of these crimes (over 85 percent) had been com- mitted by the army and related paramilitary forces, less than 10 percent by the URNG (see ODHA 1998).

"Peacetime violence" was nothing new; in Guatemala, as in the early years of all postwar transitions, social violence increased exponentially. But this was a different kind of peacetime crime: As the highest-level po- litical assassination in recent Guatemalan history, it left the nation in a state of shock. Nothing after the assassination would be quite the same as before. Perhaps because the wounds of war were so far from being healed, it raised the specter of a return to the past. In its aftermath, many habits and behaviors engrained from thirty-six years of war reemerged, making the challenges of building (or even thinking about) a new society much more daunting than previously. By mid-1999, the murder remained unsolved and strong leads pointing to army or EMP involvement had not been followed up. The government's failure to solve the crime reinforced the view that impunity would never be eradicated in Guatemala and that the rule of law remained precarious. Certainly it cast a long shadow over the entire peace process during the rest of 1998 and the first half of 1999, with skepticism about the process driven by suspicions that the government was covering up the crime and that army hard-liners could still (quite literally) get away with murder. And internationally, Guatemala was once again a focus of attention for an unspeakable human rights crime.

Delays, Detours, and Near Derailments in Compliance

"Citizen Security" and the Army's "New Missions"

One of the major underlying goals of the peace accords was the subordination of the military to civilian authority and control. The mechanism for consolidating this goal was a series of constitutional reforms that would profoundly change the army's role and functions (see below). The de-centaurization of state and society involved dismantling all of the counterinsurgency structures, separation of external defense from internal security tasks, reduction of the army's numbers and budget, and limitation of its functions to guarding the national borders ("defense of State sovereignty and territorial integrity"). Despite the clear provisions of the peace accords on the issue of demilitarization, their implementation continued to be seriously threatened by delays. While sharply delimiting the army's role, the accords had never been very clear about the issues of citizen security during the "transition period" (both until the new civilian police was fully constituted and until the constitutional reforms limiting the army's functions were approved). This legal-juridical vacuum was filled by events on the ground and the interpretations of those events by political forces with their own agendas, separate from (in some cases, opposed to) the peace agenda.

Like other countries emerging from protracted civil wars,[7] Guatemala faced new sources of violence and insecurity. Systematic state-sponsored terrorism was replaced by a massive wave of kidnappings, armed assaults and robberies, and other forms of criminal activity, both spontaneous and organized. This phenomenon led many Guatemalans to conclude that things were going from bad to worse in their daily lives. Not all "common crime" was spontaneous or poverty driven: In many cases, it was carried out by groups that were well organized, well financed, and well armed.[8]

The responses to this epidemic of common crime in postwar Guatemala came to pose serious challenges to peace accord implementation. Although the accords called for internal security functions to be carried out by the new civilian police, such a force of 20,000 would not be fully constituted until the end of 1999 (see below). For the interim, the "security vacuum" became an excuse for preserving a dominant army role in policing. In response to public pressure (coming not only from citizens in general but also from CACIF, with its members determined to continue having army protection for their property and against kidnappings), the government determined that the army should participate in internal security jointly with the PNC. In practice, the "joint" PNC/army patrols were dominated by the army: As one international official put it, "the PNC supplies the vehicles, the army the personnel." In effect, then, the army was assigned to continue patrolling the streets in the cities at least until the end of 1999; and in the rural areas, a number of military bases and *destacamentos* (detachments, stations) previously closed (after December 1996) were reopened. As of the end of 1998, only four of the nineteen bases remained closed—in itself, a failure to comply with the accords and a prolongation of the counterinsurgent deployment scheme of "social control" over the population, as both MINUGUA and the URNG have charged (MINUGUA 1998b; URNG 1998a). In short, almost no lasting progress was made on redeployment of the armed forces in function of the new role envisioned for them in the peace accords.

Some argued in favor of army involvement in crime control because the alternatives were worse: Guardianes del Vecindario (a network of neighborhood patrol groups that was molded into an ultra-rightist political/ideological movement) and private security forces controlled by large property owners. In a number of rural communities, meanwhile, in the absence of effective public security, there were citizen lynchings of criminals or suspects. No one could argue that these were acceptable alternatives; but in Guatemala it was equally unacceptable to rely on the army for policing as the default solution.[9] As pointed out by Arévalo (1998b, 8), in the absence of any clear civilian policy, army involvement was carried out in a way that implied "re-operationalizing the military structures . . . at the heart of the counterinsurgency state." In short, there was a generalized tendency to revert to old ways of doing things—ineffective ways, as MINUGUA pointed out in its verification reports, given that the Guatemalan counterinsurgency army had no technical training to fight common crime or protect citizen security.[10] Furthermore, extensive reliance on the army patrols in urban centers and the reopening of military bases and stations in the countryside added to skepticism among pro-peace sectors of the population. The resources used to reopen military bases could have been redirected toward high-quality training and rapid deployment of the new civilian police, in keeping with the clear stipulations of the peace accords that public security should be a function of the police, not of the army as an institution.

To the extent that the accords permitted the president to call upon army personnel in *support* (not substitution) of police operations during this transition period, MINUGUA experts proposed that specific criteria be developed to determine the exceptional and temporary conditions under which soldiers could serve under the control of *civilian* authorities. In each of those cases, after consultation with the community affected, it could be spelled out in advance and made public how many soldiers were needed, for how long, and for what specific functions. In these situations, in short, army personnel would be held accountable to public regulations about their functioning and to a preestablished deadline for ending their support of the police. Compliance with these guidelines would be closely monitored and verified. Norms of this kind would have been key elements of a serious transition plan for public security designed not to undermine demilitarization, but such a plan never materialized in Guatemala.

The demilitarization provisions of the accords were also stretched or violated in other ways. The one-third reduction in size of the army was accomplished, but the reductions were made almost entirely among foot soldiers, leaving the officer corps virtually intact (except for those under criminal prosecution for corruption). Units such as the EMP and Military Intelligence that were to be reorganized or dismantled actually increased their power—according to one explanation, as part of the fallout from the early July 1997 changes in the army high command and, specifically, the promotion of (EMP chief) Espinosa. On paper, the mandated one-third reduction of the budget for the armed forces was carried out (allowing for inflation). However, the military budget remained secret (not subject to congressional supervision), and there were arguments coming from the Defense Ministry that the army's budget would have to be increased in absolute terms, as the necessary cost of "professionalization."

Meanwhile, under cover of the argument that it was still the only efficient institution, important sectors in the army officer corps continued to identify "new security threats" and to seek new missions. Tasks of "guarding the border" were stretched to require opening up a series of new military installations in border areas, supposedly charged with preventing drug trafficking across borders and piracy from archaeological sites. (Regarding the U.S. role in promoting army involvement in counternarcotics, see Chapter 5.) In short, the military continued to assert its prerogative in carrying out tasks that were not within its competence as defined in the peace accords and occupying spaces that should have come under the mandate of civilian institutions. And while seeking out new missions for itself, the army made virtually no move to carry out the accords' mandate to define a new "military doctrine" for a peacetime era, and the government undertook no civilian initiative toward that goal (Arévalo 1998b, 10).

Finally, the Arzú government continued to rely heavily on the EMP, making no moves and giving no timetable for its abolition and replacement, as stipulated in the accords.[11] Nor were any advances made on the reforms of intelligence—for example, substitution of military intelligence by a civilian unit based in the Interior Ministry, and the supervision of all intelligence activities by Congress. Ongoing press reports revealed that the EMP maintained a monopoly on intelligence operations that were supposed to be conducted by the PNC. Furthermore, units such as the EMP's "anti-kidnapping commando" were left to their own methods, without regard for violations of due process and other legal restrictions (as criticized by MINUGUA) and without being subordinated to civilian control. The above patterns continued despite public opinion polls indicating a clear desire that the EMP be abolished and the army restructured (*Inforpress Centroamericana* 1996, 102; *Prensa Libre*, Aug. 2, 1998).

In sum, as stated clearly by Arnault in presenting MINUGUA's third verification report on October 16, 1998, the demilitarization accord was the one that had suffered the most from the delays in the constitutional reforms. Despite some troop reductions, virtually all of the qualitative reforms—including the crucial redefinitions of *doctrina militar* (to replace the brutal counterinsurgency doctrine) and of the army's functions in a democratic, demilitarized society—were postponed to some indefinite future. The momentum for implementing one of the principal accords was being lost.

Militarization of the New Civilian National Police

The very creation of a new civilian police force designed to be the only armed body charged with protecting citizen security, and mandated to be autonomous from the army, was an advance. In theory, it finally put to rest the idea that the army should carry out internal security functions. Not surprisingly, then, the PNC was widely received with high hopes. Other positive elements in the restructuring of the police were the plans for new facilities, a new police academy, and significantly increased spending on police training, professionalization, and salaries.

Despite these advances toward formation of a professionalized police force, there were serious problems in the constitution and functioning of the PNC. As mentioned above, the law that was to serve as the basis for the PNC was sent to Congress unilaterally by the Arzú government in February 1997, without incorporating key elements of the demilitarization accord, without seeking input from civil society, or being approved by the Comisión de Acompañamiento. (In fact, the Comisión de Acompañamiento had not yet been constituted at the time.) Furthermore, the accord itself contained important lacunae, particularly regarding the PNC's composition: It did not explicitly exclude members of previously existing police units (which were militarized and untrained in police work), nor did it provide clear mechanisms to evaluate or retrain members of those units before allowing them to be "recycled" into the new PNC. The government promised to rectify these problems through subsequent modifications of the law. But when the Comisión de Acompañamiento recommended fourteen amendments, the government adopted some but not all of them; and even the changes that the government issued by executive decree had yet to be consolidated into law by Congress and become operative by the middle of 1999.

From the very beginning, the police reform was predicated upon "recycling" (presumably after thorough reeducation and training) up to 90 percent of the members of the old, corrupt National Police (PN), despite their lack of training to qualify for the PNC. Rather than insisting that basic standards be met, the PNC lowered the standards. Worse still, in violation of the accords and over the strong protests of MINUGUA, 40 ex-army officers—some of them posing as members of the old PN—including 22 ex-officials of the EMP, and 180 ex-PMA agents were accepted into the PNC. Meanwhile, provisions for recruiting and assuring the participation of indigenous community members (and hence, the multiethnic character of the police force) were inadequately and halfheartedly implemented, with the exception of one pilot project in the Ixil area. (On the above, see *Prensa Libre*, July 15, 1998; *Inforpress Centroamericana*, November 6, 1998).

In short, despite the transformation projected in the peace accords, on the ground, PNC forces remained subordinated to the army during the "transition" period. One critical assessment (WOLA 1998) identified army control at three levels: ex-military officials becoming officers in the PNC; the use of Military Intelligence in criminal investigations (and the postponement in creating a Directorate of Civilian Security and a civilian Advisory Council, as provided in the peace accords); and, as described above, use of army forces together with police in "joint patrols" dominated by army troops as a routine rather than exceptional practice in crime control.[12]

Finally, it must be noted that many aspects of the police reform plan were predicated on the constitutional reforms—not only those regarding public security and the PNC itself but also those affecting the army and the justice system. In addition to (and independent of) the delays in the constitutional reforms, there were problems stemming from the government's attitude of giving higher priority to quick results on crime control than to carrying out the drastic reforms needed for an effective civilian police force.[13]

Delays in Reforming the Justice System

After the signing of the peace accords and as stipulated in the accord on demilitarization/strengthening of civilian power, a multisectoral commission on strengthening of the justice system held extensive hearings throughout the country. Its first report (August 1997) made recommendations for the necessary constitutional reforms; in April 1998 the commission issued a comprehensive and far-reaching final report with recommendations on the steps to be taken. A plan for modernizing and professionalizing the judiciary also began to be implemented, and initial steps were taken in related areas of the justice system.

Despite widespread agreement in principle on a number of the major issues (since impunity had negative effects for virtually everyone)—in Guatemala, a clear advance over the past—actual change moved at a snail's pace. The impasse on constitutional reforms, combined with what MINUGUA (1998a, 13) identified as "institutional resistance to change," virtually assured that it would take a long time to eliminate the entrenched corruption and intimidation and to train personnel at different levels of the justice system. In the meantime, the government did not make it a priority to develop a long-range strategy adequate to the task or to resolve the most outrageous cases from the past involving impunity for human rights violators.

As a result, domestic and international human rights organizations, as well as MINUGUA and the URNG, continued to identify impunity and the serious structural weaknesses and resistances in the judicial system as major obstacles to full democratization and normalization of Guatemala's human rights situation. They also highlighted the deficiencies in fulfillment of such basic principles as an independent judiciary, separation of powers, and equal access of all citizens to the justice system. These criticisms, as well as numerous suggestions for solutions, were repeated by donor countries and agencies at the various Consultative Group (CG) meetings and were emphasized in an ongoing way in MINUGUA's periodic reports both on human rights and on implementation of the peace accords. In the end and underlying all else, the transformation of the justice system remained pending until after the final approval and implementation of the constitutional reforms. (On the above, see Pásara 1998; *Inforpress Centroamericana*, June 19, 1998, and Oct. 30, 1998).

Truth Commission:
"Memory of Silence," Memory of Genocide

Among the most controversial underlying issues was justice for victims of the war—as addressed in the Truth Commission accord of June 1994 and the partial amnesty provision of the December 1996 accord on reinsertion of the URNG. The Truth Commission or Historical Clarification Commission (CEH) was empowered neither to take judicial action nor even to name individually those responsible for human rights crimes. These weaknesses were compounded by the partial amnesty negotiated in December 1996, covering war-related crimes—excluding genocide, torture, and forced disappearances but not excluding extrajudicial killing. In practice, however, the worst fears of the human rights organizations that criticized these accords did not materialize: By mid-1999, although impunity continued, amnesty had not been granted to military officers on trial for human rights crimes—and especially not in the high-profile cases, such as Myrna Mack and Jorge Carpio, in which lawyers for the accused military officers attempted to gain such amnesty. Nevertheless, as in other post–civil war situations, including South Africa, the issues of justice and elimination of impunity remained among the most complex and threatened to haunt Guatemala for years to come.[14]

Meanwhile, the Truth Commission, after experiencing initial funding problems, was constituted and began functioning with great energy on July 31, 1997. The commission was headed by German human rights expert Dr. Christian Tomuschat, who had served as the UN's human rights monitor of Guatemala during the 1980s (named by the UN secretary general, following the suggestion of the government and the URNG). The other members were two moderate, highly respected Guatemalans, indigenous educator Otilia Lux de Cotí and ladino lawyer Alfredo Balsells Tojo (also proposed by the URNG and the government). During the next year, the CEH took testimony from 9,000 war victims, who massively came forward to tell their stories, as had been the case with the ODHA report; and in May 1998 the commission conducted a public forum to get input from civil society organizations. Testimony was even obtained from "binational" Guatemalan individuals and communities in the United States, as illustrated by one remarkable example (see Conclusion). The commission also sought written documentation from all domestic and foreign players in the war; although it received cooperation from the URNG and the U.S. government (see Chapter 5), it ran into stone walls in attempting to gain access to Guatemalan army documents. On numerous occasions, Tomuschat publicly expressed the commission's exasperation at this resistance—a criticism echoed also by MINUGUA (1998b). In typical old-speak discourse, the defense minister mockingly shrugged off the requests for information, claiming that the files from the crucial 1979–1982 period just happened to have been destroyed. Worse yet, this peacetime excuse for noncooperation turned out to be a lie.[15]

However, there was at least one significant break in the army's ranks during the summer of 1998. Colonel Otto Noack had been a Kaibil field commander during the worst years of the scorched-earth counterinsurgency war, followed by a career in military intelligence and as army spokesman. In July 1998, by this time commander of a military base, Noack stated to a Dutch radio station that in view of the deplorable excesses it had committed during the war, the army (and particularly those who had positions of command) should publicly accept their moral and juridical responsibility for those excesses. The army leadership responded by having Noack arrested and jailed for thirty days for having made these statements "without authorization." When Tomuschat visited him in jail and publicly suggested that others in the army should come forward, the government accused him of *extralimitando* (overstepping) his function. Symbolically, this incident revealed how brittle (and how absurd) were the army's defenses.

The CEH received an extension of its mandate in order to fully prepare its report, "Memory of Silence," which was finally presented on February 25, 1999, to a packed audience of 10,000. No one—not even the many interviewees, human rights groups, and analysts who had contributed to sections of the report—was prepared for the magnitude and scope of its findings. The packed audience repeatedly interrupted the presentation, particularly Tomuschat's speech (1999), with applause and calls for justice. Beyond dramatic, it was an emotionally electrifying experience for thousands of victims in the hall, who felt vindicated by this formal indictment of what everyone already knew intuitively. It was an afternoon of "pain, shame, and tears," an "anguishing surprise" (Hernández Pico 1999a).

It is beyond my scope here to present an in-depth analysis of the report (CEH 1999), as will doubtless be done by others. I summarize here only the highlights of its findings and recommendations. Among the most important findings were the following:

- The historical roots of the conflict were germane to understanding its excesses, and this involved many sectors of society beyond the two armed forces (URNG and army).
- Both the magnitude and proportionality of the crimes were even more overwhelming than previously known: The long debate over the number of people killed (see Chapter 1) was put to rest, as the CEH report (like the ODHA report before it) concluded that over 200,000 had been killed or "disappeared." State forces were found to have committed 626 massacres, the URNG 32. Of the total atrocities documented, 93 percent had been carried out by state security forces and paramilitary groups linked to them (e.g., PACs), the URNG was responsible for 3 percent, and the remaining 4 percent was carried out by unidentified "other" forces. (See Appendix to Chapter 6.)

- Although the entire war was marked by acts of extreme brutality and cruelty, it was primarily during the scorched-earth war in the indigenous highlands (1981–1983) that state forces committed acts of *genocide*, as defined by international law (indiscriminate extermination of indigenous groups *as such*, intentional elimination of entire Maya communities, including pregnant women and babies); furthermore, these massacres were not simple "excesses" but were carried out as part of state policies. This particular finding was central, given that genocide is excluded from the amnesty law and therefore, according to the CEH, can (should) be prosecuted.
- Rape and sadistic acts of sexual assault and torture against women were routine and systematic—part of soldiers' instructions; this was, according to an interview with Tomuschat, the most "frightening" part of the report.
- As with the army, responsibility for URNG atrocities was attributed to the top leadership and could not be dismissed as "excesses" or "errors" by rogue elements.
- The report made a strikingly harsh indictment of U.S. policy, beginning with its active involvement in developing the counterinsurgency capabilities and policies of the Guatemalan army during the 1960s. During the 1970s–1980s dirty war, the United States directly and indirectly supported some of the Guatemalan state's illegal operations; the United States was fully aware of the massacres and other atrocities during that period of scorched-earth warfare and did nothing to stop them.[16] The report also mentioned Cuban support for the guerrillas, but the difference in proportionality between the Cuban and U.S. roles was notable.

On the basis of its findings, and in order to begin meeting the massive challenges of reconciliation, the report made recommendations for major obligations to be undertaken by the two parties (beyond reemphasizing the commitments already in the peace accords):

- Both sides should formally accept responsibility for the atrocities determined in the report and seek forgiveness from their victims' families and from the Guatemalan people.
- The government should establish a National Reparation Program, to be (democratically) run for at least ten years; this program of individual and collective reparations to victims should include not only financial compensation and restoration of land but also programs of rehabilitation and restoration of dignity to

the victims—for example, through special ceremonies and monuments in their honor.

- As part of the above program, there should be a national search for the over 40,000 "disappeared" people, as well as recovery of their remains and determination of the whereabouts of those still alive (e.g., children); in addition, there should be an active program of finding and conducting exhumations of clandestine cemeteries.

- Active measures should be taken to promote a culture of tolerance and respect for human rights and cultural diversity, including multilingual dissemination of the contents of the CEH report and specific initiatives to strengthen the observance of human rights.

- Similarly, measures should be undertaken to strengthen democratic processes and to foster respect for traditional (indigenous) methods of conflict resolution.

- Most centrally, the president should establish a commission (accountable to him) to examine the conduct of individual army officials, with the objective of purging ("cleansing") the army and security force of officers guilty of human rights atrocities.

- The state should carry out the National Reconciliation Law's provision to investigate and bring to justice those responsible for crimes of genocide, torture, and forced disappearance, which are not eligible for amnesty.

- The EMP should be eliminated, all intelligence and all police functions should be civilianized and subject to civilian control, and military doctrine and curriculum should be reformed—all of these (and other measures) in keeping with the provisions in the demilitarization accord.

- In case the constitutional reforms limiting the role of the army in internal security matters were not approved in the (May 1999) referendum, Congress should take the necessary legislative actions to separate the functions of the army and the police, "limiting the participation of the army in the field of public security to an absolute minimum."

- In conjunction with the indigenous accord, there should be ongoing efforts to combat the racism that led to the genocide and special measures to ensure participation by indigenous peoples in all spheres of public activity.

- Congress should create a nonpartisan (multiparty) commission ("Foundation for Peace and Harmony"), charged with the task of following up and guaranteeing implementation of the recommendations in the CEH report.

The findings and recommendations of the report sparked a broad range of responses. Two weeks after the release of the report, President Clinton, during his (prescheduled) March 1999 trip to Guatemala, made the historic gesture of acknowledging responsibility for U.S. actions and complicity with human rights crimes and pledged that the United States should never again repeat such errors (see Chapter 5). For its part, on March 12, the URNG unconditionally sought forgiveness for atrocities it had committed and pledged to follow the commission's recommendations.

By stark contrast, the Guatemalan government responded—initially through a paid ad/statement in the newspapers and subsequently through formal statements rejecting specific CEH recommendations (e.g., the establishment of a follow-up commission and a commission to investigate army officers)—by arguing that most or all of the recommendations had already been implemented. Particularly in regard to those recommendations concerning demilitarization, the government asserted that the army was a "renovated" institution that had already transformed itself internally—referring no doubt to the 1996 purges (carried out against officers involved in corruption and drug trafficking, not against human rights violators). In addition, the government argued, since it had already asked forgiveness on the second anniversary of the peace accords (December 29, 1998), it had no obligation to make any further such statements in response to the CEH report. Finally, in late June 1999, Arzú rejected the CEH finding that genocide had occurred. The tone and wording of the government's statements conveyed the clear message that it did not even consider the CEH report to be an impartial or definitive interpretation of the war, but one interpretation among others that might emerge. Even sharper was the government's emphasis that the CEH recommendations were not binding.

Despite the government's refusal to implement its recommendations, the Truth Commission report dealt a serious moral blow to the peace resisters. CACIF and right-wing press commentators charged that the report was biased; the army itself repeatedly threatened to publish its own counterhistory. But the report's finding of genocide left the door open to prosecutions of responsible individuals through the normal legal mechanisms. Doubtless for this reason, the army closed ranks and hardened its overall stance after the release of the CEH report and the "Death Squad Dossier" in May 1999 (see Note 15). But this stance was in reality an attempt to mask the army's further delegitimation and structurally defensive position (as after the 1995 CIA scandal—see Chapter 5).

Additionally, in the popular imagination, the CEH report, together with the ODHA report, will go down in history as the authoritative *lectura* (interpretation) of the war. Reacting to the government's stance, a broad range of civil society organizations formed an *Instancia Multi-Institucional,* or multisector coalition, to maintain public pressure on the government and to insist that the report's recommendations were binding. Ironically, then, what had appeared to be the weakest aspect of the peace accords turned out to be one of the most significant. Some have even argued that the restriction of not naming names actually enabled the commission to be more devastating in its analysis and more forceful in its institutional recommendations.

Finally, the CEH report had international repercussions. For one thing, it was implicitly accepted by President Clinton and sparked the first U.S. acknowledgment of its role in Guatemala. Additionally, because of its forcefulness and the unspeakable crimes it revealed—and perhaps as well because it coincided with the international prosecution initiated against Chile's General Pinochet for torture and crimes against humanity—the CEH report had an impact in many corners of the world. Painful as its findings are, it will doubtless be remembered as one of the lasting contributions of Guatemala's peace process.

Indigenous Rights and Indigenous Protagonism

One of the most significant gains of the peace process was the 1995 Accord on Identity and Rights of Indigenous Peoples. As written, it went far beyond antidiscrimination protections of Guatemala's indigenous majority; if fully implemented, it would make profound reforms in the country's educational, judicial, and political systems. The initial phases of implementation saw the establishment and active functioning of *comisiones paritarias* (joint commissions with representatives of the government and indigenous organizations) and other indigenous "permanent commissions" to propose reforms on a broad range of issues: officialization of indigenous languages, educational reform, preservation of sacred places, rights of indigenous women, land for indigenous peoples, and "reform and participation" (i.e., reforms needed to create a multiethnic, multicultural state—e.g., at the municipal level and through the multilevel "development councils"). Some of these commissions completed their work and made recommendations within the first year, whereas others continued their work throughout 1998.

Indigenous organizations also took the initiative to gain implementation of relevant provisions in the other accords—for example, the recognition of indigenous customary law (the principle of juridical plurality in the accord affecting reform of the justice system) and land-related rights (in the accords on resettlement and socioeconomic issues). On another

In postwar Quetzaltenango, mixed messages on indigenous rights. A series of regional *consultas* for the entire highlands region, bringing together Maya and non-Maya organizations, provided opportunities for different social sectors to discuss accord implementation. (These photos were taken at a *consulta* of Maya priests and priestesses in 1997, hence the banner reading *"Espiritualidad Maya."*) But at the same time, Quetzaltenango's indigenous mayor, Rigoberto Quemé, elected in 1995, was the target of racist wall graffiti: "Fix up the streets for me, you Indian!"

front, as is discussed in more detail in Chapter 8, the various indigenous organizations grouped in COPMAGUA (Coordinadora de Organizaciones del Pueblo Maya de Guatemala—Coordinating Office of Organizations of the Maya People of Guatemala) worked intensively on proposals for the constitutional reforms, particularly regarding indigenous customary law.

Taken as a whole, the initiatives and ongoing work of these commissions to realize the great promise in the indigenous accord pointed toward a far-reaching reconceptualization of the state, and the process itself represented an impressive exercise in *concertación interétnica* (reaching interethnic agreement), as noted by MINUGUA director Arnault in October 1998. But the great challenge was to realize this potential in practice, even in the face of (predictable) resistances in the name of "preserving national unity." Actual on-the-ground progress was uneven; land conflicts and other conflicts between indigenous demands and state institutions continued. (For details, see MINUGUA 1998a and 1998b, HI 1998, CNEM 1998, Cojtí 1998, and Plant 1998.) In part, these conflicts expressed the discrepancies between the broader indigenous interpretations of the accord and the narrower governmental interpretations. These discrepancies were not surprising, given the centuries of systematic discrimination against indigenous peoples and of mutual distrust and antithetical relations between the ladino-dominated state and Guatemala's indigenous majority. Even more important, real progress on many of the indigenous issues awaited approval of the constitutional reforms.

But apart from these struggles over accord implementation, what stood out most strikingly was the level of energy, organization, and protagonism displayed by the indigenous organizations and coalitions in seizing the space for taking initiatives. Even before the signing of the final accords, they had come together to work out joint strategies and resolve differences of approach among themselves (e.g., within COPMAGUA). Differences of interpretation and strategy among and within organizations persisted during the period of accord implementation. Nevertheless, these organizations continued in a proactive mode, always one step ahead of everyone else, in their work through the various commissions and particularly in regard to the constitutional reforms (see Chapter 8).[17] They also took responsibility for dissemination of and education about the accords.

MINUGUA's third verification report, presented in October 1998, noted the progress made through COPMAGUA/SEPAZ efforts to reach consensus on the constitutional reforms and on rescheduling implementation of some provisions of the indigenous accord. In reality, however, the indigenous organizations remained critical of the government for interpreting the accords as minimally as possible—while the indigenous organizations consistently pushed for maximum gains from the peace accords overall. Even beyond the indigenous accord itself, COPMAGUA's commission on land rights developed proposals for mechanisms to resolve land conflicts and to deal with a broad range of land issues. To take another example, COPMAGUA and other indigenous organizations (e.g., the association of indigenous mayors) pushed to expand and further institutionalize the juridical rights of *comités cívicos,* which functioned independently of the traditional political parties, through the proposed electoral law reform (see *Alerta Legislativa,* July 1997).

It is no exaggeration, then, to say that the indigenous movements were among the great protagonists of peace accord implementation and, through their activism, converted such implementation into the patrimony of a large sector of the population. In contrast to the critics who asserted that the accords were nothing more than inter-elite pacts between the government and the URNG, the indigenous organizations made it their goal to prevent such an outcome. As discussed in Chapter 8, nowhere was this clearer than in their mobilizations for the constitutional reforms.

Appendix

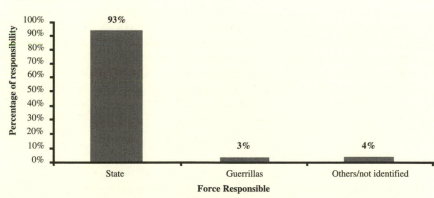

FIGURE 6.1   **Responsibility for Human Rights Violations and Acts of Violence, Guatemala (1962–1996)**

SOURCE: Comisión para el Esclarecimiento Histórico Report (February 1999).

The categorization of group responsibility yields the following data: 93% rests with the agents of the state, including in this category the Army, security forces, Civil Patrols, military commissioners, and death squads; 3% rests with the guerillas; the remaining 4% rests with the other unidentified armed groups, civilian elements, and other public officials.

Notes

1. Most obviously and seriously, the Mincho Affair further damaged the credibility of URNG leader Gaspar Ilom (Rodrigo Asturias), who was perceived as collaborating with the government in denying the existence of the assassinated ORPA militant. Beyond the specific problems of Asturias (who found it politically infeasible to return to Guatemala until September 1997), the repercussions of the affair affected the functioning of the URNG overall. Although the URNG's negotiating strategy from 1990 to 1996 had been brilliant overall, the Novella affair seriously weakened its hand in the final (operational) accords, and the Mincho sequel had the same effect during the first year of implementation. In short, the URNG paid a very heavy price, several times over, for this (still unexplained) debacle.

2. The URNG suffered two subsequent blows in 1998, the first being its worse-than-expected showing in the elections at the national university (Universidad de San Carlos), and the second being the death in September 1998 of EGP founder and leader and, after 1997, URNG secretary general Rolando Morán (Ricardo Ramírez).

3. In fact, this was more bluff than real threat, since any "revision" of MINUGUA's mandate would have been impossible without concurrence of the URNG—an unthinkable prospect. Nevertheless, on several occasions President Arzú and/or foreign minister Eduardo Stein took their case to UN headquarters in New York, accusing MINUGUA of overstepping its mandate. Perhaps one reason for such boldness on the government's part was the changing of the guard at the UN, with some recently arrived top officials being relatively unfamiliar with the byzantine and labyrinthian workings of the Guatemalan system. (However, it should also be remembered that the Guatemalan government had a history of such actions—e.g., getting rid of Francesc Vendrell as UN "observer" of the Guatemalan peace talks in the early 1990s. On the other hand, Jean Arnault's appointment as the new head of MINUGUA after having been moderator—an unusual departure from UN procedure—came at the request of the government and the URNG.) In any case, although New York was not perceived as taking any actions to strengthen MINUGUA's hand vis-à-vis the Guatemalan government in 1997, these dynamics had changed by the time of UN secretary general Kofi Annan's visit to Guatemala in July 1998.

4. One clear statement of this position was an op-ed article ("Para Qué Sirve MINUGUA?") published in the newspaper *elPeriódico* on August 19, 1997, written by Edgar Gutiérrez, one of Guatemala's most prominent human rights activists.

5. In regard to divisions within the government and within the PAN, virtually all of the members of the "Peace Cabinet"—presidential aide Gustavo Porras, foreign minister Eduardo Stein, SEPAZ head Raquel Zelaya, and SEPAZ adviser Ricardo Stein—were non-PAN government appointees and were always viewed as "outsiders" by the more conservative cabinet members and PAN party leaders. The more conservative wing of the PAN came to be known as the "Club de Paris"; this wing included, among others, Vice President Luis Flores, powerful congressional leader (later education minister) Arabella Castro, and Guatemala

City Mayor/1999 presidential candidate Oscar Berger. Many in this sector of the PAN had the closest alliances with conservatives in the private sector and the army; while uniting against the FRG for electoral purposes, they demonstrated very little loyalty to the peace agenda. As the 1999 elections approached, this sector of the PAN increased its influence, with Berger becoming the PAN candidate for president and choosing Castro as his running mate.

6. The promotion of Espinosa, combined with a temporary restitution of Col. Julio Alpírez, implicated in the DeVine and Bámaca murders (see Chapter 5), left the definite impression that the government was deliberately defying the international community and/or possibly catering to hard-line pressures. Two years later—in a typical example of the nontransparency of Guatemalan politics—it remained unclear to what extent this major army shake-up represented a change of line on peace accord implementation (mainly on demilitarization), a more subtle change of emphasis, an establishment of the president's personal authority over the armed forces, or a disguised capitulation by the president to certain forces in the army—even a "technical" coup of a new type. According to the official explanation, it was a simple routine "rotation" of command, combined with the president's decision to put an end to the rivalries between the previous two top officials. More plausible explanations revolved around the possibilities of a power struggle between the army hierarchy and the EMP, and/or Arzú's particular relation to Espinosa. (For a variety of interpretations of the 1997 changes, see *Inforpress Centroamericana*, July 11, 1997, *Cronica*, July 11, 1997, HI 1998, 62.) The debate resurfaced in June 1999, when Arzú promoted Espinosa to defense minister over loud objections from some top army sources, as well as human rights groups. (*Prensa Libre*, June 24, 1999; for a more detailed analysis, see *Inforpress Centroamericana*, July 2, 1999.)

7. Some analysts suggest that this situation is particularly typical of post–civil war conflicts. More than seven years after the signing of its peace accords, El Salvador today has been identified as the most violent society in the hemisphere. (See discussion in Conclusion.)

8. Guatemalan newspapers and other media cited considerable evidence that much of the violence was not spontaneous—indeed, that military, ex-military, or ex-paramilitary units or officers were directly linked to organized crime rings carrying out kidnappings, assassinations, car thefts, and other contraband operations.

9. At one point, there was even talk of taking such drastic measures as declaring a state of siege or reviving the PACs. (Either of the last two options, obviously, would imply a return to the darkest practices of the past and would be a total violation of the peace accords.) In regard to the continued existence or reconstitution of PACs and their ongoing links with the army, there have been contrasting views (see HI 1998, 28–29). The controversy resurfaced in the spring of 1999, when twelve ex-PAC members imprisoned for human rights abuses were freed from their Huehuetenango jail in a mob action, allegedly with a great deal of help from army members disguised as civilians (*Inforpress Centroamericana*, May 5, 1999). This incident also called attention to ongoing organizational links and control mechanisms exercised by units that were supposed to have been abolished.

10. The complex issue of public security was manipulated by peace resisters in yet other ways. Military Intelligence took advantage of the situation to allege

(without proof) the responsibility of ex-URNG members in criminal activities. In fact, it was notable that demobilized members of the URNG did not undertake such aggressive actions as the PMA, ex-PAC, and other military groups. Even more disturbing were overt charges (in the press) that conflicts and lynchings in rural areas were a result of "popular justice"; and this in turn was attributed in indigenous areas to *derecho consuetudinario* (indigenous customary law). In short, the peace resisters took advantage of the contradictions of the postwar situation to mount a massive offensive against change and to further destabilize the country during its most sensitive transition moments.

11. In the late spring of 1999, after the Truth Commission report and after the defeat of the constitutional reforms, and with only six months left in his presidency, Arzú made two contradictory moves regarding the EMP: On the one hand, he finally announced that the EMP would be abolished at the end of his term and its members reassigned to other army units. On the other hand, he named EMP-identified hard-liner Espinosa to be defense minister (see Note 6).

12. Critics have maintained that some of these problems resulted from the Guatemalan government's decision to adopt wholesale the militarized Spanish Guardia Civil model. The bilateral cooperation agreement between Guatemala and Spain was made even before the peace accords were signed. Other European Community sources, the United States, and MINUGUA worked more indirectly on projects related to police reform.

13. Regarding all of the above and other irregularities in the functioning of the PNC, see MINUGUA 1998a and 1998b; WOLA 1998; Garst 1997 and 1998; HI 1998; Instituto de Estudios Políticos, Económicos y Sociales (IPES) 1998b; and *Inforpress Centroamericana*, Nov. 6, 1998. For an excellent analysis of the problems (and the goals) of building a truly demilitarized and effective PNC, as well as a comparison with the Salvadoran experience, see Kincaid 2000. On the Salvadoran case, see also Costa 1995.

14. For a comparison of Guatemala's National Reconciliation Law with the blanket amnesty law in El Salvador, see Popkin 1996. For other comparisons and references to the comparative literature, see Conclusion, especially Notes 16 and 17.

15. According to a U.S. Defense Intelligence Agency "secret message" (Nov. 24, 1994, declassified and made public by the National Security Archive in 1999), in response to the growing 1994–1995 CIA/Bámaca scandal, "the [Guatemalan] army high command orders military personnel to destroy any 'incriminating evidence' . . . ." In addition to destruction of documents relevant to that case, "the army has designed a strategy to block future 'UN investigating commissions' from entering bases to examine army files." An op-ed by Archive analyst Kate Doyle (*New York Times,* Mar. 1, 1999) mentioned that orders for destruction of files came from then defense minister Mario Enríquez Morales. Note that such orders were given shortly after the signing of the Truth Commission accord in June 1994—indicating that, having signed the agreement, the army never had any intention of cooperating.

A new dimension of the army's resistance—peacetime resistance—to the CEH efforts surfaced in May 1999. On May 20, the Washington-based National Security Archive released a logbook from the Guatemalan army, "detailing the fate of scores of Guatemalan citizens who were 'disappeared' by security forces during the mid-1980s . . . The 54-page document was smuggled out of the Guatemalan army's intelligence files" and sold to the Archive for $2,000 in February 1999, only two days prior to release of the CEH report. Aside from its shocking contents, this document, which came to be known as the "Death-Squad Dossier," proved that the army had *not* destroyed all of its records and therefore was lying outright to the Truth Commission in saying it had no documents to turn over to the commission.

16. The finding of genocide cannot have come as any surprise to the United States. A secret CIA cable of February 1982, among those declassified in 1999, stated: "The well-documented belief by the army that the *entire* Ixil Indian population is pro-EGP has created a situation in which the army can be expected to give no quarter to combatants and non-combatants alike" (emphasis mine).

17. To cite only two specific examples: Indigenous organizations came together for a January 1998 national seminar to analyze the accords; the proceedings were published in CNEM 1998, in both Kaqchikel and Spanish. For the constitutional reforms, the indigenous "permanent national commission" on the constitutional reforms did impressive work to map out the legally complex terrain of these reforms (summarized in Comité para el Decenio del pueblo Maya 1998; see also Chapter 8).

High Hopes and Stark Realities: Obstacles to Sustainable Development

Guatemala's Window of Opportunity

The signing of the accord on socioeconomic issues in early May 1996, after a year of difficult negotiations, raised expectations for some limited but important advances. The accord had the stamp of approval of Guatemala's big business umbrella organization, CACIF, as expressed publicly the day after it was signed. From the other side, the accord initially sparked very strong criticisms from some popular organizations, and even dissension within the URNG. Eventually, however, after two months of discussions, the Assembly of Civil Society, which included the major labor unions as well as peasant and indigenous organizations, was persuaded to endorse the accord.

Furthermore, and no less important, the United Nations negotiators had been in close contact with the international financial institutions (IFIs)—the International Monetary Fund (IMF), World Bank (WB), and Inter-American Development Bank (IDB)—as well as the UN Development Program (UNDP) during the negotiation process. The goal was to avoid the "El Salvador problem"—the conflict between the UN-brokered peace agenda negotiated between the government and FMLN and the neoliberal economic agenda negotiated between the government and the IFIs. (See de Soto and del Castillo 1994; Boyce 1996, 1998.) In principle, then, all of the major players, both domestic and international, were in agreement in affirming the compromises embedded in the accord, and Guatemala stood to benefit through a process of collective learning from the problems in El Salvador.

Some international and domestic participants spoke optimistically of the accord as an experiment in sustainable development, combining social goals with economic growth. In their view, it embodied an alternative to stark neoliberal orthodoxy by positing a specific mix of state and market measures, with some indirect redistributive provisions. Without pretending to abolish Guatemala's gross social disparities (among the worst in the hemisphere), the accord did express a commitment to "integral human development," combined with sustainable productive investment. It did not promise to provide land or decent jobs outright, but in principle, it assumed governmental responsibility for the well-being of the population. It established a clear direction for socioeconomic policy, with an emphasis on creation of a functional state, increased social spending targets, and a more progressive tax system—although without specifying precisely which sectors would bear the primary burden of increased taxes.

The accord was also notable in its provisions for political participation and empowerment of the traditionally excluded sectors of society. Without spelling out precisely what sustainable development would mean in Guatemala, it established mechanisms by which a definition could presumably emerge from dialogues among all social, political, and cultural sectors of Guatemalan society. International agencies and donor governments saw the opportunity to encourage the development of new approaches for participation by historically marginalized groups and for conflict resolution and consensus-building among actors with very different interests in an extremely polarized society. Finally, as emerged from interviews with a variety of UN and IFI officials, despite the country's limited capacity to absorb or manage resources, Guatemala was also being seen as an experiment for the international community itself. For one thing, there was a deliberate attempt to avoid competition between the UN system agencies (UNDP as well as MINUGUA) and the IFIs and instead to establish a division of labor among them. And if the new approach could be made to work, some thought Guatemala could even become a point of reference for international involvement in other postwar situations in Latin America and the world.[1]

The concrete expression of these high hopes came two weeks after the signing of the final peace accords in December 1996. At the January 1997 Consultative Group meeting in Brussels, donor countries and the IFIs pledged nearly $2 billion in aid for implementing the accords. Specifically, of the total cost of implementing the peace accords during the next four years, the international community was promising to provide $1.9 billion—over 70 percent of the total—far more than had been thought possible anywhere and a strong show of confidence. These pledges were accompanied by a pledge from the Guatemalan government (in the socioeconomic accord) to raise the ratio of internal taxes to gross domestic product (GDP) from 8 percent to 12 percent by the year 2000. As noted above, a striking level of attention, energy, and resources was given to

Guatemala by the IFIs (particularly at a time when they were dealing with major crises in Asia and elsewhere) and by the donor governments. Apart from funding, Guatemala was already benefiting from substantial UN institutional expertise (e.g., through the UNDP, the UN High Commissioner for Refugees [UNHCR], and others) for projects linked to the peace accords.

A final factor in Guatemala's favor was that despite the astounding poverty levels, it was by no means a resource-poor country—as is shown later in this chapter. This being the case, the right set of policies could address the massive poverty. In the words of a top UN official, the problem in Guatemala "isn't lack of resources but poor governance." Indeed, the main policy issue in question was the age-old issue of taxes. But that policy issue could be resolved if the political will shown in the last phase of the negotiation process could be maintained for the implementation phase.

In sum, even though it could not eliminate Guatemalan poverty, the socioeconomic accord was viewed by some international and government officials as more than "the best under the circumstances." They saw it as an agreement that all Guatemalans could support; indeed, this would be necessary, since it involved sacrifice from all social sectors, as well as their empowerment. They also recognized the difficulties involved and the extremely high stakes. As one UN official expressed it to me in an interview,

> If this approach doesn't work, there will be a lot of soul-searching: the danger is that this is a fully comprehensive approach to peace-building, since the internal funding for all aspects of the peace accords is embedded in provisions for raising taxes; but the more comprehensive it is, the more chance that there will be one weak link. For this reason as well, everything rides on the socioeconomic accord: either a dent will be made in Guatemala's extreme poverty levels, or not. The scaffolding of a coalition against poverty is being created, but we'll see whether or not it holds up.

Tax (Non)Reform

In this analysis of the implementation of the socioeconomic accord, whose content is summarized in Chapter 3, I am highlighting the story of the tax (non)reform because it is paradigmatic: It reveals the systemic obstacles to change in Guatemala and the workings of a dysfunctional state. Increasing taxes was the linchpin in guaranteeing the viability of the peace accords as a whole—first, because it would provide the mechanism for internal financing of the hundreds of commitments in the accords; and second, because it was an implicit precondition for disbursement of the international funds promised at the Consultative Group meeting. However, tax reform has been one of the most difficult and hotly contested issues in Guatemala since the 1960s.[2]

From the beginning, international funders emphasized the importance of Guatemalan compliance with the target of increasing the tax to GDP ratio from just over 8 percent in 1996 to 12 percent by 2000, with an interim target of at least 10 percent by the end of 1998. Why, they argued, should taxpayers from other nations finance the development of a country whose private sector has historically refused to pay taxes? Guatemala's overall tax ratio was the lowest in the hemisphere—far below the average for developing countries as a whole (14 percent), and even further below the rest of Latin America, where some countries have ratios of up to 20 percent.[3] The accord did not specify precisely where the increase should come from, but it did endorse the principle of progressive taxation. Given that Guatemala's system is among Latin America's most regressive, it seemed logical that raising the income, business, and property taxes of the privileged would have to be a substantial part of the package.

The IFIs had been following the peace negotiations closely since 1994 and participated quietly in discussions with both sides and with the UN moderator about the socioeconomic accord (see details in Boyce 1998, 9). They became more deeply involved in planning for the postwar January 1997 Consultative Group (CG) meeting. Unlike many other Latin American countries, Guatemala was viewed as having been managed prudently and responsibly on macroeconomic issues during the past twenty to thirty years; yet this "prudence" was combined with many of the continent's lowest social indicators. Hence, the IFIs saw an opportunity to mobilize resources for peace accord implementation and poverty reduction without threatening macroeconomic stability, an ongoing concern expressed in structural adjustment measures. This opportunity was among the factors that inspired the IFIs to give disproportionate attention to Guatemala.

The $1.9 billion pledged at the CG meeting was viewed as important but only temporary;[4] the key would be gaining a solid basis in domestic funding through taxes and strengthening social programs for the long haul. This seemed logical since Guatemala was starting from such low levels of taxation and social spending. The IFIs and donor governments saw the need for a balance between direct taxes (expanding income and business taxes and eliminating the loopholes and exemptions) and indirect taxes (increasing the value-added sales tax (VAT), known as IVA in Guatemala, and excise taxes). Even the VAT, recently raised from 7 percent to 10 percent, was considered low. To implement this mix would require as broad a consensus as possible among Guatemala's social sectors (business, labor, peasants, and so on).

By the spring of 1997, the IMF thought it had reached an agreement with Guatemalan authorities that could be the basis for a stand-by arrangement—the only condition being fulfillment of the tax and social spending targets in the socioeconomic accord. In May 1997, the IMF issued a report with specific recommendations for achieving the desired targets (IMF 1997). At the same time, IMF executive director Michel Camdessus made a special visit to Guatemala—in itself, a striking gesture—and stated that this new approach was being tried for the first time in IMF history. But during the visit, he was told by government officials that it was not politically feasible to raise the VAT any more—or to meet targets simply by raising direct taxes. Camdessus responded to these expressions of gridlock with unusually strong public statements diagnosing *los siete mitos de los guatemaltecos*—the seven myths and excuses (in his words, *mentiras* or "lies") he encountered to avoid full compliance with the fiscal reforms mandated in the peace accords—for example, "no new taxes—we only need to improve tax collection"; "we are already overburdened and cannot afford to pay more taxes." (See chapter Appendix.)

An attempt to restore some momentum, worked out informally during the summer of 1997, was *recalendarización* (rescheduling), with Guatemalan government officials maintaining that they had been too optimistic in setting targets and asking the IMF and the international community to be "more flexible"—though the IMF, the UN, and others considered the 12 percent target to be extremely low. The IMF agreed to go along with the rescheduling if the rest of the international donor community accepted it. At the September 1997 mini–Consultative Group meeting in Antigua, Guatemala (an interim meeting to assess progress on the accords), the Guatemalan government insisted it was "trying"—even though its 1998 budget request to Congress did not reflect the 10 percent target for 1998. Donor countries and agencies criticized the lack of progress: U.S. and European officials, high-level World Bank functionaries, and the in-country directors of the UNDP and MINUGUA were among those who noted that Guatemala still had not presented a credible plan for significantly increasing tax revenues. Despite these criticisms, the September mini-CG resulted in the signing of loans and grants totaling $395 million, according to government figures (*Inforpress Centroamericana*, Sept. 19, 1997)—an attempt to encourage and to give Guatemala the benefit of the doubt.

During the winter of 1997–1998, the government moved to comply with its obligation to raise taxes, but the problems became more severe rather than being resolved. In late 1997, Congress passed a government-initiated property tax law (Impuesto Unico Sobre Inmuebles (IUSI)—Single Property Tax Act) that was significantly more progressive than its predecessor because it affected large property-owners much more than small or medium landowners. It was projected to collect revenues three times as high as under previous property tax laws (*Inforpress Centroamericana,* Dec. 12, 1997). But the government made virtually no effort to explain its provisions to the Guatemalan population (especially in rural areas) or to counter disinformation campaigns by opponents. As a result, the passage of IUSI sparked widespread protests in early 1998. The anti-IUSI campaign was organized/supported not only by the FRG and conservative "independents" in Congress but also by Nobel Laureate Rigoberta Menchú and a number of rural mayors—the latter on the grounds that it would benefit national rather than local government and violate municipal autonomy.[5] Beyond organizing aggressive street protests, the anti-IUSI forces took the law to the Constitutional Court to have it annulled. In response to widespread opposition, and in order to avoid violent outbreaks of social discontent, President Arzú stunned peace accord supporters on February 25, 1998, by having Congress repeal the reformed IUSI. Critics of this move maintained that he could have modified the law rather than withdrawing it. Beyond its fiscal ramifications, this capitulation signified a political defeat for the government, showing an inability or unwillingness to hold its ground regarding a cornerstone of the peace accords.

Well before the IUSI disaster, it had been clear that the government would not meet the tax targets specified in the socioeconomic accord. Even while assuming that IUSI would be implemented, MINUGUA's verification report of early 1998 (1998b) had expressed concern that the entire fiscal package did not meet the progressivity guidelines established in the accord and that the social spending targets were not being met.[6] After the government's retreat on IUSI, during the spring of 1998, the entire international donor community and MINUGUA pressured the government to come up with a new proposal that would avoid the projected *decline* in the tax ratio for 1999–2000 (see Note 6) and would meet the 12 percent target by the rescheduled date of 2002. Subsequently, they conveyed a clear message to the government that in view of its capitulation on tax reform, as well as the lack of progress on constitutional reforms and the unresolved Gerardi assassination of April 1998, the CG meeting scheduled for June 1998 would best be postponed until October, so that the government could come with something to show.

At the same time, during the late spring/early summer of 1998, the Comisión de Acompañamiento made a comprehensive new tax proposal to the government, generally relying on progressive measures to reach the tax goals. The commission included not only the URNG and other sectoral representatives but also prominent Guatemalan economist Gert Rosenthal, who had been head of the UN Economic Commission for Latin America for the previous decade; it was one of the only entities that

could make proposals to save the situation. Rather than accepting its proposal, however, the government did nothing—doubtless, by this time,
measuring any possible tax reform in terms of its effect on the 1999 elections. The only initiative was to appoint a new finance minister, Pedro
Miguel Lamport, an ex-president of CACIF who had been serving as ambassador to the United States and hence had good ties both with
Guatemala's economic elites and with the Washington-based IFIs. Presumably, his charge was to salvage the tax situation; by this time, however, the goal had shifted from meeting the original (already quite low)
accord targets to meeting the targets as rescheduled for 2002 and avoid-
ing the projected declines for 1999–2000. (See Note 6.)

By late summer/early fall 1998, in preparation for the postponed CG
meeting, the government had published a document that included the
following proposals: (1) developing a new version of IUSI, this time *con-
sensuado* (agreed-upon) with social sectors before being sent to Congress;
(2) maintaining but gradually reducing the Special Tax on Merchant and
Agricultural Enterprises or IEMA (a business tax) until 2002 ; and (3)
above all, counting on improved functioning of a new Superintendancy
of Tax Administration (SAT) in tax collection. Both civil society organizations and the URNG were skeptical about the ability of these measures to
meet the targets even in 2002—a rescheduling that had never even been
approved by the Comisión de Acompañamiento—and called on the government to add further progressive tax measures. MINUGUA was
equally skeptical and challenged the government's financial projections,
as well as its ability to meet the social spending targets mandated in the
peace accords.

In its pre-CG report of September 1998, the URNG proposed a process
designed to reach a national *pacto fiscal,* a multisectoral agreement on
further tax measures, involving civil society and emphasizing the accords' principle of progressive taxation. The government, eager to look
cooperative on the eve of the CG meeting, accepted the idea in exchange
for implicit acceptance by other players of the rescheduling. In spite of
all the criticisms (e.g., from MINUGUA)[7], the government once again
managed to come out of the CG with the international community's
stamp of approval for a rescheduling of tax targets—assuming that it
would make good on its commitment to a fiscal consensus with all sectors of civil society and to a series of concrete measures designed to reach
the target by 2002. However, plans were made to monitor progress at
two interim mini–CG meetings during 1999, in preparation for the next
full meeting in 2000.

Following the CG meeting, the government sought congressional approval for indefinite extension of the IEMA, a business tax, which would
permanently make the tax system more progressive. As a result of the

(predictable) opposition from CACIF and the FRG, it was extended for only five years. CACIF also demanded that Congress reject the principles inherent within IEMA; the FRG took up CACIF's demand in Congress, asserting demagogically that the measure would hurt small and medium producers. A second proposal, to modify the income tax (ISR) by eliminating deductions, was defeated in Congress.

By the end of 1998, then, virtually the only visible progress on this issue was creation of the SAT as an administrative unit—independent from the civil service and highly professional—to improve tax collection. Although this represented a step forward, by itself it could not begin to resolve the problem. The promise to begin a dialogue during the first half of 1999, to reach a *pacto fiscal* or agreement on tax measures that would be binding on the next government, was a further step in the right direction, but it was far too vague to be considered solid progress.[8] The sustainability of the peace process required a far-reaching effort to mobilize internal funds in order to strengthen long-range social programs and fulfill the hundreds of commitments in the peace accords. As MINUGUA warned in its October report (1998a, 7), if the government does not meet the 12 percent target by 2002, it "will have seriously failed to comply with the peace agreements and to take advantage of this historic opportunity to correct a profound distortion in Guatemala's socioeconomic policy."

Deconstructing the Debacle: Visible and Less Visible Players

From the perspective of 1999's stark realities, the idea that Guatemala might have served as an example of postconflict sustainable development appears somewhat absurd. Under the circumstances, it seems more appropriate to ask whether the tax (non)reform debacle was fated to happen or whether it could have been avoided. This question raises broader issues regarding the Guatemalan power structure, the relations among its main players, both visible and less visible, and their relation to a dysfunctional state.

The most visible players in the IUSI fiasco—those whose actions led the government to repeal IUSI—have been described above. The FRG's motivations were more or less clear: a combination of ideological opposition to increased taxes and a political stance of opposing/obstructing any government initiative. The "popular-sector" opponents (Rigoberta Menchú, the rural mayors and their followers) were in part acting on the basis of their own calculations about who stood to gain and lose by IUSI and in part being misinformed by the FRG's populist rhetoric. Above all, they were reacting to an inaccurate perception that IUSI would affect small and medium property owners as much as (hence, proportionately more than) large landowners.

And what about CACIF? (I refer here to the CACIF "position": What-ever the internal debates, it has generally closed ranks publicly on tax is-sues.) In the IUSI battle, CACIF kept a relatively low profile; after all, the FRG and others were carrying on the overt resistance battle, and there was no need for CACIF to get *visibly* involved. In addition, IUSI was less harmful to them than a significant increase in business taxes would have been. The role of CACIF emerges more clearly, however, if we focus not simply on IUSI but on the broader tax picture.

Indirect taxes account for over 75 percent of all taxes in Guatemala, di-rect taxes only 20–25 percent. Yet direct taxes actually declined as a pro-portion of government income between 1997 and 1998 (*Inforpress Cen-troamericana,* Oct. 23, 1998)—despite the fact that the socioeconomic accord mandated reform of this skewed tax structure through the institu-tion of specific measures leading to a globally *progressive* tax system. Al-though having presumably accepted this principle when the accord was signed, CACIF continued to resist the shift toward a more equitable tax structure—for example, by opposing a permanent business tax (IEMA). And in March 1999, the new president of CACIF proposed that in honor of the newly initiated SAT, business be granted a "fiscal amnesty" on un-paid back taxes! CACIF's general stance is, "We produce the wealth for Guatemala, so why should we have to pay taxes?"

By itself, perhaps, CACIF would not be able to maintain such a stance; but the dysfunctional state and the entire Guatemalan "system" has insti-tutionalized CACIF's ability to resist and obstruct change, particularly where its interests are most directly affected. For example, the 1985 Con-stitution establishes the absolute right of private property, with no men-tion of any "social function" of property; this was not changed by the peace accords. The system also ties the hands of the executive branch of government in raising taxes, since *all new taxes are subject to challenge in the Constitutional Court*—an anachronistic device taken advantage of by IUSI opponents in 1998, just as had been the case with every single attempt to reform Guatemala's tax structure in recent years (see Note 2).

This explains how CACIF has been able to operate within the protec-tions of a semifeudal system. But such a stance has costs and risks that would not be associated with a more enlightened view of the elites' self-interests. Why does CACIF see no benefit in modernizing the country so that it can participate more actively in the global economic system of the twenty-first century? Logically, that might be the stance of the "modern-izers" in CACIF. But overall, Guatemala's business elites appear to have a different view: By refusing to modernize the tax system, they may lose an intangible benefit (future opportunities), but nothing tangible (privilege and untaxed profits). They can buy time and force the government to play the game of waffling ("we're working on it") while resisting serious changes. As one international official put it, they see no reason to facilitate the government's ability to receive funds for social programs that they don't benefit from or support.[9]

One interpretation of this behavior is that CACIF's initial embrace of the socioeconomic accord was not a good faith action (except on the part of a few individuals) but rather, a gesture made with very little intention of compliance, once the war was over and there were no more disruptions or URNG "war taxes." But even as peace was being signed eight months later, CACIF publicly expressed an openness to the peace accords (e.g., in newspaper ads). This suggests that the upbeat, pro-peace dynamic at that time (which does not exist today) influenced the CACIF leadership to be more open. Even at that "modernizing moment," doubtless CACIF had its own reading of how the peace accords should be implemented. In any case, the Guatemalan ruling class is used to a level of "stability" and political power imposed by military force; it makes concessions only to the degree that it feels organized pressure from other social sectors.

Let us turn now to the most visible player: Why was the Arzú government unable or unwilling to take on the (quite predictable) battle on taxes, in which the government itself initially stood to gain a great deal without making major changes or sacrifices? Why didn't the government move on tax reform in January 1997, immediately following the Brussels CG meeting, a good two years before the 1999 election campaign made raising taxes so difficult? And why did it back down during the winter of 1997–1998, when IUSI had already been passed by Congress and there was still "political time" to recover from (or amend) an unpopular/misunderstood tax measure?

The answer is generally assumed to be some combination of political expediency and weakness in the face of pressures. When it comes to taxes, it seems almost every year in Guatemala is an election year. Furthermore, the PAN had an extremely credible argument, which was the electoral threat from the ultra-rightist FRG; armed with this specter, the PAN government was consistently able to gain a reluctant nod of approval from the international community, even in the face of progress backwards.

A second factor that undermined the PAN government stemmed from divisions within the PAN itself (see Chapter 6, especially Note 5, and Chapter 8); the "Club de Paris" within the PAN had very little commitment to the peace accords and doubtless limited the government's political choices on socioeconomic issues of the peace agenda. Another factor was the government's inability (whether by ineptitude or design) to project its goals in a convincing way so as to win over support from the less privileged sectors that objectively stood to gain from an improved tax system. Given the level of rising expectations generated by the peace accords among the popular sectors and their long-standing resentments against an entrenched system of privilege and exclusion, the government needed to develop a strategy to persuade the popular sectors as well as CACIF. Presenting them with the credible promise of a "peace dividend" would have been a necessary part of building a pro-peace coalition strong enough to overcome the institutional resistances. The peace accords provided a series of mechanisms for dialogue that the government could have used. Its failure to do so suggests that integrating the poor (mainly indigenous) majority of the population was a very low priority.

Finally, and perhaps most important, the government's attitude can be characterized as a kind of "peace opportunism," that is, being more than happy to accept international praise for the easier advances in compliance, but without being willing to fight for (or to pay any domestic political price for) the truly difficult advances. Of course the "Peace Cabinet" seriously embraced the goals of the accords. But other government officials were counting on the international community's generosity toward Guatemala to finance all the social projects (public education, health, and so forth) mandated by the peace accords to benefit the poor and indigenous—hence letting Guatemala's elites off the hook. No one in the government explicitly expressed such attitudes publicly or in my interviews with them; however, it is difficult to understand the government's contradictory behavior without positing that it implicitly operated out of some such mentality. This would explain why the government concluded that it could do without an IMF stand-by arrangement (see below)—meaning that it could muddle through without making any real tax reform. Muddling through in this way means maintaining a *dysfunctional* state—that is, a state designed to be weak, to deliver no services, to defend privilege, and to obstruct access except for the elites. The above pattern also explains why, on several occasions, government officials preferred to risk losing international support (assuming that they could win it back), rather than antagonize the domestic elites.

International Players and Peace Conditionality

None of the above-mentioned calculations by the Guatemalan government could have persisted for so long if they had not had at least some basis in reality; and this leads us to examine briefly the role of different players in the international community: the IFIs and the donor governments. What went wrong in Guatemala differs greatly from what had gone wrong in El Salvador. First, in hindsight, some players in the international community may have been overly optimistic in assuming that having endorsed the socioeconomic accord, Guatemala's elites would support its implementation—and/or that the government would be sufficiently committed to the peace agenda to persuade CACIF (an important part of the PAN's base) and stand up to the FRG in Congress. This was understandable enough, given the broad consensus in the international community in favor of helping to implement Guatemala's peace accords. And even those who were less optimistic and/or knew just how difficult the process would be viewed the accords as having opened a small window of opportunity to begin that process and to support social programs that would have been previously unthinkable.

Second, even though the international donors were pushing for more state spending on social programs and higher taxes, the case of Guatemala yields some interesting lessons about the specific stances of the IFIs and other international players and about "peace conditionality" more generally. The latter concept has been spelled out by Boyce (1998, 21): "the use of informal policy dialogue and/or formal performance criteria to tie access to external resources to specific steps by the recipient to implement peace accords and to consolidate peace processes"—in brief, conditioning assistance funds on peace accord compliance and using this leverage to create a balance more favorable to compliance among the various internal players.

Given the correlation of forces within Guatemala, as one IFI official put it, the government would have had to feel strong, unified, and consistent pressure from the IFIs and the donor governments. Instead of agreeing to the government's terms (rescheduling, lowering targets) and being super-flexible, giving Guatemala every benefit of the doubt, at some point the donors might have had to call the government's bluff. As one Guatemalan insider commented wryly after the October 1998 CG: "Things went well for the government—in fact, too well." Furthermore, the entire international donor community would have had to send a clear and consistent message. One rather imagines that the IFIs would have sent an extremely clear, consistent, and unified message if the Guatemalan government were refusing to privatize or repay the foreign debt, rather than refusing to tax the rich.

Several cases illustrate the point.[10] The IMF stood its ground in not finalizing a stand-by arrangement unless certain minimal conditions were met (i.e., meeting the tax targets). However, the IMF did not commit itself on the question of what *kinds* of taxes were needed and did not insist on meeting the progressivity guideline in the socioeconomic accord.[11] As one analyst put it, in the Guatemalan case, many IMF staff believed that distributional inequalities should be addressed through spending more than through progressive taxes. Hence, even at the October 1998 CG meeting, the IMF statement encouraged, among other measures, an increase in the VAT, which most affects consumers (IMF 1998). But this approach was politically problematic in postwar Guatemala, and it was rejected by Guatemala's own Comisión de Acompañamiento.

The World Bank (WB) consistently emphasized the need to increase Guatemala's domestic tax base and on occasion suggested that it would lower its lending if the government was not making progress on compliance with the socioeconomic accord (see Boyce 1998). But at the same time, in the face of delays and noncompliance by the Guatemalan government (e.g., just after its retreat on IUSI), the WB resident representative in Guatemala hastened to give reassurances that the Bank's funding for peace-related projects would not be affected. Like other international donors, the WB faced the classic dilemma of pressuring the government without punishing the beneficiaries of social projects for the government's noncompliance.

Meanwhile, the Inter-American Development Bank (IDB), which was the highest lender in Guatemala (its pledges came to $800 million), chaired the CG meetings and often set the tone for them. The IDB generally projected a softer line in Guatemala, seeming at times to proceed as if there were no problem; its public statements usually "accentuated the positive" and praised the government's (virtually imperceptible) steps forward. The IDB (as well as the WB) was willing to accept an increased VAT, rather than pushing for more progressive measures to meet tax targets (arguing that a VAT increase is more efficient and less regressive than an uncollected income tax—see Ruthrauff 1998, 11).

What kind of peace conditionality was exercised by the donor countries? The United States criticized Guatemala's refusal to make a serious tax reform (e.g., at the September 1997 mini-CG meeting and throughout 1998) but did not back up its criticisms by threatening to hold up any project funding. The United States was perceived by other international officials as being reluctant to pressure the PAN government, particularly before the 1999 election. By 1999, that would be a reasonable stance, given the very real threat from the FRG; but a strategic decision could have been made in 1997 or 1998 to use the leverage that Washington always had (and retains) in Guatemala. If sanctions and threats did not work, for example, or would raise the dilemma of withholding aid from the neediest sectors of the population, the United States might have induced the Guatemalan elites to cooperate through promises of increased trade and trade preferences.

The Europeans, especially the Nordic governments, generally took a stronger line—conveying their disapproval symbolically by signing virtually no loans at the September 1997 mini-CG meeting (in contrast with some other donors). By the October 1998 CG, they were relieved that the constitutional reforms had finally been approved by Congress (see Chapter 8); hence, they could give Guatemala the benefit of the doubt, encouraging advances and minimizing obstacles. Nevertheless, the Europeans made clear statements at that meeting that they would monitor closely and on an ongoing basis the creation of a more just and effective tax system, as a key indicator of the political will to comply with the accords.

More generally, the Guatemala experience of 1997–1998 reveals two contradictory trends in regard to peace conditionality. On the one hand, peace conditionality did function, if we judge by the concrete figures. Of the $1.9 billion pledged by the international community in January 1997—the general idea being to disburse around $460 million a year—only $320 million had been disbursed as of late 1998, with $926 million committed but undisbursed; in Guatemala, this was interpreted as a message regarding delays in compliance (*Inforpress Centroamericana*, Nov. 13, 1998; Fuentes and Carothers 1998, 277). But on the other hand, peace conditionality functioned only relatively, if we judge by Guatemala's conduct. In a sense, the Guatemalan government ended up using the international community (at CG meetings) more than being pressured by it. Of course, the international donors' desire to give Guatemala the benefit of the doubt is quite understandable. Who can fault them for wanting a success in Guatemala, Latin America's equivalent of a beautiful but long-battered woman finally trying to break free from her abusers?

The Guatemala experience also suggests some general reflections about peace conditionality. To begin with, some have opposed peace conditionality on the grounds that it interjects politics into financial decisions; but the absence of conditions is just as political as the attachment of conditions. Second, we can see clearly the limits of international leverage, particularly when the recipient is prepared to forgo an IMF stand-by arrangement, as in Guatemala.[12] Third, peace conditionality functions indirectly, not linearly as a club over the recipient's head at CG meetings. Rather than pressuring the government into doing something it does not want to do, it can work as a pre-CG prod or catalyst for the government to accomplish whatever it has already decided it wants to accomplish. In such cases, conditionality can be useful by strengthening the government's hand against resisters, in essence, tipping the balance among internal players. (An example of this, as well as a counter-example, is discussed in Chapter 8.) Peace conditionality is generally most useful when it strengthens internal forces committed to peace accord compliance.[13]

Land, Jobs, and Other
Socioeconomic Issues

In addition to taxation, the socioeconomic accord addresses numerous other issues. I shall not provide a systematic assessment of government compliance on each of these issues, as several other reports have done quite comprehensively (e.g., MINUGUA 1998a and its annex on the socioeconomic accord; URNG 1998a; HI 1998). For the purposes of this book, the above account of the tax reform battles may be taken as an indicator of the stances of the major players and the complex dynamics among them. An additional prominent actor on other issues (especially land) that I shall discuss briefly has been the organized indigenous/popular component of civil society, as represented by their organizations and NGOs, both inside and outside the ASC.

Let us begin with social spending. According to World Bank and CEPAL figures, Guatemala has the lowest rate of social spending in Latin America—both as a percentage of GDP and on a per capita basis (under $50 per capita, as compared with $400 in Costa Rica). As of the mid-1990s, spending on health and education was less than 2 percent and 3 percent of GDP respectively. Education and health were two of the main areas prioritized in the accord, with each slated for a 50 percent increase in government expenditures in relation to GDP, while the military budget was to be cut back significantly. In its third verification report, based on preliminary information from the government, MINUGUA (1998a) noted some progress in spending on both education and health. However, MINUGUA warned that real progress could not be sustained without the tax reforms as a source of revenue, nor without maintaining an active and appropriate government presence/performance in these areas. The latter issue was a reminder that in the Guatemalan case, state "modernization" and "restructuring" should be measured in terms of effective performance rather than streamlining or downsizing.

On the crucial issue of land, Guatemala's land tenure system is the most unequal in Latin America (WB 1995, 11). After the signing of peace, the main advances were made in establishing multisector commissions (including a *comisión paritaria* on land, as stipulated in the indigenous accord) to discuss and hammer out the specifics of accord implementation. Furthermore, within the framework of a market-oriented modernization of land tenure—by no means a land reform in the older sense—the accord mandated creation of some new institutions. Most notable among these was the Fondo de Tierras (Land Trust Fund) that would make certain categories of land available to peasants at low prices (see details in Chapter 3). After a long and difficult battle, the law structuring the fund was finally approved in May 1999, on the eve of a CG meeting. Other measures projected in the accord included a national land survey and registry, protection of indigenous communal lands, and a tax on unused land. But these were only the most initial steps, and although some consensus was achieved about creating new institutions, there were no mechanisms for internal financing, leading once again to an overreliance on international funds. The URNG and MINUGUA reports of September/October 1998, as well as other studies (e.g., Hernández 1998), all concluded that the progress made was glaringly insufficient, considering the magnitude of the problem. MINUGUA officials stressed the importance of developing a comprehensive and integral rural development policy.

As a result of the above (unresolved) situation—the persistence of an inadequate land-titling system, combined with rising expectations about what peace could bring—land conflicts continued after the end of the war. Despite the creation of commissions to resolve these disputes, real solutions would necessarily be long-range and expensive. Meanwhile, the government exacerbated the level of violence associated with land disputes through forcible evictions of peasants involved in land occupations. In this always-sensitive area, then, peace brought more new conflicts than conflict resolution, particularly in areas affecting the indigenous population.

Equally as significant as landlessness has been the continuing scarcity of decent jobs in both countryside and city. This has been expressed in the alarmingly high rate of unemployment and underemployment: Less than one-third of the workforce holds formal, stable jobs paid at the minimum-wage level or higher, with such benefits as health coverage. The most recent UNDP figures (1998, 57) show a decline in formal employment from 31.6 percent in 1990 to 27.4 percent in 1996. (Not surprisingly, then, only 27 percent of the economically active population lives above the poverty level). The absence of any strategy for generating jobs was partly a consequence of the lack of a comprehensive rural development plan; according to one UN official, this affected 400,000 families (2.4 million people) living at the bare subsistence level in the countryside. These figures were bound to worsen in the wake of Hurricane Mitch (fall 1998), which in Guatemala took its worst toll on rural jobs. One inevitable result has been ever-increasing migration to the cities (where there is also no strategy for job creation)—and frequently, migration abroad.

These issues were never addressed in the socioeconomic accord—in part, because CACIF regarded job creation as the domain (even "contribution") of the private sector, while all other parties accepted a somewhat reductionist or limited approach to land-related issues. A comprehensive rural development strategy would have included job creation and would have been part of a global development strategy for both countryside and city. Although it is common to think of Guatemala as still primarily rural, the population has become nearly half urban (counting only the two largest cities—Guatemala City at 35 percent, Quetzaltenango at 11 percent—not to mention Los Angeles at around 5 percent). And although primary attention must be focused in the countryside, where poverty is worst, fundamental problems such as job creation cannot be addressed by separating out rural from urban.[14] To mention only the most visible indicators, rural and urban sites are integrally connected through internal migration circuits as well as links in production processes.

The failure of the socioeconomic accord to address explictly the issues of investment and employment is one of the main reasons why people's daily lives have not improved directly as a result of the accords. In the longer range, this is symptomatic of the absence of any coherent mechanism for creating a stronger internal market in the economy, that is, a larger internal population with purchasing power. Meanwhile, privatization is cutting jobs in the public sector. In short, the ongoing lack of economic opportunity for a majority of working Guatemalans is a major reason why the accords have not been more actively defended by those who could be beneficiaries. It also has destabilizing consequences that range from increased migration, both domestically and internationally, to increased social violence and common crime. The latter, as discussed in Chapter 6, has undermined even the political gains for democracy by raising the temptation to do things in the old way: Use the army to repress social unrest.

Prognosis: Dysfunctional Development

Guatemala is at a crossroads, facing a choice between two very different development routes, one more appropriate to the nineteenth century, one to the twenty-first. How viable is the current path, that is, maintaining the old power structures for as long as possible? Technically, it may be viable in the sense that no apocalyptical collapse is on the horizon. However, it is in no way "sustainable" (much less a model for sustainable development) and has some very dysfunctional consequences.

The backdrop for all of the above is Guatemala's structural situation of poverty and inequity. Guatemala is by no means the poorest country in Latin America: It is in the "middle" group (in the World Bank's categorization of forty-four "middle-income/lower-middle-income" countries). Within that group, however, it has the highest incidence of poverty when compared with countries whose populations have a similar level of purchasing power. According to the most recent available data, in the 1990s, Guatemala has had one of Latin America's highest poverty rates, with 80–90 percent of the population living in poverty (figures vary) and up to 75 percent living in extreme poverty (that is, without access to the *canasta básica*, unable to afford a basic minimum diet). These figures are even more extreme in relation to the indigenous population and women. A 1998 UNDP study on poverty among Guatemala's Mayas revealed that only 10.5 percent of the indigenous population lives above the poverty level, in contrast with 26 percent of the ladino population (cited in *Prensa Libre*, Oct. 13, 1998). According to World Bank figures, Guatemala is also one of the three Latin American countries with the greatest disparities between rich and poor, and within the middle-income group, the third most unequal in the world (cited in *Inforpress Centroamericana*, Nov. 6, 1998). Also within the middle-income group, Guatemala ranks far below the median on literacy and access to health services. According to the UNDP's Human Development Index, Guatemala has fallen significantly since 1990—out of 175 countries, from #100 in 1990 to #117 in 1997; in Latin America, only Nicaragua and Haiti are lower (UNDP figures, cited by Hernández Pico 1997b).[15]

This objectively alarming situation is compounded in postwar Guatemala by the fact that the peace accords raised popular expectations for a peace dividend that would improve the quality of people's lives—but without developing the capacity to meet those rising expectations. The peace accords and the international enthusiasm they inspired provided a historic opportunity for change, but the magnitude of the obstacles is overwhelming. Certainly, the Guatemalan economy will continue to function even if much of the aid pledged does not materialize—but at a considerable cost. Never again will the conditions be as favorable as they have been in the late 1990s. The argument sometimes heard in Guatemala, that the next government can pick up where this one leaves off, is not necessarily valid; the next government is likely to feel less committed to the peace agenda than the government that negotiated the peace. Furthermore, it is unlikely that the extraordinary generosity of the international community, based on the signing of the peace accords, will last beyond the year 2000; for the medium and long run, Guatemala's social programs will have less financial support from the international community. Doubtless, Guatemala's elites do not think they need to make a serious effort to fulfill social goals. However, the scenario of maintaining the status quo would certainly lead to increased land and labor conflicts, crime and ungovernability. Ultimately, such instabilities could have negative economic consequences (less investment). And in the absence of other solutions (above all, decent jobs in Guatemala), people vote with their feet. As is discussed in the Conclusion, migration to the United States has become an inevitable grassroots response to unsustainable development in Guatemala.

What is the alternative scenario for the coming years? In theory, there is still an (ever-smaller) window of opportunity for the government to take a risk on a "peace dividend" strategy, including a reasonably progressive tax reform, in time for the full CG meeting scheduled for 2000. Particularly if agreement is reached on a *pacto fiscal*, such a strategy would doubtless be rewarded by the international community. Domestically, spring and summer 1999 opinion polls show that economic issues, especially jobs, have become the most important (surpassing "security"). Given the electoral context, this could conceivably make all parties rethink their economic programs—although that possibility seems ever more remote except for the electoral Left. Perhaps a new government will have the energy to take new initiatives and/or will be under pressure to do so. Indeed, the experience from the Arzú government is that on those occasions when it acted decisively (e.g., a proactive peace negotiation strategy, the initial purges in the armed forces), it came out ahead.[16]

The broader irony is that the socioeconomic accord, particularly its tax reform mandate, was designed to strengthen and modernize an archaic state, to make it functional—not necessarily "statist" or interventionist in the traditional sense, but no longer the exclusive preserve of the privileged. Instead, the Guatemalan state has remained dysfunctional, particularly in regard to the tax (non)reform, and hence incapable of—in fact, an obstacle to—implementing a strategy for sustainable development. The modernizers who designed the peace accords with such care hoped to open the door to a new future through constitutional and tax reforms, and together with their international supporters, they have made extraordinary efforts to implement these reforms. But as of mid-1999, the best-case scenario is agonizingly slow progress; the worst case would be a slow, also agonizing death of the peace process.

Appendix

Guatemala's "Seven Myths"

In May 1997, Michel Camdessus, executive director of the International Monetary Fund (IMF), visited Guatemala to meet with government officials. He spent much of his time urging Guatemalans to comply with the tax increases agreed to in the socioeconomic accord. In a press conference, Camdessus criticized what he called the "Seven Myths of the Guatemalans"—the excuses (mentiras, or "lies," as he called them) he encountered to avoid compliance with the accord. The myths and his rebuttals were reproduced in the Guatemalan daily, Siglo Veintiuno (May 27, 1997), as follows:

- "Closing our borders and giving more protection to national industry will be enough to improve the country." Mentira. With globalization, any country that closes its borders loses out. All members of the IMF that have opened their borders have been successful.
- "It is possible to grow, with a little pain, if there is more inflation, and a little unbacked currency emission." Mentira. It would be a flash in the pan, because soon the growth would slow and there would be more inflation, which would punish the poorest sectors of the population.
- "The country is already overburdened and cannot afford to pay more taxes." Mentira. Guatemala's neighbors, who are even poorer, have a higher ratio of taxation. The majority of countries in Latin America have tax ratios of 14%, 17%, 20%, and even 21% [of gross domestic product].

- "There's no need to increase taxes, since improving tax collection will be enough." *Mentira*. It's important to improve tax collection, but the tax ratio must be increased.
- "Let others pay taxes but not me." *Mentira*. Everyone must pay taxes, in proportion to what they are able to pay. The rich want the sales tax increased but not the income tax, while the unions want the opposite. A "cocktail" of direct and indirect taxes must be formulated, but everyone must pay.
- "Even if it's not possible to increase the tax ratio, international aid will arrive anyway." *Mentira*. The international community is willing to cooperate with Guatemala, as long as the Guatemalans themselves make their own best efforts.
- "The government will be able to resolve the situation on its own." *Mentira*. The participation of all Guatemalans is necessary in order to resolve the country's problems. With the peace accords, quite a bit has been done, but there is still much left to do.

Notes

1. Guatemalan foreign minister Eduardo Stein stated after meeting with UN secretary general Kofi Annan in June 1997 that in spite of the country's well-known "institutional difficulties" and rigidities, Guatemala could be a testing ground in the field where UN agencies could put into practice new forms of collaboration, cooperation, and project execution (*Prensa Libre*, June 17, 1997).

2. For details on the tax battles involving the government and the private sector since the 1960s, see Jonas 1991, 59, 155–56, 168–69, 178. The use of the Constitutional Court to block new taxes since the 1980s is summarized in *Inforpress Centroamericana*, Mar. 6, 1998.

3. During the negotiations, the URNG's initial proposal was for a 17 percent tax ratio; its backup proposal of 14 percent was supported by the IMF (Boyce 1998, 11). The final target of 12 percent was regarded as far too low by both the IMF and the URNG (Camdessus, quoted in the Guatemalan press, May 27, 1997). The Arzú government's chronicle of the negotiations claims that raising the tax ratio was the government's initiative (GG 1997c, 33–34); however, the December 1995 "Documento Consolidado," a summary of where the socioeconomic accord negotiations stood at the end of the de León Carpio term, indicated (p. 46) that the tax targets under discussion ranged from 12 to 14 percent by 1998 (not 12 percent by 2000 or 2002).

4. Regarding the figure of $1.9 billion (one study cites an even higher figure of $2.47 billion—see Fuentes and Carothers 1998, 275): This figure is symbolically important but not totally precise; it does not represent entirely "new" funds pledged at the CG meeting, but rather a mixture of funds already in the pipeline for ongoing projects and new funds specifically tied to peace accord implementation.

5. Popular opposition was also attributed to generalized distrust of the central government and a fear that local governments would bear the principal burden and blame for raised property taxes.

6. According to IFI and MINUGUA calculations, the tax ratio was expected to increase from 8.5–9 percent in 1997 (largely a result of the temporary indirect Solidarity Tax) to at most 9.7 percent by the end of 1998, falling short of the initial 10 percent target. (The government had previously acknowledged that it could not meet the 10 percent target in 1998.) Worse yet, the tax ratio was slated to *decline* in 1999 and 2000, largely as a result of the fact that the commercial and agricultural enterprise tax would be deductible from income tax, beginning in mid-1999—a scenario that would seriously threaten the financial sustainability of peace accord implementation. (See MINUGUA 1998b, 8.)

7. MINUGUA's third verification report (1998a, 7), released just before the CG meeting, concluded that the tax ratio was falling far short of the target for 1998, could be expected to decline in 1999 and 2000, and would not even reach the 12 percent target for 2002.

8. By March 1999, a commission of five highly respected Guatemalan professionals and experts was set up to prepare the multisector discussions of the *pacto fiscal*. The commission held preliminary meetings in different areas of the country, as well as with different sectors and political parties; the goals were to define the agenda and to come up with a preliminary discussion document and a methodology for the negotiations that would take place after a new government took office in 2000. The mandate for these discussions went beyond tax measures per se to include broader aspects of fiscal policy as a whole. In the view of one commission member, such an approach should have been adopted from the beginning. Meanwhile, it was hoped that the process could have a favorable impact for the 1999 presidential election.

9. For examples of CACIF resistance to peace accord implementation on political issues, see Chapter 6 (e.g., on use of the army for internal security) and Chapter 8 (on the constitutional reforms).

10. The following assessments are based on statements issued by the various agencies, generally around the time of CG meetings, as well as on interviews and the secondary sources cited in the text.

11. From his interviews, Boyce (1998, 11–12)—confirmed by my own interviews and in documents—noted differences in emphasis between Camdessus's stance during his May 1997 visit and that of some IMF staff subsequently. Although Camdessus held to the 12 percent target, some IMF staff were more "flexible" about the targets, and by the time of the October 1998 CG meeting, the IMF team said that they expected Guatemala to reach only a 10.2–10.5 percent tax ratio by 2002 (IMF 1998). In addition, staff members were more interested in a VAT increase as the mechanism, whereas Camdessus had stated that it should be a "cocktail" or mix of measures to be determined by Guatemalans—see Appendix to this chapter.

12. Some analysts have suggested that the international community could have promoted creative ideas to cut through traditional impasses; for example, if some IFI officials supported VAT increases, they could make this politically palatable to the majority of Guatemalans by heavily emphasizing luxury taxes on imports (Boyce 1998).

13. A more detailed and extensive summary of lessons about peace conditionality based on the Guatemalan experience has been developed by experts Fuentes

and Carothers (1998, 290–311). Even in the case of Guatemala, they argue, where there exists a synthesis between peace and economic conditionalities (itself a novel and positive situation), its effectiveness can be limited by a number of factors: (1) especially when the accords have not been accepted by powerful sectors of society, peace conditionality can be challenged by those sectors (even within the government) as "imposing external priorities"; because of widespread hypersensitivity to outside influences, the government may then use such reactions to strengthen its own resistance or foot-dragging on compliance; (2) threats of withholding resources for noncompliance are less credible because of the diversity of external funders; (3) coordination among donors (hence, sending a unified message) is more difficult because there are different kinds of donors; some institutions have a long-range relationship with Guatemala (WB, IDB), whereas others are more conjunctural (including MINUGUA, and even the IMF) or more politicized by bilateral interests (donor governments); (4) more extreme measures such as trade sanctions can be used only in very dire circumstances (e.g., Guatemala's 1993 *Serranazo*).

But Fuentes and Carothers also see positive lessons from the Guatemalan experience: (1) CG meetings provide a good occasion to monitor and denounce noncompliance; (2) when MINUGUA (as verifier) and the IMF are in agreement and working together (i.e., the same "condition," accord compliance), the combination can have a very positive effect—hence the contrast between Guatemala and El Salvador; (3) the most effective strategy by international donors is to use their leverage not directly but to strengthen the internal supporters of the peace accords—particularly, in the Guatemalan case, to create mechanisms to strengthen social beneficiaries of the accords. In any case, this leverage may be most effectively exercised not by withholding funds but by continuing them while pointing out the areas of noncompliance; at the same time, funds can be channeled preferentially to strengthen pro-peace forces and especially to strengthen the proactive capabilities of civil society organizations representing historically marginalized social sectors.

14. The comprehensive UNDP studies (e.g., UNDP 1998) point out that Guatemala has a strikingly high percentage (52 percent) of its labor force in the countryside. But this can also be read as emphasizing the lack of real jobs in the urban areas. Another study (IDEA 1998, 263) emphasizes that the search for solutions should avoid an "agrarian fundamentalism," that is, strategies that tie rural Guatemalans exclusively to the land, rather than viewing the land as a "platform" to open new opportunities of various kinds in an integral rural development strategy.

15. For a more complete statistical profile, see documents such as UNDP 1998 and 1999; WB 1995; IDEA 1998; annual CEPAL reports; statistics available in the early 1990s are compiled in Jonas 1991, 177–180.

16. Closely related to the issues of political will discussed above are issues of the government's capabilities to carry out change. UNDP and World Bank analysts, among others, have noted that a major problem of public investment in Guatemala is the weakness of public administration and trained human resources to implement projects.

8

The Hijacking of the Constitutional Reforms

Underlying most of the delays and detours in the implementation of the peace accords on political issues, as traced in Chapter 6, was a far more serious problem: There was no legal basis for changing the role of the army or the judicial system or for fully realizing indigenous rights until the constitutional reforms were in place. Those reforms were the linchpin of the entire peace process because they could remove the legal and political bases for the peace resisters' arguments that the accords were only conjunctural agreements between the Arzú government and the URNG. Furthermore, those reforms could unblock, assure, and consolidate change in the most crucial areas of the accords. (Regarding the content of the constitutional reforms, primarily in the areas of indigenous rights and strengthening civilian power, especially in the army and judicial system, see Chapter 3.) It is worth recounting here the convoluted story of the constitutional reforms not only because of their centrality to the accords as a whole but also because the story, like that of the tax (non)reform, is paradigmatic regarding what can (and generally does) go wrong in Guatemala.

The First Hijack Attempt

Formally, the Arzú government complied with its obligations by presenting proposals for constitutional reforms to Congress in May 1997. Since the PAN also held a majority in Congress, it should have been relatively easy, together with the other pro-peace forces (minimally, the FDNG), to steer these reforms through Congress—even though they required approval by a two-thirds majority (at least 54 votes)—by the deadline of the end of 1997, as stipulated in the Timetable. In Guatemala, however, nothing is ever easy. The government made a convincing argument that it had to develop a strategy for reaching consensus with opposition parties in Congress (mainly the FRG) in order to broaden the legitimacy of the reforms and to prevent those parties from sabotaging them later in the game, during the referendum.

Initially, the Legislative Commission of the Congress began discussing the reforms in August 1997. No sooner had the discussion begun when other proposals, some of them unrelated to the peace accords, were submitted for discussion. The head of the PAN congressional delegation and president of Congress then announced the creation of a new "Instancia Multipartidaria" (IM) or Multiparty Forum, with representation for all political parties in Congress, to discuss the proposals; the ostensible purpose was to reach a consensus with other parties, so that the reforms could be unanimously approved. Immediately after formation of the IM, opposition parties began insisting that its proposals should be binding on the Congress as a whole; despite the dubious legal nature or political viability of that stipulation, the PAN congressional leadership accepted it (although they subsequently denied having accepted it). Meanwhile, the FRG and other rightist forces tried to block the reforms tactically by insisting on the need for a full-fledged National Constituent Assembly (ANC)—a proposal that would have meant sure death for the reforms.[1]

From the very beginning, then, the constitutional reforms fell hostage to interparty and intraparty political maneuvers and skirmishes. For the next nine months, the reforms disappeared from public view into the IM swamp. In these murky waters, significant constitutional reforms that could consolidate the peace process were mixed with proposals by the political parties that were more marginally related or unrelated to the peace accords but served partisan purposes. Rather than facilitating consensus about the reform process, the IM became a place where the constitutional reforms were sent to die. Some critics dubbed it the "Instancia Multi-Porquería."[2]

Who was responsible for this first hijack attempt? On the surface, the most obstructionist force was the rightist FRG. The FRG had always been ideologically opposed to the peace accords, dating back to before the signing of the accords. During the Arzú government, in addition, the FRG defined its function as the principal opposition party in Congress as obstructing any progress for which the PAN could take credit. This politically motivated self-definition was crucial in holding up the constitutional reforms (and tax reforms—see Chapter 7) that were the pillars of the peace accords. But none of this stopped the FRG from using the debate over constitutional reforms to push its own agenda: annulment of the constitutional provisions that prevented its leader, Efraín Ríos Montt (who had led the 1982 military coup), from being a presidential candidate once again. Aside from the FRG, peace resisters and peace opportunists were hiding out in the ranks of several other opposition parties, with the notable exception of the FDNG.

Whether by design or ineptitude, whether as a result of internal divisions, weak leadership, or all of the above, the government party, PAN, was also responsible for problems at several key moments. On the one hand, PAN leaders could claim credit for the advances; after all, the Arzú government had done its part by sending the package to Congress and attempting to gain support from other political parties. But on the other hand, some sectors of the PAN (including its congressional leaders) had their own conservative agendas, which had little to do with the peace agenda. (See Note 5 in Chapter 6.) Finally, the PAN as a whole and the PAN government became a less effective force for peace following the tax reform debacle of February 1998 (see Chapter 7); also by this time, all else was subordinated to the 1999 election.

It was not until May 1998 that the government and the PAN congressional bloc, facing the prospect of a June Consultative Group (CG) meeting without having made any progress, took decisive actions to advance the reforms. First, they determined that the pro–Ríos Montt articles would not be included—doubtless, payback for FRG sabotage of the government's tax reform in February. Second, they dissolved the IM and returned discussion of the reforms to Congress as a whole. Finally, they sent their proposals to Congress, prioritizing those reforms stemming directly from the peace accords. The government pushed the reforms in its package part of the way through the cumbersome approval process, but Congress took a summer recess without having finalized the reforms. Largely for this reason and because of the setback on tax reform, the URNG refused to go to the CG meeting scheduled for June 1998; for the same reasons, the international community also urged that the CG meeting be postponed until October 1998. Even after Congress reconvened in August 1998, the approval process took three more endless months of maneuvers and contortions on a daily basis. By this time, there was a much larger package of reforms to be approved, going beyond those most central to the peace accords and many of them containing legal problems.

At this point as well, several major issues reemerged center-stage to be negotiated between COPMAGUA and the PAN. From the earliest days of the congressional discussion in 1997, COPMAGUA (with the necessary 5,000 signatures) had submitted proposals giving a broader interpretation than the government proposals to extending indigenous rights regarding land, officialization of indigenous languages, and indigenous *derecho consuetudinario* or customary law, as mandated in the peace accords and in Convention 169. (The 1985 Constitution recognized exclusively the authority of the national legal system.) The entire discussion of *derecho consuetudinario* had aroused opposition from the Right and more reluctance than enthusiasm from government/SEPAZ officials, who feared that this issue could block the entire package of reforms. The COPMAGUA proposals would make customary law *part of* Guatemalan jurisprudence, rather than subordinate to it.[3] In mid-September 1998, with the deadline of the October CG hanging over them, COPMAGUA (with support from the FDNG in Congress) and the PAN reached an agreement, with compromises on wording from both sides. This cleared the way for approval of the entire package of reforms by the necessary two-thirds congressional vote in mid-October, despite the abstention of the FRG. By this time, the package had mushroomed from the original thirteen reforms mandated by the peace accords to fifty (thirty-seven added in by the political parties in Congress, some unrelated to the peace accords). Thus, the first hurdle was cleared less than a week before the previously postponed CG meeting, doubtless in response to the pressures from the international community as well as domestic civil society organizations.[4]

In his October 16, 1998, speech presenting the third verification report, MINUGUA director Jean Arnault highlighted the historic significance of the long-awaited congressional approval of the constitutional reforms. Aside from the import of their specific contents for Guatemala, given the multiple delays in accord implementation during 1998, he hoped this would relaunch and unblock the whole peace process. In addition, he pointed out, their approval preempted the argument that the peace process was simply a deal between the government and the URNG; as a result of the prolonged process of their adoption in Congress, fundamental aspects of the accords could now be regarded as a national pact—to be consolidated by the referendum, which would show that "the peace agenda is the agenda of all Guatemalans." On the other hand and for the same reasons, the innumerable delays in their approval had caused a deterioration in the situation and significantly increased public distrust of political institutions.

Aside from demonstrating the endlessly convoluted and byzantine nature of Guatemalan politics, this tale of the first attempted hijacking is instructive regarding the agendas of different political forces. While the PAN was prone to tailor the specific language of the reforms to its particular assessment of what could (or should) be approved, some of the political opposition forces masked their opposition to the reforms in purist posturing. Some claimed, for example, that this was such an important exercise in democracy that it should take as long as needed. Others insisted that the process was "unrepresentative" because it did not involve the entire citizenry and hence should be submitted to a National Constituent Assembly (see Note 1). Once the reforms had been approved in Congress, many of these same forces were among those urging further postponement of the referendum and/or a "No" vote. Meanwhile, the whole process had become hopelessly distanced from the project of political-social transformation represented by the constitutional reforms in the accords.

The fact that it was only international pressure in the context of the upcoming CG meeting that finally broke the logjam in Congress demonstrated once again a pattern that had been clear during the peace negotiations: The internal pro-peace coalition in Guatemala was not strong enough *by itself* to counter the pressures from the peace resisters; hence, even on the issues that it was committed to, the government needed pressure from the international community. Furthermore, the roller-coaster dynamics of this process were very much reminiscent of the peace accord negotiations. In fact, this entire saga left no doubt that this second stage of the peace negotiations was every bit as contested as the six years prior to December 29, 1996.

Mitch, "Calamity," and the Appearance of the Dinosaurs

When he awoke, the dinosaur was still there.

—Augusto Monterroso[5]

Less than a week after the Guatemalan government triumphantly took the constitutional reforms to the CG meeting, Central America was hit by the most devastating hurricane in its recent history. Guatemala was spared some of the natural disasters that befell Honduras and Nicaragua. Nevertheless, Hurricane Mitch became the basis for the next postponement of the constitutional reforms—a juxtaposition that could happen, I am convinced, only in Guatemala. The Arzú government, while presumably committed to rapid approval of the reforms, decided to declare a "state of calamity" in Guatemala—nominally to prevent looting. But the declaration also contained restrictions on constitutional guarantees and political liberties. No such restrictions had been imposed in the other (much harder hit) Central American countries, and they were widely perceived as unnecessary for keeping order in Guatemala.[6] The extension of these restrictions through the end of December was criticized by MINUGUA, sparking the usual complaint by the Guatemalan government that MINUGUA was overstepping its mandate.

Meanwhile, since the political restrictions that accompanied this "state of calamity" prohibited the Supreme Electoral Tribunal (TSE) from calling the referendum, two crucial months were lost—a truly calamitous delay, given the upcoming general elections, and a sign that the government made peace a very low priority. By the time the "state of calamity" expired at the end of 1998, the referendum had to be called for the spring of 1999, an election year in which everything was bound to be politicized. This also assured that the reforms, if approved, would not take effect until 2000, under the new government. Even before the "state of calamity," the opponents of the reforms had begun their campaign, arguing that the reforms had been approved by a process that was both undemocratic and unconstitutional. The opponents lining up their guns against the reforms included, in addition to the FRG, several conservative "constitutionalist" organizations: CEDECON (Center for the Defense of the Constitution), Liga Pro-Patria (Pro-Fatherland League), and Asociación de Dignatarios de la Nación (Association of Dignitaries of the Nation). They were joined by the right-wing Protestant fundamentalist Alianza Evangélica (Evangelical Alliance), Guardianes del Vecindario (Neighborhood Guardians— see Chapter 6), Asociación de Amigos del País (Friends of the Country Association), and other organizations that opposed the accords or viewed them as political (nonbinding) accords.[7] Their cause was championed by a series of conservative columnists in nearly every national newspaper. This marked the appearance of the "Dinosaurs": Presenting themselves as the guardians of the Constitution and the legal order, they intended to keep Guatemala exactly as it had been for decades. In regard to the peace accords, then, they were the natural allies of the latter-day centaurs and peace resisters.

Even before the "state of calamity" was lifted on December 30, the opponents took their case to the Constitutional Court (CC) to have the entire package of reforms declared unconstitutional. While claiming to base their case on procedural grounds (that Congress had followed incorrect procedures), their real target was the content of the reforms. On January 5, 1999, the CC provisionally suspended the referendum. While the CC deliberated a final resolution, the activist advocates of the reforms—COPMAGUA, the FDNG, the URNG, the ASC (in particular its women's sector), progressive labor union federations, student and religious organizations—held demonstrations and blocked highways in various parts of the country in order to pressure the CC to deliver a ruling favorable to the reforms. (Some pro-reform advocates later questioned the choice of these tactics as unnecessarily divisive and alienating to ordinary citizens trying to get somewhere on the highways.) During this period, the political polarization concerning the reforms intensified and evolved into a classic Left-Right split. Heating up the environment were rumors that some sectors of the PAN and of the government actually wanted to postpone the referendum, to hold it simultaneously with the general elections later in 1999, for their own political gain.

In early February, the CC ruled in favor of the CEDECON's procedural suit of unconstitutionality, sending the reforms back to Congress.[8] After further deliberations, Congress reformulated the fifty reforms into four thematic blocs of questions concerning, respectively (1) the (re)definition of the Nation and social rights (recognition of indigenous peoples and their rights); (2) reforms to the legislative branch; (3) reforms to the executive branch (primarily the army); and (4) reforms to the judicial branch.

This finally cleared to road for the Supreme Electoral Tribunal (TSE) to set a date (May 16) for the vote. However, the legal wrangling resurfaced later: At several points the TSE prohibited various branches of the government (executive, Congress *as such*) from publicizing the content of the reforms, allegedly to avoid partisanship (urging a "Sí"(yes) vote); technically, they were allowed to resume educational activities but without taking a position.[9] In any case, shortly after the campaign began, some began to fear that the complexity of the package of fifty reforms, combined with the relatively short period of time (seventy-six days) available for educating the electorate about their content, could so confuse voters as to lead to the defeat of the reforms. In the reformulation of the questions into four blocs, the few original peace accord reforms were totally mixed in with the thirty-seven others added on by political parties in Congress.

Dinosaurs and Centaurs Block
La Avenida de las Reformas

"La Avenida de las Reformas: Abstencionismo amenaza consulta popular" ("Abstentionism threatens referendum"). So read the headline (*Prensa Libre*, Apr. 18, 1999), making a play on words: Avenida La Reforma is the main boulevard leading from downtown Guatemala City to the wealthier neighborhoods.

Once the campaign got under way, it became clear that pro-reform educational activities were much less of a problem than the lack of them (except by MINUGUA, which did extensive dissemination). The two major political parties, the PAN and the FRG—the latter by early April having switched to the "Sí" camp for opportunistic political reasons—did very little to actually promote the reforms. Many believed, in fact, that both were engaging in a kind of "double discourse," with their formal "Sí" masking indifference and internal divisions (PAN) or opposition (FRG). The only political parties that were unconditionally in favor of the reforms were the FDNG and the newly legalized URNG; but they were so confident that the reforms would pass and so busy with other activities that they did not set aside all else until after May 16. The main push for the Sí was conducted by the indigenous and popular organizations and by some parishes of the Catholic Church and progressive evangelical churches. During the campaign, the Sí picked up support from the Colegio de Abogados (Lawyers' Association) and a broad "Citizens for Sí" front, which included conservative/centrist figures such as ex-CACIF head Luis Reyes Mayén and ex-defense minister Julio Balconi, together with trade union and other popular leaders.

Far more coherently than the organizations favoring the reforms, the "No" forces massively escalated their campaign during the last three weeks. Millions of quetzales were invested in a television and press blitz against the reforms. *Less than a week before the referendum*, in an absurd (but typically Guatemalan) battle of legalisms among the Constitutional Court, the Supreme Electoral Tribunal, and the Supreme Court, the CC ruled in favor of an "unconstitutionality" suit by the Liga Pro-Patria. Although this action failed to postpone the referendum any further, several of the Dinosaurs made clear their intention to raise legal challenges to the content of the reforms if they were passed—particularly those concerning indigenous rights. Francisco Bianchi, a right-wing evangelist who had played a very prominent role in the Ríos Montt government of 1982–1983 and now headed a political party to the right of the FRG, stated that if the reforms were passed, he would campaign for president on a promise to convoke a Constituent Assembly to nullify the reforms. Some sources reported subterranean support for the No coming from army bases (*Inforpress Centroamericana*, May 28, 1999, quoting the Myrna Mack Foundation).

Two days before the vote, on the last day that campaigning was permitted, CACIF published a newspaper ad pronouncing its strong opposition to the reforms—ostensibly in defense of democracy (fifty reforms crafted into four blocs was a "violation of the people's will"). The CACIF ad also denounced "meddling" by international organisms.[10]

"Balkanization" and Other Myths

—What is the origin of the constitutional reforms?
   The origin was an illegal negotiation between public functionaries and guerrillas.
—What is the purpose of the reforms?
   To convert Guatemala into an indigenous state, marginalizing the non-indigenous population.
—What is the most important part?
   That it divides our citizens between indigenous and non-indigenous and gives the indigenous more rights than the other citizens have.
—Vote No.

—Liga Pro-Patria leaflet, May 14, 1999

So went the discourse of the No blitzkrieg: The Sí would "Balkanize" Guatemala (turn the country into "another Yugoslavia"), rekindle the war, turn over the country to Indians (or, alternatively, to the URNG), force everyone to learn obscure Mayan languages (rather than a modern second language like English), and replace the legal system with indigenous customary law. Teachers who spoke only Spanish would lose their jobs. Private property would be confiscated if located on Mayan "sacred sites." The reforms would convert Guatemala into a racist state (dominated by indigenous peoples); the redefinition as a multiethnic nation would violate the principle of equality by giving extra "privileges" to the indigenous population. And (from the evangelical churches) the reforms would permit exotic Mayan religions to take over and persecute good Christians. Vote No to ward off the anti-Christ and "the sign of the devil."

Dire predictions emerged from the newspaper columns and speeches of some of the most activist opponents. Well-known ultra-conservative Armando de la Torre emphasized the need to send a message to MINUGUA and other organisms of the international community to stop meddling in Guatemalan internal politics. Antonio Arenales (who had been one of the key players—the éminence grise—in COPAZ during the de León Carpio government and who was known to have very close ties to some sectors of the army) called the reforms a "monstrosity" and called for a full-fledged National Constituent Assembly (ANC). Other columnists warned that the reforms threatened such basic liberties as the free press—a gross distortion.

The mostly submerged theme of maintaining intact the functions of the army ("protector of the people") surfaced in indirect warnings—for example, that the reforms would convert the Constitution into the ideological program of the URNG. This was certainly a motivating factor in the minds of some of the anti-reform crusaders; however, no one was prepared to campaign openly on a pro-army theme, since all recent public opinion polls demonstrated the strong public desire for demilitarization (see Chapter 6) and the Truth Commission report was still fresh in the public mind. The army high command was intelligent enough to keep a low profile regarding the constitutional reforms. It is another question altogether why the Sí forces did not make a strong argument in favor of the demilitarization reforms.

Meanwhile, the political context surrounding the reforms became increasingly polarized. The spring of 1999 was marked by large popular mobilizations—at the presentation of the Truth Commission report (February 25), on the anniversary of the Gerardi assassination (April 25–26), and on May Day, the last with an openly pro-Sí message. The countermobilizations by centaur/dinosaur forces and their allies were less massive, but the messages they sent were chilling. On April 30, a mob liberated several ex-PAC members from their Huehuetenango jail, with participation by army personnel disguised as civilians; this suggested a subterranean existence or recomposition of the PACs. And three days before the vote itself, two important leaders of leftist and indigenous movements were assassinated: Roberto González, deputy director of the FDNG, who had been campaigning actively in the capital for the Sí, and seventy-one-year-old indigenous leader Juana Lucía ("Mama Lucía," accused in the 1980s of being a guerrilla) in Alta Verapaz.

Predictions and Results

Throughout this period, there were periodic public opinion polls regarding the constitutional reforms—virtually all showing a sizable preference for the Sí among the "informed" public, as shown in the following examples:

- August 2, 1998: A poll for *Prensa Libre* found 79 percent Sí, 20 percent No—and 89 percent in favor of recognizing Guatemala as multiethnic.
- November 17, 1998: A poll by CID/Gallup found among the 51 percent of those asked who knew about the vote, 37 percent Sí, 32 percent No (although only 9 percent said they would vote No—suggesting that the supporters of No would likely stay home).
- March 28, 1999: A poll by CID/Gallup found 17 percent Sí, 4 percent No; all the rest didn't know or were indifferent.
- April 18, 1999: A poll by Borge & Assoc. for MINUGUA found 64 percent Sí, 13 percent No, 23 percent "no response"; in addition, 60 percent of those polled believed the reforms would consolidate the peace process. The vote in favor of the reforms would be concentrated in the central and eastern part of the country and among those with a university education. The main threat was abstention. It was concluded from this poll, as well as previous ones, that there were very few voices for the No.
- Late April 1999: An unpublished poll for MINUGUA on all four referendum questions found 50 percent "don't know/no response," 30–37 percent Sí, 13–19 percent No (specific percentages varying by question).
- May 1999: In one Guatemala City poll conducted by the (anti-reform) newspaper *Siglo Veintiuno* during the last weeks, 86 of 100 people interviewed said they would vote, with 44 of them planning to vote No (*Washington Post*, May 17, 1999).

What stood out in all the polls, aside from the Sí/No, was the generalized lack of information and understanding. It was for this reason that the main fear, going into the May 16 referendum, was a high rate of abstention—at least 75 percent. Although it was still generally expected that the reforms would be approved by a narrow margin, in the last two weeks, the possibility of a victory for the No became much more real to close observers—particularly to those who had access to private government polls.

The actual vote on May 16 far surpassed the worst predictions. Less than 758,000 people—18.55 percent of Guatemala's (4.085 million) registered voters (11–13 percent of the voting age population)—went to the polls. Clearly, the main winner of this vote was abstention, with an overwhelming 81.45 percent of registered voters. Contrary to all the predictions, among those who voted, the No prevailed over the Sí by a margin of 55 to 45 percent of valid votes. The Sí won in most rural indigenous areas of the country, despite the difficulties of getting to the polls and the many other obstacles to voting; but numerically, the outcome was decided in Guatemala City.

Breakdowns of the vote, based on official information from the Supreme Electoral Tribunal (including the null/blank ballots as well as Sí and No) revealed some variations on the different questions. Of the four questions, the closest vote came on Question 1 regarding indigenous rights; it lost by 5 percent—43/48. Question 2, on legislative branch reform, lost by 15.5 percent—37.5/53. Question 3, on executive branch reform, including the role of the army, lost by 12.7 percent—39/51.7. Question 4, on judicial branch reform, lost by 7.5 percent—41.7/49.2.

Some aspects of the "geography" of the vote were startling (See map 8.1):

- First, the overall results virtually divided the country in two (most western and northern departments voted Sí; Guatemala City and environs, the eastern and southern coast departments voted No). The most striking case of support for the No in the indigenous highlands was Quetzaltenango, which contains Guatemala's second largest city.
- Most (but not all) indigenous departments—above all, those most affected by the civil war during the 1980s—inclined to the Sí and had higher than average participation rates; the department of Sololá had a 30 percent voter participation rate—much higher than the national average and higher than the 20 percent participation in the department containing Guatemala City. The decisiveness of this factor—having been affected by the war—explains the striking victory of the Sí in the primarily ladino department of Petén.
- The other striking and unpredicted result was the urban/rural split (urban areas voting for No, rural for Sí). Even in departments where the Sí prevailed, the No tended to win in the most

urbanized areas (department capitals); and although the No won with nearly 75 percent of valid votes in Guatemala City, it was 63 percent in the smaller surrounding municipalities of that department, and the Sí even won in its rural municipalities.

- The municipality with the highest participation was in Sololá, with 44.6 percent participation—a huge difference from the national norm of 18.55 percent; the lowest participation was in southeastern Jutiapa (3.3 percent).
- The vote made clear the overwhelming electoral primacy of Guatemala City: Excluding the vote in the municipality of Guatemala City (where nearly 75 percent voted No), the overall result (in the remaining 329 municipalities) would have favored the Sí on Questions 1 (indigenous rights) and 4 (justice system).[11]

Post-*Consulta* Postmortems

"No" to What? Major Factors in the Vote

"Guatemalans Turn Thumbs Down on Multiculturalism." Thus read the headline of the *Wall Street Journal* op-ed analysis (May 28, 1999), one of the few to appear in the U.S. press. In contrast to this simplistic headline (the article itself is not as reductionist), I shall try to present a more complex analysis that emerges from interviews and written materials (including the press) from Guatemala. The important starting point is to emphasize that the real winner of the referendum was not No but abstention; it was only among the 18.55 percent of registered voters participating that the No prevailed. *In total percentages, then, the results were 81.45 percent abstention, 9.4 percent No, 7.5 percent Sí, and 1.65 percent null and blank. If one considers additionally that 35–40 percent of those eligible to vote were not registered* (IDEA 1998, 5—higher than in the early 1990s), *the percentages (slightly over 6 percent for No, just under 5 percent for Sí, 1 percent null/blank) that so critically affected the future of the peace process become truly alarming.* One analyst (Hernández Pico 1999b) concluded that the results were "a legal vote but not a representative one." Hence, one must analyze not only why the No prevailed but also why abstention turned out to be even higher than predicted.

The Super-Organized Campaign for the No

The campaign for the No demonstrated remarkable strength, vehemence, and ideological cohesion, combined with multimillion quetzal financial

KEY

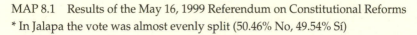

■ Sí (yes)
☐ No

MAP 8.1   Results of the May 16, 1999 Referendum on Constitutional Reforms

* In Jalapa the vote was almost evenly split (50.46% No, 49.54% Sí)

resources to spread disinformation—a task made much easier by the complexity of the reforms and the scarcity of solid information about them. The media (press, TV, radio) were the main public sources of information, and with a very few exceptions, they were heavily penetrated by publicity and columns for the No. The fact that urban centers (not only Guatemala City) tended to vote No, even in departments in which more rural surrounding municipalities voted for Sí, suggests that the Sí did best in areas outside the reach of the press and TV.

In some rural areas the No campaign worked through the Protestant fundamentalist churches, which, as one analysis pointed out, assured a "disciplined" vote. In other rural areas, organizations such as the Liga Pro-Patria followed the line from the capital, also with considerable discipline. In some areas, they drew on ex-PAC networks, which were galvanized to vote by the ultra-right Association of Military Veterans (IPES 1999)—and, many believe, with a good deal of help from military intelligence. In short, the "technicians of the No," as one well-informed, prominent Maya intellectual called them, worked methodically with opinion-makers and leaders around the country to create a climate of opinion against the reforms—as part of their timetable to delegitimate and ultimately to roll back the peace accords.

The vehemence of the No campaign was likely a response to the mid-April polls showing a significant victory for the Sí. In the last month, the No forces left no stone unturned, no quetzal unspent, no distortion untold in the media, no fear unexploited—including xenophobia (against the international community). It was, in the words of one analyst, an "ideological event" more than a political one. The crusadelike quality of the No campaign was striking: One (pro-reform) member of Congress said he had not felt such a polarized ideological climate since the 1954 overthrow of Arbenz; another analyst likened it to the "aggressive language of the Cold War." Indigenous leaders referred to it as "psychological warfare."

In speaking with people about the *consulta* experience two months later, I was struck by the "embeddedness" of the No campaign: It was deeply rooted in the workings of Guatemalan society, through small everyday circles of influence, and it showed a deep understanding of the social fabric of urban ladino Guatemala (across classes). I heard countless stories about why Guatemalan staff members at Friend country embassies and UN organizations, or maids (poor ladinos) working in people's houses, voted No. Many were influenced to vote No because they heard ominous warnings about the reforms from their pastors, their neighbors, their children (who were told at school that parents should vote No). Despite several university rectors' endorsements of the reforms, it was passed around student circles at the national university that students should vote No if they didn't want corrupt congressmen to earn higher salaries. These undercurrents were particularly effective in the capital, which had not fully felt the civil war since the 1980s and did not fully appreciate the peace.

Overall, by running an extremely intelligent as well as massive campaign, those who mobilized the "hard No" vote—the vote against the peace accords—were able to get many additional votes from "soft No" voters (those fed up with politicians—see below) and/or undecided voters, especially in Guatemala City. They pulled off a major feat in mobilizing No sympathizers to go out and vote No, rather than staying home as was predicted. Bianchi and others even used such arguments as the following: "If you're unsure or confused about the reforms, vote No," and (the ultimate doublespeak) "If you want peace, vote No."

The *Voto de Castigo* (Punishment Vote) Against the Politicians

The morning the results came out, FLACSO director René Poitevín analyzed the results as a rejection of the political class (the politicians and the mess they had made of the reforms in Congress) more than of the peace process itself (*Prensa Libre*, May 18, 1999). The noncredibility of the politicians rubbed off onto the reforms, since the major political parties were formally identified with the Sí. Several particulars are worth mentioning:

- The lack of transparency to the general public about what was being put together in Congress occurred in a climate where Congress was already delegitimized and distrusted. With the reforms (as had been the case with the IUSI tax reform), PAN's idea of "building consensus" was limited to the other political parties in Congress, with very little input from or dialogue with other sectors of society, aside from the negotiations with COPMAGUA. This fed a general sentiment that the whole process had not been democratic.
- The result of the congressional mélange (the mixing together of peace accord reforms with other items, in fact swamping the former with the latter) was total confusion on the part of voters, making it nearly impossible to be "informed." The great majority of voters, who had not managed the extraordinary feat of becoming informed, either stayed home or voted No. This was especially important as a source of abstention.
- Some measures added on in Congress sparked opposition to the reform package. First, some of the add-ons had legal problems or elements of unconstitutionality. Second, the mixing of the most

significant peace reforms with add-ons led some peace supporters to vote No because of the add-ons. In the most notable example, the mixing together, in Question 3, of the demilitarization reforms with reforms affecting municipal authority led Rigoberto
Quemé, the indigenous mayor of Quetzaltenango, to oppose the
reform, which was key in the victory of the No there. *Many analysts believe that the major peace accord reforms would have been approved if they been on the ballot alone.*

The Weak Campaign for the Sí

The pro-reform forces bear a heavy responsibility for not having carried
out an effective campaign—in effect, leaving the Sí an "orphan." The centrality of their failure is highlighted by postreferendum polls showing
that the main factor in the outcome was the lack of information (far more
than opposition to change) (*Prensa Libre*, June 18, 1999). Furthermore, the
lack of information left a space open for disinformation (*Prensa Libre*, May
19, 1999); as the Myrna Mack Foundation (1999) had warned, an unin-
formed public would not take risks and would tend to vote against
change. As analyzed by the Instituto de Estudios Políticos, Económicos y
Sociales (IPES 1999), the URNG's think tank, disinformation was well
used by the No campaign, and the Sí campaign was left on the defensive,
(belatedly) responding to it. Furthermore, "while the forces for the No
concentrated concepts and ideas in their attack, the forces for the Sí became dispersed in their information and explanations in the last stage of
the campaign."

Beyond these general factors, it is necessary to distinguish among three
different camps within the Sí forces: the politicians, particularly the PAN
and the FRG; the political Left; and indigenous and popular organizations.

The Politicians.   The two major political parties, the PAN and the FRG,
did virtually nothing to conduct a responsible campaign for the Sí, even
among their own followers. At best, given that the polls were showing a
victory for the Sí, they preferred to conserve their financial and political
capital for the presidential election in November; at worst, they were not
honestly interested in a victory for the Sí.

The FRG clearly engaged in double games throughout the entire
process. While having opposed the reforms from the start, having held
them up for months, and having then abstained in the final congressional
vote, the FRG leaders finally held a press conference to announce their
support for the Sí in early April 1999, when it appeared that the reforms
would win. This was also necessary to maintain support in indigenous
communities and to enhance the FRG's status with the international com-

munity as a credible contender for the presidency. At the same time, it was well known that FRG local leaders were organizing their followers to vote No or to "vote their conscience" and that some of the No forces had links to the FRG. Not surprisingly, the day after the defeat, the FRG vice-presidential candidate denied that the FRG had ever supported the Sí; in reality they had just urged people to vote. There is no reason to believe that the FRG ever really changed its earlier position of regarding the peace accords as nothing more than statements of "good intentions," as one FRG leader put it (*Siglo Veintiuno*, Aug. 24, 1998).

The case of the PAN (and the PAN government) is more complicated. Whereas some analysts conclude that the PAN was also engaging in a double game, others put more emphasis on the PAN's indifference ("apathy") toward the reforms and on the internal divisions within the PAN. It is clear that the PAN politicians did the minimum possible for the Sí— even less, some say, than the FRG during the last month. (This is confirmed by the resounding vote for the No in Guatemala City, historically the PAN's political base.) The PAN government, meanwhile, which was prohibited from carrying out a partisan campaign, essentially sat on its hands and did not go out of its way to publicize or explain the content of the reforms to voters (much less in languages other than Spanish). It simply was not a priority.

The PAN's ambiguity and internal divisions about the peace agenda also became clear through its conduct—beginning with the creation of the IM and culminating in the president's decision to declare an unnecessary "state of calamity" in November 1998. This held up the entire process for two months, which was disastrous, given the dynamic of the upcoming election, particularly when combined with the predicted legal challenges to the reform process. Four months were lost, interrupting the momentum for the Sí.

The Political Left. The leftist parties (the URNG and the FDNG) unconditionally supported the reforms but squandered the advantage that the Sí had demonstrated in all the polls. Rather than pressing their advantage, they allowed themselves to be lulled into complacency, in part, by those polls. After taking their victory for granted and underestimating their enemy, they had no backup plan for mobilizing their constituencies when the blitzkrieg by the Right began. In a sense, their triumphalism blinded them to the sophisticated war of images that the Right was waging, and by the time they recognized what was happening, it was too late. These attitudes may also have blinded them to another potential but unrealized advantage for the Sí: The Truth Commission report of late February had put some of their enemies on the defensive, but they did not recognize this opportunity to translate human rights sentiment into support for the Sí. A proactive educational campaign focusing on the crucial reforms for demilitarization and civilian control of the army might additionally have changed the focus of the entire campaign away from the racist offensive by the No forces.

In addition, the URNG and the FDNG were preparing for their own electoral campaigns, and the URNG was completing its legalization as a party. These activities became a higher priority than doing voter registration in rural areas, grassroots education, and massive GOTV (get-out-the-vote) on May 16, to compensate for the difficulties that their constituencies faced in getting to the polls. More broadly, as their own self-critical postmortems pointed out (e.g., IPES 1999; Molina 1999; FDNG International Bulletins—in addition to interviews), their strategy toward the referendum was more reactive than proactive. They took no educational initiatives, such as proposing televised debates. They failed to mobilize in time against the enemy of abstentionism or to recognize that it could lead to the defeat of the Sí. If they had foreseen this, they might have put more energy into mobilizing new voters from their own base. Above all, once they saw the blitzkrieg from the Right, they needed to get every Sí supporter to the polls. They were unable to create enthusiasm or momentum for the Sí among their own rank and file and mass organizations, much less to reach out to autonomous organizations and constituencies. As several URNG leaders acknowledged, "We never really led the campaign for the Sí."

The URNG and the FDNG did invest some energy in the Sí (although insufficient), and they participated in the demonstrations in January and February. But the politics of street protest does not translate into votes. Obviously, the parties of the Left did not have resources at anywhere near the level available to the major political parties; perhaps they were counting on the PAN to invest in the Sí, at least for its own partisan purposes. But, as seen in Chapters 6 and 7, they had just spent two years trying to force government compliance on other peace accord implementation issues. Long before the referendum—since the IUSI defeat of February 1998—things were going badly enough that they had no reason to entrust the fate of the constitutional reforms to the government or the PAN. Especially to the URNG, which had put the better part of eight years into the peace negotiations and accord implementation, it should have been obvious that the government/PAN would not make this a priority.

But beyond the critique of what the Left did (and mostly didn't do) for the *consulta*, this experience raised much more serious questions about its capabilities as a political force. The URNG and FDNG demonstrated an alarmingly low ability to mobilize a grassroots support base and to translate their social base into an electoral base—a task they would have to undertake in any case, in order to get support from new voters in the November 1999 elections. They could not and cannot rely on the "historic vote" (those accustomed to voting in the past): In 1995 that base voted nearly 90 percent for the PAN and the FRG, as compared with 8 percent for the FDNG. In sum, this was a new kind of battle for the Left, a battle of the transition period, which they did not know how to fight. Given the high levels of disenchantment with the current political spectrum, there is a huge potential space in Guatemalan politics for a center-left movement; but the existing Left has not yet been able to occupy that space.

Indigenous and Popular Organizations or "Social Left." From the very beginning, even while the reforms were still stuck in Congress,[12] the indigenous and popular organizations, primarily the Mayan groups in COPMAGUA, took the initiative to lobby for the reforms—and, when necessary, took to the streets (e.g., during January and February, when the CC was deliberating the suits brought by the Liga Pro-Patria and CEDECON). Overall, the indigenous organizations took more initiatives than any others and worked with local groups. Doubtless, the fact that these organizations mobilized intensively in the indigenous communities explains (1) the much higher vote for Sí on Question 1 (47/53) than on any of the others—even though this was also the main target of the crusade for the No, and (2) the higher participation rates (and vote for Sí), on all four questions in many rural indigenous or mixed areas (generally the areas that had been most affected by the war) than in other areas of the country; in these areas, they mobilized both Mayas and non-Mayas for the Sí. Nevertheless, as many Mayan leaders were the first to acknowledge, the campaign also revealed the serious limits of the Mayan organizations' representativity and of their capacity to mobilize a base for electoral politics, which was a new experience for them.[13]

Popular organizations in other sectors (trade unions, human rights, development, and student organizations) did less outreach for the Sí than would have been expected—in part, a measure of their priorities and their level of engagement with the peace accords, and in part a measure of their political weight by 1999 (as compared with the ASC years). One refreshing contrast was the activity by the more recently formed Women's Forum. Finally, it is worth mentioning that the Catholic Church, which in the past had been central in working with civil society organizations, has been weaker and less unified since the Gerardi assassination. For the *consulta*, it used its considerable resources to urge people to vote, but not systematically, nationwide to vote for the Sí—a marked contrast with the disciplined No campaign conducted by fundamentalist Protestant sects. In short, the *consulta* revealed the fault lines of the social Left; the ASC or a substitute for it will have to be reinvented.

Structural Factors, Beyond the *Consulta* Dynamics

Racism and Fear of the Mayan Population.   Especially in Guatemala City, racism was stoked by the No campaign, which played to the fears of the ladino population. Such racism has always been latent in Guatemala, and the No organizers were able to bring it out into the open through dire warnings that the reforms would turn the country over to the Mayan population and give them exclusive "privileges."[14]

Related to the above, although not totally attributable to *active* racism (anti-indigenous prejudice and behavior), was a structural aspect of the peace accords themselves: While the indigenous population gained new rights, the urban upper- and middle-class ladinos did not perceive themselves to have gained anything from the accords. Additionally, the fact that the accords brought no immediate socioeconomic improvement to people's lives made many working-class ladinos more open to anti-reform arguments and disinformation in the press. A final related factor is a general conservatism and fear of change that permeates many sectors of the urban ladino population in Guatemala. (As one analyst suggested to me, this same tendency to oppose change if it meant uncertainty had been a critical factor influencing the "fearful" urban middle and lower-middle classes to desert Arbenz forty-five years earlier.) These attitudes made them extremely susceptible to the kind of campaign being waged by the No forces, with their images of "social chaos" and division of Guatemala into two countries with two cultures.

Given these conditions, and given the vast disparity between the makeup of the population and the makeup of the voting population,[15] the most fundamental structural problem was the very requirement that the reforms be approved in a referendum. To make a rough analogy, if the federal Civil Rights bills of the mid-1960s United States had been submitted to a direct vote in Mississippi or Alabama, they would doubtless have been massively defeated.

Obstacles in the Electoral System.   The limited reach of the peace process in this case was largely a function of the limited reach of the political process overall. In many respects, Guatemala's electoral system seems designed to prevent people from voting rather than encouraging them. Major problems include the following:

- Voter registration rates are historically low and worsening. In the mid-1990s, over 35 percent of adults eligible to vote were not registered, and by 1999, this had reached 40 percent, the highest in Latin America and the second highest in the world (IDEA worldwide study in 1998, cited in *Prensa Libre,* Aug. 1, 1999); TSE officials claim nonregistration is "only" 25 percent.

- Abstention has been increasing among registered voters since the 1980s (see Chapter 4), especially in referendum votes. The previous referendum (January 1994) had a scant 16 percent turnout among registered voters.
- Reforms to the Electoral Law, as mandated in the peace accords, were defeated (or indefinitely postponed) in Congress because the PAN and the opposition parties were unable to reach agreement on them. (Many claim the PAN blocked them.) Among other things, these reforms would have corrected some of the historic obstacles to voting, especially in rural areas (e.g., very long distances between people's homes and their voting sites in municipal capitals, combined with lack of free transportation to the polls). In presidential/congressional elections, the political parties generally provide transportation for their supporters, but the referendum was not an election in which the parties chose to expend those resources.
- The system of voter registration needs reform. Under the current system, for example, workers who migrate from the indigenous highlands to do seasonal labor on the southern coast cannot vote during the months of harvest (including May) without making the long trip home.
- The system makes it much easier to confuse voters about complex issues than to educate them. Since most information comes from conservatively biased media (which, in this case, became vehicles for disinformation), the lack of anything like an impartial, universally available, multilingual voter information handbook can have decisive consequences.
- The electoral system makes it easy for conservative organizations like CEDECON to carry out legal challenges in the name of defending the Constitution.

From the combination of all of the above-mentioned factors, one can begin to understand why the reforms were defeated. The tragedy is that this was a case where political space existed to vote for change. Unlike previous elections, voters were not physically intimidated, and the broader political context was less repressive than in the past. The space existed, but it was not fully used. Although many have concluded that the defeat of the reforms was inevitable, it is difficult to avoid a nagging feeling that a proactive, intelligent campaign for the Sí could have overcome the odds.

In contrast to the above, one very positive and very important lesson emerges from the referendum experience (in particular, from the areas where the Sí won): Where there was active education and mobilization for the Sí, people who objectively stood to gain from the peace accords voted on the basis of their real interests and were not confused or tricked by the No propaganda. In fact, contrary to the predictions by the polls, it was often those with the least formal education who had the keenest sense of their interests. Theirs were highly conscious votes, in many cases, well-informed by discussions at the local level.

What, then, emerges regarding our original question, "No" to what? To what extent was it a "No" to peace? Clearly, there was a "hard No" vote, that is, by people opposed to the peace accords. That vote was well organized by hard-line peace resisters, who became more cohesive in the face of the threat from the Sí; hence they were able to move from the margins to the center of *consulta* politics. They were also able to turn a large neutral/indifferent bloc (especially in the capital) into a "soft No" constituency. The "soft No" was largely rejecting the bloated, confusing congressional package and the politicians more than the peace accords; those voters could be persuaded to abstain or to vote No because they felt no direct benefit from the peace accords. In sum, taking all of these complexities into account and looking at the "geography" of the vote lead to a more nuanced analysis than the simple explanation that the entire urban ladino middle class is racist. (For analyses that come to the same conclusion, see Solares 1999; Hernández Pico 1999b.)

These factors also help explain why, the day after the defeat of the constitutional reforms, the main presidential candidates felt somewhat constrained to state that they would push for reforms stemming from the peace accords to be passed in Congress through ordinary legislation (*Prensa Libre,* May 18, 1999). (Whether those statements are believable is another question.) Even more significant was a poll conducted one month after the referendum: In response to the question, "Do you believe that the next government should continue with the peace process?" 83.9 percent answered Sí, 6.4 percent No (*elPeriódico,* June 19, 1999)—a point to which I return in the Conclusion.

Culture Clash: Contested Interpretations

A final piece of this picture that emerges from interviews and from reading the Guatemalan press is the inevitable aftermath of the referendum, the contention among the major political actors over how to interpret the results and what conclusions to draw specifically in relation to the peace accords. Although this discussion will doubtless continue for a long time, the outlines became clear soon after the referendum. Without going into all of the possible interpretations, I focus here on three of the most prominent actors in regard to the peace process—the principal dynamic being the political/cultural interaction among Dinosaurs, politicians, and Mayan organizations as new political actors.

Dinosaurs (Peace Resisters)

Not surprisingly, the tone and discourse of the peace resisters were triumphalistic, and their message simple: "The people have spoken—this is the end of the peace process." One example, taken from a newspaper column, declared, "It is impossible to pass up this opportunity today to congratulate the Guatemalan people for the triumph of the NO. . . . The messages to the government, to the foreign interventionists, and to the ex-guerrilla and to the supposed 'friends of peace' are clear: We don't believe in them. No more deceptions" (*Prensa Libre*, May 18, 1999). In short: We are finally rid of these peace accords, which have been imposed on us by the international community and were never accepted by more than a handful of Guatemalans.[16]

Some of the No forces went further, seeming almost to threaten the PAN and the government that if they tried to pass any of the peace accord reforms through ordinary legislation, it would constitute a violation of the will of the people and they would pay for it in the November election. Some even embarked on a campaign to press their advantage and roll back the peace accords altogether: A group of jurists sought to take all of the laws already passed to implement the peace accords to the CC, to have them declared unconstitutional. Others argued that the results of the referendum were binding, whereas the peace accords never were: "The peace accords, and the attempt at constitutional reforms coming from them, contradict our Constitution. Therefore, they violate the higher norms that govern the rule of law in Guatemala. In consequence, the only possible response is to nullify them; the alternative is the destruction of the juridical system that sustains Guatemalan democracy" (*Crónica*, May 21, 1999).

The referendum also evoked a strong xenophobic response. In its aftermath, there was an intensified campaign to get MINUGUA expelled from the country.[17] Once the reforms had been approved in Congress, MINUGUA had undertaken an extensive educational campaign; and no matter how much it insisted that the campaign was informational, not for the Sí, the No forces attacked its efforts relentlessly. Given the long history of MINUGUA-baiting by peace resisters (since late 1994), this was predictable, but its vehemence was striking. Although MINUGUA was the most active, other international donors attracted attention to their role by taking credit for their pro-reform activities, despite pleas from Guatemalans not to do so.[18] And when a U.S. State Department spokesman stated publicly the day after the referendum that the high abstention and the defeat of the reforms were a "step backward in the consolidation of peace," this provoked a vehement reaction in Guatemala—from the peace resisters, but also from the government—denouncing foreign interference and the violation of Guatemalan sovereignty. Following this, the Europeans decided to make their observations privately.

PAN/Government (Peace Opportunists)

Reading this as a political defeat, the PAN and the government were primarily concerned about how to recover from its effects in time for the November 1999 election. Rather than worrying about the consequences for the peace process, the PAN and most of the government virtually deserted the peace agenda—in part, a reflexive caving in to the threats from the peace resisters and in part a response driven by their own ambiguity about the peace agenda. Within this overall response, however, one can detect a range of positions.

The clearest expressions of peace opportunism occurred the day after the referendum. The PANista president of Congress declared that he considered "the legislative agenda of the peace accords to have been aborted" or canceled; as promised, he moved to eliminate legislation dealing with the peace accords from the congressional agenda. The vice-president of the PAN congressional delegation went further, commenting that very few of the reforms could be passed through ordinary legislation—a statement tantamount to openly abandoning the peace agenda altogether. Meanwhile, the PAN's 1999 presidential candidate, Oscar Berger, declared that although he had supported the reforms, he felt "pleased" with the result of the referendum and "proud" of Guatemalan voters, and considered the whole experience to be very positive for Guatemalan democracy. At the meeting of the Consultative Group in Stockholm—held the week after the *consulta*, focusing generally on Hurricane Mitch assistance, but in the Guatemalan case raising many questions about the implications of the No for the future of the peace process—Vice President Luis Flores said nothing more than, "This is democracy; we must respect the will of the people."

The official reaction to the referendum result (representing President Arzú) was somewhat more nuanced, promising to respect the will of the people but also to continue the application of the peace accords within the framework of the (existing) constitution. But some members of the Peace Cabinet cautiously expressed their concerns about the future. In several interviews, SEPAZ head Raquel Zelaya seemed genuinely troubled by the results (especially the lost opportunity to restrict the functions of the army); the peace process will continue, she added, but much more slowly. Foreign minister Eduardo Stein's statements at the CG meeting, as he tried to give explanations to the donor governments and institutions, struck a similar tone. Finally, the Comisión de Acompañamiento (not representing the government per se but speaking for the government representatives to the commission) issued a statement that it planned to develop an agenda for implementing the peace accords through ordinary legislation; it emphasized the strong support demonstrated in favor of continuing the process and presented a view of the No as imposing "temporary limits" on what could be done.

New Political Actors (Peace Supporters)

I focus here on the most visible actor in the aftermath of the *consulta*: the coalition of Mayan organizations, which, despite the defeat, emerged as a most energetic defender of the reforms and, more generally, as a potentially significant new force in Guatemalan politics. Following the vote, COPMAGUA immediately issued a statement declaring that "we will continue our work" to concretize the accords, some of which build on the recommendations of *comisiones paritarias* (e.g., on officialization of Mayan languages and educational reforms). COPMAGUA emphasized that the constitutional reforms were only part of the peace agenda on indigenous issues and that even recognition of customary law could possibly be achieved within the existing constitution.

The Defensoría Maya made an even stronger statement on May 18—almost a direct response to the peace resisters: "The defeat of the reforms is not the end of the peace process, as the ultra-right is trying to achieve, but the renovation of the fulfillment of the accords." The statement went on to reject all the lies from the campaign (regarding indigenous desires to divide the country) and to emphasize the achievements in mobilizing people to vote for the Sí, even in the face of the "psychological warfare conducted against the indigenous population." Finally, the statement made a series of concrete proposals for continuing the peace process—in both a national peace agenda and a peace agenda specific to the Maya movement—and listed a series of initiatives that indigenous organizations intended to take, including a national dialogue with the political parties and their presidential candidates to establish agreements about continuing the peace process. It concluded: "We learned that there is a minority power group that still lives in the colonial era of 1524, and that we must situate it in the year 2000, in relation to the . . . configuration of relations in today's world and within countries whose territories are populated by diverse peoples with different identities and rights." (See Defensoría Maya 1999.)

The dinosaur is still there. But it is not alone.

Notes

1. This was not a good-faith argument, because an ANC (requiring the election of delegates and an entire redrafting of the Constitution) is needed only to reform

the articles that are specifically denominated as "nonreformable" by any other means—which was not the case of those stemming from the peace accords.

2. The role of the IM is a much-debated point. Some point out that the IM was created as a stipulation of the peace accords (*Inforpress Centroamericana*, Feb. 12, 1999). The Accord on Strengthening Civilian Power (para. II, 6–7) mandated creation of a multiparty "agency" or forum to work with legislative commissions in Congress on accord implementation for one year, as needed. Other analysts consider that the IM was a good mechanism for promoting interparty consensus. In theory, all of this could have been the case. But certainly no one imagined that it would turn into a backroom forum, nontransparent to the public; as described by one opposition congressman, the PAN used it to find out from each of the other parties what they wanted to add on—presumably, to get their votes in favor of the reforms. MINUGUA analysts maintain that most of the fifty reforms were in some way related to the accords; however, I would add, some were very tenuously and unnecessarily related, that is, not requiring constitutional reform.

3. Some of the specific disputes concerned how precise to make the definitions of territorial jurisdiction where customary law would be applied, and the nature and specific powers of local indigenous authorities within that jurisdiction (*Inforpress Centroamericana*, May 8, 1998). More important for the overall political battle, some key participants and analysts argue that in attempting to expand the content of the reforms beyond what was strictly contained in the accords, the indigenous organizations opened up the Pandora's box, indirectly paving the way for what later occurred in Congress.

4. My sources for constructing the story as told above were mainly interviews with participants from all sides. In addition to these interviews and the particular sources cited, see *Inforpress Centroamericana* and *Alerta Legislativa* (May 1998); and Comité para el Decenio del Pueblo Maya (1998).

5. Thanks to Juan Alberto Fuentes for calling my attention to this short story by Guatemalan writer Augusto Monterroso.

6. In asking government officials why this action was taken, I got responses ranging from bewilderment about my question, to dismissals of its relevance as a factor affecting the referendum, to indirect hints that military officials may have been key in painting scenarios of disorder and land takeovers. Other (nongovernment sources) believe that the measure was decreed in order to boost the image of an efficient government in this preelection year.

7. These organizations, although unified in the campaign against the reforms, should not all be lumped together indiscriminately. Whereas the extreme rightist Liga Pro-Patria maintained that the peace accords were meant only to disarm the URNG (see Note 17 below), others (e.g., CEDECON) were more concerned about legalities and legalisms. Regarding Guardianes del Vecindario, see Chapter 6. The Alianza Evangélica had been part of the ASC (as had other conservative parties and organizations) but by 1999 felt threatened by the reforms' proposal to recognize Mayan spirituality.

8. It is worth noting that among the magistrates sitting on the CC at this time were several founding members of CEDECON (*Inforpress Centroamericana*, Feb. 19, 1999).

9. Numerous analysts have pointed out that such a prohibition preventing the government from promoting a substantive reform (as opposed to a candidate) is virtually unparalleled anywhere else in the world—one more example of the endlessly byzantine nature of the Guatemalan "system."

10. Nevertheless, CACIF said it would have supported a package of reforms limited strictly to those stemming from the peace accords. According to virtually everyone I interviewed, including CACIF members, there was considerable debate and lack of consensus within CACIF as to whether to take a public stance for the No. They ultimately did so, some believe, because the implied changes in the balance of power in Guatemalan society were too threatening to their interests and to their worldview. (See Conclusion.) In any case, well-informed observers maintain that many CACIF members were financing the No all along.

11. Sources for the above include official results from the Supreme Electoral Tribunal (TSE); also (for the "electoral geography,") Lizardo Sosa, *Siglo Veintiuno*, May 24, 1999; *Inforpress Centroamericana*, May 28, 1999; and unpublished analyses, all using TSE information.

12. An August 28–29, 1998, meeting of social organizations, a "National Consultation for Peace," issued the "Declaration of Mazatenango" and appeared to be a promising effort toward broad discussion and participation.

13. It should be noted that a few Mayan intellectuals and newspaper columnists opposed the reforms. Rigoberta Menchú, although a Sí supporter, was in Europe on May 16.

14. Hernández Pico (1999b, 16) extends the latent racism factor to explain the defeat of the army reform: "Fear of being left without an army, whose mission is to guarantee the country's internal security, influenced the votes of the many Guatemala City residents who are afraid of the indigenous population's growing influence."

15. This disparity is nowhere clearer than in Guatemala City and its surroundings: Its overwhelmingly ladino electorate contrasts sharply with the fact that "indigenous people now form the majority, following the massive internal displacements of the 1980s" (Hernández Pico 1999b, 12).

16. In another example, the Association of Military Veterans published a press release on May 17, reading the results as a vote of confidence in the army (with all of its current functions) and of support "for our soldiers, PAC members, military commissioners, and civilians working with the army who gave their lives to defend democracy and the fatherland." The army leadership said nothing publicly but held parties to celebrate the victory of the No, which they saw as vindicating the army's role.

17. In a widely viewed post-*consulta* television program ("Libre Encuentro") focusing on the role of MINUGUA, the Liga Pro-Patria representative maintained that MINUGUA has had no legitimate function in Guatemala since the URNG was disarmed (which effectively was the end of the peace process). The message from the *consulta*, he continued, is that MINUGUA should get out of Guatemala; its continued presence only "violates our laws, protects criminals, and accompanies land invaders." He repeatedly accused MINUGUA of trying to impose "a socialist agenda" on Guatemala.

18. In the heat of the campaign, for example, television ads ended, "This has been a message from" U.S. AID or the European Union. As one pro-reform Guatemalan put it, these indiscretions became ammunition not only against the reforms but the entire peace process, reinforcing the old argument of the peace resisters that the process had been imposed by the international community.

Conclusion: "Reinvention" or Lost Opportunity? Global, Comparative, and Imaginary Perspectives

Writing about El Salvador, Roberto Turcios (1997) captured an essential dilemma of interpreting postwar transitions: "Looking back over the past twenty-five years, you can see a gigantic leap forward; but looking ahead, what stands out is uncertainty." Perhaps this helps explain the striking juxtaposition in the Guatemalan case of how minimal the advances seem—yet at the same time, how remarkable.

The underlying question is whether the Guatemalan peace process can "work," beyond ending the civil war, and what kind of society postwar Guatemala will be. My (inherently contradictory) task here is to conclude a book about an ongoing, unfinished process and to address problems that have no clear solutions. Without claiming to make definitive interpretations, this Conclusion offers some interim reflections concerning Guatemala's peace process. However, these interim reflections are being made at a particular moment—the most dangerous moment since the signing of peace—following the defeat of the constitutional reforms, when peace accord implementation has been put on hold until after the November 1999 presidential election. Why, then, when it appears so obviously a "lost opportunity," is there any question about "reinvention"? It seems almost impossible to answer this question directly. But if we take a less linear approach and visit several other conceptual realms or perspectives—in effect, using several wide-angle lenses after so many close-ups of the peace process—this exercise may shed new light on Guatemala's prospects.

This Conclusion begins by analyzing briefly the structural changes in the world-economy (globalization, neoliberalism, and transnationalization) that have bearing upon the prospects for postwar Guatemala. It then briefly examines the Guatemalan experience as part of a worldwide learning process of peace negotiations and their aftermath. This loosely "comparative" perspective can help us assess the extent to which current implementation problems in Guatemala are typical of postwar reconstruction experiences—or more precisely, *which* of these problems are typical and which are specific to Guatemala. The "imaginary" perspective refers to a more symbolic realm or space for visions of a "new Guatemala" and construction of full citizenship. The final section of this Conclusion explores scenarios for really-existing postwar, post-*consulta* Guatemala. If the "imaginary" perspective reminds us of what is the *project* of the peace accords, the reality reveals itself to be *postwar*—which overlaps with but falls far short of the peace project.

Postwar Guatemala Faces Globalization, Neoliberalism, and Transnationalized Actors

During the most violent phase of its civil war, Guatemala was somewhat insulated and cut off from the world because of its "pariah" status. This began to change when the international community (the UN and the Friend countries) became involved in Guatemala's peace negotiations and subsequently in facilitating implementation of the accords through the Consultative Group meetings and peace conditionality—in a sense, bringing the world into Guatemala. The peace process was also accompanied by Guatemala's incorporation into the world-economy; but by this time (the late 1990s), the world-economy had undergone significant structural modifications that affected postwar Guatemala.

What kind of a world is Guatemala being integrated into and what are the implications for the peace process? First, it is an ever more "globalized" world, meaning one in which nations and economic enterprises are increasingly integrated into the world market and across borders through commercial ties, networks, and relations. The most commonly recognized expressions of this tendency are related to the drive for free trade and reduction of trade barriers. However, it also has repercussions in many other areas, such as reorganization of production processes and labor markets, migrations, communications, consumption patterns, and cultures.[1]

Second, the "rules of the game" governing the globalization process in this post-socialist era can be broadly characterized as "neoliberal." That term refers to a general set of policies: privatization of state-owned enterprises; deregulation, that is, elimination of state "interferences" with market operations; liberalization of trade and finances and lifting of protectionist trade barriers; an almost exclusive focus on export to the world market, accompanied by a harsh critique and dismissal of earlier strategies oriented toward building internal markets; dismantling of welfare institutions, including drastic cutbacks in state-supported social programs and "social subsidies"; structural adjustment and austerity policies, prioritizing balanced budgets. These are all viewed as requisites for the ultimate imperative: attracting investment by foreign capital. Ideologically, neoliberalism has become a new orthodoxy in the post-socialist era. It presents itself as unipolar and monolithic, and there are no competing centers of power. Hence—especially for Latin American countries, located in the sphere of influence of the United States, which has espoused the most extreme version of pure market economics (versus "welfare-state" capitalism)—there are virtually no choices, but only one hegemonic development strategy, that of the unregulated market.[2]

The neoliberal policy recipe implies abandoning internal market-oriented policies of national development identified as Keynesian and, in Latin America, associated with the UN Economic Commission for Latin America (CEPAL). It rejects policies of industrialization for the internal market and other forms of state capitalism and planning. Neoliberalism is "post-Fordist" in discarding the (Fordist) assumption that linked economic growth to broadening the consumer market, so as to include workers and peasants. Rather than treating workers as consumers needing a decent (higher) income in order to consume (as in the internal market model), now the incentive is for the lowest possible wages. Hence, it is essentially a *cheap-labor* model, which reduces industrialization to maquiladora operations. The effect of this policy approach has been to increase the concentration of wealth at the top and to cut jobs as well as spending on popular needs. These effects have been even more notable in Latin America because the adoption of neoliberal policies coincided with a generalized regionwide economic crisis, making the 1980s the "Lost Decade" in Latin America. The neoliberal policy response to the "Lost Decade" did not alleviate but worsened the spread of poverty and unemployment/underemployment.

Although it is not organically related to neoliberal economic policies, there is an *ideological* association of unregulated free markets and free enterprise with democracy. "Democracy" is interpreted, however, in the most minimalist terms (strictly procedural/electoral)—resulting in "democratic forms that reinforce the political dominance of one community over another" and often "produce democratic rules with undemocratic outcomes" (Crighton 1998, 76). Despite the common association of free markets with democracy, a number of experts on Latin America (e.g., Stark 1998; Borón 1998) argue convincingly that neoliberalism in practice has become a "fault line" of democratic governance, undermining rather than accompanying it.

Without entering into the extensive discussions about all of the above (on some issues, see Chapter 4), I shall focus here on the debate most relevant to this book: the effects of globalization and neoliberalism on peace processes in general and the Guatemalan peace process in particular. This debate is broadly framed in terms of "neoliberal peace"—or as some (e.g., Paris 1997) call it, "liberal internationalist peace"—in which "the goal is to maintain a minimalist definition of peace (the absence of armed conflict) and to move as quickly as possible to promote a transition to democratic governance and a market economy" (Crighton 1998, 76). A neoliberal peace "seeks to put into place instrumental arrangements that will lead not to a more equitable distribution of resources or power or the settling of festering differences, but instead to the institutionalization of the appearance of political equity and the promise of economic opportunity" (Lipschutz 1998, 14).

Official policy communities and their defenders avoid using the pejorative term "neoliberal": They prefer the discourse of "market reform" or "market-friendly policies" (versus "statism"), "trade liberalization" (versus outdated "protectionism"), "fiscal discipline," "structural adjustment," and "healthy economy." They also generally deny that these policies impose any negative constraints on peace (or democracy). From their perspective, the critique of neoliberalism is an intellectual construction and oversimplification by ideologically dogmatic leftists or outmoded welfare statists, a kind of "straw man." Particularly in the case of Guatemala, they point to the fact that the allegedly "neoliberal IFIs" have pushed for strengthening the state through higher taxes and are financing social programs oriented toward poverty reduction.

This last point is true enough, but it does not fully address the contradictory dynamics affecting Guatemala. Indeed, the policies for Guatemala have been more nuanced than in other cases—in part, learning from previous experiences, and in part because the Guatemalan state was almost nonexistent and therefore did not need to be downsized. But at the same time, the world into which Guatemala is being integrated operates on neoliberal principles that undermine state strengthening and have some negative consequences for peace accord implementation—above all, for redistributive goals. (The Guatemalan government [GG 1997c, 35] acknowledged that its premise in negotiating the socioeconomic accord was "acceptance that there are iron laws in the world economy which no one can escape, much less small countries like Guatemala.") For example, the emphasis on fiscal discipline and budget deficit reduction precludes unorthodox policies that might be needed to ensure stability in the postwar period (see Boyce in Arnson 1999, 439–440). To take another example, the prevailing emphasis on export to the world market precludes consideration of internal market–oriented policies as being equally central to a sustainable development strategy.[3]

Indeed, these contradictions have shown up in virtually all postwar societies of the 1990s, with the result that they are all plagued by similar socioeconomic problems. In fact, the problems are generally aggravated in these postwar situations. The case of South Africa is particularly instructive. Here, the negotiated transition led to a postwar government headed by the former African National Congress insurgents, led by a unique historical figure, Nelson Mandela. Additionally, South Africa is important and independent enough to "matter" to the world community and economy in ways that El Salvador and Guatemala can never matter because of their small size. Yet even in this best of cases, some of the most entrenched problems we have seen in Guatemala are fully evident. For example, socioeconomic deterioration, growing unemployment, and poverty are equally serious; and these, in turn, lead to high crime rates, social violence, and generalized citizen insecurity. Postwar peacetime crime waves—in large part linked to "the old order or the fallout from its collapse" (Gordon 1998)—have been the Achilles' heel in South Africa and in virtually all of the 1990s peace settlements. As Scheper-Hughes (1997, 493) points out, the explosion of postwar violence makes democratic transition a "dangerous hour."

In South Africa and elsewhere, then, the neoliberal policies of the 1980s and 1990s have created an international environment that is much less "friendly" to the peace agendas emerging from national liberation and revolutionary struggles of the mid- to late twentieth century. These policies have also tended to destabilize and fuel social discontent and unrest (see Paris 1997)—hence undermining or limiting gains for democracy. To return to the concerns raised at the end of Chapter 4, it seems clear that the unresolved question of social justice is being resolved increasingly in the wrong direction. It remains an unmet challenge for the future, as one analyst put it, "to secure a distribution of economic benefits which will sustain the balances of power on which the peace process rests and redress the social tensions which fueled the war" (Boyce 1998, 1; see also case studies in Lipschutz and Jonas 1998).

Returning to Guatemala: Perhaps we can best answer, What kind of world is Guatemala being integrated into? by recalling briefly the program of the Arbenz government (1951–1954)—a program that led to his overthrow but was being implemented in the larger countries of Latin America, such as next-door Mexico. In today's world, agrarian reform (à la Arbenz) is not seen as "pro-communist"; it has simply disappeared from the vocabulary. In today's world, the idea of regulating or competing with foreign monopolies (the Arévalo/Arbenz program) has been replaced by a scramble to attract foreign capital (monopolistic or otherwise) and to offer special privileges. It is a world in which "tax reform" is no longer assumed to mean *progressive* tax reform. It is a world in which the Arbenz government's strategy of raising wages for workers and peasants to create an internal market is dismissed as anathema, while "low-wage labor" is regarded as Central America's "comparative advantage." In today's world, policies that promote the organization of labor and peasants or build a social safety net, as Arbenz's did, are seen as statist interferences with free market operations. It is a world in which poverty statistics are geometrically higher than those under Arbenz or even the counterrevolutionary Castillo Armas (1954–1957). Today's discourse is about reduction—more often, alleviation—of extreme poverty, not socioeconomic equality, justice, or equity. Even the discourse has been appropriated: "Reform" has come to mean market reform, not land and tax reform. It is a world with no socialist bloc to provide moral support for reformist governments. It is a world in which full democracy and sustainable development have replaced social revolution as the goal of revolutionaries.

Can the Peace Project Survive Neoliberalism?

Given the situation described above, some analysts view peace processes as doomed to failure in the current neoliberal climate. This argument is developed comprehensively in the Central American cases by Robinson (1996, 1997, 1998). In this view, the peace negotiations were primarily a mechanism through which the transnationalized elites (those linked to world markets) were able to eliminate an obstacle (internal armed conflict) to their agenda; hence, virtually nothing was gained for the majority of the population beyond polyarchy, that is, elections that are formally fair but structurally stacked against popular forces and the ex-insurgent Left. The implication is that even if Guatemala complied with all of the accords, the result would be little more than fair elections combined with neoliberal economic policies. In short, the Central American peace settlements were a victory for the elites and a defeat for popular and revolutionary forces.

I would suggest a slightly different approach regarding neoliberalism's effects for peace processes. First, if neoliberalism presents itself as the universal solution, some of its critics also paint with too broad a brush, as if neoliberalism's effects were the same in all countries. In fact there are differences even within the Central American region, among Nicaragua, El Salvador, and Guatemala. Timing accounts for some of the differences: As discussed in Chapter 7, the IFIs have nuanced their approach somewhat by the late 1990s;[4] in Guatemala, moreover, there was (theoretically) an opportunity for some collective learning from the social disasters in El Salvador and Nicaragua. (For reasons specific to Guatemala, as we have

seen, that opportunity was not used.) More important, even if its proponents had wanted to impose the same policy formula on all countries and
even if the outcomes in Nicaragua, El Salvador, and Guatemala have been
broadly similar, internal factors (class structure, ethnic composition, and
so on) lead to some differences in their specific functioning.

To take an example: According to Robinson (1997, 144; 1998), the
Guatemalan peace accords, like its predecessors, "set the basis for the hegemony of the transnational elite project for Guatemala." But the issue of the
transnational elite project is somewhat more complex in Guatemala than it
was in El Salvador. Somewhat like Cristiani's ARENA in El Salvador,
Arzú's PAN in Guatemala represented a (partial) recomposition of the ruling class, and one of its projects was to facilitate the negotiations to end the
war. But as seen in the last three chapters, the PAN has been far from unified in support of implementing the peace accords, with the "Club de
Paris" doing more to resist than to fulfill them. And unlike the Salvadoran
situation, the PAN did not represent the entire ruling class; some of its
fractions have supported the FRG. Even the modernizing/transnational
sectors in CACIF did not support the peace process for several years after it
began; they eventually did so, but it was not their preference or initiative.
And after the signing of peace, CACIF reverted to peace resistance, for example, in relation to tax and constitutional reforms stemming from the accords. If the peace accords were their agenda or project, why have they
been resisting and sabotaging? At best, their stance toward making the
changes required for integration into the world-economy is schizophrenic.
If there was any doubt about this, the May 1999 referendum brought the
still-prevalent oligarchical worldview out of the woodwork. (See Chapter
8, Note 10.) This, in turn, sent a message to foreign investors and financiers:
Guatemala is not ready to "modernize" and remains a risky place for investment. In short, powerful sectors of the Guatemalan elites are too "illib-
eral" (Pearce 1998a, 171) and backward-looking to accept the transnational
project; the transnational elite has *not* been as hegemonic in Guatemala as
in El Salvador.[5] Hence, Guatemala has been much more resistant to being
incorporated into the world-economy than El Salvador and continues to
have a peculiarly convoluted relationship to the world.

If Guatemala's domestic elites were to support the implementation of
the peace accords (which has not been the case to date) and *if* the accords
were implemented as written, we would see some incompatibilities between peace and neoliberalism. First, although the socioeconomic accord
was far less than a program for full social justice, it was more than a simple platform for the application of neoliberal policies; its full implementation would create some conflict with such policies. Second, the logic of
the peace accords as a whole brings rising popular expectations and ultimately implies raising the price of labor (among other things, by remov-

ing the repressive apparatus that has maintained cheap labor and by respecting labor rights). Paradoxically, the accords that would in some respects improve Guatemala's "foreign investment climate" would at the same time create new challenges to investors from a more empowered labor force.

A second question about the interaction between neoliberalism and peace processes is the degree to which all windows of opportunity have already been closed by international constraints and dominant domestic elites. Robinson and others have accurately characterized the *agenda* of the transnationalized elites; however, this is a process rather than a finished product. At the heart of this process is the interaction between neoliberalism and popular demands arising from the peace accords. It is a tug-of-war, with contingent outcomes. Countries like Guatemala, where unpredictability is the norm, require an approach that illuminates the many contradictions, crosscurrents, and social contestations, allowing us to see the range of options available to all players—including the nonelite players of civil society, even when they are weak and disorganized. As Portes (1997, 254) has theorized it, a series of *contingent* forces or internal social structures (including, in the case at hand, ethnic composition) "determine variations in the outcomes of a uniform neoliberal policy package applied in different national contexts, and unexpected responses by the groups most directly affected." To put it another way, even under the constraints of globalization and neoliberalism, the peace accords have created margins for maneuver. In the long range, it makes sense to consider agency as well as structure.[6]

But in the end, the constraints remain very powerful. There is no question that globalization and neoliberalism have dramatically increased Guatemalan poverty, both nationally and locally, during the peace process years as well as the decades of war. (See UNDP 1998 and 1999; Abell 1999). Furthermore, independent of the resistances of both oligarchical and indigenous/popular sectors to being incorporated, the world-economy is coming to Guatemala—very likely in the form of a major economic/financial crisis whose impact will be most fully felt in 2000. When this crisis hits, we will finally see the interaction between neoliberalism and peace in all its dimensions. At that point as well, we will see whether the IFIs (and the United States) value a substantive peace in Guatemala (including its premise of a stronger state) as highly as macroeconomic stability.

Binational Guatemalan Communities

There is another dimension (and effect) of globalization that must be taken into account, especially because the peace accords as implemented have *not* led to sustainable development in Guatemala. If Guatemala were to use the socioeconomic accord to generate a "peace dividend" and create stable, decently paid jobs—now the primary concern of most Guatemalans—the country could modernize its dysfunctional socioeconomic system and resolve the problems of its working population within its borders. But in the likely continuance of dysfunctional development— that is, if there is no tax reform to finance the social goals of the peace accords and no peace dividend in the form of land, jobs, or basic services— the only recourse for thousands of Guatemalans will be the transnational solution they have chosen during the past two decades: migration to the United States. The decline in refugees fleeing political violence today is counterbalanced by several factors that promote migration: Borders have already been opened up to capital and commodities;[7] the networks formed during the war are now the social infrastructure for new migrants; and while revolution (in Guatemala) is no longer a viable strategy for achieving socioeconomic redistribution, remittances from Guatemalans working in the United States can contribute. To put it another way, when revolution is not a collective option, many more individuals are likely to choose the exit option—all the more so because their labor is very much needed in the United States.

In short, Guatemala's working/indigenous populations, as well as elites, are being transnationalized by (and responding transnationally to) the new world order. This dimension of Guatemala's incorporation into the world represents a grassroots strategy for mitigating the effects of dysfunctional development—across borders, if not within Guatemalan borders. At least 10 percent of the Guatemalan population now lives in the United States: Commonly used figures range from 1 to 1.2 million.[8] Through the remittances they send back home (approaching $1 billion a year—*Prensa Libre*, Sept. 6, 1999), they have become significant contributors to the Guatemalan economy. Remittances from Guatemalans in the United States have become the second-largest source of foreign exchange after coffee exports. Indeed, when the international community's contributions to postwar Guatemala begin to dwindle, the role of binational Guatemalans will become even more evident. (See Rincón et al. 1999; Jonas 1996b.)

Beyond their economic contributions, the diverse binational Guatemalan communities in the United States constitute new collective "social actors" whose impact will increasingly be felt on Guatemalan local and national politics. Even during the peace negotiations of the mid-1990s, a group of "Displaced Guatemalans Living in the U.S." obtained representation in the ASC. More broadly, it can be argued that the Guatemalan diaspora (primarily in the United States, but also in Europe) played a central role in determining what stance the international community would take in relation to Guatemala's peace negotiations. The fact that the Guatemalan diaspora was so largely made up of victims of army brutality delegitimated the army and indirectly helped the URNG win the international diplomacy wars; this was one of the factors that compensated for the URNG's relative military weakness vis-à-vis the army. (A counterexample is the Middle East—a case in which not only military strength and political intractability but also international legitimacy—through the Jewish diaspora, with its collective identity as victims of the Holocaust—has strengthened the hand of the Israeli government against the PLO.)

Portes (1999) refers to this influence of Guatemalan refugee organizations in the United States as "externalization" of the Guatemalan conflict, putting the Guatemalan government more sharply under the glare of world opinion. Others have identified it as a "transnationalization" of the movements for human rights and justice. A notable example during the war was the $47.5 million judgment (ordered by a U.S. federal judge in 1995) against former defense minister Héctor Gramajo on behalf of a community of Kanjobal Indians living near Davis, California, for a massacre carried out in their home village during the early 1980s *(Xuncax v. Gramajo)*. To cite a more recent example, on the occasion of the 1999 anniversary memorial of the Gerardi assassination, 500 bishops from around the world came to Guatemala (the world in Guatemala); at the same time, Guatemalan communities throughout the United States organized their own memorial masses (Guatemalans in the world). The articulation between domestic and international criticism has at least made it more difficult for the government to cover up its mishandling of the Gerardi case.

In the late 1990s, the signing of the peace accords has strengthened binational Guatemalan communities by making it possible for groups in the United States that were traditional enemies—political refugee organizations and government consulates—to work together in coalitions and national networks on issues affecting the status of Guatemalans in the United States (immigrant/refugee rights). By 1999, under pressure both from Central American governments and Central American organizations in the United States, the White House was supporting legislation to regularize the legal status of over half a million Central Americans (primarily Salvadorans and Guatemalans) living and working in the United States as of December 1995—thus equalizing the treatment given to Cubans and Nicaraguans in 1997. If enacted into law, this measure (the proposed Central American and Haitian Adjustment Act of 1999) would enable a large number of legalized Guatemalans to travel back and forth freely. As a result, these binational Guatemalans would doubtless play a much more significant role in Guatemalan domestic politics (through the circulation of new ideas and social practices, and possibly electoral participation); hopefully, this would strengthen democratizing trends.

In Guatemala, then, although it imposes very clear constraints, globalization broadly understood has been a complex and multidimensional process whose effects are diverse, contradictory, and not always easy to predict.[9]

Guatemala in the World Cycle of Peace Processes

Earlier chapters, as well as this Conclusion, have mentioned relevant comparisons to experiences in other peace processes. A full-fledged, formal comparative analysis is far beyond my scope here—in part because the outcome in Guatemala is still so highly uncertain. Furthermore, after looking at a number of cases in the vast comparative literature on peacemaking and peacekeeping experiences, I have been increasingly struck by the *specificity* of each—an observation reinforced by Arnson's collection (1999) about these processes in Latin America. Hence, my use of a "comparative perspective" is more heuristic than literal; my focus is on Guatemala as part of a regional and worldwide learning process about negotiated peace settlements.

I am situating Guatemala as one of a particular "generation" of conflicts during the second half of the twentieth century, which I refer to as "Cold War civil wars"—meaning not that they were caused solely by the Cold War but that they were very much affected by occurring within that broader context. In the generation of ideologically polarized Cold War civil wars, leftist revolutionary forces fighting for socialism and/or national liberation—and, more importantly, excluded from the political process—confronted counterinsurgency forces backed by antisocialist great powers, primarily the United States. The cycle of peace processes ending these wars is by and large a "post–Cold War" phenomenon because it required openness to the ideas of negotiation and compromise—mutual concessions rather than "winners versus losers."[10] For my purposes here, despite the centrality of its ethnic dimension, Guatemala's civil war and its peace process has had more in common with (and can better be understood in comparison with) El Salvador, South Africa, and the Middle East than with the post–Cold War ethnic conflicts, such as Rwanda, Bosnia, and Kosovo.[11]

The Guatemalan experience shares with other revolutionary or national liberation insurrections during the Cold War, and their subsequent resolution by internationally mediated negotiation processes, a set of framework questions: Can former revolutionary movements win anything for their constituencies—or more accurately, *what* can they win—once they opt for peace negotiations? Do the political and social gains of such peace processes compensate for the human cost of the wars? What did Guatemala learn from other, relatively "successful" experiences (South Africa, El Salvador)? What does it have in common with the semi-"failed" (or failing) peace process in the Middle East (see Beinin 1998)? What can other countries learn from Guatemala, despite its particularities? And what are the ripple effects of the Guatemalan experience for the collective history of the Western Hemisphere at the end of the twentieth century?

Guatemala, El Salvador, and Beyond

As seen in Chapter 2 and elsewhere in this book, in practice, the major point of reference for Guatemala has been El Salvador. Methodologically, this makes sense: Because of the elements of common history, the contrasts stand out more clearly. The idea of negotiating to end a civil war first arose in the region in the 1987 Central American Peace Accords. These accords (known as Esquipulas II) formed the context for the Sandinista/Contra settlement in Nicaragua at the end of the 1980s. Subsequently, a model of UN-mediated negotiations going far beyond a cease-fire to address profound substantive issues (demilitarization, civilian police, legalization of former insurgents, Truth Commission, and so forth) was more fully developed in El Salvador. Despite the initially fierce resistances by its elites, Guatemala eventually followed a path similar to the Salvadoran. There were also major negative lessons from El Salvador (mainly, on socioeconomic issues), which were taken into account in the Guatemalan negotiations.

During the implementation phase, as during the negotiations, the problems in Guatemala have been significantly greater than in El Salvador. First, both of the major actors—the government and the insurgents—are less hegemonic in Guatemala. Second, in contrast with El Salvador, multiple players have participated in building Guatemala's peace, as in negotiating it. In El Salvador, everything was worked out among the ARENA government/army (and behind them, the United States), the FMLN, and a cohesive UN team. Theoretically, the broader range of social actors in Guatemala could be quite positive; this certainly ended up being the case during the negotiations. But in the implementation phase, it has had contradictory consequences. A positive aspect has been the proactive involvement of a wide range of indigenous organizations and the emerging protagonism of women's organizations, with important implications for the construction of citizenship (see below).

But the negative aspects have become painfully clear, primarily with the constitutional reforms. The need to ratify the reforms electorally held out the promise of national legitimation of the peace accords, but it posed risks that were far greater than the promise—particularly given the chasm between who votes and who benefits from the peace accords. One wonders whether any peace process other than the South African, under Mandela's leadership, could have successfully survived such a challenge—especially in a society characterized by the structural divisions of Guatemala. Like El Salvador, and in sharp contrast to South Africa, Northern Ireland, and the Middle East, Guatemala has an alarmingly low voter participation rate, lower yet among constituencies that stand to benefit from the peace process. This widespread noninvolvement in the political process was bound to damage the peace process if it was put to a vote (which El Salvador was fortunate to avoid). Compounding this and unlike El Salvador, Guatemala has to contend with a political culture permeated by multidimensional racism as well as oligarchical recalcitrance.

Once again, the question arises: If the 1964 Civil Rights Act passed by the U.S. Congress had needed ratification in a Mississippi referendum, would it have done any better than Guatemala's? And once again, we should remember the 1996 Israeli election, in which the Jewish majority of the Israeli electorate essentially voted down the Oslo peace process. These quandries have led a number of participants and observers in the Guatemalan case to question whether negotiated peace settlements always go hand in hand with "democratization," narrowly defined. In fragile peace processes, democratic forms can produce undemocratic outcomes. In Guatemala's referendum, electoral democracy defeated multicultural, demilitarized democracy.

Finally, the Guatemalan accords are far more ambitious than the Salvadoran, particularly the socioeconomic and indigenous accords; even the demilitarization accord is more ambitious, given that the Guatemalan army was (and remains) much more difficult to reform than the Salvadoran. But the fact that they are broader also makes them more complex to implement. In El Salvador, there was a very clear trade-off between the FMLN's military demobilization and a thorough (although difficult) demilitarization of the state. In Guatemala, by contrast, demilitarization, which is a precondition for all else, has been overshadowed by other issues; certainly that was the case in the referendum.

The upshot of this comparison with El Salvador is that the stakes are higher in Guatemala, but the capacity of domestic Guatemalan actors *by themselves* to deliver is lower. Nevertheless, it is important not to distort this delicate balance into a (commonly heard) false comparison that belittles or dismisses the Guatemalan experience relative to the Salvadoran.[12] By contrast, leading Salvadoran analyst Héctor Dada captured the essence of the Guatemala conundrum when he commented at the January 1998 FLACSO forum, "In Guatemala (unlike El Salvador), as I realized when I read the accord on indigenous rights, you negotiated an entire revolution." From this perspective, even the very limited achievements in Guatemala are significant—taking into account as well that the starting point (Guatemala during the 1980s) was so much worse, that the levels of resistance were (and remain) so much higher, and that the Guatemalan "system" throws up so many more obstacles.[13] Now, as during the negotiations, Guatemala's peace process still calls to mind the endless resistances, minefields, volatilities, fragilities, and zigzags of the Middle East peace process. If most of the problems faced by Guatemala are typical of postwar situations, the responses to those problems have been made more difficult by Guatemala's particular political culture. Perhaps, then, a Guatemala/El Salvador comparison should be accompanied by an effort to assess what came out of the two experiences *taken together* as two tracks of the *camino centroamericano*.

Finally, this quasi-comparative exercise is a reminder that despite the enormous investment by domestic actors and the international community in dozens of conflict situations, the successes are painfully slow and minimal in almost all cases. Seen in this light, Guatemala's problems are greater than (and not necessarily typical of) other cases; but what stands out *grosso modo* is the Herculean effort that must be made to gain a few millimeters of social or political change in almost any situation. Even from South Africa—the best of cases, where the most difficult problems have been addressed in a civilized way—the message that emerges (particularly in the post-Mandela era) is not clear-cut success but mixed results and the need to fight some battles over and over again. From the other side, the events of 1995–1999 in that most intractable case of all, the Middle East, is a reminder that no matter how bad things get, tomorrow could conceivably be another day. Above all, the actors in and chroniclers of any peace process have to take a very long view, to think "in Maya time."

Ripple Effects for Latin America: Against All Odds

I move now to a brief assessment of the ripple effects of Guatemala's peace process for the hemisphere—both its symbolic significance and its practical impact. My starting point is that Guatemala's has been the longest, bloodiest, and most CIA-intervened civil war in Latin America— far more so than El Salvador's, in which the U.S. involvement and the war itself were highly intense, but for a much shorter period of time. Guatemala's peace accords ended the cycle of Cold War counterinsurgency wars in the hemisphere. From the viewpoint of Latin America, *the Cold War both began and (with the exception of Cuba) ended in Guatemala.*

The signing of the Guatemalan peace accords closed the cycle of Central American peace processes. Viewed in its totality, this cycle, which be-

gan with the 1987 Esquipulas II accords, relativized the U.S. role in its historic "backyard" (Central America), opened the door to UN peacemaking
in the region, and shifted the overall balance of forces in the hemisphere.
The Central American experiences also gave Latin America the model of
political negotiations as a path for ending internal armed conflicts—the
model of no winners/no losers, concessions from all sides. Ironically, this
model was fully developed in the tiny Central American countries and, to
the surprise of many, was successfully applied in Guatemala; it could
eventually be useful for negotiations between governments and insurgents in larger Latin American countries.

Regarding implementation, there are mixed messages from Guatemala.
On a negative note, the defeat of the constitutional reforms and the difficulties of demilitarization could have an adverse impact on the entire
Central American region and beyond. As long as the Guatemalan army
remains a bastion of autonomy from civilian control, Central America
cannot be fully consolidated as a region of peace and democracy. Particularly in El Salvador, given the long history of ties between the military
and civilian right-wing forces in the two countries, the dangers of a re-
militarization should not be discarded—using, for example, the argument
that only the army can truly maintain order in the face of the peacetime
crime wave. In short, El Salvador's peace resisters may be learning from
their Guatemalan counterparts. On the other hand, if the obstacles to demilitarization are ever overcome in Guatemala, if this most brutal of
counterinsurgency armies is finally defanged, other Latin American
armies would feel added pressure to submit to civilian control.

There are other ripple effects for Latin America. First, some elements of
the Guatemalan and Salvadoran experiences can be seen in Colombia,[14]
and a number of pro-peace Colombians have taken inspiration from those
peace processes. When he took office in 1998, incoming President Andrés
Pastrana looked very much like Alvaro Arzú in his determination to negotiate peace. A mechanism something like the Asamblea de la Sociedad
Civil has been invented in Colombia for civilian input. Nevertheless,
Colombia today looks more like Central America during the 1980s wars,
with deepening U.S. involvement and a peace process that does not yet
have a forward dynamic. Furthermore, what stands out increasingly in
1999 is the complexity and specificity of the Colombian situation, as well
as a resistance to foreign involvement or models—something like the
"never in Guatemala" syndrome in the early 1990s.

This last point becomes even clearer in the case of Guatemala's next-
door neighbor, Mexico. Given that Mexico was such a key player in the
Guatemalan peace negotiations and that President Zedillo enjoyed such a
high profile at the peace-signing in Guatemala, the Mexican government
acquired an indirect moral obligation to negotiate seriously in its own internal conflict, with the Zapatista rebels and indigenous communities in

Chiapas. But the Mexican government is always resistant to outside pressures and comparisons, especially involving its "junior" neighbor, as it regards Guatemala. In any case, as of mid-1999, the Mexican government has not seriously begun to negotiate. And neither side has publicly embraced Guatemala's indigenous accord. Some observers and advisers to the Zapatistas view it as an "input," but not a model. Perhaps over time that accord may come to have a "demonstration effect," in part because of the real connection between Mayan Guatemala and Mayan Chiapas.

Looking beyond war-torn societies to all of Latin America, where virtually every country is riddled with social conflicts, what emerges from Guatemala are some of the process-related participatory gains. The multisectoral Asamblea de la Sociedad Civil is an example that should be relevant in a great variety of situations. And Guatemala's postwar commissions and other mechanisms for interchange, negotiation, conflict resolution, and eventual consensus-building and policy initiatives are broadly applicable. In this sense, Latin America as a whole can benefit from the major investments made in Guatemalan peace-building. On a symbolic level, a positive message emerges from the very occurrence of the negotiated peace process in this most difficult country and *against all odds*. If Guatemala can undertake and sustain a reform project, then reformers in other Latin American countries can take heart.

Finally, for reasons peculiar to its tragic and dramatic history, Guatemala remains a touchstone or point of reference for Latin America: "The Guatemala solution," indigenous rights, Jacobo Arbenz, CIA intervention, Rigoberta Menchú, to name only a few examples, have become code words signifying experiences throughout the hemisphere. Guatemala even appears with striking prominence in an article on the life of Che Guevara (Guillermoprieto 1997, 110–111)—perhaps for the same reason that Uruguay's Eduardo Galeano once called Guatemala "the key to Latin America," and elsewhere referred to Guatemala as "a source of great lessons painfully learned." Guatemala is *patrimonio latinoamericano*.

The Realm of the *Imaginario* and the Construction of Citizenship

"What is a man on the road?" asks a sacred Maya book. And answers, "Time." [In]
. . . Guatemala on the road, the tormented present remembers a different possible future.

—Eduardo Galeano

Like other peoples emerging from decades or centuries of oppression, Guatemalans have a space of the *imaginario*—loosely translated, the future that they envision, that they dream of creating or inventing.[15] Indeed, they have had to train themselves in mental gymnastics in order to keep their eyes on the prize during the forty years of extreme terror—and for the indigenous majority, added onto five hundred years of domination. The peace process has fortified the visionary space of the *imaginario*—*that realm, beyond everyday ordinary politics, of hopes, aspirations, dreams, and fears.* Before returning to really-existing Guatemala, I briefly visit this realm of the imaginary, because it suggests what has advanced in Guatemala— even when structurally, the pace of change has been so glacial and the gains so minimal. This seems particularly appropriate to understanding the dynamics of a transition period in which the old order is obsolete (but has not finished dying), and the new order has yet to be born.

In the spirit of Martin Luther King's "I have a dream" speech, the imaginary of Guatemala's majority populations serves as a counter-hegemonic space of resistance to intolerable realities. (The hard-line peace resisters, obviously, have their own imaginary, of a return to the past.) Given that elite minorities control the levers of power in Guatemalan society, the imaginary is a space where subalterns have not capitulated and have maintained their alternative vision. It (deliberately) does not reflect, conform to, or obey the existing structure of power relations; in fact, it is the antithesis of those relations. Theoretically, it does not accept the constraints of minimalist concepts of democracy.

The imaginary is a symbol of *inclusive* nationhood, a negation of nationhood violently imposed by a minority on the majority and maintained through repression; it exposes the failure of the dominant elites to create an inclusionary nation. But it does not remain purely symbolic: Some expressions of subaltern self-organization, based in part on the collective social memory of resistance, inspired the recent decades of Mayan organizing. And in the context of the peace process, new hopes and aspirations have been awakened in the hearts and minds of many Guatemalans. The peace accords are a Bill of Rights for the hitherto most excluded sectors of the population.

But especially after the May 1999 referendum, how can we argue that subjective indicators so intangible and elusive as rising expectations, inclusionary visions, and a gradual decline of fear constitute an advance? For one thing, they are the basis for new forms of behavior. Many individuals and organizations are acting as if the peace accords were in place *as rights.* In the 1997–1998 negotiations for the constitutional reforms (particularly on customary law), for example, Mayan organizations were acting on the basis of those rights. As a consequence, the ruling political power (PAN) had no choice but to negotiate with the indigenous coalition COPMAGUA, as well as with the traditional elite actors that have always been their negotiating partners. Even though the constitutional reforms were not approved, it is highly unlikely that organized sectors of the indigenous population will demobilize or accept the exclusionary *status quo ante*. New social demands are also arising from the peace accords' legitimation of the *idea* of social spending and governmental responsibility for generalized well-being; these social and political demands cut across ethnic lines to mobilize poor ladinos as well as Mayas. At another level, the ODHA and Truth Commission reports crystallized the demand for justice; the historical memory they preserve is an essential part of the "different possible future."[16] These examples remind us that even where revolutions fail, people's hearts and minds are often transformed by the experience.

I have found it impossible to explain the stakes in Guatemala's peace process in material terms alone. While rooted in structural/material conditions, the peace process also has a less measurable side—a collective social vision, a "politics of rights" that goes far beyond the traditional condemnation of human rights violations. At the heart of this politics of rights is a comprehensive notion of *citizenship*, that is, beyond the formal legal status, belonging and inclusion, entitlement and full equality—in sharp contrast to the historic exclusion and dispossession of great majorities of the population (the poor, the indigenous, women). (See Poitevín 1999.) Active participation by these constituencies is a necessary basis for building democracy *with* citizenship (as contrasted with the monster of "democracy without citizenship" discussed in Chapter 4).

Beyond negotiating an end to wars, then, long-range peace processes are largely about constructing citizenship. In his call for a binational state as the basis for a settlement and reconciliation in the Middle East, Edward Said (1999, 39) has written:

> The beginning is to develop something entirely missing from both Israeli and Palestinian realities today: the idea and practice of citizenship, not of ethnic or racial community, as the main vehicle for coexistence. In a modern state, all its members are citizens by virtue of their presence and the sharing of rights and responsibilities. Citizenship therefore entitles an Israeli Jew and a Palestinian Arab to the same privileges and resources.

Implicit within a broad conception of citizenship, as well, is a belief in individual potential—not only for the privileged but for everyone, as evoked in Nelson Mandela's 1994 inaugural words:

> Our deepest fear is not that we are inadequate. Our deepest fear is that we are powerful beyond measure. . . . We ask ourselves, who am I to be brilliant, gorgeous, talented, and fabulous? Actually, who are you *not* to be? You are a child of God. . . . We are born to make manifest the glory of God that is within us. It is not just in some of us; it is in everyone. And as we let our own

light shine, we unconsciously give people permission to do the same. As we are liberated from our own fear, our presence automatically liberates others.

A second fundamental element of the visionary politics associated with peace processes is *social reconciliation*. I am using the conceptualization by Lipschutz (1998, 9 ff.): "a long-term process, involving therapy, social work, and the building of trust between formerly warring communities." (See also Scheper-Hughes 1998, and the discussion by Wilmer [1998, 102 ff.] of how a postconflict "civil society is constructed, destroyed, and rebuilt.") In Guatemala, this is part of the healing process that must take place in hundreds of communities where, for example, ex-PAC members live side by side with their victims. It will also involve a long process of bringing out the truth, as the initial step toward reconciliation and human reconstruction, a measure of justice, and possible eventual forgiveness. As related in the South African case, "the Truth and Reconciliation Commission process has, in fact, opened up new emotional spaces where conversations and actions that were once impossible, even unthinkable, are now happening" (Scheper-Hughes 1998, 138).[17] However distant this seems in Guatemala, since the army has taken no responsibility for its war crimes, this goal and this demand will be central to the struggle for the soul of postwar Guatemala.

A final element of social reconciliation in Guatemala concerns Maya/ladino relations. Coming from a totally exclusionary past, the peace accords projected the vision of a multiethnic, multicultural society. The "multi" discourse emphasized a reappropriation and revalidation of indigenous cultural identities and the right to "difference" (versus "ladinization," which is a form of homogenization). But even coming from Mayan leaders who were clearly not separatists (but seeking equality and recognition for autonomous practices within the national state framework), this provoked among many ladinos fears of ethnic conflict or "privileges" for the Mayas (something like anti-affirmative action sentiments in the United States). At the same time, the strengthening of Mayan movements led progressive nonindigenous intellectuals to explore more constructive responses (e.g., Marta Elena Casáus interview in *Crónica*, Sept. 16, 1996). In the wake of the *consulta*, the search for *intercultural* dialogue and political practices has become a much more conscious goal of both Mayan and progressive ladino actors (see Solares 1999). Whereas "multi" emphasizes diversity, "inter" adds process-oriented values of interaction, *convivencia* (living together), articulation of differences in an ongoing discussion, tending toward possible alliances. Both emphases will have to be included in a culturally pluralistic vision that departs radically from Guatemala's past and points to a new social contract.

Really-Existing Postwar
Post-*Consulta* Guatemala

"De-centaurization" Revisited

The most dangerous immediate consequence of the referendum was the loss of the historic opportunity to constitutionally limit the functions of the army and subordinate it to civilian authority.* This is also the principal constitutional reform that technically cannot be changed through ordinary congressional legislation but would require another referendum or ANC. In contrast with the *imaginario*, which projects a very broad democratic vision (construction of full citizenship), de-centaurization is the minimalist bottom line for Guatemalan democracy. Because it lies at the very heart of the peace process and of this book, it merits a final discussion.

The most direct referent for de-centaurization is the content of the Accord on Strengthening Civilian Power. As analyzed in one report by the URNG think tank IPES (July 5, 1999), by mid-1999, the army had complied with only three of the twelve specific commitments in the accord; among those commitments that had not been met were the most important reforms, particularly the redefinition of the functions of the army, which was tied up with the constitutional reforms, and redefinition of "military doctrine." We have seen in previous chapters that even after the accords were signed, the majority of the army high command (with very few individual exceptions) did not really unite with the peace project and the changes it implied—above all, civilian control and reduction of the army's autonomy. After July 1997, the army's posture ranged from open or sub-rosa resistances to a low-profile stance of "outwaiting" the peace process and the MINUGUA presence.

This last point is important in contesting the thesis that the Guatemalan army initiated the peace process or turned the peace accords into its own project—which would imply that Guatemalan society stood to gain almost nothing from the peace accords. Schirmer (1998, 270), for example, states that the accords, particularly the Accord on Strengthening Civilian Power, "represent for the army the final institutionalization of their strategic project to win the war militarily and politically by 'neutralizing' and reinserting the guerrillas into political life." As discussed in Chapters 1 and 2, the army's goal for many years (including the early years of the

---

*Although not totally surprised, I was stunned by the outcome of the May 16 referendum. While I intended to end this book with the referendum, I realized that I could not fully interpret its consequences in a nuanced, balanced way from outside Guatemala. What follows here is based largely on the many conversations I had during a final summer 1999 trip to post-*consulta* Guatemala.

peace negotiations) was to annihilate the URNG and to *prevent* its political reinsertion. It is quite true, as Schirmer argues (1998, 2), that the army's goal before, during, and after the peace accords was continued domination through "appropriation of the imagery of the rule of law," and this included its claims to be the author of both the 1980s democratic transition and the 1990s peace accords. However, having this goal does not make it a reality—as seen from the army's continual passive (sometimes active) resistance to accord implementation.[18] If most army officials continue resisting, there must be something to resist and some reason why they celebrated on the night that the constitutional reforms were defeated.

Interpretations that overestimate the army's role in the peace process risk underplaying the role of other actors and accepting the desires and posturing rhetoric of army officials at face value (e.g., claims that the *consulta* result was a vote of confidence in the army [*Inforpress Centroamericana*, Aug. 13, 1999]). Beyond academic interpretation, this stance has implications for public action. The argument that even full implementation of the accords would be insufficient to establish civilian authority (Schirmer 1998, 274)—a view that resonates among some sectors in Guatemala—can make civil society actors less willing to take on the battle. It is indeed a fierce battle, but it can be won by advocates of civilian control only if they believe that their efforts to force compliance with the accords will make a difference.

Indeed, the obstacles to implementation of the demilitarization accord are so great precisely because, beyond the specific commitments contained in the accord, it is inspired by a broader, more integral goal: dismantling the hybrid "centaur" bred by the counterinsurgency war and decisively changing the relation of civilian to military power. This requires fundamental changes by many players other than the army in order to strengthen civilian authority in the state and society. Drawing on a wide body of literature about this process in Latin America, Arévalo (1998a, ch. 9; 1998b) has spelled this out for Guatemala to mean development of a comprehensive "military policy"—that is, an integral policy of civilian authorities toward the army, combined with a military doctrine appropriate for a democratic society.[19]

It is also important to remember that demilitarization has been a Herculean task throughout Latin America. (See, for example, McSherry 1998 and other articles in that collection.) These experiences have demonstrated that (particularly postauthoritarian) civilian governments and politicians generally do the minimum necessary unless they are under strong pressure from civil society. In Guatemala, as in El Salvador, the peace accords provided important mechanisms for translating the desire for civilian control over the army into a reality. But in Guatemala, whether by design,[20] omission, or weakness, the URNG did not use its own demobilization as leverage to force governmental compliance with the demilitarization accord—which would have meant passage of the constitutional reforms affecting the army simultaneously with and/or as a condition for URNG demobilization. Indeed, the URNG was not alone in failing to foresee the problems: Former negotiators for the government say they had assumed that approval of the constitutional reforms in both Congress and the referendum would be accomplished during the first year. It is in hindsight that all pro-peace forces see this as a strategic error of the accord negotiation per se. Compounded by Arzú's increasing tendency after mid-1997 to grant the army its autonomy and by the lack of full discussion about demilitarization before the *consulta*, this could lead to one of the great lost opportunities of Guatemala's peace process if it is not corrected soon.

What can be done in the absence of the constitutional reform of the army's functions? From my summer 1999 interviews, a number of ideas emerged: (1) above all, the issue must be restored to the forefront of the public agenda before and after the November 1999 elections, obligating candidates (and the president-elect) to specify their demilitarization programs; (2) according to numerous experts, including two former defense ministers (*Prensa Libre*, May 20, 1999, and *Siglo Veintiuno*, May 24, 1999), Congress could legislate the de facto separation of military and police functions by strengthening and professionalizing the PNC as fast as possible and sharply delimiting the army's role in internal security; this was the essence of the Truth Commission's prophetic recommendation (para. 78) in the event that the *consulta* was lost; (3) there are proposals for a new referendum to deal solely with the issue of the army's functions; (4) in support of domestic efforts, international actors (above all, the United States and European "friend" armies) can actively promote these changes with Guatemalan army officials, holding them to their public statements accepting the reforms; they can take demilitarization as a litmus test for compliance with the peace accords and a condition for all future international cooperation. Until the army's mandate is limited, Guatemala risks ending up as a semi-failed peace process.

Mixed Signals: Uncertainties and Continuities

As discussed in Chapters 6 and 7, the peace accord implementation process was already in serious trouble before May 16, 1999; but the constitutional reforms were supposed to fix all that and establish national "ratification" of the accords. Now, however, the *consulta* outcome has provided an excuse for questions to be raised about the very continuity of the implementation process. This situation has led some participants and observers to conclude that the Guatemalan peace process is over and that the peace accords cannot be regarded as "accords of state." Although it is logical for hard-line peace resisters to make this argument, it is a misinterpretation and an unnecessary capitulation when it comes from peace supporters. The lack of guarantees does not mean the end of the peace process. It does subject all future gains to the ups and downs of the "normal" political arena, rather than the certainties of a controlled negotiating environment. The continuity of the accords will have to be established by making them sustainable in the political arena—primarily Congress, in interaction with various pro-peace constituencies of civil society.[21]

In short, the forms and mechanisms of the peace process are changing, and this will affect the lineup of players as well as the pace of change and the degrees of certainty. The process will also be affected by two major late-1999/early-2000 contingencies external to the peace process: (1) the outcome of the general (presidential, congressional, mayoral) elections of November 1999, mainly a contest between the PAN and the FRG at the presidential level, but with important stakes for the pro-peace Center and Left; and (2) the likelihood of a major economic/financial crisis during the winter of 1999/2000—the "wild card" that is bound to have direct and indirect effects for the peace process.

Within this context, we can project several possible medium-range scenarios.[22] The most negative scenario would be explicit noncontinuity of the peace accord implementation process by whatever new government takes office in January 2000—total stagnation or fade-away of the peace accords, or even a rollback or reversal of some kind—for example, premature termination/expulsion of MINUGUA. In this nightmare scenario, Guatemala could be in for another half century of reaction, repression, and racism—something like the Jim Crow period following Reconstruction in the U.S. South, or another rollback experience (the first being the 1954 overthrow of Arbenz).

An alternative, less drastic scenario (and probably more likely) is the *institutionalization of uncertainty*.[23] A transition such as this is best understood through the lens of a filmmaker rather than a still photographer. I am reminded that in the dynamics of the peace negotiations, there was no predicting exactly how the parties would get out of each impasse. The implementation process has also had a dynamic of obstacles and impasses, but with fewer breakthroughs. In part this is because the postwar negotiations involve an even broader spectrum of social and political actors than the peace negotiations—on the one hand, sectors of civil society strengthened by the peace process, on the other hand, political parties, especially the FRG. As in the past, some apparent dead ends may turn out to have an unexpected, previously unseen way out; but in Guatemala, these are generally discovered or invented only at ten minutes before

Monuments to Guatemala's peace: The "Flame of Peace" is in the Central Plaza, just outside the National Palace, and was lit on the night of December 29, 1996, when the peace accords were signed. The sculpture of the hands, the "Monument to Peace," is in the courtyard of the National Palace of Culture, which is the new name and function of what was formerly the National Palace.

midnight. As SEPAZ head Raquel Zelaya (WWICS 1999, 24) described the dynamics of 1997–1998, "the friends of the peace process are very timid during the periods without major difficulties. We see their solidarity with the process only when we are up to our necks in water. It's a very Guatemalan way to act."

One reason why the enemies of the peace process are so much more visible than the friends is that after thirty-six years of war, virtually all nongovernmental players distrust the state. The private sector opposes state regulation, as well as any special arrangements with its historic enemy, the URNG. Urban ladinos of all classes see no direct benefit to themselves from the peace accords. The social sectors that stand to gain from the accords see the state as an essentially repressive apparatus and, in any case, have had a difficult time maintaining a united front, given the history of strong divisions and the precariousness of new attempts at unity on the Left.[24] These contradictions, deeply ingrained in Guatemala's political culture, have been particularly apparent in regard to the constitutional reforms and the tax reform, both of which implied strengthening the state, but both of which had to be agreed upon with sectors that distrust the state and/or want it to remain weak and dysfunctional. As seen in previous chapters, the political system seems designed to undermine the state's ability to promote change.

Particularly in the absence of the constitutional reforms, many of the formal mechanisms established by the peace accords to ensure government accountability are losing force, and new ones will have to be invented. First, of the dozens of commissions and *comisiones paritarias* established by the accords, many have finished their work, although a major new one was created for the *pacto fiscal*. Second, the URNG's relatively privileged position in the negotiation process and its leverage over government policies, through the Comisión de Acompañamiento and through the Consultative Group meetings, will decline over time.[25] Longer range, the URNG will have to exert its influence as a political force—hopefully as part of a strong pro-peace opposition bloc in Congress that can exert pressure on an indifferent or hostile government; but that force remains to be built, as URNG leaders have acknowledged. Third, there is no formal entity to represent pro-peace civil society organizations that is as cohesive as the ASC was during the 1994–1996 peace negotiations. Although some sectors (indigenous, women's) are growing rapidly, others (e.g., labor unions, the Catholic Church) have been declining in influence. "Civil society," then, has not been a cohesive pro-peace force, as became painfully clear during the *consulta*.[26] There exists a huge space in Guatemalan politics for a leftist force;[27] but even with the FDNG political representation in Congress since 1996, the political Left is still far from having learned how to occupy that space.

If some of the formal mechanisms for holding the government account-able are losing force over time, what factors can reinforce the continuity and sustainability of the peace process? First, leaving aside the peace re-sisters and their lawyers, there is a strong current of expert opinion that the accords are, in the words of the Mack Foundation (1999), "political commit-ments of the Guatemalan state . . . negotiated with the URNG by three con-secutive elected governments over the course of six years, with UN media-tion and participation by various social sectors"; hence, they are accords of state, independent of changes in government. Second, even the constitu-tional reforms that were defeated in the referendum did have the stamp of congressional approval by the necessary two-thirds majority.[28] Third, sev-eral basic mechanisms of the peace accords—MINUGUA, CG meetings, Comisión de Acompañamiento, the Timetable, and some of the participa-tory commissions (e.g., *pacto fiscal*)—remain in place at least through the end of 2000 (possibly 2001). They can be used intelligently and strategically to broaden the support base for the accords (e.g., by incorporating repre-sentatives of major opposition parties into the Comisión de Acom-pañamiento) and to achieve legislative implementation of the accords.

Fourth, public opinion has given positive as well as negative messages. Very shortly after the *consulta,* a poll showed that 83.9 percent favored continuation of the peace process by the next government.[29] A July 1999 message of the Catholic Church Bishop's Conference about the upcoming elections stated clearly, "the peace accords remain the great national agenda for achieving a better future," and it will be the duty of the next government to fulfill them (*Prensa Libre,* July 21, 1999; see also *Prensa Li-bre,* July 27, 1999). Finally, some who ended up supporting the No but were not ideologically anti-peace have begun to view the *consulta* results as a Pyrrhic victory. Even some representatives of CEDECON and CACIF are having to explain that it was not their intention to destroy the peace accords. They might even look at the map of the *consulta* vote and recog-nize that the peace process offered the best chance for a smooth, gradual transition to a less exclusionary society.[30] But the "modernizing Right" will never move or make any concessions unless it feels pressured by so-cial and political forces of the Left (see below).

Given all of the above factors, it seems worth suggesting that despite all odds (and even amid a major economic crisis), there might be a more pos-itive version of the uncertainty scenario: beyond *consulta* damage control, a "relaunching" of the peace process during the critical year 2000 (and ex-tension of MINUGUA's mandate through 2001). This would have to be the project of a very proactive multisector pro-peace coalition. Clearly, the URNG and other pro-peace forces in the political Left will remain central to any peace-related initiatives, but they have a great deal to learn from the *consulta* experience—above all, how to work within a coalition.

Decisive actors in such a coalition would come from the pro-peace social Left (different constituencies of civil society)—especially those open
to learning from the *consulta* experience. During the summer of 1999, I
found a widespread ferment of ideas and self-criticisms and a search for
new ways of engaging and effectively influencing the political process. A
number of Mayan and popular organizations (and individuals) are using
this key moment as a mirror to see their weaknesses as well as their
strengths—as they did after the 1993 *Serranazo*.[31] Some of them understand the need to develop strategies for increasing grassroots participation that is not just nominal but effective. They can also build on experiences from the participatory peace accord commissions that were
designed to incorporate previously excluded sectors (e.g., indigenous
people, peasants, women, refugees and displaced populations, ex-
combatants) and to engage them in dialogue and interaction with government agencies, both locally and nationally.

Also essential to a "relaunching" coalition would be players not identified with the Left or grassroots civil society—among the most important,
a number of thoughtful pro-peace professionals (some of them with experience from the peace negotiations, the Comisión de Acompañamiento, or
other commissions). Beyond bridge-building, these individuals can contribute a pro-peace "strategic intelligence," a pragmatic ability to translate visions into feasible projects.[32]

This pro-peace coalition would have several major goals and priorities.
The first would be to relegitimate the peace process (after the *consulta*
seemed to have made peace a dirty word) and to establish its continuity
and political sustainability by broadening the political base of the existing
peace mechanisms. Ultimately, the goal is to build a social-political force
broad enough to make the peace agenda more nearly a national agenda.
The second priority would be massive political education to involve the
huge numbers of abstainers and nonregistered potential voters—to extend the reach of the political process and pressure for the long-overdue
electoral reforms. The third goal would be to present the new government
with a prioritized agenda for accord implementation (through legislation
and administrative initiatives) in the key areas of indigenous rights, demilitarization and public security reform, justice strengthening and reform, progressive tax measures (emerging from the *pacto fiscal*), and land-
related measures.[33] The ongoing task of this coalition would be to
pressure for and contribute to implementation of the peace agenda.

A final key player affecting the prospects for Guatemalan peace remains the international community. The Guatemalan government continues to have a contradictory relation with that community. This was
highlighted once again at the May 1999 (Stockholm) CG meeting for
Central America, when Guatemalan officials had to "explain" to skepti-

cal donors the *consulta* results—as well as the unresolved Gerardi case, resistance to the CEH recommendations, and lack of progress on tax reform. International pressures may become even more important in the context of an economic crisis. It goes without saying that the IFIs will have to resist the temptation, when the crisis hits, to prioritize macroeconomic stability and reduced state spending over peace implementation and peace conditionality.

Medium-range, the specific forms of conditionality are likely to change, with CG meetings becoming less central and donor governments—with the important exception of the United States—exercising their influence more strategically, less frequently, and with a lower profile.[34] There will likely be occasional collective interventions by the international community, in coordination with MINUGUA, to ensure accord compliance and internal financing for peace-related projects, to untangle impasse situations among domestic players, and to strengthen internal pro-peace forces with raised expectations.[35] International influence will also come through foreign trade and investment, which require a far better political/social climate than currently prevails in Guatemala. Peace conditionality may take new forms, but it is more necessary than ever.

Michelangelo's "Prisoners"

Guatemala's peace accords reached very high—too high, some would say. Beyond correcting the distortions from the decades of repression and war (that is, making Guatemala a normal country), they attempt to turn a society that was racist and exclusionary to the core into a fully democratic and multicultural/intercultural society. The magnitude of this enterprise is daunting, and the difficulties have been far greater than expected. No one ever thought it would be easy; but some previously hidden costs of having lived through decades of civil war are only now emerging in their full complexity. As one participant put it, "the peace process will have to be reinvented over and over again." The elements for such a reinvention exist in Guatemala, with its great human, cultural, and natural resources, and its particular component of magic. Therein lies the vision and the drive to develop a workable solution, despite the Sisyphus-like obstacles.

Even though accord implementation has not even begun to meet the much-raised expectations, the accords remain the core agenda for those who seek Guatemala's reinvention. Even with all its impossible problems, the peace process remains the best available option and the only way forward. There was no choice but to make that effort, and there is no choice but to keep making it. This is the only historical opportunity Guatemala has had since 1954, and the best one it will have in the next half century.

Whatever the outcome, it has been and remains an extraordinary effort at human engineering. It seems unlikely that history will be harsh in judging those who made the effort. All who have contributed to this epic effort are heroes, because it is better to have tried and failed than not to have tried.

The Guatemalan experience is a painful reminder that anything worth doing involves endless struggle. In an essay written just after the referendum, reflecting on its meanings for the Mayan movement, Jorge Solares (1999, 19) takes us to Florence, to visit the Gallery of the Academy of Fine Arts:

> At the end of a half-lit corridor, a cascade of brilliant light falls from the dome over the perfectly finished white sculpture of David by the genius sculptor Michelangelo. As if guarding both sides of the gallery and in the shadow, are enormous stones of unpolished marble—from which, struggling to emerge with titanic boldness . . . are the unfinished, tragic, colossal and unresolved figures of four prisoners, struggling to get out of the prison of the unfinished rock.
>
> One has the feeling that the great Michelangelo was suggesting that any birth of a free and dignified existence is a difficult process, in which nothing can be taken for granted and nothing is gratuitously conceded. Any struggle for dignity and liberty bears the face of the pain and the passion contained in these marble figures by the genius of Florence. The Maya movement, as the counterpart in jade, is struggling to free itself from the unpolished stone that the centuries of mistreatment and exploitation represent. We can only hope that on this path will be found a resolution as brilliant as that which triumphs in that famous museum in Florence.

Notes

1. The term "globalization" has been used by different analysts to mean many different things. My encrypted summary of this very complex phenomenon is taken from the following analyses, among others: Chase-Dunn (2000); Robinson (1997); Portes (1997, 1999); Kay (1998); Stark (1998); and Borón (1998).

2. Two distinctions deserve mention. First, neoliberalism is not a simple continuation of earlier (1945–1970s) U.S./IFI approaches to Third World development during the Cold War era, when the West was competing with the socialist bloc and when its development policies were laced with the mitigating rhetoric of "trickle-down" benefits for the working class and poor. The more extreme neoliberal fundamentalism is partly an artifact of the post-socialist, post–Cold War era. (For a different view, see Petras and Veltmeyer 1999.)

Second, neoliberalism is often referred to as the "Washington Consensus," having its principal authors and proponents in the U.S. and the Washington-based IFIs. European-promoted development policies are generally more rooted in welfare state capitalism. For example, Crighton (1998, 77 ff.) argues that British policy for peace in Northern Ireland has not shared the "neoliberal illusion that free markets and elections can build peace" and has followed a more "state-centered" route.

3. I am using "sustainable" very broadly to refer to development that addresses the "social debt" owed to the poor and working classes (jobs as well as services); since it would relate to the world-economy on a basis sustainable for *all* sectors of society, it incorporates a role for the internal consumer market as well as competitiveness in the world market. (Some Latin American analysts refer to this as a "neostructuralist" approach—see Kay 1998). Boyce (1998, 4) adds a component of "democratic accountability" that would "protect the property rights of the poor and middle classes from the predations of the rich and powerful." Beyond the socioeconomic dimension, some of its other parameters include political accountability and a responsible state. In the Guatemalan case, it would also necessarily include a democracy that is multicultural and intercultural. A program for sustainability, broadly defined, would provide a progressive alternative for middle-class voters concerned about the quality of life for the country as a whole—for example, viewing the elimination of poverty and unemployment as the best way to combat the wave of common crime.

4. After having to respond to the contradictions of growing impoverishment caused by their structural adjustment programs, the IFIs have become somewhat less fundamentalist in their programs. For example, the "poverty reduction" and human resource development emphases and a return to the discourse of "trickle-down" were necessary correctives to the excesses of neoliberalism. (See Ruthrauff 1998; Fuentes and Carothers 1998, 313, n. 26). An important pressure on the IFIs has come from the UNDP reports showing inexorably, year after year, that globalization has widened the gap between rich and poor nations (and between rich and poor within nations). A 1999 study also highlighted growing U.S. economic and cultural dominance (*New York Times,* July 14, 1999).

5. A reading of Paige (1997) suggests the origin of this difference between the ruling elites in El Salvador and Guatemala (the rupture between agrarian and agro-industrial fractions in El Salvador but not in Guatemala); however, this contrast is not developed in full detail, since Guatemala is not a major focus of his study.

6. Regarding this point, as well as the complex relation of civil society to IFIs in Guatemala and elsewhere in Central America, Pearce (1998a and 1998b) argues that the IFIs have created a window of opportunity that can be used by civil society organizations. To be sure, progressive forces are far behind CACIF in developing a concrete program for development; they are under increasing pressure to do so, in response to rising expectations from the peace process.

7. More generally, it has been convincingly argued in the migration literature (by Alejandro Portes and Saskia Sassen, among others) that globalization generates migration: The freer movement of capital across borders generates cross-border movements of labor—despite the (ironically) statist attempts by the advanced industrial nation governments to control the latter.

8. Sources for this figure range from the U.S. embassy in Guatemala to the Guatemalan foreign ministry and embassy and consulates in the United States.

Official INS figures are considerably lower, since they count only those who come in contact with U.S. authorities (Rincón et al. 1999).

9. Some analysts (e.g., Chase-Dunn 2000) refer to a related but broader pattern of "globalization from below," which includes such transnational activities as cross-border organizing in support of minimum wages for maquiladora workers. In a sense, cross-border organizing is the only way to offset the effects of neoliberal globalization, such as drastically reduced unionization rates (the result of privatizations and anti-union models of labor relations). Although cross-border organizing has not yet become a systematic strategy in Guatemala, there have been important specific cases: the campaign in support of Coca Cola workers (late 1970s through mid-1980s); the successful campaign by U.S. activists, eventually involving the AFL-CIO, pressuring the U.S. Trade Office not to extend preferential trade status to Guatemala until improvements were made in labor practices (late 1980s through mid-1990s); and the (late 1990s) campaigns in support of coffee workers for suppliers to Starbucks Coffee and maquiladora workers at the Phillips Van Heusen plant.

10. Even during the Cold War there were negotiated solutions to conflicts, the main example being Vietnam. However, that was more the exception than the rule, a result of the United States not having "won" the war. The general paradigm was "winners versus losers," as opposed to concessions from both sides. There is another group of cases that I am deliberately not including here: cases such as Nicaragua and Angola, which were Cold War civil wars, but whose dynamics were somewhat different because anti-communist "Contra"-style forces with U.S. backing were attempting to overthrow revolutionary or nationalist governments, rather than vice versa.

11. The distinction between Cold War and post–Cold War insurgencies in Latin America is made by analysts in Arnson (1999, ch. 8 and 457). For an argument that the difference between Cold War and post–Cold War civil conflicts is more a matter of discourse than reality, see Lipschutz (1998, 11–13).

12. This tendency seems to be particularly pronounced among some non–Central Americans who went from studying or working in El Salvador during the 1980s to Guatemala in the 1990s. In their minds, the Salvadoran model—and particularly the military stalemate in El Salvador—became the standard for measuring everything in Guatemala. The essence of their argument is that unlike the FMLN, the URNG was militarily defeated during the 1980s (an exaggeration); hence, the peace accords are *substantively* weaker (not true) and the peace process never really "took root" in Guatemala (an oversimplification). On the last point, careful analysts emphasize that Guatemala's peace accords are organically rooted among sectors of the population that were most affected by the war, while far less so among Guatemala City residents. (This was the great lesson from the *consulta*.) My point is that although the comparison is inevitable and useful, it should be made carefully and with respect for each process—as did Héctor Dada, cited in the text. In comparing Guatemala with El Salvador, Arnson (1999, 8–9) warns against reifying military balance as *the* determining factor in peace negotiations. (See also last section of Chapter 2.)

13. To mention only one example, although the FMLN was legalized as a political party without much ado in 1992, the URNG had to spend over two years ful-

filling the endlessly byzantine requirements for becoming a political party. If the peace accords had attempted to make an exception for the URNG, the peace resisters would probably have taken the entire peace accord arrangement to the Constitutional Court in December 1996 or January 1997.

14. The irony is that Colombia played an important role as one of the four "Contadora Group" countries that made peace proposals for Central America in the mid-1980s; subsequently, Colombia was a member of the "Friends" Groups for the Salvadoran and Guatemalan negotiations.

15. I am using the term in its broadest sense. For a variety of articles developing the concept in relation to one of its original referents, in the literature about Latin American indigenous movements, see Dary (1998). Also central is the literature emerging from women's movements.

16. There is a growing literature on the politics of memory and the role of Truth Commissions in generating counter-hegemonic *imaginarios*. See, for example, Jelin 1998 (and other articles in the same collection); Hale 1997; Hayner 1994; Kaye 1997; several articles in Arnson 1999—and on South Africa's Commission, Rosenberg 1996; Ignatieff 1997 (also, Note 17 below). Reverberations of Guatemala's CEH Report, and of the international prosecution of Chilean dictator Pinochet in 1998–1999, have spilled across borders to impact the entire hemisphere. Even the U.S. government has been pressured to participate in the process, leading to President Clinton's Guatemala apology (see Chapter 5) and to U.S. declassification of documents that are key to the reconstructions of history throughout Latin America.

In Guatemala, historical memory as recorded in *testimonio*—the genre most used by Truth Commissions—has also become the subject of a 1999 debate, sparked by Stoll's (1999) questioning of the world-famous autobiography of Nobel Laureate Rigoberta Menchú (1984). (These issues will be fully explored in several forthcoming books.) At the center of the storm lie deeper issues such as the use of testimony as history and conflicting interpretations of the last twenty-five years: Who writes history and how is it written? Which (and whose) version(s) of history will be read and believed two decades from now? (See also last section in Chapter 1.)

17. Sometimes the attempt to make sense of social suffering (e.g., through the South African Truth and Reconciliation Commission, as recounted by Scheper-Hughes [1998]) brings out the best in people. Such was the case of Amy Biehl's parents, who favored amnesty for the black youths who killed their daughter. (See also Biehl and Biehl 1998).

18. My point here is made very precisely by Kincaid (2000) in an article comparing public security reform in Guatemala and El Salvador: "As opposed to an interpretation emphasizing the resourcefulness of the Guatemalan armed forces in defending their long-standing dominance of society (cf. Schirmer 1998), the argument here is that a variety of factors—such as external pressures, generational transitions of leadership, and growing assertiveness among new social actors—will make further demilitarization irresistible," although with delays caused by the public security crises in Guatemala, as in El Salvador. For a pre-peace process discussion of the extent and limitations of Guatemala's counterinsurgency state, see Jonas (1991, 171 ff.).

19. Williams and Walter (1997, 8–12) have developed the concept of a "military policy" in regard to El Salvador: a policy that would "address all aspects of the military's traditional domination of the political sphere" and initiate a process of "decolonization of the state apparatus and of everyday life."

20. According to one top URNG leader, the FMLN advised the URNG, on the basis of the Salvadoran experience, to avoid the complications of a long, drawn-out demobilization. In hindsight, of course, URNG leaders can see the much more serious complications of the route that was taken.

21. Several Guatemalans expressed it in more theoretical terms: Changes in the constitution have to be the expression (and result) of a broad national political consensus or agreement, rather than vice versa. (See Poitevín 1999, 5.)

22. I say "medium-range" in order to avoid the teleological danger of a long-range view that Guatemala will necessarily ("*en última instancia*") be better off with the accords on paper and will eventually move in a forward direction. Although this might be true at one level, it does not capture the continual dangers of a lost opportunity, or the roller-coaster ups and downs, or the comparison between what exists and what was envisioned.

23. In one of his last speeches as secretary general of the URNG, and in my last interview with him in August 1998, the late Rolando Morán (1998a) emphasized that uncertainty is the hallmark and the norm of a transition of such major proportions; instabilities, problems with no short-range solutions, and even periods of stagnation are its essence. In his words (months before the *consulta* defeat), "It's like a soccer game: everything has to be won yard by yard in order to get a goal."

24. For heuristic purposes, I am defining "leftist" forces broadly, to include progressive intellectuals and human rights and other social movement organizations/NGOs as well as the URNG and its supporters. Although logically the entire Left stands to gain from the peace process and accords, some unaffiliated forces were critical of the URNG during the 1980s through the mid-1990s for holding out to negotiate, or for other reasons never really believed in the peace process. Today, some of these same forces are critical of the URNG for making compromises, and a kind of all-or-nothing maximalism is combined with a deep pessimism (see Chapter 6). From the URNG side, as discussed in Chapter 8, the *consulta* experience revealed an inability to reach out to its natural base or to engage skeptics or critics in a serious dialogue about wartime (and postwar) errors or crucial tasks of peace-building.

25. Actually, in the view of knowledgeable participants in the peace process (e.g., Arnault in Arnson 1999, 293–294) and as seen throughout this book, the URNG was less hegemonic, "privileged," and insulated from civil society pressures both before and after the signing of peace than is commonly believed. We have seen the role of the ASC during the negotiations; during the implementation phase, COPMAGUA carried out its own negotiations with the PAN about the constitutional reforms on indigenous issues. In any case, the URNG can hardly be accused of having negotiated "behind the backs" of civil society or engaged in a simple "pact between elites," as critics from all sides have charged.

26. From a variety of different viewpoints, generally as the alternative to "top-down" strategies, there is a tendency to idealize (and thereby reify) "civil society." Pearce (1998b, 7 ff.) critiques this tendency on the part of donor agencies (and on

the part of some popular or civil society organizations themselves), showing how it reduces the very plurality and complexity of civil society to a "reified subject." A separate issue now receiving more attention is the vulnerability of grassroots organizations and NGOs when they become overly dependent on international funding that will eventually dry up.

27. According to a mid-1999 poll, 25.9 percent of Guatemalans define themselves as having leftist sympathies, as compared with 25.4 percent rightist, 24.4 percent centrist, and the rest undecided (*Prensa Libre,* Aug. 10, 1999).

28. According to several key peace negotiators, the constitutional reforms had originally been assumed to be the last of the *short-range* commitments (i.e., to be passed by Congress either at the time of the peace signing or during the first year)—in which case, most observers agree, they would have had the momentum for approval in a referendum.

29. In another mixed message, the same (August 1999) poll that showed an advantage for the FRG presidential candidate also registered an 82 percent rejection (87 percent among women) of the idea that ex-military officers who had committed war crimes, a number of whom were on the FRG congressional slate, should participate in electoral politics (*Prensa Libre,* Aug. 25, 1999).

30. This logic has been explained to me as follows: Thus far the Mayan movement has not been anti-ladino or separatist. Furthermore, the last three years, since the signing of the accords, have been years of relative social peace. The more thoughtful "modernizers" on the Right might also eventually realize that all the new roads and other infrastructural improvements being made to attract increased foreign investment, tourism, and so forth, are useless unless the country becomes more civilized. From this perspective, their real adversary is not a reasonable indigenous/popular movement but the hard-line peace resisters.

31. For example, a panel at the August 1999 Congreso de Estudios Mayas on "The State and the Mayas" turned into a fascinating debate regarding the lessons of the *consulta;* amid considerable disagreement (including some who had opposed the reforms!), there was a surprising degree of consensus regarding the long-range need for ladino allies and about the need for "*inter*cultural" (Maya/ladino) as well as "*multi*cultural" dialogues and solutions. These ideas were expressed also in interviews.

32. As one example, after the *consulta,* a group of these professionals and practitioners designed the project "Visión Guatemala." Drawing partly on experiences from South Africa, the architects of this project see their role as setting the stage for dialogues between former antagonists, soliciting "trickle-up" input from nonelite constituencies, while developing a methodology to "get things done." Another emphasis is the ever-elusive articulation between visions and daily realities. (See Visión Guatemala 1999.)

33. The closest to any interim strategy is the workplan of the Comisión de Acompañamiento, which sees two phases: (1) during the 1999 electoral period, to take "bridge actions," convoking a broad-based Peace Congress, getting political candidates and parties committed to continuity of the peace process (such an event took place in October 1999); and (2) long-range, to create favorable conditions for continuity of the process (rescheduling commitments, forging links for interaction with political parties and civil society, taking multisectoral initiatives

to breach the Maya/ladino gap)—the overall political goal being to restore peace to the center of the national agenda. Among the Comisión de Acompañamiento's specific goals is implementation of the CEH recommendations (which the Arzú government rejected).

34. The United States is a case apart because, in addition to a general peace agenda, the United States always has a separate bilateral agenda with Guatemala (regarding immigration, drug wars, and military aid/training). In addition, because of its political and financial battles with the UN, the United States remains key to decisions about renewing the MINUGUA mandate.

35. In a paper on the IFIs' approach to civil society in Guatemala, Jenny Pearce (1998b, 19) put it as follows: "Donors themselves need to sort out their own ambivalence between encouraging a self-determining democratic process and assuming that the outcome will not challenge the present form of Guatemala's integration into global capitalism." In their paper on peace conditionality, Fuentes and Carothers (1998, 310–311) recommend that, particularly if faced with government noncompliance, donor countries and agencies should channel assistance "preferentially," to strengthen nongovernmental actors in their ability to negotiate with the government (i.e., pressure for governmental compliance).

Epilogue

As this book goes to press, Guatemala's general elections of November 1999 have given a strong victory (just short of an absolute majority) to Alfonso Portillo, the presidential candidate of the FRG; the final outcome, pending the result of a December 26 run-off election between the FRG and PAN candidates, will be known only after this book is at the printer. Assuming a victory for the FRG, the party founded by former dictator Efraín Ríos Montt—following only six months after the defeat of the constitutional reforms—this election could be portrayed as a triumph of the iron fist and a slap in the face of the peace accords. But the complexities of this election result should not be reduced to one dimension; they should be read structurally as well as politically.

Politically, the FRG victory resulted from an astute populist campaign by Portillo, combined with a "punishment vote" against the Arzú government—primarily for the PAN's failure to take even the most basic measures to improve people's daily lives (socioeconomic situation and personal security), while maintaining the privileges of the rich. In this sense, it was a vote about people's most immediate concerns, not about the long-range structural issues addressed in the peace accords (indigenous rights, demilitarization, human rights, judicial and tax reform, etc.). Nevertheless, late in the campaign, pro-peace forces in Guatemalan civil society successfully pressured the major candidates to make commitments to maintain the continuity of the peace process, to honor the accords as accords of state, and to complete the implementation process that the Arzú government had left in limbo. And the day after the election (November 8, 1999), Guatemala's conservative newspaper *Prensa Libre* pointed out that "the peace accords are commitments of state," whose implementation must be on the agenda of the next government.

The other notable (surprising) element in the election was the much stronger than expected showing of the Alianza Nueva Nación, the leftist coalition constructed by the newly legalized URNG together with other progressive forces. Despite its scarce resources and many other disadvantages, the Alianza won around 13 percent of the national vote and nine seats in Congress. Structurally, the consolidation of the Left as the third force is a major step toward "normalizing" Guatemalan politics; for the first time since 1954, all political/ideological tendencies are represented. If the Left was already the natural defender of the peace accords, it now becomes a force that the two rightist parties will have to negotiate with. By issuing a stinging critique of peace accord noncompliance by the Arzú government during the campaign, the URNG evolved from the PAN's partner in signing the accords to its future role as central participant in a serious leftist opposition coalition.

In any case (and regardless of the run-off election result), the year 2000 will be a critical opportunity—perhaps the last—for the peace process: Either the accords will be taken off the back burner to which the PAN has opportunistically relegated them since 1997, or they will die an agonizing death and Guatemala will remain unchanged. On the negative side, implementing such aspects as the Truth Commission recommendations and major transformations of the army appears highly problematic—even endangered—given the strength of retrograde army forces in the FRG. Within the FRG delegation that will dominate the new Congress are key architects and henchmen of the scorched-earth dirty war of the 1980s—not to mention Ríos Montt himself, who will preside over Congress. How can the centaurs be expected to de-centaurize Guatemala?

On the more positive side, in addition to the Left's growing presence in Congress, two other elements could make a major difference: First, the pro-peace forces in civil society and the entire "relaunching coalition" have the opportunity (and the challenge) to be strongly and ongoingly proactive, as they were toward the end of the election campaign. Second, the international community will have considerable leverage with the new government, given the latter's financial crisis. Paradoxically, it could even have more leverage over an FRG government precisely because of the FRG's record as the party of human rights violators and peace resisters. If they remain interested in changing Guatemala, the donor institutions and governments can use their leverage strategically and intelligently (but uncompromisingly, immediately during the first few months, and ongoingly) to pressure the new government and Congress—and, behind them, the army and CACIF—to meet the demands for peace accord compliance.

The year 2000 marks the beginning of a new stage whose parameters are not yet clear. In defiance of any attempts to predict the dénouement of the peace process drama (Act V), Guatemala remains the country where anything can happen.

November 1999

Acronyms

AEU	Asociación de Estudiantes Universitarios (Association of University Students)
AID	U.S. Agency for International Development
ANC	Asamblea Nacional Constituyente (National Constituent Assembly)
ARENA	Alianza Republicana Nacionalista (Republican Nationalist Alliance) (El Salvador)
ASC	Asamblea de la Sociedad Civil (Civil Society Assembly)
CACIF	Comité Coordinador de Asociaciones Agrícolas, Comerciales, Industriales y Financieras (Coordinating Committee of Agricultural, Commercial, Industrial and Financial Associations)
CC	Corte de Constitucionalidad (Constitutional Court)
CEDECON	Centro para la Defensa de la Constitución (Center for the Defense of the Constitution)
CEH	Comisión de Esclarecimiento Histórico (Historical Clarification Commission—Guatemala's Truth Commission)
CEPAL	Comisión Económica para América Latina (U.N. Economic Commission for Latin America)
CERJ	Consejo de Comunidades Etnicas Runujel Junam (Council of Ethnic Communities "Everyone Is Equal")
CG	Consultative Group
CIA	U.S. Central Intelligence Agency
CNR	Comisión Nacional de Reconciliación (National Reconciliation Commission)
CONAVIGUA	Coordinadora Nacional de Viudas de Guatemala (National Coordinating Committee of Guatemalan Widows)

CONDEG   Consejo de Desplazados Guatemaltecos (Council of Displaced Guatemalans)

COPAZ   Comisión de la Paz (Peace Commission of the Guatemalan Government)

COPMAGUA   Coordinadora de Organizaciones del Pueblo Maya de Guatemala (Coordinating Office of Organizations of the Maya People of Guatemala)

CPR   Comunidad de Población en Resistencia (Community of People in Resistance)

CUC   Comité de Unidad Campesina (Peasant Unity Committee)

DEA   U.S. Drug Enforcement Agency

EGP   Ejército Guerrillero de los Pobres (Guerrilla Army of the Poor)

EMP   Estado Mayor Presidencial (Presidential "Chief of Staff" or Military Guard)

ESF   U.S. Economic Support Funds

FAR   Fuerzas Armadas Rebeldes (Rebel Armed Forces)

FDNG   Frente Democrático Nueva Guatemala (New Guatemala Democratic Front)

FLACSO   Facultad Latinoamericana de Ciencias Sociales (Latin American Faculty of Social Sciences)

FMLN   Frente Farabundo Martí de Liberación Nacional (Farabundo Marti National Liberation Front) (El Salvador)

FRG   Frente Republicano Guatemalteco (Guatemalan Republican Front)

GAM   Grupo de Apoyo Mutuo (Mutual Support Group)

GDP   gross domestic product

GV   Guardianes del Vecindario (Neighborhood Guardians)

IDB   Inter-American Development Bank

IEMA   Impuesto de Empresas Mercantiles y Agropecuarias (Tax on Commercial and Agricultural Enterprises)

IFI   international financial institution

ILO   UN International Labor Organization

IM   Instancia Multipartidaria (Multiparty Forum)

IMF   International Monetary Fund

INS	U.S. Immigration and Naturalization Service
IOB	U.S. Intelligence Oversight Board
ISR	Impuesto Sobre la Renta (income tax)
IUSI	Impuesto Unico Sobre Inmuebles (single property tax)
IVA	Impuesto Sobre Valor Agregado (value-added tax)
MINUGUA	Misión de Naciones Unidas de Verificación en Guatemala (UN Verification Mission in Guatemala)
MR-13	Movimiento Revolucionario 13 de Noviembre (November 13 Revolutionary Movement)
NAFTA	North American Free Trade Agreement
NGO	nongovernmental organization
OAS	Organization of American States
ODHA	Oficina de Derechos Humanos del Arzobispado (Archbishop's Human Rights Office)
ORPA	Organización del Pueblo en Armas (Organization of the People in Arms)
PAC	Patrulla de Auto-Defensa Civil (Civilian Self-Defense Patrol)
PAN	Partido de Avanzada Nacional (National Advancement Party)
PGT	Partido Guatemalteco de Trabajo (Guatemalan Labor Party) (Communist Party)
PMA	Policia Militar Ambulante (Mobile Military Police)
PN	Policia Nacional (National Police)
PNC	Policia Nacional Civil (National Civilian Police)
SAT	Superintendencia de Administración Tributaria (Superintendancy of Tax Administration)
SEPAZ	Secretaria de la Paz (Peace Secretariat of the Guatemalan Government)
TSE	Tribunal Supremo Electoral (Supreme Electoral Tribunal)
UN	United Nations
UNDP	United Nations Development Program
UNHCR	United Nations High Commissioner for Refugees
URNG	Unidad Revolucionaria Nacional Guatemalteca (Guatemalan National Revolutionary Unity)

USAC	Universidad de San Carlos (University of San Carlos, Guatemala's national public university)
VAT	value-added tax
WB	World Bank

References

As is explained in detail in the Prologue, this book is based primarily on interviews with a wide range of Guatemalans and others who have been involved in Guatemala's peace process from the late 1980s through 1999. Their generosity and cooperation made this book possible.

Abell, John. 1999. "The Neoliberal World Order: The View from the Highlands of Guatemala." *NACLA Report on the Americas* (July-August).

Adams, Richard. 1995. "Ethnic Conflict, Governance, and Globalization in Latin America, with Special Attention to Guatemala." Latin American Program Working Paper Series #215, Ethnic Conflict and Governance in Comparative Perspective (September), pp. 51–69.

_____. 1994. "A Report on the Political Status of the Guatemalan Maya." In Donna Lee Van Cott, ed., *Indigenous Peoples and Democracy in Latin America*. New York: St. Martin's Press.

Aguero, Felipe, and Jeffrey Stark, eds. 1998. *Fault Lines of Democracy in Post-Transition Latin America*. Coral Gables, FL: North-South Center Press.

Aguilera, Gabriel. 1997. "Negociar lo imposible: El proceso de paz en Guatemala." Manuscript. Cited by permission.

_____. 1996a. "El proceso de paz en Guatemala." *Estudios Internacionales* (July-December), pp. 1–19. Guatemala: Instituto de Relaciones Internacionales y de Investigación para la Paz (IRIPAZ).

_____. 1996b. "Democracia y elecciones en Guatemala." *FLACSO Cuaderno de Trabajo no. 14.* Guatemala: FLACSO.

_____. 1995. "El camino desconocido: Las nuevas funciones de los ejércitos centroamericanos." *Nueva Sociedad* (Caracas, Venezuela) (July-August), pp. 120–131.

_____. 1994. "Los temas sustantivos en las propuestas para la paz." *Debate* no. 24. Guatemala: FLACSO.

_____. 1993. "Guatemala: Transición sin llegar a ninguna parte." *Nueva Sociedad* (January-February), pp. 6–11.

_____. 1990. "The Armed Forces, Democracy, and Transition in Central America." In Louis Goodman, Johanna Mendelson, and Juan Rial, eds., *The Military and Democracy: The Future of Civil-Military Relations in Latin America*. Lexington, MA: Lexington Books.

_____. 1986. "Notas sobre elecciones y transición en Guatemala." *Economía* (Guatemala), no. 88 (April-June).

Aguilera, Gabriel, and Karen Ponciano. 1994. "El espejo sin reflejo: La negociación de paz en 1993." *Debate* no. 23. Guatemala: FLACSO.

Aguilera, Gabriel, Rosalinda Bran, and Claudinne Ogaldes. 1996. "Buscando la paz. El bienio 1994–1995." *Debate* no. 32. Guatemala: FLACSO.

Aldana, Carlos, Juan Quiñónez, and Demetrio Cojtí. 1996. "Los acuerdos de paz: Efectos, lecciones y perspectivas." Debate no. 43. Guatemala: FLACSO.

Alvarez, Sonia, Evelina Dagnino, and Arturo Escobar, eds. 1998. *Cultures of Politics, Politics of Cultures: Re-visioning Latin American Social Movements*. Boulder: Westview Press.

Americas Watch. 1996. *World Report 1996: Events of 1995*. Washington, DC: Americas Watch, pp. 93–100.

Amin, Samir. 1991. "El problema de la democracia en el Tercer Mundo contemporaneo." *Nueva Sociedad* (March-April).

Arévalo, Bernardo. 1998a. *Sobre arenas movedizas: Sociedad, estado y ejército en Guatemala, 1997*. Guatemala: FLACSO.

_____. 1998b. "Apuntes sobre una tarea inconclusa: La reconversión militar en Guatemala, 1998. *Diálogo* (October). Guatemala: FLACSO.

Armon, Jeremy, Rachel Sieder, and Richard Wilson. 1997. "Negotiating Rights: The Guatemalan Peace Process." Accord no. 2. London: Conciliation Resources.

Arnson, Cynthia, ed. 1999. *Comparative Peace Processes in Latin America*. Palo Alto and Washington, DC: Stanford University Press and Woodrow Wilson Center Press.

Asamblea de la Sociedad Civil. 1995a. "Propuestas para la paz." *Debate* no. 27. Guatemala: FLACSO.

_____. 1995b. "Documentos: Sector Mujeres, 1994–1995." Guatemala: Asamblea de la Sociedad Civil.

Asociación de Investigación y Estudios Sociales (ASIES). 1998a. *XIII Seminario sobre el rol de los partidos políticos (1997): Regimen electoral y organización política: Instrumentos de transformación democrática en Guatemala*. Guatemala: ASIES.

_____. 1998b. *XIII Seminario sobre realidad nacional: Guatemala frente a la globalización (1997)*. Guatemala: ASIES.

_____. 1997. *XII Seminario sobre el rol de los partidos políticos (1996): La paz: Un proyecto incluyente*. Guatemala: ASIES.

_____. 1996a. *XII Seminario sobre realidad nacional: Vision integral de los acuerdos de paz*. Guatemala: ASIES.

_____. 1996b. *Memoria de la Conferencia: Procesos de paz comparados*. Guatemala: ASIES.

_____. 1996c. *Acuerdos de paz: Aspectos socioeconómicos y situación agraria*. Guatemala: ASIES.

_____. 1995. *XI Seminario sobre el rol de los partidos políticos: Partidos políticos, programas de gobierno y acuerdos de paz*. Guatemala: ASIES

_____. 1993. *El proceso de paz: Encuesta a nivel nacional*. Guatemala: ASIES.

Azpuru, Dinorah. 1999. "Peace and Democratization in Guatemala: Two Parallel Processes." In Cynthia Arnson, ed., *Comparative Peace Processes in Latin America*. Palo Alto and Washington, DC: Stanford University Press and Woodrow Wilson Center Press.

_____. 1993. "Procesos de negociación comparados: El caso de Guatemala." Guatemala: ASIES.

Ball, Patrick, Paul Kobrak, and Herbert Spirer. 1999. *State Violence in Guatemala, 1960–1996: A Quantitative Reflection*. Washington, DC: American Association for the Advancement of Science and Cento Internacional de Investigaciones Sobre Derechos Humanos.

Baranyi, Stephen. 1995. "The Challenge in Guatemala: Verifying Human Rights, Strengthening National Institutions, and Enhancing an Integrated UN Approach to Peace." London: Centre for the Study of Global Governance, London School of Economics. Updated version in Spanish in Leonardo Franco, Jaime Esponda, and Stephen Baranyi, "La ONU y el proceso de paz en Guatemala." *Debate* no. 33. Guatemala: FLACSO.

Barrientos, César. 1998. "Las Reformas Constitucionales: Alcances y Problemas." *Aportes* (Guatemala), May 14, pp. 16–21.

Bastos, Santiago, and Manuela Camus. 1993. *Quebrando el Silencio*. Guatemala: FLACSO.

Beinin, Joel. 1998. "Palestine and Israel: Perils of a Neoliberal Repressive Pax Americana." In Ronnie Lipschutz and Susanne Jonas, eds., "Beyond the Neoliberal Peace: From Conflict Resolution to Social Reconciliation." Special Issue of *Social Justice* (Winter).

Biehl, Peter, and Linda Biehl. 1998. "The Story of Linda and Peter Biehl: Private Loss and Public Forgiveness." *Reflections* (Fall).

Bittar, Jorge, ed. 1992. *O Modo Petista de Governar*. São Paulo: Teoria y Debate.

Boff, Leonardo. 1986. *E a Igreja se Fez Povo*. Petrópolis, Brazil: Voces.

_____. 1981. *Igreja: Carisma e Poder*. Petrópolis, Brazil: Vozes.

Booth, John, ed. 2000a (forthcoming). "Globalization and Democratization in Guatemala." Special Issue of *Journal of Interamerican Studies and World Affairs*.

_____. 2000b. "Global Forces and Regime Change: Guatemala Within the Central American Context." In John Booth, ed., "Globalization and Democratization in Guatemala." Special Issue of *Journal of Interamerican Studies and World Affairs*.

_____. 1995. "Introduction. Elections and Democracy in Central America: A Framework for Analysis." In Mitchell Seligson and John Booth, eds., *Elections and Democracy in Central America: Revisited*. Chapel Hill: University of North Carolina Press.

_____. 1989. "Elections and Democracy in Central America: A Framework for Analysis." In John Booth and Mitchell Seligson, eds., *Elections and Democracy in Central America*. Chapel Hill: University of North Carolina Press.

Booth, John, and Mitchell Seligson, eds. 1989. *Elections and Democracy in Central America*. Chapel Hill: University of North Carolina Press.

Borón, Atilio. 1998. "Faulty Democracies?" In Felipe Aguero and Jeffrey Stark, eds., *Fault Lines of Democracy in Post-Transition Latin America*. Coral Gables, FL: North-South Center Press.

_____. 1993. "Estado, democracia y movimientos sociales en América Latina." *Crisol* (Mexico) no. 5 (Summer).

Boutros-Ghali, Boutros. 1996a. *An Agenda for Democratization*. New York: United Nations.

_____. 1996b. "Global Leadership After the Cold War." *Foreign Affairs* (March-April), pp. 86–98.

_____. 1995a. *An Agenda for Peace 1995*, 2nd ed. New York: United Nations.

_____. 1995b. *An Agenda for Development 1995*. New York: United Nations.

Boyce, James. 1998. "Reconstruction and Democratization: The International Financial Institutions and Post-Conflict Transitions." Manuscript. Cited by permission.

Boyce, James, ed. 1996. *Economic Policy for Building Peace: The Lessons of El Salvador.* Boulder: Lynne Rienner.

Boyce, James, and Manuel Pastor. 1998. "Aid for Peace: Can International Financial Institutions Help Prevent Conflict?" *World Policy Journal* (Summer), pp. 42–49.

Bran, Rosalinda, and Claudinne Ogaldes, eds. 1996. *Los retos de la paz, la democracia y el desarrollo sostenible en Guatemala.* Guatemala: FLACSO.

Bruck, Connie. 1996. "The Wounds of Peace." *The New Yorker* (October 14), pp. 64–91.

Buergenthal, Thomas. 1994. "The United Nations Truth Commission for El Salvador." *Vanderbilt Journal of Transitional Law* (October), pp. 497–544.

Byrne, Hugh. 1997. "The First Nine Months of the Guatemalan Peace Process: High Expectations and Daunting Challenges." Washington, DC: WOLA.

_____. 1996. "The Guatemalan Peace Accords: Assessment and Implications for the Future." Washington, DC: WOLA.

Cahill, Kevin, ed. 1996. *Preventive Diplomacy: Stopping Wars Before They Start.* New York: Basic Books.

Cameron, Maxwell. 1998. "Self-Coups: Peru, Guatemala, and Russia." *Journal of Democracy* (January), pp. 125–139.

Canadian Foundation for the Americas (FOCAL). 1997. "Managing the Peace: Building Consensus on Economic Reforms in Guatemala." Ottawa: FOCAL.

Castañeda, Jorge. 1990. "Is Squeaky Clean Squeaky Fair?" *Los Angeles Times* (November 18).

Cavarozzi, Marcelo. 1992. "Beyond Transitions to Democracy in Latin America." *Journal of Latin American Studies* (October), pp. 665–684.

Centro de Reportes Informativos sobre Guatemala (CERIGUA). 1997a. "Peace in Guatemala: The Accords." Guatemala: CERIGUA.

_____. 1997b. "Paz en Guatemala: Documentos y acuerdos históricos." Guatemala: CERIGUA.

_____. 1991a. "Discursos de las delegaciones participantes en la reunion de Cuernavaca, México, Junio de 1991." Guatemala: CERIGUA.

_____. 1991b. "Proceso de diálogo y negociación." Guatemala: CERIGUA.

Chase-Dunn, Christopher. 2000. "Globalization from Below in Guatemala." In John Booth, ed., "Globalization and Democratization in Guatemala." Special Issue of *Journal of Interamerican Studies and World Affairs.*

Chinchilla, Norma Stoltz. 1997. *Nuestras utopías: Mujeres guatemaltecas del siglo XX.* Guatemala: Tierra Viva/Magna Terra.

Clinton, William. 1999. "Remarks by the President in Roundtable Discussion on Peace Efforts." Transcript (March 16).

Cojtí, Demetrio. 1998. "Gobernabilidad democrática y derechos indígenas en Guatemala." In Rachel Sieder, ed., *Guatemala After the Peace Accords.* London: Institute of Latin American Studies.

_____. 1991. *La configuración del pensamiento político del pueblo maya*. Guatemala: Asociación de Escritores Mayances de Guatemala.

Collier, David, and Steven Levitsky. 1997. "Democracy with Adjectives: Conceptual Innovation in Comparative Research." *World Politics* 49 (April), pp. 430–451.

Comisión de Acompañamiento del Cumplimiento de los Acuerdos de Paz. 1997. "Valoraciones de la Comisión de Acompañamiento sobre el cumplimiento de los compromisos de los acuerdos de paz." Guatemala.

Comisión de Fortalecimiento de la Justicia. 1998. *Informe Final: Una nueva justicia para la paz*. Guatemala: Magna Terra.

_____. 1997. *Informe y recomendaciones sobre Reformas Constitucionales referidas a la Administración de Justicia*. Guatemala: Magna Terra.

Comisión de Reforma Electoral. 1997. "Comités cívicos electorales (documento para discusión)." Guatemala (June).

Comisión Especial de Incorporación (CEI). 1997. "Balance del Programa de Incorporación de la URNG a la Legalidad." Guatemala: CEI.

Comisión Nacional de Reconciliación (CNR). 1992. *La paz firme y duradera, un proyecto nacional*. Guatemala: Ediciones América.

_____. 1991. *Diálogo Nacional*. Guatemala: Ediciones Américas.

Comisión para el Esclarecimiento Histórico (CEH). 1999. *Guatemala: Memory of Silence*. Guatemala: CEH.

Comité para el Decenio del pueblo Maya. 1998. "El Derecho Indígena ante el debate para su Reconocimiento Constitucional y Legal." *Aportes* (Guatemala), May 14.

Congreso de la República de Guatemala. 1998. "Documentación: Reformas Constitucionales." Guatemala: Congreso de la República.

Consejo Nacional de Educación Maya (CNEM). 1998. *Análisis del proceso de paz desde la perspectiva indígena*. Guatemala: CNEM.

Coordinating Committee of Agricultural, Commercial, and Financial Associations (CACIF). 1995. "Guatemala: Reflections on the Past, Considerations about the Present, and Recommendations for the Future." Guatemala.

Costa, Gino. 1995. "The United Nations and Reform of the Police in El Salvador." *International Peacekeeping* (Autumn), pp. 365–390.

Crighton, Elizabeth. 1998. "Beyond Neoliberalism: Peacemaking in Northern Ireland." In Ronnie Lipschutz and Susanne Jonas, eds., "Beyond the Neoliberal Peace: From Conflict Resolution to Social Reconciliation." Special Issue of *Social Justice* (Winter).

Crónica. 1998. "Guatemala en números" (August). Guatemala.

Cruz Salazar, José Luis. 1991. "El Proceso Electoral Guatemalteco, 1990–1991." Guatemala: ASIES. Manuscript.

Dagnino, Evelina. 1993. "An Alternative World Order and the Meaning of Democracy." In Jeremy Brecher, John Brown Childs, and Jill Cutler, eds., *Global Visions: Beyond the New World Order*. Boston: South End Press.

Dary, Claudia, ed. 1998. *La construcción de la nación y la representación ciudadana*. Guatemala: FLACSO.

Davis, Shelton. 1997. "The Guatemalan Peace Accords and Indigenous Communal Lands." Manuscript.

Defensoría Maya. 1999. "Comunicado nacional e internacional." Guatemala. (May 18).

de Soto, Alvaro. 2000. "International Missions and the Promotion of Peace and Democracy." In Tommie Sue Montgomery, ed., *Peacemaking and Democratization in the Hemisphere: Multilateral Missions*. Coral Gables, FL: North-South Center Press.

_____. 1992. "The Negotiations Following the New York Agreement." In Joseph Tulchin and Gary Bland, eds., *Is There a Transition to Democracy in El Salvador?* Boulder: Lynne Rienner.

de Soto, Alvaro, and Graciana del Castillo. 1994. "Obstacles to 'Peace Building.'" *Foreign Policy* (Spring), pp. 69–83.

Development Associates, Inc., University of Pittsburgh, ASIES. 1998. "La cultura democrática de los guatemaltecos (Tercer Estudio, 1997)." Guatemala: Development Associates. (January).

Diamond, Larry. 1997. "Consolidating Democracy in the Americas." *Annals of the AAPSS* 550 (March), pp. 12–41.

Diamond, Larry, and Marc Plattner, eds. 1996. *Civil-Military Relations and Democracy*. Baltimore: Johns Hopkins University Press.

_____. 1993. *The Global Resurgence of Democracy*. Baltimore: Johns Hopkins University Press.

"Documento Consolidado, no. 2." 1995. Working Document. (December).

Domínguez, Jorge, and Marc Lindenberg, eds. 1997. *Democratic Transitions in Central America*. Gainesville: University Press of Florida.

Domínguez, Jorge, and Abraham Lowenthal, eds. 1996. *Constructing Democratic Governance: Mexico, Central America, and the Caribbean in the 1990s*. Baltimore: Johns Hopkins University Press.

Doyle, Kate. 1998. "Getting to Know the Generals: Secret Documents on the Guatemalan Military." Manuscript. Cited by permission.

_____. 1997. "The Art of the Coup: A Paper Trail of Covert Actions in Guatemala." *NACLA Report on the Americas* (September-October), pp. 34–41.

Drake, Paul, and Eduardo Silva, eds. 1986. *Elections and Democratization in Latin America, 1980–1985*. San Diego: University of California, Center for Iberian and Latin American Studies.

Dunkerley, James. 1994. *The Pacification of Central America*. London: Verso.

Economic Commission for Latin America and the Caribbean (ECLAC). 1997. *Preliminary Overview of the Economy of Latin America and the Caribbean 1997*. Santiago, Chile.

Elon, Amos. 1993. "The Peacemakers." *The New Yorker* (December 20), pp. 77–85.

Escobar, Arturo, and Sonia Alvarez, eds. 1992. *The Making of Social Movements in Latin America*. Boulder: Westview Press.

Escobedo, Sonia. 1997. "Análisis de los acuerdos de paz." Guatemala: Asamblea de la Sociedad Civil-Sector Mujeres.

Esquit, Alberto, and Victor Gálvez. 1997. *The Mayan Movement Today: Issues of Indigenous Culture and Development in Guatemala*. Guatemala: FLACSO.

Fagen, Richard. 1986. "The Politics of Transition." In Richard Fagan, Carmen Diana Deere, and José Luis Corragio, eds., *Transition and Development*. New York: Monthly Review.

Falk, Richard. 1993. "The Making of Global Citizenship." In Jeremy Brecher et al., eds. *Global Visions: Beyond the New World Order*. Boston: South End Press.

_____. 1989. "Group Claims and the Nation-State Within the United Nations System." Conference on Ethnic Conflict and the UN Human Rights System. Oxford: St. Ann's College.

Falla, Ricardo. 1998. *The Story of a Great Love*. Washington, DC: EPICA.

_____. 1994. *Massacres of the Jungle*. Boulder: Westview Press.

_____. 1978. *Quiché Rebelde*. Guatemala: Editorial Universitaria.

Felice, William. 1996. *Taking Suffering Seriously: The Importance of Collective Human Rights*. Albany: State University of New York Press.

Fernández, Damián, ed. 1990. *Central America and the Middle East: The Internationalization of the Crisis*. Miami: Florida International University Press.

Figueroa, Carlos. 1986. "La centaurización estatal en Guatemala." *Polémica*, no. 19 (January-April).

Finkelstein, Norman. 1998. "Securing Occupation: The Real Meaning of the Wye River Memorandum." *New Left Review* (November-December).

FLACSO (Facultad Latinoamericana de Ciencias Sociales)/El Salvador. 1998. "De los Acuerdos de Chapultepec a la construcción de la democracia." San Salvador: FLACSO.

_____. 1997. "De la experiencia Salvadoreña a la esperanza Guatemalteca: Acuerdos de Paz en El Salvador y Guatemala." San Salvador: FLACSO.

FLACSO/Guatemala. 1997. "Fortalecimiento del proceso democratizador y de paz." Guatemala: FLACSO.

_____. 1992. "La paz en El Salvador: Repercusiones en Guatemala." Guatemala: FLACSO.

Flores Alvarado, Humberto. 1997. *Significado político-social de los acuerdos de paz*. Guatemala: Artgrafic de Guatemala.

Foley, Michael. 1996. "Laying the Groundwork: The Struggle for Civil Society in El Salvador." *Journal of Interamerican Studies and World Affairs* (Spring), pp. 67–104.

Fox, Jonathan. 1996. "How Does Civil Society Thicken? The Political Construction of Social Capital in Rural Mexico." *World Development* 24 (no. 6), pp. 1089–1103.

Franco, Leonardo. 1996. "Human Rights Verification in the Context of Peace: The UN Experience in Guatemala." Manuscript. Presented to the United Nations Commission on Human Rights (April).

Franco, Leonardo, Jaime Esponda, and Stephen Baranyi. 1996. "La ONU y el proceso de paz en Guatemala." Debate no. 33. Guatemala: FLACSO.

Fuentes, Juan Alberto, and Thomas Carothers. 1998. "Luces y sombras en la cooperación internacional." In International IDEA, *Democracia en Guatemala: La Misión de un Pueblo Entero*. Colombia: Tercer Mundo Editores.

Fundación Myrna Mack. 1999. "Notas de Coyuntura de la Fundación Myrna Mack." Guatemala: Fundación Myrna Mack.

_____. 1996. "Resumen ejecutivo de la encuesta 'Amnistia-impunidad.'" Guatemala: Fundación Myrna Mack.

Fundación para la Paz, la Democracia y el Desarrollo (FUNDAPAZD). 1994a. *Documentos de la Asamblea de la Sociedad Civil (Mayo-octubre 1994)*. Guatemala: FUNDAPAZD.

_____. 1994b. *Documentos básicos del proceso de paz*. Guatemala: FUNDAPAZD.

Gaitán, Claudia. 1997. "Analisis de los acuerdos de paz." Guatemala: Sector Mujeres-Asamblea de la Sociedad Civil.

Gálvez, Victor. 1995. *La gobernabilidad en centroamérica: Sectores populares y gobernabilidad precaria en Guatemala*. Guatemala: FLACSO.

_____. 1991. "Transición y régimen político en Guatemala, 1982–1988." *Cuadernos de Ciencias Sociales* 44. San José: FLACSO.

Gálvez, Victor, and Roberto Camposeco. 1996. *Guatemala: Políticas de descentralización y capacidades de gestión administrativa y financiera de las municipalidades*. San Salvador: FLACSO.

Gálvez, Victor, Claudia Dary, Edgar Esquit, and Isabel Rodas. 1997. *Qué sociedad queremos?* Guatemala: FLACSO.

Gálvez, Victor, Carlos Hoffman, and Luis Mack. 1998. *Poder local y participación democrática*. Debate no. 40. Guatemala: FLACSO.

Garretón, Manuel Antonio. 1995. "Transiciones Ambivalentes." *Memoria* 80 (August), pp. 39–44. México: CEMOS.

Garst, Rachel. 1998. "Continuing Military Power in Guatemala." *NACLA Report on the Americas* (November-December).

_____. 1997. "The New Guatemalan National Civilian Police: A Problematic Beginning." Washington, DC: WOLA (November).

_____. 1995. "Guatemala: United States Policy and the Guatemalan Peace Process." Washington, DC: WOLA (March).

Global Exchange. 1996. "Guatemala: The Long Road to Peace." San Francisco: Global Exchange.

Gobierno de Guatemala (GG). 1997a. "Programa de Paz: La oportunidad para Guatemala: Invirtiendo en la Reconciliación Nacional, Democracia y desarrollo Sostenido." *Informe a la Reunión de Seguimiento del Grupo Consultivo de Bruselas*. Guatemala (September).

_____. 1997b. "Nota estratégica de Guatemala." Guatemala (January).

_____. 1997c. *Crónica de la paz 1996*. Guatemala: Presidencia de la Republica, Coordinación de la Crónica Presidencial.

_____. 1992. "Response to the Global Proposal Made by URNG in May of 1992." Guatemala (June).

González Casanova, Pablo. 1995. "La democracia de los de abajo y los movimientos sociales." *Nueva Sociedad* (March-April), pp. 37–40.

_____. 1989. "La crisis del Estado y la lucha por la democracia en América Latina." *Nueva Sociedad* (November-December), pp. 95–104.

González Casanova, Pablo, and Marcos Roitman, eds. 1996. *Democracia y Estado multiétnico en América Latina*. México: La Jornada Ediciones.

Goodman, Louis, William Leo Grande, and Johanna Mendelson Forman, eds. 1990. *Political Parties and Democracy in Central America*. Boulder: Westview Press.

Gordon, Diana. 1998. "Crime in the New South Africa." *Nation* (November 9).

Goulding, Marrack. 1996. "Observation, Triage, and Initial Therapy: The Role of Fact-Finding Missions and Other Techniques." In Kevin Cahill, ed., *Preventive Diplomacy: Stopping Wars Before They Start*. New York: Basic Books.

Gramajo, Héctor Alejandro. 1995. *De la guerra . . . a la guerra*. Guatemala: Fondo de Cultura Editorial.

Guillermoprieto, Alma. 1997. "The Harsh Angel." *The New Yorker* (October 6).

Gutiérrez, Edgar. 1997. "¿Para qué sirve MINUGUA?" *elPeriodico* (August).

Hale, Charles. 1997. "Consciousness, Violence, and the Politics of Memory in Guatemala." *Current Anthropology* (December).

Hayner, Priscilla. 1994. "Fifteen Truth Commissions—1974 to 1994: A Comparative Study." *Human Rights Quarterly* 16, pp. 598–675.

Hemisphere Initiatives (HI). 1998. "Promise and Reality: Implementation of the Guatemalan Peace Accords." Cambridge, MA: Hemisphere Initiatives (August).

Herman, Edward, and Frank Brodhead. 1984. *Demonstration Elections*. Boston: South End Press.

Hernández Pico, Juan. 1999a. "'Memory of Silence': A Stunning Indictment." *Envio* (April), pp. 17–28.

_____. 1999b. "Why Was the Referendum Defeated?" *Envio* (July), pp. 12–17.

_____. 1998. "A Year Without War: Low Intensity Peace." *Envio* (March), pp. 16–21.

_____. 1997a. "The Left: A Past with No Present but with a Future?" *Envio* (November), pp. 19–26.

_____. 1997b. "Poverty: Protagonist of the Post War." *Envio* (August), pp. 10–14.

_____. 1997c. "Peace Accords: Return of the Quetzal." *Envio* (February-March), pp. 14–21.

_____. 1993. "Guatemala: ¿Fructifir la democracia?" *Estudios Centroamericanos* (ECA). El Salvador (June).

Hernández, Rosalinda. 1998. *La tierra en los acuerdos de paz: Resumen de la respuesta gubernamental*. Guatemala: Inforpress Centroamericana (May).

Hinkelammert, Franz. 1994. "Our Project for the New Society in Latin America." In Susanne Jonas and Edward McCaughan, eds., *Latin America Faces the 21st Century*. Boulder: Westview Press.

Hobsbawm, Eric. 1992. "The Crisis of Today's Ideologies." *New Left Review* (March-April), pp. 55–64.

Holiday, David. 1997. "Guatemala's Long Road to Peace." *Current History* (February), pp. 68–74.

Holiday, David, and Tania Palencia. 1995. "Organización ciudadana y estado en Guatemala." Manuscript.

Holiday, David, and William Stanley. 1993. "Building the Peace: Preliminary Lessons from El Salvador." *Journal of International Affairs* (Winter), pp. 415–438.

Hombres de Maíz. 1998. "Guatemala: El primer año de paz." *Hombres de Maíz* (July-August). San José, Costa Rica.

Hovsepian, Nubar. 1996. "The Intellectual and the Challenge of Palestine." *Monthly Review* (May), pp. 53–60.

Huntington, Samuel. 1991. *The Third Wave: Democratization in the Late Twentieth Century*. Norman: University of Oklahoma Press.

Ignatieff, Michael. 1997. "Digging Up the Dead." *The New Yorker* (November 10), pp. 84–93.

Ilom, Gaspar. 1992. "El difícil camino de la negociación." *Noticias de Guatemala* (August). México.

Inforpress Centroamericana. 1996. *Compendio del proceso de paz II: Análisis, cronologías, documentos, acuerdos, 1995–1996.* Guatemala: Inforpress Centroamericana.

_____. 1995. *Compendio del proceso de paz I: Análisis, cronologías, documentos, acuerdos, 1986–1994.* Guatemala: Inforpress Centroamericana.

_____. 1985. *Guatemala: Elections 1985.* Guatemala: Inforpress Centroamericana.

Instituto Centroamericano de Estudios Políticos (INCEP). 1993. *Al rescate de la democracia en Guatemala.* Guatemala: INCEP.

Instituto de Estudios Políticos, Económicos y Sociales (IPES). 1999. "6 razones para entender las causales de una derrota." Guatemala (May 17).

_____. 1998a. "Pulso temático: Reformas Constitucionales." Guatemala (August).

_____. 1998b. "Pulso temático: Seguridad Ciudadana." Guatemala (July).

Instituto de Relaciones Internacionales y de Investigaciones para la Paz (IRIPAZ). 1995a. *Construcción de la paz, cultura de paz y democracia. Primer Congreso Latinoamericano de Relaciones Internacionales e Investigaciones para la Paz.* Guatemala: IRIPAZ.

_____. 1995b. *Función del ejército en una sociedad democrática.* Guatemala: IRIPAZ.

Inter-American Development Bank (IDB). 1998. "Justice and Development: The Inter-American Development Bank and Reform of the Judicial System." Washington, DC: IDB (April).

_____. 1996a. "The IDB in Guatemala: Supporting Peace and Development." Washington, DC: IDB (December 10).

_____. 1996b. "Frame of Reference for Bank Action in Programs for Modernization of the State and Strengthening of Civil Society." Washington, DC: IDB (March 11).

_____. 1995. "Informal Donors Meeting: Summary Report for Guatemala." Washington, DC: IDB (June).

International Human Rights Law Group and Washington Office on Latin America (IHRLG/WOLA). 1985. *The 1985 Guatemalan Elections: Will the Military Relinquish Power?* Washington, DC: IHRLG and WOLA.

International IDEA (IDEA). 1998. *Democracia en Guatemala: La Misión de un Pueblo Entero.* Colombia: Tercer Mundo Editores.

International Monetary Fund (IMF). 1998. "Statement by the IMF Staff Representative at the Consultative Group Meeting on Guatemala." Brussels (October 22–23).

_____. 1997. "Guatemala: Rompiendo la barrera del 8 por ciento." Washington, DC: IMF (May).

Isacson, Adam. 1997. *Altered States: Security and Demilitarization in Central America.* Washington, DC: Center for International Policy.

IXIMULEW. 1997. "A un año de la firma de la paz." IXIMULEW (Guatemala), December 29.

Jelin, Elizabeth. 1998. "The Minefields of Memory." *NACLA Report on the Americas* (September-October), pp. 23–29.

_____. 1995. "Building Citizenship: A Balance Between Solidarity and Responsibility." In Joseph Tulchin and Gary Bland, eds., *Is There a Transition to Democracy in El Salvador?* Boulder: Lynne Rienner.

_____. 1990. "Citizenship and Identity: Final Reflections." In Elizabeth Jelin, ed., *Women and Social Change in Latin America*. London: ZED & UN Research Institute for Social Development.

Jelin, Elizabeth, and Eric Hershberg, eds. 1996. *Constructing Democracy: Human Rights, Citizenship, and Society in Latin America*. Boulder: Westview Press.

Johnson, Kenneth. 1973. "On the Guatemalan Political Violence." *Politics and Society* (Fall), pp. 55–82.

_____. 1972. "Guatemala: From Terrorism to Terror." *Conflict Studies* (May), pp. 1–19.

Johnstone, Ian. 1995. *Rights and Reconciliation: UN Strategies in El Salvador*. Boulder: Lynne Rienner.

Jonas, Susanne. 1999. "'National Security,' Regional Development, and Citizenship in U.S. Immigration Policy: Reflections from the Case of Central American Immigrants and Refugees." In Max Castro, ed. *Free Markets, Open Societies, Closed Borders?* Coral Gables, FL: North-South Center Press.

_____. 1998. Review of Yvon Le Bot's *La Guerra en Tierras Mayas*. *American Historical Review* (February).

_____. 1997. "Guatemala's Peace Accords: An End and a Beginning." *NACLA Report on the Americas* (May-June).

_____. 1996a. "Dangerous Liaisons: The U.S. in Guatemala." *Foreign Policy* (Summer).

_____. 1996b. "Transnational Realities and Anti-Immigrant State Policies: Issues Raised by the Experiences of Central American Immigrants and Refugees in a Tri-national Region." In Roberto Korzeniewicz and William Smith, eds., *Latin America in the World Economy*. Westport CT: Greenwood.

_____. 1995. "Electoral Problems and the Democratic Project in Guatemala." In Mitchell Seligson and John Booth, eds., *Elections and Democracy in Central America: Revisited*. Chapel Hill: University of North Carolina Press.

_____. 1994a. "Guatemala: Encrucijada entre la guerra y la paz." *Espacios* no. 2 (October-December). FLASCO/Costa Rica.

_____. 1994b. "Text and Subtext of the Guatemalan Political Drama." *LASA Forum* (Winter).

_____. 1992. "Salvadoran Peace Accords: Can the Fragile Balance Hold?" *Nation* (June 1).

_____. 1991. *The Battle for Guatemala: Rebels, Death Squads, and U.S. Power*. Boulder: Westview Press.

_____. 1990. "Reagan Administration Policy in Central America." In David Kyvig, ed., *Reagan and the World*. New York: Greenwood.

_____. 1989. "Elections and Transitions: The Guatemalan and Nicaraguan Cases." In John Booth and Mitchell Seligson, eds., *Elections and Democracy in Central America*. Chapel Hill: University of North Carolina Press.

_____. 1988. "Contradictions of Guatemala's Political Opening." *Latin American Perspectives* (Summer).

_____. 1981. *Guatemala: Plan Piloto para el Continente*. San José: EDUCA.

Jonas, Susanne, and Edward McCaughan, eds. 1994. *Latin America Faces the 21st Century*. Boulder: Westview Press.

Jonas, Susanne, and Nancy Stein, eds. 1990a. *Democracy in Latin America: Visions and Realities*. New York: Greenwood/Bergin & Garvey.

_____. 1990b. "The Construction of Democracy in Nicaragua." *Latin American Perspectives* (Summer), pp. 10–37.

Jonas, Susanne, and David Tobis, eds. 1974. *Guatemala*. Berkeley: NACLA. Spanish edition, *Guatemala: Una historia inmediata*. México: Siglo XXI, 1976.

Joxe, Alain, et al. 1993. "Reconversión militar: Elementos para su comprensión." *Debate* no. 19. Guatemala: FLACSO and Fundación Friederich Ebert.

Karl, Terry. 1995. "The Hybrid Regimes of Central America." *Journal of Democracy* (July), pp. 72–86.

_____. 1992. "El Salvador's Negotiated Revolution." *Foreign Affairs* (Spring), pp. 147–164.

_____. 1990. "Dilemmas of Democratization in Latin America." *Comparative Politics* (October).

Kay, Cristóbal. 1998. "Estructuralismo y teoría de la dependencia en el periodo neoliberal." *Nueva Sociedad* (November-December).

Kaye, Mike. 1997. "The Role of Truth Commissions in the Search for Justice, Reconciliation, and Democratization: The Salvadorean and Honduran Cases." *Journal of Latin American Studies* (October).

Kincaid, Douglas. 2000. "Demilitarization and Security in El Salvador and Guatemala: Convergences of Success and Crisis." In John Booth, ed., "Globalization and Democratization in Guatemala." Special Issue of *Journal of Interamerican Studies and World Affairs*.

Kirkpatrick, Jeane. 1979. "Dictatorships and Double Standards." *Commentary* (November).

Kumar, Krishna, ed. 1997. *Rebuilding Societies After Civil War: Critical Roles for International Assistance*. Boulder: Lynne Rienner.

Lane, Charles. 1999. "TRB: From Washington: Sorry About That." *New Republic* (April 4).

Last, D. M. 1995. "The Challenge of Interagency Cooperation in International Peace Operations: A Conference Report." *Peacekeeping and International Relations* (January-February), pp. 5–7.

Lawyers Committee for Human Rights. 1995. *Improvising History: A Critical Evaluation of the United Nations Observer Mission in El Salvador*. New York: Lawyers Committee for Human Rights.

Le Bot, Yvon. 1995. *La guerra en tierras mayas: Comunidad, violencia y modernidad en Guatemala (1970–1992)*. México, D.F.: Fondo de Cultura Económica.

Lechner, Norbert. 1997. "Los condicionantes de la gobernabilidad democrática en la América Latina de fin de Siglo." *Diálogo* (November), Guatemala: FLACSO.

Lindenberg, Marc. 1993. *Democratic Transitions in Central America and Panama*. A World Peace Foundation Report (January).

Lipschutz, Ronnie. 1998. "From Conflict Resolution to Social Reconciliation." In Ronnie Lipschutz and Susanne Jonas, eds., "Beyond the Neoliberal Peace: From Conflict Resolution to Social Reconciliation." Special Issue of *Social Justice* (Winter).

Lipschutz, Ronnie, and Susanne Jonas, eds. 1998. "Beyond the Neoliberal Peace: From Conflict Resolution to Social Reconciliation." Special Issue of *Social Justice* (Winter).

Lopes, Gilberto, ed. 1998. *Los Acuerdos de Paz y el proceso de democratización en Guatemala: Seminario–25 al 29 de marzo de 1998*. San José: Fundación ACECOD, Unión Europea.

Lowy, Michael, and Eder Sader, eds. 1985. "The Militarization of the State in Latin America." *Latin American Perspectives* (Fall).

Lungo, Mario. 1994. "Redefining Democracy in El Salvador." In Susanne Jonas and Edward McCaughan, eds., *Latin America Faces the 21st Century*. Boulder: Westview Press.

Mack, Helen. 1998. "Reforma Constitucional: Construyendo la Institucionalidad Democrática." *Aportes* (May 14).

MacPherson, C. B. 1973. *Democratic Theory: Essays in Retrieval*. Oxford: Claredon Press.

Makovsky, David. 1996. *Making Peace with the PLO: The Rabin Government's Road to the Oslo Accord*. Boulder: Westview Press.

Marini, Ruy Mauro. 1994. "Latin America at the Crossroads." *Latin American Perspectives* (Winter), pp. 99–114.

_____. 1980. "The Question of the State in the Latin American Class Struggle." *Contemporary Marxism* 1.

Martínez, Juan, and Ian Bannon. 1997. "Guatemala: Consultation for the Indigenous Development Plan." Washington, DC: World Bank (June).

Marx, Anthony W. 1997. "Apartheid's End: South Africa's Transition from Racial Domination." *Ethnic and Racial Studies* (July), pp. 474–495.

McCleary, Rachel M. 1997. "Guatemala's Postwar Prospects." *Journal of Democracy* (April), pp. 129–143.

_____. 1996. "Guatemala: Expectations for Peace." *Current History* (February), pp. 88–92.

McSherry, Patrice. 1998. "The Emergence of Guardian Democracy." *NACLA Report on the Americas* (November-December).

Meisler, Stanley. 1995. "Dateline U.N.: A New Hammarskjold?" *Foreign Policy* (Spring), pp. 180–197.

Menchú, Rigoberta (with Elisabeth Burgos-Debray, ed.). 1984. *I, Rigoberta Menchú*. London and New York: Verso.

Millett, Richard. 1991. "Guatemala: Hopes for Peace, Struggles for Survival." *Survival* (September-October), pp. 425–441.

Mingst, Karen A., and Margaret P. Karns. 1995. *The United Nations in the Post–Cold War Era*. Boulder: Westview Press.

MINUGUA-PNUD and Comisión Legislativa de Estudios para la Paz del Congreso de la República, eds. 1997. *La construcción de la paz en Guatemala*. Guatemala: Serviprensa.

Misión de Naciones Unidas de Verificación en Guatemala (MINUGUA). 1998a. "Third Report, Verification of compliance with the commitments made in the Agreement on the Implementation, Compliance and Verification Timetable for the Peace Agreements." New York: United Nations (September 28).

_____. 1998b. "Second Report, Verification of compliance . . . ." New York: United Nations. (February 4).

_____. 1997. "First Report, Verification of compliance . . . ." New York: United Nations (June 20).

Molina, Raúl. 1999. "Análisis de coyuntura al concluir la consulta popular." Guatemala. (May 19).

Monsanto, Pablo. 1994. "Una negociación con contenido." Guatemala: URNG.

Montenegro, Arturo. 1998. "El tema fiscal en Guatemala." *Diálogo* (May). Guatemala: FLACSO.

Montgomery, Tommie Sue, ed. 2000 (forthcoming). *Peacemaking and Democratization in the Hemisphere: Multilateral Missions.* Coral Gables, FL: North-South Center Press.

Montobbio, Manuel. 1999. *La Metamorfosis de pulgarcito: Transición política y proceso de paz en El Salvador.* Madrid: Icaria.

_____. 1997a. "Guatemala y su proceso de paz." *Política Exterior* (July-August), pp. 99–116.

_____. 1997b. "La construcción de la democracia en El Salvador." Madrid: Centro de Estudios Políticas Americanas (February).

Morán, Rolando (Ricardo Ramírez). 1998a. "La Transición en Guatemala: Modalidades y Perspectivas." Guatemala: IPES (August 4).

_____. 1998b. "Reformas Constitucionales Necesidad Imperante en Guatemala." *Aportes* (May 14).

Moreno, Dario. 1994. *The Struggle for Peace in Central America.* Gainesville: University Press of Florida.

Morlino, Leonardo. 1985. *Como cambian los regimenes políticos.* Madrid: Centro de Estudios Constitucionales.

Muldoon, James, et al., eds. 1999. *Multilateral Diplomacy and the United Nations Today.* Boulder: Westview Press.

North American Congress on Latin America (NACLA). 1995. "The Left in Local Politics." *NACLA Report on the Americas* (July-August), pp. 14–44.

Nash, June. 1998. "Transnational Civil Society and the Mayan Quest for Democracy." Manuscript. Cited by permission.

_____. 1995. "The Reassertion of Indigenous Identity: Mayan Responses to State Intervention in Chiapas, Mexico." *Latin American Research Review* 30 (no. 3), pp. 7–42.

National Democratic Institute for International Affairs (NDI). 1991. *The 1990 National Elections in Guatemala: International Delegation Report.* Washington, DC: NDI.

North, Lisa, and CAPA. 1990. *Between War and Peace in Central America: Choices for Canada.* Toronto: Between the Lines.

Nun, José. 1993. "Democracy and Modernization, Thirty Years Later." *Latin American Perspectives* (Fall), pp. 7–27.

Ochoa, Carlos, Rosa Sánchez, and Armando Pacay. 1995. *Los Comités Cívicos: Gestión local de la acción política.* Guatemala: IRIPAZ.

O'Donnell, Guillermo. 1997. "Rendición de cuentas horizontal y nuevas poliarquías." *Nueva Sociedad* 152 (November-December), pp. 143–167.

O'Donnell, Guillermo, Phillipe Schmitter, and Laurence Whitehead, eds. 1986. *Transitions from Authoritarian Rule.* Baltimore: Johns Hopkins University Press.

Oficina de Derechos Humanos del Arzobispado de Guatemala (ODHA), Informe Proyecto Interdiocesano de Recuperación de la Memoria Histórica (REMHI). 1998. *Guatemala: Nunca más.* Guatemala: ODHA.

Oficina Nacional de la Mujer (ONAM). 1997. *Las obligaciones legislativas a favor de las mujeres derivadas de los Acuerdos de Paz.* Guatemala: Ministerio de Trabajo y Previsión Social.

Ogle, Kathy. 1998. "Guatemala's REMHI Project: Memory from Below." *NACLA Report on the Americas* (September-October), pp. 33–34.

Olson, Eric. 1998. "Building a New Consensus on Civil Society: Preliminary Assessment of Two IDB Loans." Washington, DC: Washington Office on Latin America (WOLA).

Olson, Joy. 1995. "U.S. Military Humanitarian and Civic Assistance Programs and Their Application in Central America." Alburquerque, NM: Resource Center Press (September).

Organization of American States (OAS). 1997. *Electoral Observation: Guatemala 1995–1996.* Washington, DC: OAS.

Oz, Amos. 1994. *Israel, Palestine, and Peace.* San Diego: Harcourt Brace.

Padilla, Luis Alberto. 1997. "Peacemaking and Conflict Transformation in Guatemala." *Estudios Internacionales* (January-July), pp. 82–108. Guatemala: IRIPAZ.

_____. 1996a. "Presentación." *Estudios Internacionales* (July-December), pp. i-viii. Guatemala: IRIPAZ.

_____. 1996b. "Las nuevas relaciones cívico-militares en el marco del proceso de paz en Guatemala." *Estudios Internacionales.* (July-December), pp. 27–41. Guatemala: IRIPAZ.

_____. 1995a. "The United Nations and Conflict Resolution in Central America: Peace Making and Peace Building in Internal Armed Conflict." *Estudios Internacionales* (July-December), pp. 92–104. Guatemala: IRIPAZ.

_____. 1995b. "La negociación bajo el signo de las mediaciones interna y externa." *Estudios Internacionales* (January-July), pp. 30–60. Guatemala: IRIPAZ.

Paige, Jeffery. 1997. *Coffee and Power: Revolution and the Rise of Democracy in Central America.* Cambridge: Harvard University Press.

Palencia, Tania. 1996. "Peace in the Making: Civil Groups in Guatemala." Manuscript.

Palencia, Tania, and David Holiday. 1996. "Hacia un nuevo ciudadano para democratizar Guatemala." Montreal: International Center for Human Rights and Democratic Development.

Paris, Roland. 1997. "Peacebuilding and the Limits of Liberal Internationalism." *International Security* (Fall), pp. 54–89.

Parlamento Centroamericano. 1995. "IV conferencia centroamericana de partidos políticos: Declaración de Contadora." Panama (August 22).

Pásara, Luis. 1998. "La justicia en Guatemala." *Diálogo* (March). Guatemala: FLACSO.

Pastor, Manuel, and James Boyce. 1997. "The Political Economy of Complex Humanitarian Emergencies: Lessons from El Salvador," Working paper no. 131. Helsinki: World Institute for Development Economics Research (April).

Pateman, Carole. 1970. *Participation and Democratic Theory.* Cambridge: Cambridge University Press.

Payeras, Mario. 1996. *Asedio a la utopía: Ensayos políticos 1989–1994.* Guatemala: Luna y Sol.

_____. 1991. *Los fusiles de octubre*. México, D.F.: Juan Pablos Editor, S.A.

Pearce, Jenny. 1998a. "Building Civil Society from the Outside: The Problematic Democratisation of Central America." *Global Society* 12 (no. 2).

_____. 1998b. "Perspectives in Paralysis: Discourse of Civil Society in Guatemala." Manuscript. Cited by permission

Peeler, John. 1995. "Elites and Democracy in Central America." In Mitchell Seligson and John Booth, eds., *Elections and Democracy in Central America: Revisited*. Chapel Hill: University of North Carolina Press.

Perera, Victor. 1993. *Unfinished Conquest: The Guatemalan Tragedy*. Berkeley: University of California Press.

Pérez Sáinz, Juan Pablo. 1998. "La nueva industrialización y el trabajo: Reflexiones desde Centroamérica." *Nueva Sociedad* (November-December).

Petras, James, and Henry Veltmeyer. 1999. "Latin America at the End of the Milennium." *Monthly Review* (July-August).

Plant, Roger. 1998. "Ethnicity and the Guatemalan Peace Process: Conceptual and Practical Challenges." In Rachel Sieder, ed., *Guatemala After the Peace Accords*. London: Institute of Latin American Studies.

Poitevín, René. 1999. "Guatemala: La democracia enferma." *Diálogo* (May). Guatemala: FLACSO.

_____. 1998. "Temas de debate: La democracia en Guatemala." Guatemala. Manuscript. Cited by permission.

_____. 1992. "Los problemas de la democracia." In FLACSO, *Los problemas de la democracia*. Guatemala: FLACSO.

_____. 1991. "En busca de la identidad." *Cuaderno de FLACSO*, no. 1. Guatemala: FLACSO.

Ponciano, Karen. 1996. *El rol de la Sociedad Civil en los procesos de paz de Guatemala y El Salvador*. Guatemala: INCEP.

Popkin, Margaret. 1996. "Guatemala's National Reconciliation Law: Combating Impunity or Continuing It?" *Revista IIDH*. San José, C.R.: Instituto Interamericano de Derechos Humanos.

Portes, Alejandro. 1999. "Theories of Development and Their Application to Small Countries: The Guatemalan Case." Manuscript. Cited by permission.

_____. 1997. "Neoliberalism and the Sociology of Development: Emerging Trends and Unanticipated Facts." *Population and Development Review* (June), pp. 229–259.

Przeworski, Adam. 1996. "Studying Democratization: Twenty Years Later." Manuscript. Cited by permission.

Quemé, Rigoberto. n.d. "La paz, desfio histórico o coyuntura?" Quetzaltenango. Manuscript.

Reyes, Miguel Angel. 1997. *Los complejos senderos de la paz: Un análisis comparado de las negociaciones de paz en El Salvador, Guatemala y México*. Guatemala: INCEP.

Richard, Pablo. 1995. "La fuerza del espíritu: Religión y teología en América Latina." *Nueva Sociedad* (March-April), pp. 128–141.

Rincón, Alejandra, Susanne Jonas, and Néstor Rodríguez. 1999. "La inmigración guatemalteca en los EE.UU. 1980–1996." Manuscript prepared for and summarized in United Nations Development Program, *Guatemala: El rostro rural del desarrollo humano*. Guatemala: UNDP.

Robinson, William. 1998. "Neoliberalism, the Global Elite and the Guatemalan Transition." *Report on Guatemala* (Winter).
_____. 1997. "Maldevelopment in Central America: A study on globalization and social change." *Pensamiento Propio* (September-December).
_____. 1996. *Promoting Polyarchy: Globalization, U.S. Intervention, and Hegemony.* Cambridge: Cambridge University Press.
Rodríguez, Alicia. 1998. "Ciudadanía y desarrollo de las guatemaltecas: Balance y perspectivas frente al próximo milenio." *Diálogo* (August). Guatemala: FLACSO.
Roht-Arriaza, Naomi, ed. 1995. *Impunity and Human Rights in International Law and Practice.* New York: Oxford University Press.
Rohter, Larry. 1997. "Whew! That War's Over. Ready for Another?" *New York Times* (January 5).
Rojas Lima, Flavio. 1995. *El derecho consuetudinario en el contexto de la etnicidad Guatemalteca.* Guatemala: Procurador de los Derechos Humanos.
Rosada, Héctor. 1997a. "El desafío de la paz." *Nueva Sociedad* (January-February), pp. 18–26.
_____. 1997b. "El lado oculto de las negociaciones." Series in *Prensa Libre.* Guatemala.
_____. 1996. "El impacto de las negociaciones de paz en Guatemala." *Estudios Internacionales* (July-December), pp. 20–26. Guatemala: IRIPAZ.
_____. 1990. "Elecciones generales en Guatemala, 11 de noviembre de 1990 y 6 de enero de 1991." *USAC: Revista de la Universidad de San Carlos,* no. 11. Guatemala (September).
_____. 1989. "Transición política en Guatemala y sus perspectivas." *USAC: Revista de la Universidad de San Carlos,* no. 6. Guatemala (June).
_____. 1986. *Guatemala 1985: Elecciones generales.* Guatemala: ASIES.
Rosenberg, Tina. 1996. "Recovering from Apartheid." *The New Yorker* (November 18), pp. 86–95.
_____. 1995. "Overcoming Legacies of Dictatorship." *Foreign Affairs* (May-June), pp. 134–152.
_____. 1991. "Beyond Elections." *Foreign Policy* (Fall).
Ruthrauff, John. 1998. "The Guatemalan Peace Process and the World Bank and Interamerican Development Bank." Manuscript. Cited by permission.
_____. 1996. "A Case Study: Influencing Consultative Group Meetings of the World Bank. Guatemala." Silver Spring, MD: Center for Democratic Education.
Ruthrauff, John, and Teresa Carlson. 1997. "A Guide to the Inter-American Development Bank and World Bank: Strategies for Guatemala." Silver Spring, MD: Center for Democratic Education.
Sader, Emir. 1992. *Governar para todos.* São Paulo: Editora Página Aberta Ltda.
Said, Edward. 1999. "The One-State Solution." *New York Times Magazine* (January 10).
_____. 1996. *Peace and Its Discontents: Essays on Palestine in the Middle East Peace Process.* New York: Vintage Books.
Sarti, Carlos. 1987. "La democracia en Guatemala: Sus contradicciones, límites y perspectivas." *Cahiers* (December). Rome: Fondation Internationale Lelio Basso.
Scheper-Hughes, Nancy. 1998. "Social Suffering and the Politics of Remorse in the New South Africa." In Ronnie Lipschutz and Susanne Jonas, eds., "Beyond the

Neoliberal Peace: From Conflict Resolution to Social Reconciliation." Special Issue of *Social Justice* (Winter).

_____. 1997. "Specificities: Peace-Time Crimes." *Social Identities* (November), pp. 471–497.

Schirmer, Jennifer. 1998. *A Violence Called Democracy: The Guatemalan Military Project*. Philadelphia: University of Pennsylvania Press.

Schmitter, Philippe, and Terry Karl. 1991. "What Democracy Is . . . and Is Not." *Journal of Democracy* (Summer).

Seligson, Mitchell, and John Booth, eds. 1995. *Elections and Democracy in Central America: Revisited*. Chapel Hill: University of North Carolina Press.

Sen, Tomás. 1998. "Constitutional Reforms and the Creation of a New Nation." *Report on Guatemala* (Fall).

Serech, José. 1998. "El desarrollo de la globalización en la población Maya." Manuscript. Cited by permission.

Sharckman, Howard. 1974. "The Vietnamization of Guatemala: U.S. Counterinsurgency Programs." In Susanne Jonas and David Tobis, eds., *Guatemala*. Berkeley: NACLA.

Sieder, Rachel, ed. 1998. *Guatemala After the Peace Accords*. London: Institute of Latin American Studies.

_____. 1996a. *Derecho consuetudinario y transición democrática en Guatemala*. Guatemala: FLACSO.

_____, ed. 1996b. *Central America: Fragile Transition*. London: Institute of Latin American Studies.

_____. ed. 1995. *Impunity in Latin America*. London: Institute of Latin American Studies.

Smith, Carol. 1995. "Race-Class-Gender Ideology in Guatemala: Modern and Anti-Modern Forms." *Comparative Studies in Society and History* (October), pp. 723–749.

Solares, Jorge. 1999. "Punto de Inflexión, Momento de Reflexión: Lo Interétnico y la Consulta Popular." *Diálogo* (July). Guatemala: FLACSO.

_____. 1992. "Guatemala: Etnicidad y democracia." In FLACSO, *Los problemas de la democracia*. Guatemala: FLACSO.

Solórzano, Mario. 1998. "El primer aniversario de la paz." *Diálogo* (February). Guatemala: FLACSO.

_____. 1987. *Guatemala: Autoritarismo y democracia*. San José: EDUCA/FLACSO.

Stalsett, Gunnar. 1996. "Towards Peace in Guatemala." Manuscript. Cited by permission.

Stark, Jeffrey. 1998. "Globalization and Democracy in Latin America." In Felipe Aguero and Jeffrey Stark, eds., *Fault Lines of Democracy in Post-Transition Latin America*. Coral Gables, FL: North-South Center Press.

Steichen, Régine, ed. 1993. *Democracia y democratización en Centroamérica*. San José, Costa Rica: Editorial de la Universidad de Costa Rica.

Stoll, David. 1999. *Rigoberta Menchú and the Story of All Poor Guatemalans*. Boulder: Westview Press.

_____. 1993. *Between Two Armies in the Ixil Towns of Guatemala*. New York: Columbia University Press.

Time. 1968. "Guatemala: Caught in the Crossfire." *Time* (January 26).

Tomuschat, Christian. 1999. "Presentación con ocasión de la entrega del informe de la Comisión para el Esclarecimiento Histórico." Guatemala (February 25). Transcript.

Torres Rivas, Edelberto. 1997. "Negociando el futuro: La paz en una sociedad violenta." *Debate* no. 36. Guatemala: FLACSO.

———. 1996. "Los desafíos del desarrollo democrático en Centroamérica." *Anuario de Estudios Centroamericanos* 22 (no. 1), pp. 7–40. Universidad de Costa Rica.

———. 1995. "Democracy and the Metaphor of Good Government." In Joseph Tulchin and Bernice Romero, eds., *The Consolidation of Democracy in Latin America*. Boulder: Lynne Rienner.

———. 1992. *El tamaño de nuestra democracia*. San Salvador: ISTMO Editores.

———. 1991. "Imágenes, siluetas, formas en las elecciones centroamericanas." *Polémica* 14–15 (May-December).

———. 1989. "Authoritarian Transition to Democracy in Central America." In Jan Flora and Edelberto Torres Rivas, eds., *Sociology of Developing Societies: Central America*. New York: Monthly Review Press.

———. 1987. *Centroamérica: La democracia posible*. San José: EDUCA and FLACSO.

Torres Rivas, Edelberto, and Gabriel Aguilera. 1998. *Del autoritarismo a la paz*. Guatemala: FLASCO.

Touraine, Alain. 1991. "Lecture for 'Tribuna 92.'" *El Gallo Ilustrado*, Supplement of *El Día* (Mexico) (September 29).

Trudeau, Robert. 1993. *Guatemalan Politics: The Popular Struggle for Democracy*. Boulder: Lynne Rienner.

———. 1989. "The Guatemalan Election of 1985: Prospects for Democracy." In John Booth and Mitchell Seligson, eds., *Elections and Democracy in Central America*. Chapel Hill: University of North Carolina Press.

Tulchin, Joseph, and Bernice Romero, eds. 1995. *The Consolidation of Democracy in Latin America*. Boulder: Lynne Rienner.

Tulchin, Joseph, and Gary Bland, eds. 1992. *Is There a Transition to Democracy in El Salvador?* Boulder: Lynne Rienner.

Turcios, Roberto. 1997. "El Salvador: Una transición historica y fundacional." *Nueva Sociedad* (July-August).

Tzuk Kim Pop. 1997. "Agenda de desarrollo social desde perscepcion del los sujetos y sectores sociales del altiplano occidental de Guatemala." Quetzaltenango.

United Nations (UN). 1995. *The UN in El Salvador, 1990–1995*. New York: United Nations.

———. 1994–1995. "Letters from the Secretary General to the Negotiating Parties in Guatemala." New York: United Nations (December 22, 1994 and February 17, 1995).

United Nations Development Program (UNDP). 1999. *Guatemala: El rostro rural del desarrollo humano*. Guatemala: UNDP.

———. 1998. *Guatemala: Los contrastes del desarrollo humano*. Guatemala: UNDP.

United Nations Research Institute for Social Development (UNRISD). 1998. "Guatemala, la construcción de la paz." Guatemala: UNRISD (March).

Unidad Revolucionaria Nacional Guatemalteca (URNG). 1998a. "Informe sobre Cumplimiento de los Acuerdos de Paz: Período enero-septiembre 1998." Guatemala: URNG (September).

_____. 1998b. "Cumplimiento de los Acuerdos de Paz: Período abril-diciembre 1997." Guatemala: URNG (January).

_____. 1997a. "Cumplimiento de los Acuerdos de Paz: Período mayo-agosto de 1997." Guatemala: URNG (September).

_____. 1997b. "Cumplimiento de los Acuerdos de Paz: En los primeros 90 días." Guatemala: URNG (May).

_____. 1996a. "Unificar a los revolucionarios y forjar su partido: Tarea histórica de URNG." Guatemala: URNG.

_____. 1996b. "Guatemala, la democracia plena: Meta revolucionaria en el fin del milenio." Guatemala: URNG (June).

_____. 1995. "Guatemala: Propuesta a la Sociedad." Guatemala: URNG (April).

_____. 1992. "Guatemala: Una paz justa y democracia: Contenido de la nego-ciación." Guatemala: URNG (April).

_____. 1991. "Situación de la democracia en Guatemala en lo político, económico, social y cultural." Guatemala: URNG (June).

Universidad de San Carlos de Guatemala. 1994. "Propuestas de la Universidad de San Carlos de Guatemala a la Asamblea de Sectores Civiles." Guatemala: Universidad de San Carlos (September).

U.S. Agency for International Development (AID). 1999. "U.S. AID Support for Implementation of the Guatemalan Peace Accords." Washington, DC: AID (June).

_____. 1997. "Peace in Guatemala: Inclusion, Local Empowerment, and Poverty Reduction. Strategic Plan, USAID Assistance to Guatemala, FY 1997–2001." Washington, DC: Government Printing Office (February 14).

U.S. Government (White House), Intelligence Oversight Board. 1996. "Report on the Guatemala Review." Washington, DC: U.S. GPO.

U.S. House of Representatives. 1993. "Guatemala: The Prospects for Peace." Hearing before the Committee on Foreign Affairs. Washington, DC: U.S. GPO (March 3).

U.S. Senate, Select Committee on Intelligence. 1995. "Hearing on Guatemala." Washington, DC: U.S. GPO (April 5).

Vesper Society and Fundación Arias para la Paz y el Progreso Humano. 1994. "Imagining a Post-War Guatemala: A Roundtable for Prosperity in the Americas." Summary Report. Oakland, CA.

Vilas, Carlos. 1997. "Inequality and the Dismantling of Citizenship in Latin America." *NACLA Report on the Americas* (July-August), pp. 57–63.

_____. 1996a. "Are There Left Alternatives? A Discussion from Latin America." In Leo Panitch, ed., *The Socialist Register 1996*. London: Merlin Press.

_____. 1996b. "Prospects for Democratisation in a Post-Revolutionary Setting: Central America." *Journal of Latin American Studies* (May), pp. 461–503.

_____. 1994. "Latin America: Socialist Perspectives in Times of Cholera." In Susanne Jonas and Edward McCaughan, eds., *Latin America Faces the 21st Century*. Boulder: Westview Press.

Visión Guatemala. 1999. *Guatemala hacia el nuevo milenio: Los escenarios del futuro*. Guatemala: Magna Terra.

Walker, Thomas W., ed. 1997. *Nicaragua Without Illusions: Regime Transition and Structural Adjustment in the 1990s*. Wilmington, DE: Scholarly Resources.

Wallerstein, Immanuel. 1996. "The ANC and South Africa: The Past and Future of Liberation Movements in the World-System." Binghamton: Fernand Braudel Center, SUNY–Binghamton.

_____. 1995. *After Liberalism*. New York: New Press.

_____. 1991. *Unthinking Social Science: The Limits of Nineteenth-Century Paradigms*. Cambridge, UK: Polity Press.

Warren, Kay. 1998a. *Indigenous Movements and Their Critics: Pan-Mayanism and Ethnic Resurgence in Guatemala*. Princeton: Princeton University Press.

_____. 1998b. "Pan-Mayanism and Multiculturalism in Guatemala." Manuscript. Cited by permission.

_____. 1997. "The Indigenous Role in Guatemalan Peace." *Cultural Survival Quarterly* (Summer), pp. 24–27.

Washington Office on Latin America (WOLA). 1998. "Memorandum to International Donors Regarding Police Reform in Guatemala." Washington, DC: WOLA (October 21).

_____. 1995. "Military Intelligence and Human Rights in Guatemala: The Archivo and the Case for Intelligence Reform." WOLA Policy Brief. Washington, DC: WOLA (March 30).

Weffort, Francisco. 1992. "New Democracies. Which Democracies?" Manuscript, prepared for East-South System Transformations Seminar.

Whitfield, Teresa. 1999. "The Role of the United Nations in El Salvador and Guatemala: A Preliminary Comparison." In Cynthia Arnson, ed., *Comparative Peace Processes in Latin America*. Palo Alto and Washington, DC: Stanford University Press and Woodrow Wilson Center Press.

_____. 1994. *Paying the Price*. Philadelphia: Temple University Press.

Williams, Philip. 1994. "Dual Transitions from Authoritarian Rule: Popular and Electoral Democracy in Nicaragua." *Comparative Politics* (January), pp. 169–185.

Williams, Philip, and Knut Walter. 1997. *Militarization and Demilitarization in El Salvador's Transition to Democracy*. Pittsburgh: University of Pittsburgh Press.

Wilmer, Franke. 1998. "The Social Construction of Conflict and Reconciliation in the Former Yugoslavia." In Ronnie Lipschutz and Susanne Jonas, eds., "Beyond the Neoliberal Peace: From Conflict Resolution to Social Reconciliation." Special Issue of *Social Justice* (Winter).

Wilson, Richard. 1995. *Maya Resurgence in Guatemala*. Norman: University of Oklahoma Press.

Woodrow Wilson International Center for Scholars (WWICS), Latin American Program. 1999. "El proceso de paz en Guatemala: Logros y desafíos." Washington, DC (April).

World Bank. (WB). 1997. "Guatemala. Investing for Peace: A Public Investment Review." Report no. 16392-GU. Washington, DC (July).

_____. 1996. "Guatemala: Building Peace with Rapid and Equitable Growth." Report no. 15352-GU. Washington, DC (August).

_____. 1995. "Guatemala: An Assessment of Poverty." Report no. 12313-GU. Washington, DC (April).

de Zarco, Teresa Bolaños. 1996. *La culebra en la corbata: Crónica del proceso de paz guatemalteco.* Mexico, D.F.: Editorial Diana.

Zelaya, Raquel. 1997. "Evaluación de los avances en el cumplimiento de los compromisos de los acuerdos de paz." Guatemala: Gobierno de Guatemala (September).

Periodic Reports and Primary Documents

Asamblea de la Sociedad Civil (ASC). 1994–1996. Propuestas de la Asamblea de la Sociedad Civil. Guatemala.

Consulta Ecuménica por la Paz y la Democracia en Guatemala. 1991–1995. Latin American Council of Churches, World Council of Churches, National Council of Churches of Christ of the United States, World Lutheran Federation.

Misión de Naciones Unidas de Verificación en Guatemala (MINUGUA). 1997–1998. Periodic Reports, Verification of compliance with the commitments made in the Agreement on the Implementation, Compliance and Verification Timetable for the Peace Agreements. New York: United Nations.

_____. 1995–1999. Periodic Reports of the Director of the United Nations Mission for the Verification of Human Rights and of Compliance with the Commitments of the Comprehensive Agreement on Human Rights in Guatemala. New York: United Nations.

United Nations. 1994–1996. Texts of the Peace Accords. New York: United Nations.

Periodicals

Acción Ciudadana, *Alerta Legislativa* (Guatemala).

Assamblea de la Sociedad Civil (ASC) *Organo Informativo* (Guatemala).

Centro Exterior de Reportes Informativos sobre Guatemala (CERIGUA). *Weekly Briefs.* (Guatemala)

Christian Science Monitor.

Crónica (Guatemala), and supplements.

Envio, Instituto Histórico Centroamericano, Universidad Centroamericana (Managua).

Frente Democrático Nueva Guatemala (FDNG), *Boletín Internacional* (Guatemala).

Guatemala Scholars Network, newsletters.

Information Services Latin America (ISLA) (Oakland).

Inforpress Centroamericana (Guatemala).

New York Times.

Noticias de Guatemala (NG) (México; Guatemala).

Prensa Libre (Guatemala).

Report on Guatemala, Guatemala News and Information Bureau (GNIB)/Network in Solidarity with the People of Guatemala (NISGUA) (San Francisco).

Siglo Veintiuno (Guatemala).

Unidad Revolucionaria Nacional Guatemalteca (URNG), bulletins (Guatemala).

Index